D0646936

World Atlas of Golf

First published in the United States in 1998 by
Thunder Bay Press
5880 Oberlin Drive, Suite 400
San Diego, CA 92121-9653
1-800-284-3580
http://www.advmkt.com/

Copyright under International, Pan American, and Universal Copyright Conventions. All rights reserved. No part of this book may be reproduced or transmitted in any form or by any means, electronic or mechanical, including photocopying, recording, or by any information storage-and-retrieval system, without written permission from the publisher. Brief passages (not to exceed 1,000 words) may be quoted for reviews.

Please direct permission inquiries to Reed Consumers Books Ltd., London, England.

Copyright ©1998 Reed Consumer Books Limited
First edition published 1976
Second edition 1988
Third edition 1991

Publishing Director: Laura Bamford
Executive: Editor Julian Brown
Editor: Trevor Davies
Assistant Editor: Tarda Davison-Aitkins
Creative Director: Keith Martin
Designer: Darren Kirk
Picture Researcher: Liz Fowler
Production Controller: Bonnie Ashby
New Illustrations: Chris Forsey and Line and Line
Fourth Edition edited and revised by Derek Lawrenson

ISBN 1-57145-166-8

Library of Congress Cataloging-in-Publication Data
World atlas of golf : the greatest courses and how they are played /
Pat Ward-Thomas . . . [et al.] -- 4th ed. / rev. and updated by Derek Lawrenson.
p. cm.
Includes index.
ISBN 1-57145-166-8
1. Golf courses--Guidebooks.   I. Ward-Thomas, Pat, 1913-1982.
II. Lawrenson, Derek.
GV975.W6 1998
796.352'06'8--dc21   98-26823
                                                    CIP

Produced by Toppan
Printed in China

1 2 3 4 5 98 99 00 01 02

World

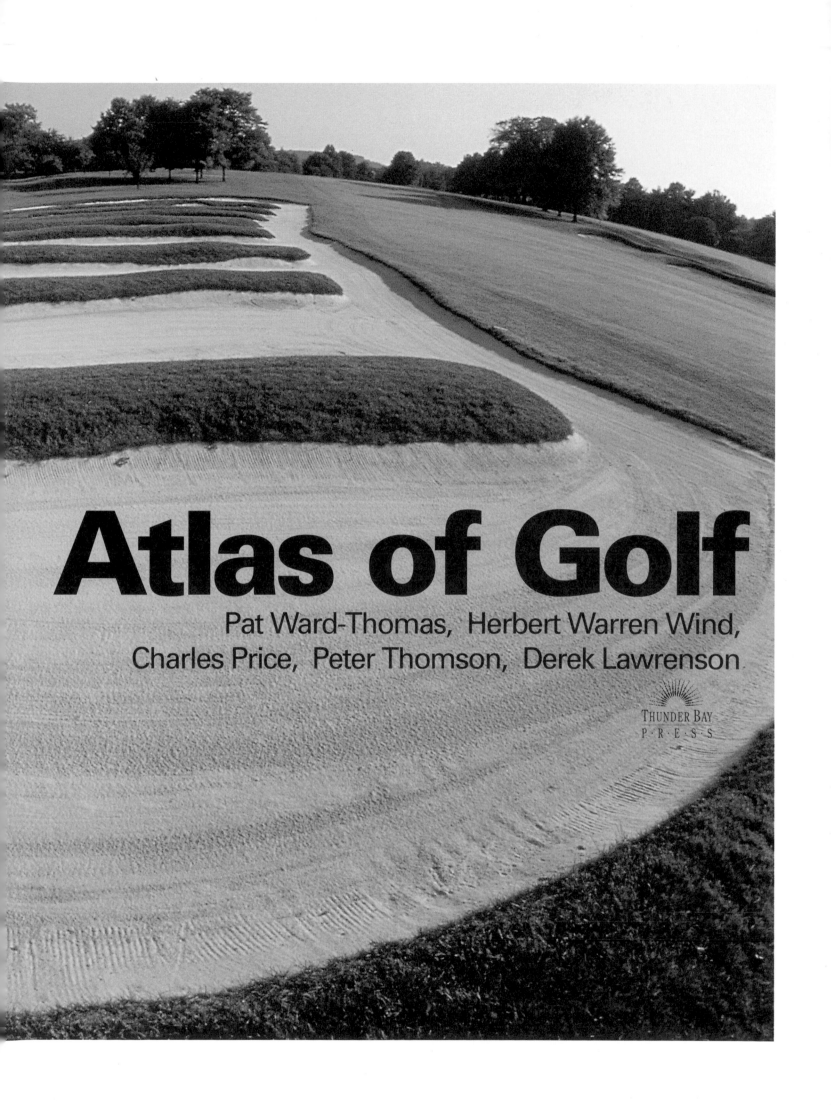

Atlas of Golf

Pat Ward-Thomas, Herbert Warren Wind,
Charles Price, Peter Thomson, Derek Lawrenson

THUNDER BAY
P·R·E·S·S

Contents

Introduction

By Derek Lawrenson

For a game that talks loud and often about upholding tradition, golf has changed a great deal in the last twenty-two years. Cast your mind back for a moment to the summer of 1976, as you stepped onto the first tee and pulled from your bag a wood that, glory be, was actually made of wood. Its steel shaft would gleam in the sunshine, and, if this was a good day, you would hope to deliver a clean blow that would not leave you wondering whether a scuff mark would appear on your clean white golf ball. A good player would drive the ball to about the 200-yard mark. Now, look at us. Only stubborn Luddites like myself still use wood; only a few of us are left who prefer steel; unless a golf ball's cover is made purely from balata you could take a machete to it these days and still struggle to leave a mark. And yes, you would hope to carry the 200-yard mark with the ball still in flight.

The World Atlas of Golf first appeared in the summer of 1976 and in the years that have passed it has come to be considered a classic of its kind. Mind you, how could it fail to be so proclaimed with such a first-rate lineup of writers such as Herb Warren Wind, Pat Ward-Thomas, Charles Price, and Peter Thomson? I remember reading it for the first time as a teenager and recall being in awe at the knowledge imparted and the quality of the writing.

All these years later, rereading it for the purposes of this revision, I was still in awe. But this time it was mixed with a few wry smiles as well. There was, for example, Herb Warren Wind's description of how to play the 11th at Augusta: a player could either head down the left-hand side with his drive and have a 4-iron to the green; or go for the big drive down the right and leave himself a 5- or 6-iron for his approach. All perfectly lucid in 1976; but in 1997 Tiger Woods went for the big drive and it was not a 6-iron he followed it with but a sand wedge. Which, so far as how it should be played is concerned, made it a completely different hole.

When Gene Sarazen holed his wooden approach to the 15th at Augusta in 1935 for what we call an albatross in Britain, a double-eagle in Georgia, Bobby Jones had just wandered down to swell the gallery to around 25 spectators. As I write this I have just had a press release from the Augusta authorities informing me that this year's Masters is already a sell-out, and not just for the tournament itself but for the practice days as well. No one but the inner clan at that famously secretive venue knows how of wood apply equally to the enjoyment of playing new courses over old. Sadly, the opposite is true. Nearly every modern course I play leaves me hankering even more for one that has stood the test of time.

This is the first real revision and update to *The World Atlas of Golf* since 1976 and it had to take into account the overwhelming changes detailed above. But I felt it was important to stay true to the original text as well—it was a revision after all, not a rewrite—and so I set myself a couple of ground rules.

One of the qualities of the book was the sidebars that accompanied the main text on each course; usually this involved taking an incident from a major championship to illustrate the strengths of a signature hole. I have stayed close to the spirit of this, while using examples from the last twenty-two years if I felt they provided a stronger case, or if they showed how a hole has changed with the advance of modern technology. The bottom line is that any book that sets out to name "the great courses" is being subjective. So, I did not think it was my job to interfere with the original authors' right to wax lyrical, say, about Medinah in Chicago while leaving Oak Hill in small print in the gazeteer section in the back, even though I think the latter is a far superior course to the former.

Two courses that were around in 1976 and were in the gazeteer section have been expanded however; it is right that Ballybunion on Ireland's west coast and Royal Troon on Scotland's western seaboard are included in full detail.

It is as much my desire not to tamper with a much-loved masterpiece as a comment on modern course architecture that only three courses that were not around in 1976 have been included now. One, The Belfry, has become famous through the Ryder Cup and is arguably the prime example of how architects these days can take an unpromising piece of land and make something of it that will lend itself to great drama.

The other two courses, Valderrama in southern Spain, and Loch Lomond in Scotland, are great in their own right. The latter, designed by Tom Weiskopf and Jay Morrish, is perhaps the finest golf course built anywhere in the past ten years and proof that modern designers can emulate the storied achievements of the past.

As for the United States, it seems astonishing to me that no unquestionably great course capable of holding major championships has emerged since this book was first published. Am I being too harsh on new tournament venues such as Shoal Creek in Alabama, Muirfield Village in Ohio, Sawgrass in Florida, or Valhalla in Kentucky? Well, maybe. A good case could certainly be made for Muirfield Village. But Valhalla was the final resting place in Norse mythology for slain heroes and if I had to choose my resting place it would be any of the courses described by Herb Warren Wind before that Jack Nicklaus venue in Louisville.

Finally, of the four authors who wrote most of the original text, Pat Ward-Thomas and Charles Price have sadly gone to their valhallas, and Herbert Warren-Wind has retired. In the field of writing as well, much has changed in twenty-two years. But the beauty of the words and the knowledge they imparted is one tradition that I hope has been upheld through this revision.

The beautiful par-four 12th hole at Lahinch, where danger lurks on both sides of the fairway. This hole is rated among the toughest in all Ireland.

many people this involves but I would be astonished to learn it was less than 350,000 spectators for the week. Everywhere the game is played has witnessed this sort of astonishing surge in popularity since the *World Atlas of Golf* made its first appearance.

In Europe it was in the 1980s as new superstars emerged from lands that had hitherto been dominated by other sports. Bernhard Langer from Germany and Severiano Ballesteros from Spain were part of a European team that won successive Ryder Cups, and proved the catalyst for a redesign of the landscape of mainland Europe. As the decade came to an end, so the Far East in general adopted what hitherto had been a largely Japanese obsession with the Royal and Ancient game. Now, as the millenium approaches, the United States is experiencing another boom. PGA Tour commissioner Tim Finchem believes that in his lifetime the game will stand alongside football, baseball, and basketball as a major U.S. sport. With Tiger Woods as totem, anything seems possible. One more change that has happened in the last twenty-two years is that the world has another 100,000 golf courses on which to practice its skills. So not only has how we play the game changed out of all recognition, and who plays the game, but where we play, too.

It would be nice to say these courses have made a huge contribution to golf course architecture; that the considerable benefits that accrue from playing metal instead

Links Courses

Nature's Gift to Golf

Golf architecture is now recognized as a distinct art, the creation of a great golf course being achieved with a subtle alchemy of skill, imagination, and technology upon which another dimension of greatness can be conferred by the staging of a championship. But not every championship setting owes its quality to the hand of man. St. Andrews, Prestwick, and Carnoustie are relics of the old, natural links on which the game first became popular. To this day nobody knows who laid them out, but even they are refinements of the earliest golfing arenas used when the game was played across country. There were no fairways, no tees, and no greens, simply agreed starting and finishing points. The game had reached St. Andrews, Carnoustie, Leith, Dornoch, Montrose, North Berwick, and Musselburgh by the beginning of the sixteenth century. Golf thus became established on linksland. These strips of coastal land, left when the seas receded after the last ice age, were once a wilderness of sand. Slowly, sparse vegetation grew up and something akin to a fairway with fine-bladed grass threaded its way among the gorse. St Andrews became—and still is—one long fairway, with nine holes out to a distant point and nine holes back. Those unfamiliar with links courses expect it to have more definition and more color. Yet the Old Course's influence on generations of golf architects has been immense—so pervasive that every golf course is essentially built in imitation. The Old Course served as a model for the early architects, Old Tom Morris, Willie Park Jr. and the Dunns, who in their early days did little more than site eighteen teeing grounds and greens on the splendid golfing ground that was put at their disposal. Unfortunately, for a period the blessings of nature were often overlooked and some courses took on a stiff and unnatural appearance. Designs incorporated stone walls, blind shots, hedges, regularly shaped mounds, and greens in geometric shapes.

Left and below: The par-four 17th (Alps) at Prestwick is typical of the many blind holes that once existed on the old links course. It used to be considered a sporting hole, but its emphasis on the vagaries of fortune—their cruelest twist epitomized by the deep bunker, below—to the almost total exclusion of skill, makes the Alps an anachronism. A number of large bunkers on courses around the world have been named Sahara on account of the vast expanse of sand. The first to be so named was the bunker that protects the 17th green at Prestwick, left.

Right: The hidden bunkers that riddle the Old Course's 12th fairway started out as natural sandy depressions and were probably enlarged by sheep sheltering from the wind. These are common on links courses where the first bunkers were not designed but evolved through use.

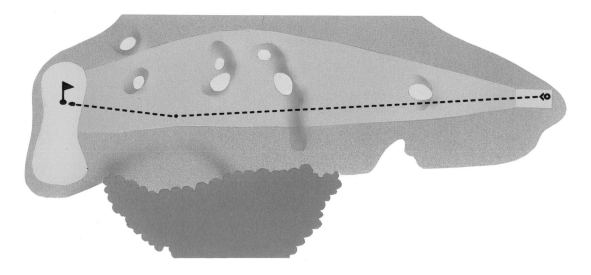

The Birth of Golf Architecture

Toward the end of the last century came a welcome return to simplicity and naturalness. Great courses continued to be built on traditional linksland (Muirfield and Portmarnock, built in the 1890s, were routed in refreshingly new ways), but due to a radical decision to build on the sandy heathland west of London, they were for the first time created inland. Courses had previously been built away from the sea—but on nonporous soil, soggy in winter and rock hard in summer; this new land was superbly drained and easy to contour, and on it the genius of Willie Park Jr., Herbert Fowler, Tom Simpson, H.S. Colt, and Charles Alison flourished. In the United

Above and right: The 2nd at Pine Valley is one of the most dramatic and fearsome holes on a course that, apart from being considered the most difficult in the world, introduced the concept of island fairways. These fairways dictate not only line but also length and are isolated among vast areas of sandy scrubland that, along with the more formal bunkers set around the greens, is never raked.

Pine Valley 1st and 2nd

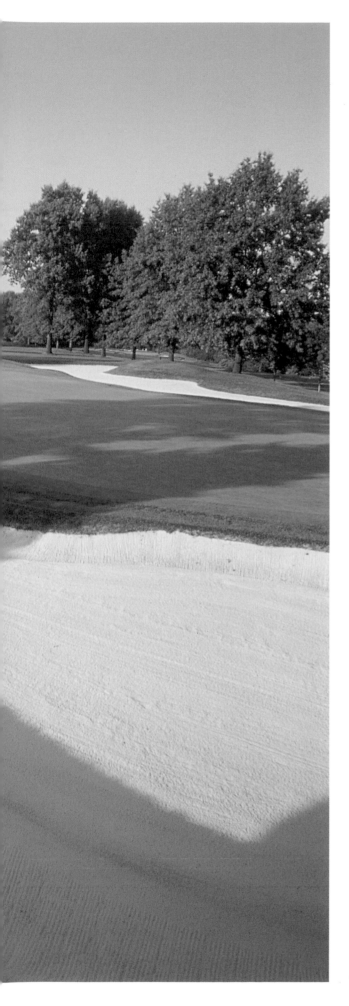

States, Charles Blair Macdonald created the National Golf Links, the first course of real quality built beyond the shores of Britain and Ireland, and in the years until the end of World War I some exceptional courses were carefully nursed into existence by truly gifted men—George Crump (Pine Valley), the Fownes family (Oakmont), A.W. Tillinghast (San Francisco GC), and Hugh Wilson (Merion).

All of these men, British and American, made careful studies of the fine old linksland courses and incorporated the best features into their designs, but they also introduced new ideas of their own and formulated two divergent schools of thought on golf architecture—the strategic and the penal. A penal hole dictates the line of play and punishes a player who strays from it out of all proportion to the degree of his error. The strategic hole offers a number of routes of varying difficulty and, while hampering the poor shot in subsequent play, rewards the good one. These men also understood the value of good drainage, the virtues of suitable grasses, the subtleties of green size in relation to the approach shot, and they did away with the lottery of blind holes, building instead holes that made no secret of their hazards. In their knowledge and its application golf architecture, part intuition, part science, was born.

Left: A feature of the daunting Oakmont layout is the bunkers that protect virtually every hole, not least the par-four 14th.

Muirfield 8th   Hagen 1929

Muirfield 8th
Although Oakmont was the first penal course, earlier individual holes were decidedly penal, including Muirfield's 8th, an example of insurance bunkering. In the 1929 Open, before trees made the shot too difficult, Walter Hagen used an ingenious route to a birdie-three.

Muirfield   Portmarnock

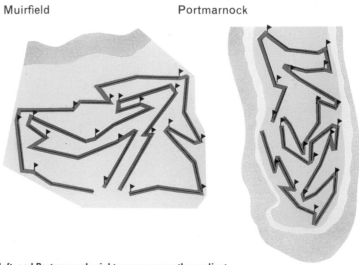

Muirfield, left, and Portmarnock, right, were among the earliest courses to depart from the then accepted principle of nine holes out to a distant point and nine holes back. On both courses only once do three successive holes pursue the same direction, forcing the golfer to play the wind from all quarters.

The Golden Age

A Universal Quest for Perfection

Golf's popularity soared in the period between the wars, particularly in the United States, where the feats of Bobby Jones caught the public imagination. Thus, when he retired and built his ideal course, it was bound to be influential. Fortunately, Augusta National, which Jones designed with Alister Mackenzie, proved to be a worthy model. Its wide fairways, sparing but telling use of bunkers, subtle mounding, huge greens, and its capacity to test golfers of all abilities, demonstrated irrefutably that strategic design was superior to penal design, which had enjoyed an inexplicable vogue in the 1920s.

Other design features emerged as, with a sounder knowledge of the technical problems of building and maintenance and with increasing subtlety, architects pitted their wits against players whose consistency was considerably enhanced by the switch from hickory to steel-shafted clubs. They patiently sculpted their greens, angled them and tilted them; they held out baits, forced decisions, encouraged boldness, indulged the growing taste for spectacular drop-shots, and popularized the heroic, all-or-nothing type of hole. Their growing preoccupation with

Left: Between the wars came the transition from hickory (left) to steel shafts. The change was dramatic because steel eliminated the torsion present in hickory, which had made the shaft twist as well as bend when swung. The changeover took time, the first perforated steel shaft (right), devised by Allan Lard of Massachusetts in 1903, proving inadequate. The breakthrough came with the development of the seamless steel shaft, legalized in Britain in 1929, which led to matched sets of clubs with consistent feel and characteristics.

Left: Pebble Beach. The 8th: 425 yards, par four.
The 8th at Pebble Beach is a magnificent example of the heroic hole that came into its own in the years between the wars. Unlike so many other death-or-glory holes the 8th does offer a less adventurous alternative to the player who has hit a bad drive: he can play to the left and get home in three. However, for those who dare to go for it, the second shot, seen from the small, heavily bunkered green, far left, is a thrilling experience, requiring a carry of some 150 yards to clear the sea and the cliff-edge bunker short of the green. Pebble Beach, on which work was begun in 1918, has eight holes set along the rock-bound coast of Carmel Bay and it was the forerunner of a host of imitative, and usually inferior, spectacular seaside courses.

balance was best summed up by Donald Ross, creator of Seminole and Pinehurst Number 2: "The championship course ... should call for long and accurate tee shots, accurate iron play, precise handling of the short game and, finally, consistent putting. These abilities should be called for in a proportion that will not permit excellence in any one department of the game to too largely offset deficiencies in another."

In those years many other architects were given marvelous land on which to build, and on it they created some unforgettable courses: Jack Neville at Pebble Beach, A. W. Tillinghast at Baltusrol, Stanley Thompson at Band, Charles Alison at Hirono, Mackenzie at Royal Melbourne. They made the period between the wars into golf architecture's Golden Age.

Right: The uncut rough at Turnberry's 7th looks (and, because of its unpredictability, can be) fearsome but it is very often possible to get the club face near the ball and impart some backspin.

The Modern Era

The Land Yields to the Machine

Few courses were built in the years immediately following World War II, the prime concern being the reinstatement of courses that had been neglected or partially destroyed. Then in the late 1950s more money, more leisure time, and the magnetism of Arnold Palmer again made golf into a boom sport.

Increased mobility led to a demand for courses in exotic vacation areas where golf had barely been heard of, and a championship golf course became an essential for every chic resort, just as it did for the proliferation of expensive real estate developments. Elaborate water systems, new construction techniques, and better machinery made them possible, just as these were instrumental in the transformation of desert, mountain, and marsh into land that was fit for golf. Some of the results have been predictably disastrous, but one welcome by-product has been the creation of a plethora of heroic holes in glorious settings around the world.

Water has become a dominant feature of design, particularly around the green. Fairway bunkers are now commonly staggered, though all too often flat and far too easy to escape from. Small greens are again finding favor, ensuring the survival of the art of chipping. Golfers of all abilities are catered to by long tees or, more imaginatively, by numerous smaller tees scattered to provide variations not only in length but also in the line of attack.

A period of undue emphasis on length seems to be drawing to a close, but throughout the modern era the contribution of the architects who have built courses of real worth has been to stay with the classic verities of the masters who preceded them while adding their own individual signatures. Among the most successful are: Tom Weiskopf (Loch Lomond), Dick Wilson (Royal Montreal), Robert Trent Jones (Valderrama), Pete Dye (Harbour Town), Pat Ruddy (The European), Joe Lee (Lagunita), Jack Nicklaus (Muirfield Village), and Peter Thomson and Michael Wolveridge (Bali).

Far left and left: The modern practice of staggering flanking fairway bunkers is perfectly illustrated by Pete Dye's 1969 design for the 13th at Harbour Town. The ideal tee shot must be threaded between the left-hand bunker and a lone oak tree but kept out of the right-hand bunker. Dye also made interesting use of trees, a device that became increasingly popular, by using two oaks to guard the entrance to the green.

The Dunes Golf and Beach Club
The 13th : 560 yards par 5

Far left and left: Robert Trent Jones has always championed strategic design, the 13th hole at Dunes being an excellent example of his approach. From every tee the golfer can decide on the extent of the challenge he wishes to take on.

Like all the early courses actually built to a design, Muirfield was constructed by hand with the help of horses pulling shallow scoops, or drag pans. The architecture benefited from the limitations of this slow but controlled method because it was easier to give earthworks constructed in this way a pleasing natural contour.

The Science that Transforms

Design Into Reality

Since World War II it has been possible to build a golf course almost anywhere—given the two major requirements, money and the technical knowledge. Swamps can be reclaimed, jungles cleared, deserts irrigated, and mountains moved. However, only in the last twenty years or so has it been necessary to even contemplate such radical action to bring a golf course into being. It was finally forced by soaring demand, combined with the rapid escalation in the cost of land and the scarcity of suitable sites. Previously, architects had, with comparative ease, found land that without too much effort could be made fit for golf. With the limited means at their disposal, usually hand labor and horses hauling drag pans, they were able to create courses with the naturalness they so coveted. Occasionally the very earliest designers were unable to route their courses around unwanted sandhills and blind holes resulted, but they were almost the only insurmountable problem.

Today the challenge is altogether different. The architect is given a piece of land, often highly unsuitable, upon which he must construct a course; occasionally, as Pete Dye was able to do at Cajuiles, he is able to search out less uncompromising ground, although even then it is likely to require considerable effort to make it into a golf course. To further complicate his problems the harsher environments of the more remote sites now frequently chosen have called for new grass strains, specially bred and selected to give the best playing qualities in extremes of climate. Thus a knowledge of agronomy, geology, drainage, engineering, forestry, machinery, and heavy construction has become an essential part of the architect's armory. But golf architecture is an art as much as a science and the aims remain the same—to blend sand, water, fairways, and greens, course and surroundings as naturally as possible into a combination pleasing to the senses and thrilling for golf.

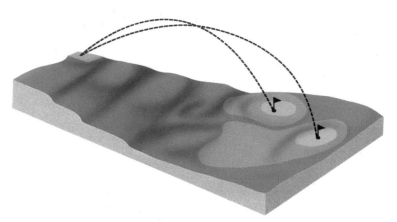

Above: The old 3rd hole at Royal St. George's offered sporting alternatives. A new green—wholly visible—has since been built on a rise.

Left: The consistency and distribution of materials in a modern green are tailored to climatic conditions, but the aim is to ensure controlled growth through use of a balanced seedbed mixture—so important that it is often imported—and good drainage. The sand absorbs excess water, which filters through gravel to be drained off through perforated piping.

Right: The 1st hole at Muirfield Village, with its numerous bunkers, rolling fairways, thoughtfully contoured green, and carefully shaped multiple tees, is typical of the course—and of what can be achieved when $2 million is spent on construction. The annual upkeep of the course costs some $300,000—almost half what it cost in 1975 to build a course with a full irrigation system and the moving of 100,000 cubic yards of earth.

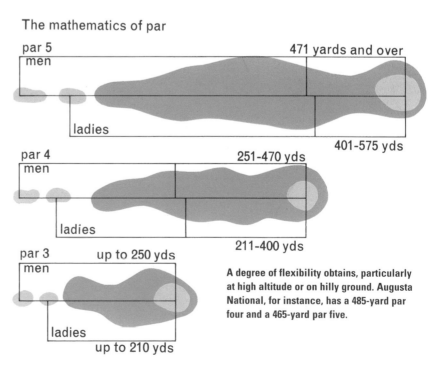

The mathematics of par

par 5
men
471 yards and over
ladies
401-575 yds

par 4
men
251-470 yds
ladies
211-400 yds

par 3
men
up to 250 yds
ladies
up to 210 yds

A degree of flexibility obtains, particularly at high altitude or on hilly ground. Augusta National, for instance, has a 485-yard par four and a 465-yard par five.

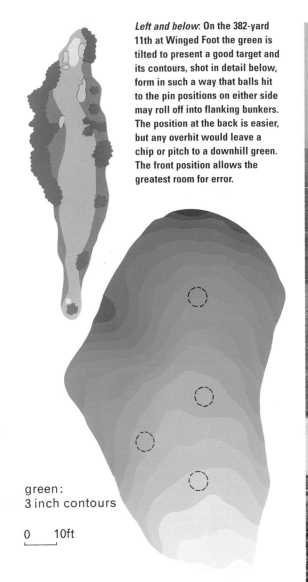

Left and below: On the 382-yard 11th at Winged Foot the green is tilted to present a good target and its contours, shot in detail below, form in such a way that balls hit to the pin positions on either side may roll off into flanking bunkers. The position at the back is easier, but any overhit would leave a chip or pitch to a downhill green. The front position allows the greatest room for error.

green:
3 inch contours

0   10ft

Greens
The Ultimate Target

No part of the golf course can have as much influence on a golfer's score as the greens—the ultimate target. They form the most important part of the construction work and often are the most costly item. No two are alike, but their nature has had an obvious bearing on the difficulty of a course ever since the principles of golf architecture became accepted.

Greens influence scoring in two ways: in the target they present for shots hit into them, and in the effect they have on putting—that controversial game within a game. At first greens were little more than cut extensions of the fairway, though sometimes they were sited in hollows or on plateaus; some were flat, others eccentrically undulating, but all were natural. It was unreasonable to expect a golfer to flight a mashie shot with a feathery or gutty over greenside bunkers and stop his ball on a rough, unprepared surface. Thus in the early days greens were relatively unguarded, but later were given protection, as a means of

calling for more control and as a counter to the ever improving clubs and balls. First sand and later water, sometimes both, were used, often completely encircling the putting surface, their severity depending on the type and length of approach to be played. Greens were angled, raised or lowered to favor those who had hit their previous shot to the ideal place.

With the advent of watering and improved strains of grass, it was not so much a question of hitting the green as one of hitting it in the right place. Pin placement became an art in itself, practiced, with weather conditions in mind, to vary the severity of the test. It came to be universally accepted that if a player aimed for the fat of the green he might face difficulty in getting down in two putts, whereas should he be bold enough to play for the pin the margin for error was slight but the potential rewards great. The putting surface itself should be receptive to the well-struck shot and, ideally, be firm, fast, and true.

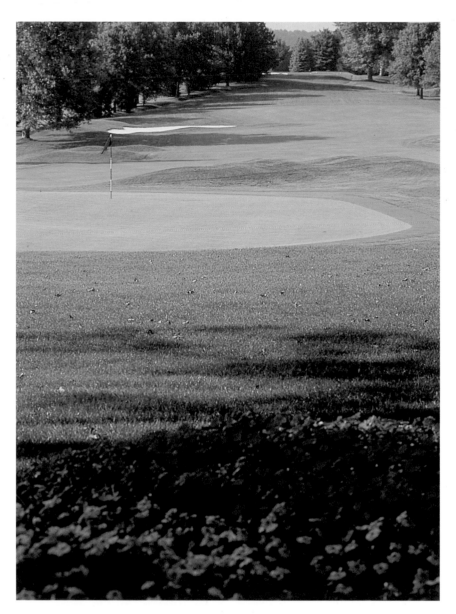

Above: The fast, undulating 18th green is typical of those at Oakmont, which are generally acknowledged to be the most terrifying in the United States, not simply because of the premium they place on putting but because they call for such perfect placement of approach shots. In spite of their fearsome contours, Oakmont's greens are fair because they contain no grain, which affects not only the distances putt will roll but also in which direction it will bend.

Above: The short 7th hole at Pebble Beach is famous for its beauty. Despite its length of only 120 yards, it is a great golf hole, its challenge lying in the size of the green—8 yards wide and 24 yards long—its siting along the line of approach, and the tight ring of bunkers that enclose it.

Right: These three very short holes, Pebble Beach 7th (left), Augusta 12th (center), and Country Club of North Carolina 3rd (right), show how the size and angling of the green can affect the difficulty of a par-three hole.

Not the least of golf's attractions is the fact that it is the one game that is played on natural terrain, or, failing that, on terrain that has been diligently molded so that it has the aspect and the feel of natural terrain. Nearly every other game is played on a court or field especially prepared for it, and whose dimensions must adhere to certain prescribed measurements. It is generally agreed that the best land for golf resembles the gently rolling terrain of the British linksland on which the game slowly developed and reached its first stage of maturity.

Today, when a golfer plays the Old course at St. Andrews and many other British or Irish links, the land, with only occasional slight alterations, twists and turns and slides and heaves very much the way it did centuries ago when uncivilized man walked it without a lofter, a baffy, a brassie, a 5-iron, or a Big Bertha driver in his hand. In the United States and other countries where there is a paucity of true linksland and where, in building a golf course, trees and underbrush have to be ripped out and the bulldozer has to be called in again to move the earth and shape the tees, fairways and greens, the desideratum, to a considerable degree—even on inland courses hundreds of miles from the nearest salt water—has been, and continues to be, to create holes that, with certain necessary variations, possess the character of the best linksland courses.

In this connection all genuinely first-rate golf courses have many traits in common, and at one and the same time

The Imperishable Genius of
the Master Architects

each genuinely first-rate golf course is astonishingly singular. Take the first great U.S. course, the National Golf Links at Southampton, on Long Island, which was opened in 1911, ten years after the idea for the course first came to its designer, Charles Blair Macdonald, and four years after the actual construction began. It probably would not have been a great course had Macdonald not been steeped in British golf—he met the game during the period he was attending St Andrews University—and had gotten to know the best one-shot, two-shot, and three-shot holes on the island so well that he frankly set out to reproduce them on his stretch of bramble-covered duneland off Sebonac Bay. It would not have been a great golf course either had Macdonald not had the excellent common sense not to try to reproduce the famous Scottish and English holes yard for yard and slope for slope, but, instead, modified his models as the land he was working with suggested. The point is not that most golf critics think that Macdonald's Redan is a much better golf hole than the original Redan at North Berwick, or that they consider that Macdonald's Road Hole at the National is not at all in the same class as the original at St. Andrews. Rather, the point is that by understanding what made great holes great, and by intelligently adapting this knowledge to his own acreage, Macdonald reached his goal, which was to have the National Golf Links "serve as an incentive to the elevation of the game in America." Until the National was built, all but a few U.S. courses were hack jobs laid out by golfing illiterates. After the unveiling of the National, the pilgrims who came from every part of the country to study it began to gain a clear idea of what golf course architecture was all about.

So much has been written about the history of golf architecture that it would be wise not to inflict another detailed chronicle upon the reader. However, I would feel remiss in a way if I did not excerpt one of the key passages from Sir Guy Campbell's account of the birth of the linksland courses, which first appeared in *A History of Golf in Britain*, published by Cassell & Co. Ltd. in 1952:

"British golf was first played over links or 'green Gelds'.... Nature was their architect, and beast and man her contractors.

In the formation and overall stabilization of our island coastlines, the sea at intervals of time and distance gradually receded from the higher ground of cliff, bluff, and escarpment to and from which the tides once flowed and ebbed. And as during the ages, by stages, the sea withdrew, it left a series of sandy wastes in bold ridge and significant furrow, broken and divided by numerous channels up and down which the tides advanced and retired, and down certain of which the burns, streams, and rivers found their way to the sea. As time went on, these channels, other than those down which the burns, streams, and rivers ran, dried out and by the action of the winds were formed into dunes, ridges, and knolls, and denes, gullies, and hollows, of varying height, width, and depth.

In the course of nature these channel-threaded wastes became the resting, nesting, and breeding places for birds. This meant bird droppings and so guano or manure, which, with the silt brought down by the burns, streams, and rivers, formed tilth in which the seeds blown from inland and regurgitated from the crops of the birds germinated and established vegetation. Thus eventually the whole of these areas became grass-covered, from the coarse marram on the exposed dunes, ridges and hillocks and the finer bents and fescues in the sheltered dunes, gul-

lies, and hollows, to the meadow grasses round and about the river estuaries and the mouths of the streams and burns. Out of the spreading and intermingling of all these grasses which followed was established the thick, close-growing, hard-wearing sward that is such a feature of links turf wherever it is found."

After getting the grass started, Sir Guy goes on to relate how, successively, heather and whins and broom took root on the linksland; rabbits were attracted to start warrens there; foxes came down the runs to hunt the rabbits; man came down to hunt the foxes; and, later when golf was just starting up and man was looking for the most suitable place to play it, the links was the obvious solution. Incidentally a rough version of the Old Course at St. Andrews had been established by 1414, the year that St. Andrews University, the oldest in Scotland, came into existence.

I was thinking about this extended essay by Sir Guy one day in the spring of 1958, I think it was, when I was en route to a resort in northern Virginia, called the Tides Inn, where Sir Guy was in the process of building a nine-hole course. On the flight to Richmond that day, as I say, I found myself thinking about Sir Guy's piece on the birth of linksland golf, and, proceeding from that I began to muse about the slow, curious, often muddled stages by which golf architecture had developed through the centuries. Those musings, among other things, touched on the following phases of golf course architecture during the past century and a quarter:

• How, shortly after the gutta-percha ball replaced the feather ball in the middle of the nineteenth century, blind golf holes were thought to be the last word in golf architecture. As a result, Prestwick, the proud possessor of the Himalayas (the short 5th) and the Alps (the long two-shot 17th)—on both of them the green is hidden behind a Brobdingnagian sand dune—was regarded in the golf world as the crème de la crème.

• How, as the game spread throughout Britain and around the globe toward the end of the century, the top pro-

fessionals became the busiest golf course architects. There followed a deplorable period of geometric, non-natural design that featured square tees, bunkers that ran the width of a fairway in a straight line, and "gun platform greens" guarded by mounds shaped like chocolate drops. (Many golf champions have proved to have a true talent for golf architecture, but it ain't necessarily so.)

• How the happy discovery was made near the turn of the century that the copious unused stretches of sand, heather, and fir outside London could be transformed into splendid courses, such as Walton Heath and Sunningdale. The porosity of the soil was a key factor. On many of the earlier inland courses built in England, the loamy earth tended to compact tightly in cold weather, and pools of water regularly collected in the fairways.

• How, shortly after the turn of the century, thanks to the tardy recognition that artificial design had no merit at all, golf course architecture came to be regarded as a respectable and useful profession. There followed in Britain a return to courses that emphasized the natural and the simple. Concomitantly, this led to a much better understanding of the principles of "strategic" architecture. In a word, the essence of a strategically designed hole is that the more accurately a golfer places his tee shot, the better his position for his approach shot to the green. Or conversely, the greater a golfer's degree of error on any shot, the more difficult the ensuing shot. A strategically designed hole encourages a golfer to take chances—to cut corners, fly hazards, go for the pin—rewarding him if he accepts a dangerous challenge and pulls it off, and punishing him when he doesn't, in a fair ratio.

• How, when the rubber-cored ball replaced the gutta-percha ball early in this century, holes had to be lengthened. In the view of H. N. Wethered and Tom Simpson, just as the gutta-percha ball had shortened the "feather holes" 20 percent, the rubber-cored ball shortened the "gutty holes" 20 percent.

The 11th hole at Augusta is a completely different challenge now than that presented to players in the 1950s. The advances made in golf club and ball technology, plus fitter and stronger golfers, often means a wedge approach to the green rather than a 3- or 4-iron. Ben Hogan used to play away from the water that protects the green's left-hand side. Now, Tiger Woods just aims straight at the flag.

• How in the United States, even after Macdonald's National had dramatized the virtues of strategic design so memorably, a strange vogue set in for "penal" design. Briefly, the essence of penal golf architecture is its insistence that a golfer follow the narrow route ordained for him to travel from tee to green. He is penalized severely if he makes a mild error—his ball will end up in one of the plethora of deep bunkers that punctuate the fairway and protect the green. The acme of penal courses, Oakmont outside Pittsburgh, at one time found room for over 200 bunkers and 21 traversing ditches. Penal architecture violates the cardinal rule of enlightened design: a first-class hole should present the player with an alternate route—or routes—to the green.

• How the most important contribution, perhaps, of the renowned course at the Augusta National Golf Club, which Bobby Jones designed in collaboration with Dr. Alister Mackenzie, the noted Scottish architect, was that, as the home of the Masters, it demonstrated forcibly and handsomely the superiority of strategic design to penal design. For instance, when the course was formally opened in January 1933, there were only about 30 bunkers on the 18 holes, and no rough to speak of. Its challenge lay in the imaginative use made of its wonderful rolling terrain and the creeks that crossed its lower stretches. Like every great course, the Augusta National could be set up so that, from the back tees, it was a formidable test for the leading professionals and, from the regular tees, a layout that the average golfer could handle and enjoy. Through no fault of its own, the Augusta National—the most influential course built in the United States since Macdonald's National—had one unfortunate effect on American golf. It started a trend toward mammoth-sized greens that, in the years following World War II, became epidemic. At the Augusta National the large greens looked right and played right since they fit in with the overall heroic scale of the course, but it is hard to think of another U.S. course where they seem natural and improve the playing qualities of the holes.

• How, during the affluent post-war period, when a good number of American architects were given the financial backing, time, land, and support (not to mention vastly improved grass strains, better irrigational methods, and all the rest of the advances in knowledge and technique) to build courses of championship standard, more often than not they botched it, chiefly because of their preoccupation with making as much money as possible, which meant becoming involved in as many as twenty projects simultaneously. Consequently, what should have been a Golden Age of Golf Architecture yielded little beyond that rhinestone jewel of a thought: the mistaken concept that a course over 7,000 yards in length is automatically a championship course and that the first tour tournament played over it is automatically entitled to call itself a Classic.

• How, today, we still have our problems—two in particular. The first is that in the United States, anyway, it now takes almost five and a half hours to play a round of golf. The second is that the inordinate distance the ranking pros hit their shots, due to more powerful clubs and livelier balls, has now reached the point where many of the celebrated championship courses no longer provide a bona fide test.

Well, back to Sir Guy Campbell standing in the alien corn in northern Virginia. Without much ado, Sir Guy whisked me out to see his nine holes. They had reached a stage of sufficient advancement—the fairways were cleared, the hazards roughed out, the greens outlined—where a golf-architecture buff like myself had no trouble reading Sir Guy's intentions clearly.

For some odd reason, though, I thought that Sir Guy had certainly gotten the most that was possible out of his lim-iting tract of land, only three holes remain fixed in my memory, one of them—the 1st—principally because it was an enigma. The terrain dictated that it be a short par four of about 340 yards. That's fair enough: nothing wrong with starting out with a short four to give a golfer a chance to get himself unwound before he faces the stern stuff. After all, the starting hole on the Old Course is only 370 yards long. However, whereas the 1st on the Old Course presents some problems—there is out-of-bounds along the right, and the Swilcan Burn separates the fairway from the green—the terrain on Sir Guy's first hole was pretty banal, and he was dissatisfied with all of the ideas for turning it into an interesting hole that he had tossed around. For example, he didn't want a golfer to be able to swat away freely off the tee with only a little flip for his second; on the other hand, he didn't want to toughen up the hole by introducing some strident fairway bunkering about 230 yards out. One doesn't like to make a golfer lay up short of a hazard off any tee or to make him hit a powerful enough opening drive to carry a major hazard.

We must have sketched out and rejected more than fifteen plans for dealing with that first hole during the two days we walked and studied Sir Guy's nine holes. My two-day visit with Sir Guy, in which he fussed with one small detail after another, also served to clarify for me why so many of the acknowledged great U.S. courses have been built by amateur architects—Oakmont (love it or leave it) by Henry C. and W. C. Fownes, steel magnates; Merion by Hugh Wilson, an insurance broker; Pine Valley by George Crump, a hotelier; and Pebble Beach (which may be the best course in the world) by Jack Neville, a real estate salesman who never built another course on his own. As amateur architects they were able to lavish on their projects the countless hours, the perfectionistic fervor, and the plain love that distinguishes the fine arts from lesser efforts.

This does not mean that professional architects do not occasionally give as much of themselves to their courses, but all too frequently, because of the crush of their schedules, the success or failure of their designs depends on how well they are executed by the construction superintendent. (One hears it was an inspired local superintendent who made Mackenzie's Royal Melbourne such a magnificent layout, and one suspects that a similarly superior superintendent followed through on Mackenzie's Cypress Point.) There really is no substitute, though, for the architect staying with the job himself and employing the most effective and not the quickest means to achieve the tiny touches that make exceptional holes exceptional.

This is probably the point at which to ask ourselves, "Why all this concern about what makes for good golf architecture? What does good golf architecture accomplish?" The answer, I think, might well begin with the statement that the average golfer, no different from a Sam Snead, a Gary Player, or a Sandy Lyle, feels in his bones whether or not a hole is laid out correctly and possesses true shot values. Both the average golfer and the champion golfer enjoy playing a sound, enticing, well-conditioned hole much more than a bland one, because a good hole makes it absolutely clear to golfers of all degrees of skill what shots he should play from tee to green and how he should handle the green. Consequently, when a golfer is able to execute the shots that are called for, the pleasure he experiences is far greater than when he merely manages to hit a fine shot on an indifferent hole though, I hasten to add, any time a golfer hits a fine shot, the satisfaction is considerable. In golf, because of the nature of the game, a beautiful hole is not one that has a lovely stream flowing across it. It is a hole with a lovely stream flowing across it at the right place.

It goes without saying, a good course is one where the fundamentals are right: where the implicit strategy of each individual hole is apparent to the golfer as he stands on the tee; where, as John Low put it long ago, "the ground determines the play"; where the hazards are frankly visible (always allowing for the exception to every rule that is the Old Course); where there is a judicious variety of fairway lies; where the holes do not present the wrong sort of difficulty—the kind that skill cannot cope with—but, rather, possess a beckoning spirit of adventure, like the cliffside holes at Ballybunion in County Kerry or at Turnberry in Ayrshire; where the routing of the holes is both thoughtful and appealing, like at Muirfield, where the first nine moves in a clockwise arc outside the counter-clockwise pattern of the second nine, and like at the Augusta National, where one does not encounter two holes with the same par back to back until the 9th and the 10th, two par fours; where the greens offer plenty of diversity in the way they are positioned, shaped, and contoured; and where, when all is said and done, the raison d'être of the course is the suitableness of the land for golf. We all know they can "hit the ball a ton" and play it high, low, left-to-right, right-to-left, straight, soft, hard—the works. What we don't know is whether they can come through with the shot that is called for when they are confronted with an arresting challenge when the pressure is on. The top courses present these challenges hole after hole, and this is why for just about a century now people who appreciate golf have turned out in large numbers to watch the championships.

For example, let's say the year is 1896 and we are at Muirfield following a young man named Harry Vardon, who has never done anything much, play the 72nd hole of the British Open. It is a long two-shotter, over 400 yards to a raised green, on which the crucial hazard is a bunker with an intimidatingly steep front wall that lies in wait just before the green. J. H. Taylor, the defending champion, is in with a total of 316. Vardon has driven well. If he can get his four, that will give him a total of 315, but the trouble is that this means he will have to carry the bunker, almost 200 yards away, with his second, and that might mean ending up with a buried lie in the face of the bunker and, eventually, with a total of 317. What a minute! Vardon, after much cogitation, elects to lay up short of the beast, make certain of his five, and take his chances on beating Taylor in a play-off. The next day he went out and won the first of his six British Opens. As the old saying goes, behind each successful champion stands a provocative, soundly strategic course that imposes difficult decisions and sometimes elicits historic shots. Let me describe another such dramatic moment.

Muirfield, the 1966 British Open, seventy years after Vardon's break-through victory. Final round. Jack Nicklaus, who has never won the championship, may have lost another wonderful chance. Leading the field by three strokes with only nine holes to go, he has tossed them away by missing his pars on the 65th, the 67th, and the 68th. Pars on the next two. To win, he now needs a birdie and a par—probably in that order, since the 528-yard 71st offers a golfer with Jack's tremendous length a good crack at a four. It's an odd hole, the 17th or 71st. The tee shot is a blind one, up and over a rising fairway that breaks to the left—bunkers in the elbow. Far away in the distance, as you walk to your ball after your drive, you take in the small, old-fashioned green, half-hidden by a rugged ridge that thrusts itself out into the fairway from the right a hundred yards or so from the green. Today, the wind is out of the west, directly behind Nicklaus off the tee. Accordingly, he decides to go with a 3-iron instead of the 1-iron he used on the first three rounds. He whacks his tee shot—following wind, small British ball, remember—a full 290 yards down the right side of the fairway. All right, where do we go from here? Wind—from off the left and a little behind. Lie all that one could ask for. Jack

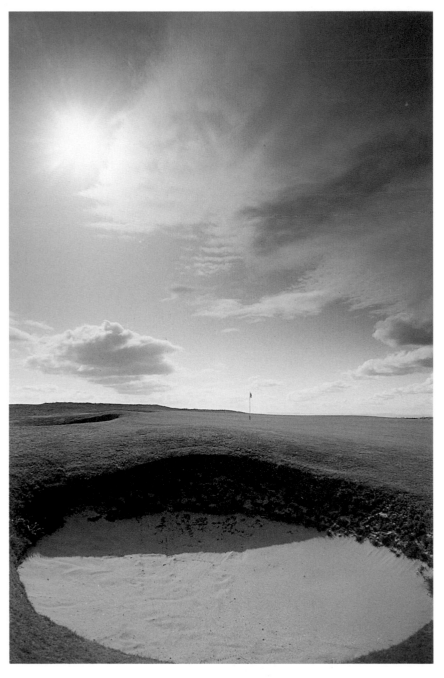

decides on a 5-iron and takes aim on the left side of the green. If he flies the ball all the way to the green, it won't hold the resilient surface. He wants to bounce it on—hence the 5-iron. His swing is very smoothly executed. Yes, he's played an extremely good-looking, high-arcing shot. The ball lands in the narrow channel of fairway about 6 yards short of the green, gets a nice slow bounce, and finishes about 20 feet from the pin. It is the winning shot, in effect. Nicklaus cozies the ball up close to the cup and gets that all-important birdie. On the tough 72nd, two more superlative irons—a 1-iron and a 3-iron banked into the wind coming off the right—and the par four that wraps up his first victory in the British Open.

On the great courses, it is a great game—as several million golfers claim, the best game ever invented.

Note: The yardages quoted throughout this book for courses and for individual holes are from the championship tees unless otherwise specified. Within the descriptive text they have, for reasons of clarity, been rounded up or down and reflect the original course design.

At the 7th at Muirfield, a par three played to an exposed green, a golfer is completely at the mercy of the elements and club selection is dictated accordingly.

Europe

Born, cradled, and nurtured on the wild coasts of Scotland, golf is native to the British Isles and an exotic plant everywhere else—although, like many exotics, it has often found conditions as much to its liking where it has been imported. Scotland's pride are the natural links where time and the seasons were the principal architects of courses like Royal Dornoch, that noble links of the north, and the austere, patriarchal St. Andrews, the shrine to which the greatest still return to pay homage. Golf began its travels when it was taken south to England by the Stuarts and then to the four corners of the earth by the men of both nations in the Empire-building days of the nineteenth century. Progress remained tardy on the European mainland until as late as the mid-1980s when the emergence of players like Bernhard Langer from Germany and Spain's Severiano Ballesteros, allied to victories for Europe in the Ryder Cup, had a dramatic effect.

Among the earliest of courses on the continent of Europe were those built during Queen Victoria's reign at watering places to which the wealthy British migrated annually to take the cure: spas like Baden-Baden in Germany, Karlovy Vary and Marienbad in Czechoslovakia (then a realm of the Hapsburgs), and Pau in the foothills of the Pyrenees, the earliest of them all (1856). At first most progress, outside Britain, was made in northern Europe—the Low Countries (where there are echoes of Scottish linksland), Sweden, and Germany.

But changing patterns of wealth and tourism have seen the emergence in more recent times of a plethora of courses at Europe's other extreme, the Mediterranean and Atlantic coastlines of the Iberian Peninsula. In 1997 the importance of Spain in particular to European golf was recognized when Valderrama, in the province of Andalusia, was chosen as the first continental venue for the Ryder Cup.

Similar in appearance and atmosphere to the resort courses of North America, these new venues have largely been built as commercial developments by entrepreneurs and have had the benefit of some of the best architects that money can buy. Their sunlit, Sybaritic ambience seems a world away from the windswept linksland of the Scottish coast where the game took root, almost organically, as part of the life of small, tightly knit communities.

1. St Andrews 2. Royal Troon 3. Carnoustie 4. Royal Dornoch 5. Muirfield 6. Turnberry 7. Loch Lomond 8. Royal Liverpool 9. Royal Lytham St Annes 10. Sunningdale 11. Royal Birkdale 12. The Belfry 13. Royal St George's 14. Royal Porthcawl 15. Royal County Down 16. Royal Portrush 17. Portmarnock 18. Killarney 19. Ballybunion 20. Kennemer 21. Royal Antwerp 22. Falsterbo 23. Club Zur Vahr 24. Olgiata 25. Chantilly 26. Valderrama 27. Vilamoura

Nature Fashions an
Ageless Masterpiece

With the patronage of King William IV in 1834 the Society of St. Andrew's Golfers became known as the Royal and Ancient Golf Club.

For centuries, the eyes and thoughts of golfers everywhere have turned toward St. Andrews: in all their world there is nothing to compare with the ancient university city and the Old Course spreading away from its doors. Here is the very heart of golf, the very breath of its history on links that, for countless ages, have known so little change. Every golfer there ever was has wanted to play at St. Andrews, and through the years it has attracted more pilgrims than any other course in the world.

At first sight, the Old Course may not seem remarkable. One will have been charmed by the intimacy of its approaches from within the city and the beauty of the spacious rectangle of green, sweeping down from the Royal and Ancient clubhouse, gray, four-square, and slightly forbidding. On one side are the smaller clubs, Old Tom Morris's shop, hotels and houses; on the other a rolling sward of putting green and beyond, the superb bay, leagues and leagues of golden sand curving away toward the distant estuary of the Tay.

The old links has been condemned as an anachronism and cursed as being unfair, but no course has commanded greater affection and respect from those who have learned to appreciate its subtleties and charms. It can be as tantalizing as a beautiful woman, whose smile at once is a temptation and a snare, concealing heartbreak and frustration for some, joy and fulfillment for others, but possession only for the very fortunate few. It does not yield its ancient secrets lightly or take kindly to contempt and impatience, but it does reward those who give their best in thought, temper, and technique. Furthermore, St. Andrews is the setting for the Royal and Ancient Club. It was founded on May 14, 1754, when 22 "Noblemen and Gentlemen, being admirers of the ancient and healthful exercise of the Golf,"

met to subscribe for a silver club, to be the trophy of an annual competition. Since then its sphere of influence has become almost universal, except in the United States, which has its own governing body in the United States Golf Association.

There is no telling when golf began at St. Andrews, but the earliest written evidence was a license, issued in 1552, that permitted the community to rear rabbits on the links, and "play at golf, futball, schuteing ... with all other manner of pastimes." The proprietor was bound "not to plough up any part of said golf links in all time coming" but to reserve them for the comfort and amusement of the inhabitants. So, for more than 400 years, every golfer has enjoyed a right to play over the course, and only within the present century has a green fee been imposed. In recent times, this has grown to the point where the cost is outside the means of many golfers, a sad development since the last thing the Old Course was meant to be was a testament to wealth.

It remains, nonetheless, a monument to the origins of golf as a game played on links by the sea. In the beginning it knew no architect but nature; it came into being by evolution rather than design; and on no other course is the hand of man less evident.

In all the years since the Royal and Ancient Club was formed, the outline of the course has never changed. It was then no more than 40 yards wide, a rolling strip of linksland between the gorse bushes in the shape of a huge billhook. There was not room for separate holes going out and home, so the golfers played eleven (later nine) out to a distant turn by the shining waters of the Eden estuary, and returned using the same fairways and greens.

St. Andrews must have had its perilous moments in those days—and it still can, for seven of the double greens remain—but nowadays there is more delay than danger on a crowded day. The double greens are so huge that only an extremely wayward shot will find its way on to another man's province. If so, the player can face a length of putt undreamed of on any other course in the world. Nowhere does the old excuse for an indifferent score of taking three putts hold more water.

The greens are further evidence of nature's bounty; most of them are on plateaus, sometimes only slightly raised above the level of their surrounds but plateaus nonetheless. When the wind stands firm and the turf is hard and swift, the man who pitches to the hole can be lost; the pitch and run or the plain running approach must be used, though such conditions nowadays are the exception rather than the rule at St. Andrews. In common with many other links it has lost something of its seaside character; the grass on the fairways is richer, the greens more holding than of old. Often enough, it is possible to pitch to them and good scoring is easier in consequence. This is most readily seen at the Alfred Dunhill Cup, which is played at St. Andrews every October, when the turf is invariably lush and the greens soft. Add a windless day and anything becomes possible: in 1987 Curtis Strange went around in just 62 strokes to set a new course record. Ten years later, a Swede named Joakim Haeggman played the front nine in level threes, a wonderful effort given the formal regulation mark of 36.

Another remarkable feature of the course is the mul-

titude of bunkers, most of which are named, ranging from vast sandy caverns to little holes of varying depth, often allowing room only for an "angry man and his niblick." All are natural, many are relics of the days when people dug for shells deposited by the sea before the links were formed, while others were made by sheep sheltering from the wind. Over the years great numbers were filled, but enough remain to test and infuriate the mightiest, because they are not always visible and seem to lurk in the most unexpected places.

Lying within the curve of a bay on the northeastern shores of Fife, the course is vulnerable to every caprice of the wind. Many are those who have played to the turn against it and then, hoping for assistance on the homeward journey, had to face it all the way back. The strategy of play can change within the hour. Such are the

The 1st and 18th holes at St. Andrews, flanked by some of Scotland's finest architecture. On the left is the magnificent clubhouse of the Royal and Ancient G. C., the governing body (with the USGA) of golf.

The Course Card

Royal and Ancient Golf Club
of St. Andrews, Fife
Old Course

Record: 62, Curtis Strange, Dunhill Cup, 1987

Hole	Name	Yardage	Par
1	Burn	370	4
2	Dyke	411	4
3	Cartgate (out)	352	4
4	Ginger Beer	419	4
5	Hole o' Cross (out)	514	5
6	Heathery (out)	374	4
7	High (out)	359	4
8	Short	166	3
9	End	307	4
10	Bobby Jones	318	4
11	High (in)	172	3
12	Heathery (in)	316	4
13	Hole o' Cross (in)	398	4
14	Long	523	5
15	Cartgate (in)	401	4
16	Corner of the Dyke	351	4
17	Road	461	4
18	Tom Morris	354	4
Out		**3,294**	**36**
In		**3,272**	**36**
Total		**6,566**	**72**

whereabouts of the hazards that the slightest variations in the wind can mean the difference between being trapped in an infuriating little bunker and having a straightforward shot to the green. There is no standard way of playing the holes, except for the first and the last. Everything depends on the wind; an approach may be a metal wood one day, a short pitch the next.

The Old Course makes a wonderful play on courage and fear but, above all, it is an examination of a golfer's thinking: he can never relax. In view of this, it is not surprising that nearly all the great golfers throughout the ages have grown to respect the place, and some, like Bobby Jones, to love it. With Jones it was not love at first sight. In the third round of the 1921 Open he was a dozen or more strokes over par and, after taking six on the short 11th, tore up his card. The world knows how he redeemed

that failure with a famous victory six years later, and another in the Amateur championship, the first stage of the "Grand Slam" in his imperishable summer of 1930. When, almost thirty years later, Jones was given the freedom of St. Andrews and made an Honorary Burgess of the city—a distinction not conferred upon an American since Benjamin Franklin—he said: "The more I studied the Old Course, the more I loved it and the more I loved it, the more I studied it, so that I came to feel that it was for me the most favorable meeting ground possible for an important contest. I felt that my knowledge of the course enabled me to play it with patience and restraint until she might exact her toll from my adversary, who might treat her with less respect and understanding."

The beginning of the course seems innocence itself. The widest fairway in existence—shared by the first and last holes—looks inviting, but at its limit winds the Swilcan Burn, an immediate menace to peace of mind for it must be carried by the first shot to the 1st green, and this invariably is longer than it looks. From the second tee the long trail outward begins down the narrow ribbon, perhaps a 100 yards across, of crumpled, saffron links, broken only by the emerald pools of the double greens and the countless folds, falls, and hummocks of the ageless land. This second hole is a perfect example of the course at its best, especially when the flag is toward the left of the green. The only reasonable approach is from the right, so either the drive risks bunkers and gorse or the second shot must be played to the right-hand part of the green, leaving a long and formidable putt.

The problem at the 3rd is the same—a measure of risk must be taken from the tee for a clear pitch to the pin; likewise at the 4th, with its drive along a valley between a plateau and the inevitable gorse and bunkers on the right. A host of bunkers awaits the drive to the 5th which is aimed too straight at the distant pin; this is the Hole o' Cross, the longest of all, which forces a decision whether to attempt to carry a hill with two large bunkers in its face or play short, leaving a longish third to the green. In the

John Daly drives off from the 18th hole on his way to an emotional victory in the 1995 Open Championship.

The 17th

Hardest Par Four in Golf

When Tom Watson stood on the 17th tee during the final round of the 1984 Open he was, unquestionably, the finest golfer in the world. In an astonishing eight-year period of supremacy he had won eight majors and he was on the point of equaling Harry Vardon's record of six Opens.

When Watson stood on the 18th tee he was a different golfer entirely. He had misjudged his second shot and with it went his dream of winning the Open at the Home of Golf. He had also lost that feeling of imperiousness, that self-belief that gave him his edge. Watson never did

win another major. Vardon continues to stand alone.

If a single hole can do that to a player of Watson's stature, what hope the rest of us? Not much, for only the best of the pros expect to walk off with a par. This is one hole that has withstood the demands of technology, offering advantage to the long hitter only if he shows the utmost courage from the tee. For John Daly to find the 17th fairway with his driver in the 1995 Open play-off, he had to practically aim at his suite balcony in the adjoining Old Course hotel. Daly plotted the route perfectly, drawing the ball back from the building and into the

——— Daly
- - - - - Safe line

1933 Open, with the ground bone-hard and a gale behind him, Craig Wood drove into one of these bunkers, almost a quarter of a mile from the tee. A slight ridge protects the 6th green and makes the approach seem shorter than it is, a common feature of the Old Course. The stranger is forever under-clubbing.

The next six holes form what is commonly known as the Loop, where the foundation of low scores invariably is made; on occasion they have been played in eighteen strokes or less. The drive to the 7th is one of the most testing, practically blind, with a sea of gorse to punish the slice—but the 8th is not a severe short hole. Good drives make threes readily possible at the next two holes, but the little approach to the 9th is dead flat. It has caught many a player in two minds as to whether to pitch or run it, and has often resulted in a scuffle.

Of all the great short holes, the 11th stands high. The green is on a considerable slope, with the waters of Eden beyond; to the left is the deep Hill bunker. The essence of the shot is to avoid these and yet not to have a fiendishly difficult putt. To finish above the hole with the wind off the estuary is to invite three putts; men have been known to putt off the green. Gene Sarazen once took six there, with three shots in the Hill bunker, and eventually lost the championship by one stroke.

There never was a hole more obviously the work of the Devil than the 12th, where seeming innocence conceals all manner of evil. However well one knows the hole, it is hard to realize that so much danger exists between tee and green, only some 300 yards away. None of it is visible, but the fairway, a gentle green slope, is infested with bunkers.

After the 13th, the task is stern indeed. No single hole in golf has brought more championship competitors to grief than the 14th; the number of great golfers who have taken sevens and worse there is legion. In any kind of wind, save a helping one, the prospect from the back tee is fearsome indeed, with the five Beardies bunkers clustered together to trap the slightest pull and a low gray

stone wall jutting into the line from the right. Only the bold or the very strong attempt to carry the great Hell bunker and its attendants, and then remains the problem of judging the third shot over a sleek, steep bank. The 15th presented no great difficulty for years, because the professionals could easily carry its main hazard, the wretched little Sutherland bunker, which stands precisely on the cautious line from the tee. But now the hole has been lengthened by 46 yards and many a pro will now find himself echoing the thoughts of one greens committee long ago, that ordered its removal. On that occasion the rebels went in the night, opened it again, and there it remains.

Similarly the 16th has been lengthened by 44 yards to bring the Principal's Nose bunker back into play. The confident or the unthinking will continue to drive between the railway and the hazard, a threateningly narrow approach. The railway, whose fences remain, is nowadays out-of-bounds. But in olden days, when it was a cart track, golfers carried a track iron, one of which can be seen in the Royal and Ancient Museum. The prudent line from the tee is to the left, but the Wig bunker by the green must be avoided. Then at last the golfer stands on the tee of the most famous hole in the world.

The drive over the corner of the hotel grounds, where black railway sheds once stood, is not as alarming as it looks, but the green on a little plateau is an awesome sight. On the left, "eating its way into its very vitals" as Bernard Darwin once wrote, is the Road bunker, while beyond the narrow green is the road itself, at the foot of a sharp little shelf with nothing to prevent the ball rolling down. The second may be anything from wood to short iron, but only the brave go for the top level of the green. The majority play short, but even the little approach is fraught with danger. The ground draws into the bunker, from where there is no more terrifying recovery, with the road awaiting any overhit.

Whatever may have befallen the golfer on the 17th the broad, guileless swoop of the last fairway is infinitely appealing. The drive can be aimed anywhere to the left;

middle of the fairway. From there he had just a seven iron to the flag.

Besides the bold second shot, where a player tries to hold the sliver of green, there are several approaches possible. A golfer can aim to take the bunker out of play, and aim for areas beside the 18th tee, as Ernie Els is prone to do. A more common route is to aim for a spot to the right of the flag, parallel to the surface from where a par four is feasible.

The 17th

A Splash Shot of the Utmost Delicacy

The Road bunker on the 17th has probably ruined more cards than any other in the world and none more so than in the 1995 Open play-off between John Daly and Costantino Rocca. An hour earlier, Rocca had holed across the Valley of Sin to reach this position. Now joy turned to heartache. Rocca's ball lay well in the sand but the bunker is small, its face steep, and the hole only a few yards beyond it. A splash shot of the utmost delicacy, one that would feather the ball over the lip and make it land softly, was demanded of him. But the instinct of

most golfers in such a situation is for a swing that is short and hurried and Rocca proved another victim. He would need three strokes in all before emerging and the four hole play-off was over as a contest without the 18th needing to be played.

The Road bunker cut into the 17th green.

to slice out-of-bounds at this point would be lunacy indeed. Only the Valley of Sin, a smooth bowl that gathers the timid approach, remains to be avoided and so on to Tom Morris's green. Always it seems there are people leaning from the windows and over the fences. Behind them rises the cloistered little city, gray, peaceful, and so very old. This was the setting for the most dramatic last hole the Open has known in modern times.

When Doug Sanders, at the end of a torturous day of wind in 1970, hit a long drive up the last fairway, victory was there for the taking; he needed a four to beat Nicklaus. The task seemed only a formality but he took three putts, finally missing from a yard—and Nicklaus had enjoyed the escape of his lifetime. In the play-off the following day, Sanders bravely fought back from four behind to one as they stood on the last tee. Nicklaus, with an unconsciously masterful gesture, took off a sweater for greater freedom and unleashed a thunderous drive that almost hit the pin. It ran through the green into thick rough, from where he chipped to 6 feet. As the putt just curled in he flung his putter high in the air, a rare show of emotion for Nicklaus and a heartbreaking moment for Sanders.

In the 1995 Open the old green saw more drama, when Costantino Rocca holed a putt from in the Valley of Sin to force a four hole play-off against John Daly. Moments earlier, Rocca had fluffed a 50-yard chip and a lifetime of regret was staring him in the face. The putt negated the tears. He fell to his knees and then pummeled his fists into the turf in jubilation. Rocca would lose the play-off but the smile would not leave his face. He had lost with honor rather than humiliation and the difference became apparent in the years that followed, as he established himself among the finest players.

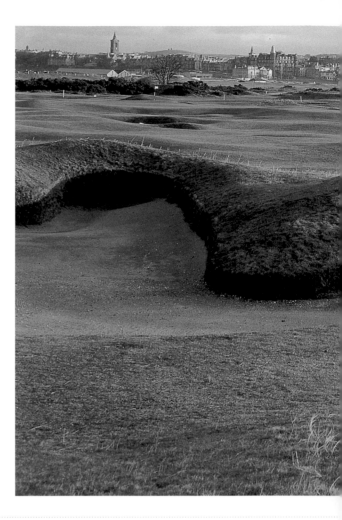

Hell bunker, which yawns so menacingly at the end of the Elysian Fields, forces the player to choose a right- or a left-hand line to the green and thereby court trouble of a different sort. The left side of the green is well protected by the Ginger Beer bunkers.

The 18th

To Pitch or Run?

Doug Sanders' approach shots at the 18th in the 1970 Open. In the final round Sanders chose to pitch over the grassy hollow of the Valley of Sin, which can be seen at the front left-hand corner of the 18th green. His pitch shot (1) was hit with loft and landed, as he intended, close to the pin, but, despite the backspin, the ball failed to stop. The following day, from a similar position, Sanders hit a classic chip-and-run shot with top-spin (2) through the Valley of Sin and up to the pin.

Perhaps no shot better illustrates the yawning difference between golf played on a traditional links and those lush venues to be found throughout the United States than the approach to the home hole at St. Andrews. The tendency among the Americans is to pitch to the hole and try to impart enough spin to keep the ball near the flag. The danger is in going too long and leaving oneself the sort of putt that is easy to misjudge. Most British players prefer the classic method of the chip and run and unless the ground is heavy and slow this is usually the safer shot. The overwhelming concern in this situation is not to fall short in the insidious grassy hollow of the Valley of Sin, from where it is also simplicity itself to take three putts.

Which is the better method? There is no better method, rather depending instead on the skills of the player involved, the conditions of the day, and whether the flag is positioned toward the front or the back. But in midsummer, when the ground is hard and baked and the pin to the front, there is no finer shot either to watch or to play than the chip and run executed with a true sense of feel. One such shot was played by Nick Faldo in 1990, when he won the Masters at Augusta and the Open at St. Andrews by five shots. In the first round his drive down the 18th left him 40 yards of ground to cover. He selected a 7-iron, and the ball crawled over the arid earth before dropping into the hole for an eagle two.

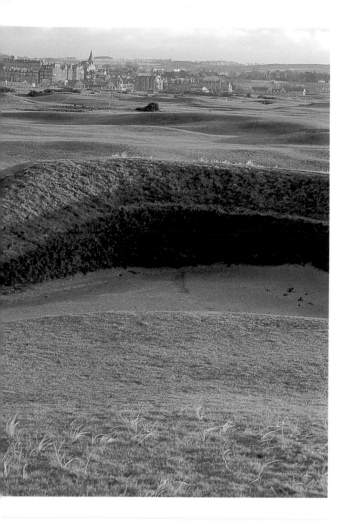

The Nose Job

For over a decade the Principal's Nose, the cluster of three bunkers that guards the 16th fairway, had failed to get up the noses of the top players, thanks to the advances of modern technology. The players had little difficulty reaching for their howitzers and blasting the ball beyond the hazard, thus destroying the hole's original concept. Now, things are somewhat different. A new tee has been introduced that lengthens the hole by 44 yards, and the effect is to restore the hole to how it was envisaged in design. Once more, players have to decide whether to take on the carry and risk plunging into the bunkers, thereby almost certainly losing a stroke, or play short and take on a long iron to a green that sits right next to the boundary wall. With the 15th similarly lengthened and the 17th always the hardest hole in championship golf, St. Andrews now possesses a trinity of punishing finishing holes that will ensure it will remain a demanding test long into the new millennium.

——— New line

--------- Old line

Much by Skill
as by Strength

The Course Card

Troon
Record: 64,
Greg Norman,
The Open 1989

Hole	Yards	Par
1	364	4
2	391	4
3	379	4
4	557	5
5	210	3
6	577	5
7	402	4
8	126	3
9	423	4
10	438	4
11	481	4
12	431	4
13	465	4
14	179	3
15	475	4
16	542	5
17	223	3
18	452	4
Out	3,583	37
In	3,682	37
Total	**7,265**	**74**

Royal Troon is rarely acclaimed among the great Open Championship golf courses. It possesses neither the beauty of Turnberry, the dunes of Birkdale, the fairness of Muirield, or the reverence of St. Andrews. But its place on the roster is deserved for all that and its motto, "Tam Arte Quam Morte" (Much by skill as by strength) was much in evidence at the 1997 Championship when the laurels were handed out not to the celebrated Tiger Woods but rather Justin Leonard, a short-hitting Texan who showed a greater awareness of its subtle demands.

Troon's most celebrated member is Colin Montgomerie, who has made his name with his accuracy and an acute sense of course management. One round over the fabled links of his home course is sufficient to understand where he learned his rudimentary knowledge of such skills. Without them, no one can hope to prosper over this dour and forbidding stretch of Ayrshire coastline.

The first six holes, though, are wonderfully inviting, and Greg Norman demonstrated the possibilities for low scoring when, in the final round of the 1989 Open, he birdied them all. The last seven offer no such prospect, however. Back into the prevailing wind, it is as much as a golfer can do to hold on to par if the elements possess any velocity. The links has more than its share of prized holes. It has both the longest and shortest holes on the Open Championship roster. The former is the sixth, an endless par five where the green has been widened in recent times to allow the pin to be tucked behind one of its infinite number of humps. The latter is the most celebrated of all short holes, the Postage Stamp, a magnificent testament to the belief that the game, indeed, is as much about skill as strength. Henry Leach described it perfectly when he wrote: "It is as full of wickedness as it is of beauty." Like many seaside courses that were formed in the closing years of the nineteenth century, Troon owed its formation to a railway line, in this instance the main

link between Glasgow and Ayr. For the citizens of Glasgow and Paisley an engaging stretch of coastline offering sandy beaches and miles of duneland was now within their grasp. It was also perfect for golf and the developers seized upon the land like prospectors at a gold mine. Their legacy is a necklace of sublime links courses, stretching one after the other: Irvine, Glasgow Gailes, Western Gailes, Barassie, Troon, and Prestwick.

Troon was formed on Saturday March 16, 1878, at the instigation of a Scot named James Dickie, who owned a summer house on Troon's South Beach and wanted to kindle the interest of some of the local people for a golf club of their own. Dickie approached the Duke of Portland, who gave permission to build a course on land between Craigend and Gyaws Burn. Craigend Burn is now piped under the road in front of the clubhouse but Gyaws Burn is turning back and forth, rather like that at the Old Course at St. Andrews. The last six all head homeward, toward a clubhouse steeped both in history and beauty.

Not even the opening hole at St. Andrews can offer a more welcoming start to a round than the first at Troon. The fairway may run close to the edge of the shoreline but it is a poor shot that locates it. The driving area is inviting and the short second shot is to a generous green. The hole runs to 364 yards and in the summer months with a helpful wind a big hitter can open his shoulders and contemplate reaching the front apron. The 2nd is almost as straightforward although Darren Clarke might be tempted to disagree after finding the beach with his tee shot during the final round of the 1997 Open. Given that he finished only three shots behind the winner, to lose two here was wasteful in the extreme. Two fairway bunkers lie in wait to capture the big hitter but with length not a factor the player with an artful sense of course management will play short and still have a small iron to the green.

Similarly the 3rd, where the Gyaws Burn crosses the fairway at 300 yards, thus taking the green out of range. Another short iron approach, nonetheless. The 4th is a long par five that did not appear very long at all after Tiger Woods launched his drive during the first round of the 1997 Open. A yardage circle painted into the turf nearby indicated that, give or take a yard, he had struck his tee shot 435 yards. For more mortal players the hole plays as a dogleg to the right. The 5th is the first of a quartet of splendid short holes. To the right are clear views of the Isle of Arran. With the wind blowing off the sea and the flag to the right the line can be the very edge that separates the green from the beach; a brave shot, to say the least.

The 5th is the one hole over the first six where a reasonable player in reasonable weather needs to be fully on his mettle. The 6th, therefore, continues the run of holes from which a golfer must make his score, a raking par five

still very much part of the layout, crossing both the 3rd and 16th holes. While Dickie was securing the land for the course a local GP, Dr. John Highet, approached a number of interested parties with regard to finance. Dr. Highet became the club's first Secretary, holding the post for fifteen years, while James Dickie was the first Captain. The Royal Seal, the most recent to have been conferred, was given on the occasion of the club's centenary, in 1978.

In common with many of the great Scottish links courses, no one architect was responsible. The initial six holes at Troon were laid out by the greenskeeper at Prestwick, Charles Hunter. As for the rest of the holes, which grew in number as more land was acquired, no-one is sure who designed them. The first man to carry out alterations was the 1883 Open Champion Willie Fernie, the Troon professional at the time. In turn he has been followed by James Braid, Dr. Alister Mackenzie, and Frank Pennink. Between them they have fashioned an honest course that requires the utmost concentration and skill to unlock a score. Even Arnold Palmer, who won the Open there in 1962, once talked of his determination "not to get locked into a life and death struggle with the course."

Troon is laid out in the manner of a classic traditional links. The first six holes head away from the clubhouse, along the shoreline. The next six holes broadly form a loop,

The 6th hole is the longest in Open Championship golf, an endless par five to a green surrounded on two sides by dunes.

The 11th

Tiger's Torment, Nicklaus's Nemesis

Not since Jack Nicklaus had any player come to his first Open as a professional with a bigger reputation than Tiger Woods. Coincidentally, both made their debuts at Troon. It is not coincidence, however, that both were humbled by the 11th. Arnold Palmer once said that he aimed to get the 11th before it got him but Woods and Nicklaus were not so fortunate. In their first encounters with the hole in serious competition, they played it in a combined total of 17 shots.

Nicklaus ran up no less than a ten on the hole and typically learned from the experience. "It taught me how much knowledge I needed to absorb before I could think of taking on the original form of golf," he would say. Woods's seven arose from hooking his tee shot into the bushes to the left of the tee. He donned his waterproofs for his recovery shot but when the ball moved but a few feet he had to concede defeat.

Palmer's strategy was clearly the correct one. Before the 1962 Open began he had identified the hole as the key one, based on where it came in the round and also its difficulty. The hole had recently been converted from a shortish par four into a par five and over the four days of the championship Palmer would birdie it three times and par it once. Thirty-five years later it was once more a par four, though, at 463 yards, not one that now lacked for length. Woods was hardly alone in suffering. The 11th was played in an average of 4.65 shots, thus easily securing its ranking as the most difficult hole on the course, and adding still further to its formidable reputation.

Tiger Woods's first Open as a professional saw him encounter difficulty with the daunting 11th hole.

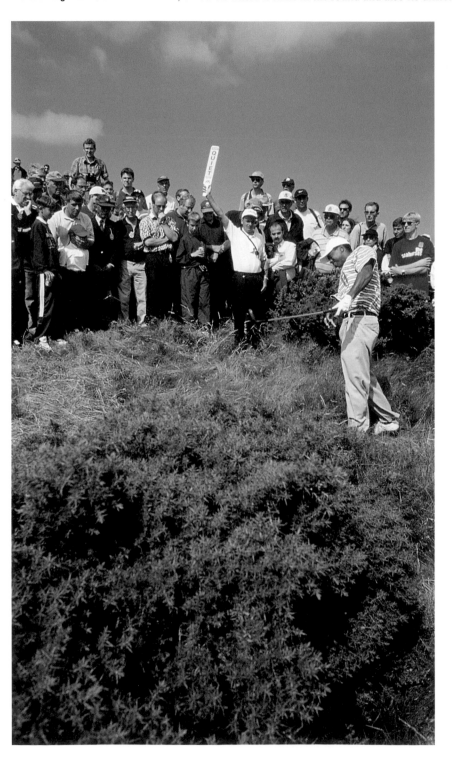

where, despite its length of 577 yards, accuracy is the prime requirement.

The 7th lies resplendent before the player as he stands on the tee. For the first time the wind is no longer in the same direction. Then, the wonderful 8th, its green tugging at a dune for protection from the sea breeze. Before they think of designing a course, all architects should stand on this tee to discover the true glory of the short par three.

The distance is just 126 yards but a friend of mine, a former Scottish amateur who still plays off scratch, has dispatched a full-blooded 3-wood from this tee and still finished short of the green. In more normal conditions it is just a 7-iron or less, and the premium on hitting the green is high. To the left of the green is not only the dune but two deep bunkers. To the right are two more cavernous sand traps, while another lurks to the rear. In the 1997 Open there was a certain poetry when the man who had struck the ball 435 yards down the 6th ran up a triple bogey six on the shortest hole on the course. As much by skill as strength, remember.

The 9th takes the golfer to the far end of the course, a par four of 423 yards that plays somewhat shorter than its yardage. The second shot is to a tricky two-tier green. The homeward nine begins with the one "blind" drive on the course, and is a foretaste of the sequence of difficult holes that follow. The second shot is invariably a long iron to another green that rejects any ball played toward its outer rim. After the 8th, the 11th is the most famous hole on the course and, since they changed the par at the 1997 Open from five to four, one of the hardest par fours in golf. From the fairway there appears little to aim at. The railway runs right along its right-hand side, but to the left the bushes make an equally troublesome prospect. Neither is there any letup with the second shot as the right-hand side of the green snuggles cozily against the railroad tracks.

The 12th hole was the scene of an extraordinary stroke of luck during the 1989 Open. Mark Calcavecchia was struggling to come to terms with Troon's ominous challenge and ready to concede defeat as he stood over his ball to the left of the green. He had already spilled several strokes and now was to lose at least one more, since there appeared no hope of getting down in two, save to

Brain Beats Brawn

Greg Norman lost the 1989 Open because he forgot the motto that lies below the club's crest at Royal Troon. Coming to the home hole, the fourth in a four-hole play-off, Norman was level with Mark Calcavecchia. The American, fearing his drive would catch the bunker down the right-hand side of the fairway, fell off his tee shot and the ball sliced badly to the right. Yet when Norman took out a wood, Calcavecchia suddenly became less worried. He knew the bunker stood 310 yards from the tee but he also knew it was in reach for such a long hitter. Such thoughts never came into Norman's strategy. He wanted to intimidate his opponent, and punish him for his errant drive. Norman caught the drive perfectly. But when, on first bounce, it veered to the right, it was Calcavecchia who was watching

closely. Sure enough, the ball bounded for an age and finished in the trap. Norman was devastated. Once more, from the trap he went for brawn, and the ball smashed into the bunker's face, and limped into another bunker. This time Norman thinned his shot and the ball careened out of bounds.

Norman had started that last day by humiliating Royal Troon with six consecutive birdies. He eventually finished with an incredible 64, as good a score as the old course has ever seen. But at the end of the day it was Troon that had delivered its telling reminder that it is not a course with which to trifle.

hole a freakish 45-foot putt. Such was the lie, Calcavecchia could not contemplate getting the ball any closer. Accordingly, he thrashed at the ball with his wedge and was happy enough to see the ball fly into the air, even though he knew he was going to be left with the long putt he had forecast in his best-case scenario. And then, just as he contemplated all this, the ball dropped from the sky and into the hole without a bounce and stayed there. A bogey at best had become the unlikeliest of birdies and when he eventually collected the title after a four-hole play-off he could not help but reflect on this moment of outrageous good fortune.

The 13th is a rarity, a par four without a bunker. For its protection it relies instead on an uneven fairway where the bounces can be capricious. In many ways it is an unfair means of defense. Golf was never meant to be a fair game and links golf is the unfairest form of all. But this crosses the boundary and the 13th has proven unlucky for many and unreasonably so. Accordingly, it is probably the least distinguished hole on the course. The 14th is another stoutly defended short hole, the premium again on a well-struck tee shot. And so to Troon's fierce finish, one to match the terrors at Carnoustie and Lytham. In poor weather the 15th and 16th can seem unremittingly bleak. Staring into the distance at the former, unable to see the green for his second shot, Lee Trevino once remarked: "I did not know the First World War was played out here." One of the difficulties common to both holes is there is little on the horizon a golfer can use for a line.

The 17th is a long par three with a vast apron and here a player must call upon all his skill to judge how far the ball will run upon landing. In the 1989 Open play-off Greg Norman misjudged it. His tee shot, a beauty from the tee, or so it appeared, ran through the back from where he chipped weakly and ran up a bogey.

The home hole is reminiscent of that at Lytham. A resplendent clubhouse stands guard in the distance. From the tee there are bunkers left and right to avoid. The green, too, is heavily protected by sand. From the tee the drive has to travel at least 230 yards to reach the fairway. From there, though, the player is faced with one of the nicest shots in golf, to a green that positively implores a good stroke.

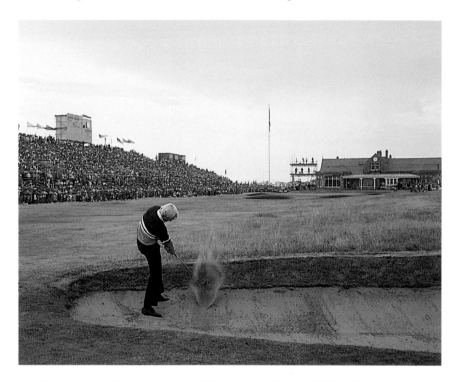

Greg Norman thought his drive down the 18th in the play-off for the 1989 Open Championship was perfect. But it never stopped rolling until it fell into a fairway bunker and the error of judgment cost him the title.

A Perfect Short Hole

Anyone who stands on the tee will not dwell to wonder why the hole is called the Postage Stamp. Even with a short-iron in one's hands the green looks impossible to hit. With the wind blowing off the sea it can prove as much, although it did not to Gene Sarazen in a lovely interlude to the 1982 Open. Sarazen had been invited back, fifty years after winning the Championship, and participated with two other former holders of yore, Max Faulkner and Fred Daly. The years might have robbed Sarazen of his length, but his feel remained intact.

In the first round he played a 5-iron which pitched short of the hole before rolling in. The following day, after finding a deep bunker to the right, the man who invented the sand wedge played the perfect shot with it, holing for a wonderful birdie two. Thus, in two rounds, Sarazen had played the hole in three strokes. If that was the sublime, the ridiculous came in the 1950 Open when a poor German amateur named Hermann Tissies one putted for a 15.

Character to Test a
Champion

In common with most of the links courses of Scotland, the beginnings of golf at Carnoustie are a matter of legend and vague historical references. Early in the sixteenth century Sir Robert Maule, one of the first known golfers, delighted in exercising the "gowf" on the Barry links, adjoining Carnoustie on the northern shores of the Firth of Tay. The club was formed in 1842, in the early years of Victoria's reign, a prolific age for the birth of Scottish clubs; in 1867 the genius of Young Tom Morris first came to light there when, aged 16, he played against and defeated all comers. Almost ninety years later a golfer named Ben Hogan came to Carnoustie and confirmed, in a masterful act of supremacy, that he was the greatest player of the age. In 1975 Tom Watson, previously known as a player who buckled under pressure, ably demonstrated that competing in a melting pot is a talent not god-given but acquired. His victory in the Open proved the making of him, for he knew that if he could conquer Carnoustie then nowhere need hold any fears. His victory would lead to him dominating the game for eight years, during which time he won no fewer than eight Major championships. Sadly Watson's year was to prove the last Open at Carnoustie until its long overdue return in 1999. In the interim years the course was allowed to fall into neglect and for many years its unkempt appearance was a pitiful sight. Happily that has been corrected in the 1990s, its condition now in accordance with its status. Even the clubhouse, so long an eyesore and easily the worst of any distinguished course in Britain, has been demolished as well.

Rarely can it be said of any course that it has no weakness, but this is true of Carnoustie. Every hole is different in character. Only three are short, and at no point during the round do more than two follow exactly the same direction. The problems set by the wind, therefore, are ever-changing and furthermore Carnoustie lies on the flatlands between the estuary and the low, distant hills, so that judgment of distance is critical. In every way it is a big course, and even from the ordinary competition tees it is a test of golf for good players. Most of the hazards, which include the sinuous menace of the Barry Burn at several holes, are placed to threaten the stroke that is slightly less than perfect, rather than one that is slightly better than awful.

The evolution from the ten-hole course made by Allan Robertson in the middle of the nineteenth century was a long one. Even after the extension to eighteen holes under the guidance of Tom Morris it knew many changes, until in 1926 James Braid made some new greens, tees, and bunkers. The result was a superb course. Within its general confines is another, smaller, eighteen-hole course—the Burnside—and both are held in trust by the town council, which provides members for a joint management committee with the four clubs that share the courses with one another. Since the last years of the nineteenth century, almost 300 young men of Carnoustie have become professionals. A great number went to the United States and three of the most notable were the Smith brothers. The eldest, Willie, won the U.S. Open in 1899; Alex was twice champion thereafter, but poor Macdonald always failed. In twelve years from 1923 he was second, third, and fourth twice each in the British Open, and was runner-up to Bobby Jones in both his victories in 1930. No more distinguished golfer ever failed to win an Open.

The early development of American golf owes much of its strength to the men of Carnoustie. It is written that, at various times, every State title had been held by one of them. Stuart Maiden, famous mentor of Jones, Archie Simpson, and many others, sought fame and fortune far from the great

Stark and severe in outline and flatter than most British championship links, Carnoustie is still a very tough course. Great demands are made by its enormous length, and many a competitor has come to grief in one—or both—of the burns that meander through the course. Jockie's Burn comes into play at the 2nd, 3rd, 5th, and 6th, the Barry Burn winds its way insidiously through the fairways, calling for both judgment and nerve, particularly at the last two holes, both long par fours.

links that had brought forth their skills. There is no gentle introduction to the course. From the long rise of the first fairway a lengthy stroke is needed to reach a hidden basin of green. In his first round in the 1953 Open, Hogan used a 2-iron, searing into the wind. The next day he was home with a pitching club; each time the ball finished in the same place on the green. Controversy—particularly among professionals, many of whom seem to think that driving should be an unthinking process—has long centered upon Braid's bunker in the middle of the second fairway, where a good straight drive may finish. There is sufficient room to either side and why, occasionally, should the drive not have to be exactly lined?

The 3rd is a beautiful little hole, with its pitch over a stream to an awkward green, and then one turns again toward the prevailing wind for a finely shaped par-four with a long second over level ground. On the left-hand side is a thick wood of firs, a pleasing break in the bleak severity of the scene, and the 5th, again angled to the right, with its approach to a raised green, runs along the wood's far side.

By any reckoning the 6th is one of the great long holes in golf. Far down the fairway, which has a boundary fence the full length on the hooking side, are two bunkers that a good drive can reach. Again hard thought is called for on the tee: to play short or to either side? The right is the safer, and from there a long second must be placed on to the left of the fairway to avoid the mean little Jockie's Burn, which cuts in from the right. Then, and only then, is the 3rd to the green fairly straightforward. The 7th, a good straight

Ben Hogan's record in the Open Championship was: played one, won one. His triumph came at Carnoustie, where the moody and magnificent golfer found contentment over a moody and magnificent links.

The Course Card

Carnoustie Golf Club, Tayside Championship course

Record: 65, Jack Newton, The Open 1975

Hole	Name	Yardage	Par
1	Cup	391	4
2	Gulley	412	4
3	Jockie's Burn	316	4
4	Hillocks	374	4
5	Brae	375	4
6	Long	500	5
7	Plantation	373	4
8	Short	157	3
9	Railway	420	4
10	South America	425	4
11	Dyke	352	4
12	Southward Ho!	462	5
13	Whins	141	3
14	Spectacles	468	5
15	Luckyslap	442	4
16	Barry Burn	235	3
17	Island	421	4
18	Home	428	4
Out		3,318	36
In		3,374	34
Total		**6,692**	**par 70**

hole, moves to the farthest corner of the course and then, at last, is the first short hole. The shot to a slightly raised plateau green is never easy to judge and here again a little thicket eases the setting. The 9th is downhill—the only perceptible change in level on the whole course apart from the 12th, which ascends a parallel course with equal gentleness. Carnoustie, mercifully, does not hasten coronaries. Many have wondered why, in this Scottish fastness, the 10th should be called South America. Seemingly, a young citizen of Carnoustie, in the days when it produced more emigrant golfers than anywhere else on earth, had hopes of reaching that continent but celebrated his departure too freely and got no farther than the thicket by the 10th before succumbing to after-effects. The green here is within a loop on the Barry Burn, which cruelly snares the underhit shot as well as the one that is sliced. One drives across it from the next tee, but at no substantial range. The real menace of the water is yet to come.

The short 13th, tightly trapped though it is, brings some breathing space before what is probably the most exacting finish in Britain. The second shot from the long, curving 14th fairway must carry a hill in which have been carved the "Spectacle" bunkers. This shot deceived Hogan into underclubbing more than once and cost him the only five in his final round of 68, but it brought lasting fame to Gary Player when he held off the challenge of Nicklaus fifteen years later. The 15th swings along a hog's-back fairway into duneland and—except in a helping wind—is a demanding four.

By modern par standards the 16th is a short hole, but only by a yard or so from the back tee; by any standards it is ferociously difficult, with its tiny entrance between bunkers to a narrow shelf of green. And then the ghoulish fun of the finish begins in earnest. A solid drive in the right

Above and right: The last time the Open Championship was held at Carnoustie was in 1975 when Tom Watson won following a play-off against the Australian Jack Newton, right. The 18th hole, above, with its second shot over the Burn, proved the key for Watson both during regulation play and in the following day's play-off.

The 6th

The Weakness Of Links Golf

Jockie's Burn winds along the right side of Carnoustie's long 6th. On a windless day, like the one Hogan encountered on the last day of the 1953 Open, it presents few problems. But against a headwind the second shot requires careful judgment and the shallow green is hard to hold with a long third shot. This could lead to trouble in the big, deep bunker at the back. Falling short means a nasty little chip with no guarantee of a par.

Memories of Hogan's conquest of Carnoustie in 1953 are indelible for the purity of his striking and the ruthless precision of his golf. He twice destroyed the 6th hole on the final day. Morning and afternoon his drives screamed through the still, gray air, perfectly lined past the right hand of the fairway bunkers and finishing in almost exactly the same spot. From there wooden shots boomed straight for the green, easily clearing Jockie's Burn and stopping some 30 yards from the hole. Each time he made his birdie.

This was an instance of modern technique and equipment rendering course design almost meaningless. For Hogan that day the hole offered little challenge beyond the hitting of two fairly straight, full shots, never a great problem to him. He played it as if the bunkers and Jockie's Burn did not exist. They came even less into the reckoning on the first three days of the

1975 Open, when the fairways were faster and a light breeze was helping. Scores of people were home with irons for their second shots. Such is the way of seaside golf in Britain, where par-fives often are defenseless against the experts because there are few features to restrain the length of the first two shots and little or no penal element around the greens, the majority of which are invitingly open.

direction from the 17th tee will carry the Barry Burn twice, but against a strong wind the tee shot must be placed on what is virtually an island amid its wicked curves.

The drive to the last, haunted by the burn and out-of-bounds, is formidable. Then comes the last challenge of the burn, which is no mere stream but twenty feet or more across. Gene Sarazen tells of how, one evening during a championship, bets were made on the possibility of jumping it. The history of the Open is as much one of tragedy as of triumph and few would wish to match the fate of Jose Jurado of Argentina in 1931. Tommy Armour had set the pace with a closing 71, but Jurado could beat him by playing the last two holes in nine strokes. After a smothered drive had cost him six at the 17th Jurado (unaware of Armour's total, for score boards did not exist then) played short of the burn, took five, and then learned that he could have tied with a four

when he had been within range to risk the carry. There was no talk of tragedy in 1937, when Henry Cotton achieved his finest hour. The whole American Ryder Cup team was competing and the weather was appalling. Cotton began his last round in a deluge and there was a danger that play might be abandoned, but he was around in 71, a tremendous performance. Al Laney, one of the finest and most perceptive of all American writers, was there and later described Cotton perfectly: "A strange, forbidding man in those days, but he could handle a golf club with his three-quarter swing more expertly than anyone I have seen since except Ben Hogan. When Cotton hit an iron to the green with chilling, humorless concentration it seemed magic. Like Hogan again, he gave the impression of coldness, but there was also the same feeling as with Hogan that the ball had been given no option, that there was nothing he could not achieve."

One Of The Great Championship Finishes

The 1968 Open was in destiny's melting pot when Gary Player and Jack Nicklaus came to the 14th in the last round. Player was two ahead and had to wait on the fairway while Nicklaus, lucky to have a wooden club lie, extricated himself from the trees on the right. He smashed a 4-wood which finished just off the green and then, even before the excitement for Nicklaus had subsided, Player hit the shot of a lifetime. The 1975 Open was also decided by a great shot, by Tom Watson at the 18th.

The 14th to the 18th

In the 1968 Open, Gary Player made a perfectly timed thrust at the 14th. He struck a magnificent 4-wood over the Spectacle bunkers to within two feet of the hole. Down went the putt for an eagle. The look of a champion was about Player that year; he was less tense, more relaxed, and philosophical than usual. He had need of it all, because from that point Nicklaus outgunned him from the last four tees with a sequence of thunderous strokes with a driver. When intent on a particularly big drive Nicklaus always took the club away from the ball even more deliberately than usual, and never hurried the first movement. It helped to ensure that no suspicion of haste marred his swing's rhythm. His most remarkable shot was at the 17th. Everyone had been playing short of the Burn, but Nicklaus was two behind and the light breeze was helping. His massive hit, all of 340 yards, soared over the Burn and left him only a wedge. But he did not make a three and Player was almost safe.

In 1975 the 18th was reduced to a par-four 448 yards. This was done to emphasize the challenge of the carrying the burn for the second shot instead of forcing the lay up short, as the longer hole often did. It also intensified the drama for the watching thousands. The decision certainly was justified as Tom Watson would agree. A golfer could ask for little more than to make a birdie on the last hole of

The 14th to the 18th — Player ------- Nicklaus

an Open aware that he needed to beat Nicklaus, who had just finished, and Johnny Miller, his companion, to win. Watson did just that with a perfect long pitch about ten feet from the hole. Then, in the play-off next day, after Jack Newton had bunkered his second shot and Watson knew that if he hit the green all the glory of victory and its manifold rewards would probably be his, he did it again. The hole was playing longer in relentless rain and Watson hit a 2-iron. Later, being the honest golfer he is, he admitted that it was struck a shade heavy; nevertheless, it flew straight and far enough over the Burn to finish in the heart of the green. The merit of the shot was that Watson took enough club to allow for any slight striking error. It proved that his swing could withstand intense pressure, something of enormous importance to one who had failed in the two previous U.S. Opens.

Above: One of the great triumphs during Gary Player's illustrious career came in the 1968 Open at Carnoustie, when he held off the challenge of a rampant Jack Nicklaus.

Historic Links and Noble Traditions

Northernmost of the world's great golf courses, Dornoch shares its latitude with the Bering Sea and Hudson Bay and its antecedents with those other places on the North Sea coast of Scotland, where golf had its beginnings. Among the early evidence of the antiquity of its links is a book, *The Earldom of Sutherland*, by Sir Robert Gordon, who was tutor to the family in the seventeenth century. Writing of Dornoch, he said: "About this town are the fairest and largest links of any part of Scotland, fitt for Archery, Golfing, Ryding, and all other exercises; they doe surpasse the fields of Montrose and St. Andrews." It is possible, therefore, that a form of golf as it is now recognized was played at Dornoch over 300 years ago, although there is no definite record of this until the autumn of 1876. The club was formed in the following spring by Alexander McHardy, pioneer of golf in the north of Scotland, and Dr. Gunn, who learned the game at St. Andrews.

For the first ten years of its life the course had only nine holes, but gradually more people were making the long pilgrimage beyond the Highlands and it was decided that old Tom Morris should be called upon to add another nine. He was charmed with the place from the outset, particularly with the presence of many natural plateaus that could serve for greens. From time to time alterations were made—notably by John Sutherland, a famous secretary—but for the most part the golf is wonderfully natural. The beautiful seaside turf, the dunes, hummocks, and undulating fairways owe little to the hand of man. Because of its remoteness, many golfers may not be aware of Dornoch's existence; others, aware of its fame, have never ventured so far in search of their game, for it is some sixty miles north of Inverness. Those who have speak of its glory with one voice. Dornoch stands comparison with all the finest in Britain. It curves along the shores of Embo Bay at the mouth of Dornoch Firth, a setting of wondrous isolation from the foulness of the cities —London is over 600 miles away—and a place of madly contrasting moods. The wind may be firm, bringing forth the golf at its splendid best; it can be a roaring gale, thundering down the valleys through the old western mountains, making the course a fear-some test of all the strength, purpose, and technique that a man can muster; or its voice may be stilled and the day alive with sunshine.

On such a day the golfer is reminded of the words of a man who visited Dornoch long ago and wrote: "Looking westward and, indeed, bounding the view from the Ord of Caithness on the northeast to the far away hills of Aberdeenshire, in the south, there is a grand circle of highlands before us, embracing all the finest 'Bens' in Suther-land, Ross, and Inverness. On fine summer days the play of cloud shadows and sunlight gleam on these distant mountains is a very remarkable feature of the scenery." Let it not be thought that Dornoch is normally afflicted with tempest and extremes of climate. It can often be more temperate the farther north one travels—but how swiftly it can change, as the golfer discovers when enduring the challenge of the ferocious wind. This can be fun for the average golfer, except perhaps in competition, for rare pleasure can be had in improvising the strokes necessary to combat a wind.

The 1st, along a shallow rippling valley, and the 2nd, a pitch to a table green, are tricky rather than severe, especially if the turf is keen. From the 3rd tee the course falls away to the great curving basin of the links itself. Now follow two lovely holes of medium length, then a pitch to a long, narrow green high above the fairway and a beautiful short 6th, with its green a shelf hard against the flank of a heathery hillside. This must be climbed to the 7th tee, and for a moment the golf is that of open heathland. But the drive to the 8th plunges toward a green in a secret hollow.

To the golfer at one with his game, and helped perhaps by a prevailing breeze, the course thus far may not seem unduly difficult; but thence-forth his task begins in earnest with one of the most glorious stretches of seaside golf to be found anywhere in the world. From the 9th tee one turns for distant home and the next seven holes follow the gentle left-handed curve of the bay—a great scimitar of blue and silver and gray. This is true linksland golf, compelling not only strong, accurate driving but fine judgment of long approaches if par is to be achieved. Should the wind be against the golfer, or from either hand, control of flight and

Royal Dornoch is a links of splendid isolation rather than the bustle of championships, but two great golf architects, Pete Dye and Donald Ross, have bestowed on it the accolade of imitation. Dye's short par-four 5th at the Columbus Golf Club, Ohio, is patterned after Dornoch's 15th, while the basic character of Ross's famous Number 2 course at Pinehurst, North Carolina, also derived from Dornoch —where Ross was born and learned his golf under Old Tom Morris, four times British Open champion, in the 1890s.

length will be examined to the utmost. There is respite of a kind at the short 10th and 13th, but their greens are far from generous targets and true strokes alone will prevail.

The one hole that does not instantly appeal is the 16th, with its steep, mounting fairway and no sight of the green unless the drive is very long; but the 17th is dangerously attractive with its drive to an unseen valley, where the pitch must be truly struck or it will not reach the table-land of green. Two good shots will see one home at the last. The length of the second can be deceptive but the green stands free and open, inviting a good bold stroke. Analyze and examine the course as you will, the conclusion is inescapable that it is sufficient to test the most accomplished golfers in the world. There is little hope that it will, because of its remoteness. In 1984 the Amateur Championship did extend beyond its natural parameters and an Irish Walker Cup player Garth McGimpsey will always treasure, in particular, the decision to do so. Now Dornoch has returned to its blessed place in the game's roster, a place for pilgrims and the many distinguished golfers that have come to love it. Perhaps it is fitting that it remains in such splendid solitude, far removed from the turmoil and the excitement of championships.

The 14th

Character for Export

The 14th is the greatest of all Dornoch's holes and the most demanding. Long known as "Foxy," it measures 445 yards and requires two outstanding shots. The fairway swings to the left at about the range of a solid drive, then pursues its original direction before moving to the right again and rising to the plateau green. The beauty of the hole is its simplicity of design and the way in which the natural feature of a formidable hummock of dune on the right has made possible the two changes of direction. It has no need of artificial hazards and there is not a single bunker. Ideally, the drive should draw slightly with the tilt of fairway into a position from where a wood or long iron can be faded over the corner of the hill to the green. For those whose approaches fall short of the green there is the alternative of pitching their third shot or nursing it up the slope with a running shot. Although few modern links play as fast as they once did, the pitch and run is still essential to the successful golfer's armory.

Undoubtedly the natural character and subtlety of Dornoch had a great influence on Donald Ross, who was professional and head greenskeeper there before going to the United States at the turn of the century and becoming one of the greatest architects. Numerous examples of his work there remain, including Pinehurst, the venue for the 1999 U.S. Open. One of Ross's basic principles in designing a green was to raise its surface slightly—three or four feet— above the level of the fairway and then fashion subtle undulations. This meant that the slightly erring shot would tend to roll off.

Above: Many a U.S. green was inspired by the character of the 14th at Dornoch, and Pinehurst Number 2 is regarded as one of the most exacting tests of chipping in the United States because of its Dornoch-style crown greens. Harry Vardon, in his prime when the fame of Dornoch spread at the turn of the century, described the 14th as "the finest natural hole I've ever played."

The Course Card

Royal Dornoch Golf Club, Dornoch, Highland

Record: 65, Jim Miller(Am), Freser Shield 1971 66, Bernard Gallacher (Pro), Northern Open 1973

Hole	Yards	Par
1	331	4
2	177	3
3	414	4
4	427	4
5	354	4
6	163	3
7	463	4
8	396	4
9	496	5
10	147	3
11	446	4
12	507	5
13	166	3
14	445	4
15	319	4
16	402	4
17	405	4
18	456	4
Out	3,221	35
In	3,293	35
Total	**6,514**	**70**

A Punishing Kind Of
Perfection

Tucked compactly away by the shores of the Firth of Forth, Muirfield is a beautifully simple and testing links, the fairest of all British championship courses. It has one of the most exacting finishing holes in golf, a wickedly bunkered 448-yard par four. The front nine ends in an equally daunting par five of 504 yards, protected on the right by bunkers and on the left by an out-of-bounds area. Muirfield has only three successive holes that are played in the same direction—a decided asset for a course that is almost always played in windy conditions.

To define the perfect golf course is nearly impossible; so many factors of design, situation and personal taste are involved. Nevertheless, no course in the British Isles embraces more of the qualities one seeks in a great and fair challenge of skill than Muirfield, home of the Honorable Company of Edinburgh Golfers, generally recognized as the oldest club in the world. Its records are continuous since 1744, when "several Gentlemen of Honor skilfull in the ancient and healthful exercise of Golf" petitioned the City of Edinburgh to provide a silver club for annual competition on the links at Leith.

For almost half a century the Company played over the five holes there, but eventually encroachment caused difficulties and they went to Musselburgh. In time this links also became disagreeably crowded, and in 1891 the Company again moved east, down the Firth of Forth to Muirfield. At first the new course met with much abuse, partly because the club had taken the Open Championship with them. This championship had been started by the Prestwick club, and was played there for the first time on October 17, 1860. Willie Park of Musselburgh won the handsome red morocco challenge belt.

Ten years later Young Tom Morris, a supreme golfer, annexed it for himself by winning for the third successive year. There was no Open in 1871, and thereafter the Honorable Company and the Royal and Ancient joined with Prestwick in subscribing for the present trophy and in managing the Championship. For the next twenty years it was played on each of their courses in turn. The disappointment of Musselburgh in losing the championship may have prompted unkind comment about its successor, for apparently it was neither long nor testing enough, albeit surrounded by a gray stone wall and water. Andrew Kirkaldy, a famous professional of the time, notorious for his sharp tongue, was moved to dismiss Muirfield as an old water meadow. In spite of this the first championship to be played there in 1892 has a place in history. For the first time it was over 72 holes instead of 36, and was won by Harold Hilton, one of the great Hoylake amateurs. His score of 305 with the gutty ball was considered to be remarkably low; he won again five years later and since then no amateur, except Jones, has been Open Champion.

Thereafter the stature of Muirfield grew. Every few years down the generations it has been the setting for one or other of the great occasions. Harry Vardon won the first of his six Open titles there in 1896, after a play-off with J. H. Taylor. The third member of the great triumvirate, James Braid, also won his first victory at Muirfield and, just before World War I, the vast figure of Ted Ray strode the links and

the Championship. It is unlikely that he was afraid of the thick, clinging rough that, long before his time, had struck fear and fury into the hearts of golfers.

The first post-war champion to arise at Muirfield became one of the greatest amateurs of the period. Although the American challenge was not regarded by the British in the apprehensive light of nowadays, there must have been acute anxiety abroad the afternoon Cyril Tolley beat R. A. Gardner in the final. Tolley was three up and four to play, but the American squared the match on the last green. In 1920 the 1st was a short hole: Tolley followed Gardner's fine shot to the green with a better one, and eventually holed for a two and the Championship. After his first pilgrimage to Britain in 1921 Jones was beaten only once in three subsequent visits and five championships. This was in the quarter-finals of the Amateur in 1926. His conqueror was a young Scottish golfer, Andrew Jamieson, who, it is said, practiced his putting for three hours on the eve of the match. Jones previously had beaten Robert Harris, the defending champion, an occasion in itself because never before had the champions of Britain and the United States met in either event. O. B. Keeler, who for so long played Boswell to Jones's Johnson, was certain that his hero would win this championship and his agony must have been considerable,

The Honorable Company of Edinburgh Golfers, Muirfield, Lothian.

Record: 64, Rodger Davis, The Open, 1987

Hole	Yards	Par
1	447	4
2	351	4
3	379	4
4	180	3
5	559	4
6	469	4
7	185	3
8	444	5
9	504	5
10	475	4
11	385	4
12	381	4
13	159	3
14	449	4
15	417	4
16	188	3
17	550	5
18	448	4
Out	3,518	36
In	3,452	35
Total	**6,963**	**71**

Nick Faldo acknowledges the applause from the crowd after playing one of the great shots of his career, to the 18th at Muirfield in the 1987 Open Championship. Two putts meant an 18th consecutive par in that last round, good enough for a one stroke victory over the American Paul Azinger.

for he wrote later, "In all my life I have never heard anything as lonely as the cry of the peewit in that twilight on the rolling Muirfield course, nor was I ever so lonesome." The peewits and the curlews still cry over the links; it is a place that haunts the memory.

Walter Hagen's comprehensive victory in the 1929 Open Championship was a classic instance of a champion playing with great skill. While others, including most of the American Ryder Cup team, were blown to oblivion by a gale, Hagen shrewdly used less lofted clubs than previously, improvised all manner of shots under the wind, and won by a mile. The 8th hole at Muirfield is a big dogleg to the right, and within its curve there is an alarming cluster of gathering bunkers. On the last day Hagen, instead of playing down the fairway and having a long second over a great cross-bunker to the green, drove far out into the rough on the right, scorning the architect's purpose and considerably shortening the hole. He was rewarded with two threes, but soon afterward a thicket was planted to defeat such liberties.

Much of the greatness of Muirfield is in its test of driving. The fairways need not be menacingly narrow, but the rough (unlike the normal links grass) is consistently lush and tenacious. To be in it invariably means the loss of half a stroke or more. This is as it should be, for many British links do not penalize the errant stroke enough. However strong a man may be, he cannot score low without accu-

rate driving. When Henry Cotton won his third Open at Muirfield in 1948 he missed only four fairways in 72 holes. His second round of 66 was played in the presence of King George VI, which was a rare gesture to majesty. The rough caused much speculation before the 1966 Open. It had been allowed to grow exceptionally thick, and Sanders was moved to say after finishing second that he wished he had the hay concession. Never was rough more punishing; but Jack Nicklaus approached the course with a finely preserved balance between attack and defense, frequently used an iron from the tees and was rewarded, one stroke ahead of Doug Sanders and David Thomas, with a total of 282. Their closest pursuers included the most accomplished golfers in the field, proof that the course was a fair, if severe, examination. In one round P. J. Butler returned a 65, which set the record. This victory was a climax in Nicklaus's career. At the age of twenty-six he had won the four Major titles of the world: so another illustrious name was added to the roll of Muirfield's champions.

Rough is not the only problem, for the bunkering reveals an imagination of design that would be cruel if it were not so fair. Rarely at Muirfield does a ball jump a bunker; if the shot is fading or drawing toward one then in it will go, for the bunkers have been fashioned, with sleek, beautifully preserved surroundings, to gather the slightly wayward stroke. This can be maddening, but always in one's heart there is the knowledge that the stroke was

The 18th

Faldo Realizes a Famous Victory

The moment of truth in the career of Nick Faldo arrived on the 18th hole at Muirfield in 1987, and the player both recognized it and embraced it. Three years he had spent changing his swing in order to cope with pressure moments like the one he now faced and it is a measure of the confidence he had in his new method that he welcomed the opportunity to test it. The shot in front of him was almost 200 yards in length, with little margin · for error. In short it was the sort of shot that defines champions, and why Muirfield was Faldo's favorite course long before he won there. Normally he would have struck a 4-iron given the distance but this was the last round of the Open, the trophy was on the line, the adrenalin was flowing, and so he took a five. If Faldo lives to be 100 he will always remember what happened next. It was the shot of a lifetime, the ball emerging from the core of the sweetspot to never leave the flagstick for a second. In that moment all the pain and sacrifice had found their reward, and everything he achieved in his career thereafter flowed from that one life-affirming shot. It showed that he could play a perfect stroke when nothing else would do and players who reach that state of grace invariably go on to greater things. Five years later Faldo returned to Muirfield and won another Open, again with another telling blow on the home hole.

——— Faldo

---------- Azinger

imperfectly struck or aimed. The man playing good golf, or the man who knows his course and his limitations, need have no fear of Muirfield. It is a far-from-fearsome place: there are no trees, no water, no unduly strenuous carries, and only one blind stroke to play. The greens are not enormous (in fact some tend to be small), but this is another strength, for the influence of putting is kept within reasonable proportion. Those of the short holes, in particular, are sharply defined within their embracing bunkers. Always the golfer can see what is expected of him in the approach to the green: in this respect Muirfield is similar to Birkdale among the championship courses of the British Isles and for that reason likely to commend itself more readily to American eyes, used to golf on the target principle. A man gets what he hits and, what is more, can see it happen; no golfer could justly claim that the course took unfair advantage of ignorance.

All of this is contrary to the common conception of a seaside course and, in appearance, Muirfield resembles none of them. There is nothing of a long desolate sprawl of dunes and linksland, with holes that are subtle in their identity and not easily memorable for the casual visitor; there is nothing, either, of the sense of limitless freedom that one feels at Sandwich, or Carnoustie. It lies on the southern shores of the Forth and its boundaries are precise, for the gray wall patrols three sides. To the north are the dunes, protected by great banks of buckthorn, and

beyond is the great estuary—a magic stretch of water, whether dancing silver in sunshine and a brave wind, tranquil in the haze of summer, or eerily haunted as ships, booming in the mist, steal upstream to Leith and Rosyth. Across the Forth spreads the graceful coast of Fife, ever-changing in its patterned hues as the cloud shadows glide by. Along the eastern side of the course the dark gnarled trees of Archerfield heel forever from the winds—the woods of Archerfield are called Graden Sea Wood in Robert Louis Stevenson's *Pavilion on the Links*. Away to the west stands Gullane Hill, commanding not only the two splendid courses on its flanks but also a view of rare majesty, from Bass Rock, sentinel of North Berwick, to "Auld Reekie" itself, smokily enchanted in the distance.

The immediate impression of Muirfield is of a place beautifully contained and private, but spacious in its policies. The eye can roam the course in a glance, and there in is one of its greatest charms. It was laid out in two approximate loops: the first nine holes form an outer ring in a clockwise path, the homeward half runs within but is less constant in its counter arc. The result is that no hole is more than a few minutes' walk from the clubhouse, and only once, from the 3rd to the 5th holes, do as many as three consecutive holes follow the same direction. The golfer thus is never bored by having the wind against or behind him for long periods as on many links of an older

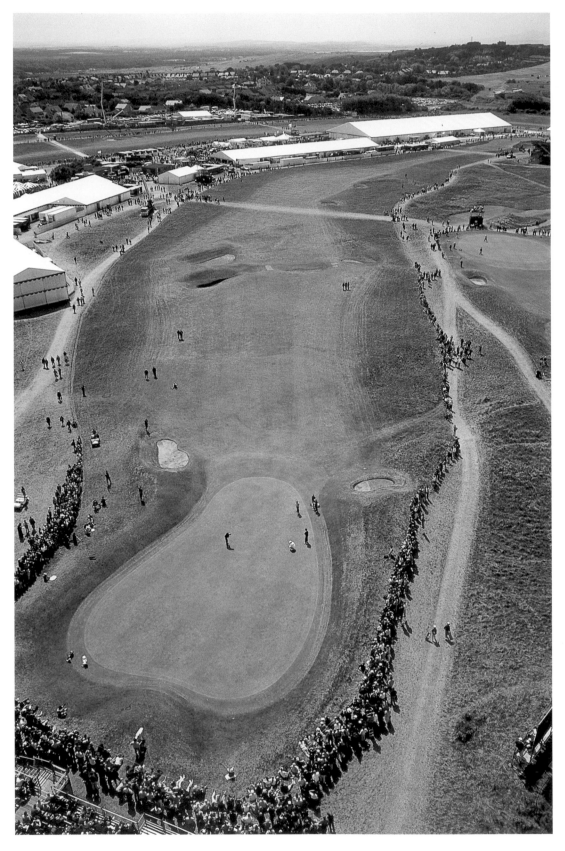

demands the greatest care; the fairway leans from right to left and the drive must hold its lower side or the pitch to a wickedly sloping green will be uncommonly difficult. A well-placed drive to the 3rd leaves a tempting view of the green through a vale between the dunes, otherwise the distance of the approach is hard to judge. The first of the short holes is at once disturbing and beautiful, for the green is a plateau closely protected at the front and on either hand by deep bunkers, and if in fear of them the tee shot is too bold, it will leave a long downhill putt. This can easily happen in the prevailing westerly wind; and there is some slight criticism of the course in that the short 13th and 16th are similarly helped and tend to play too short. Their comparative simplicity to an accomplished golfer was emphasized in 1959 when Gary Player, four strokes behind the leaders at lunch on the final day, won the Open with a memorable round of 68. He used only a short iron to these holes, pitched close at the 13th and 16th and holed for twos. This is not to say that they are all that easy, and in a cross-wind the 13th can be difficult to hit and hold. It lies in a cleft between dunes, with bunkers eating into the long narrow green; as at the 4th, the stroke finishing at the back of the green can mean a fearsome putt.

The story goes that Hagen deliberately played into one of the bunkers short of the green, preferring an uphill shot from sand to a long slippery downhill putt, but this was on a severe day. For the most part the holes offer absolutely fair targets. The remaining short hole, the 7th, faces west and also has a high plateau green exposed to all the moods of the wind. It was lengthened in preparation for the 1966 Open, and against any wind at all demands a stroke of unerring accuracy and power.

As already noted, Muirfield is a great test of driving. The long 5th curves from left to right with an obvious temptation to carry a shoulder of ground on the right and shorten the hole. Unless this tactic is resisted the drive almost certainly will vanish into one of a nest of bunkers designed to punish those who try to cheat the hole of its glory. A pull at the 6th can likewise be disastrous; the problems of the 8th have already been mentioned, and then comes one of the finest par-five holes in existence. From the far southeastern corner of the course, where Archerfield Wood comes to an end, one drives to an ever-narrowing fairway with a large bunker

The 17th hole at Muirfield is a mighty par five that extracted a costly mistake from Paul Azinger in 1987 and another from John Cook five years later, when he missed from no more than 18 inches. In both instances the beneficiary was Nick Faldo.

fashion, but always he must take heed of its changing angle of approach.

Immediately the golfer at Muirfield is made aware that he is setting forth on a considerable exercise of his powers. The opening drive must be exact to find a narrowing waist of fairway between subtly placed bunkers on the left and rough on the right; as often as not the wind will be against it, and the approach, a lovely, straight long shot, may not get home. If the greens are fast the next hole defying those who try to play the hole absolutely straight; it was not designed for this. To have a clear third to an unusually open green, the second must be played to a broad expanse of rolling fairway, but this Elysian field ends abruptly against the wall that runs the length of the hole. Now one is by the clubhouse, and the long ribbon on the 10th, a superb two-shot hole stretches away in the distance. Here again cross bunkers challenge the second shot, yet somehow at Muirfield they do not seem old-fashioned but entirely fitting; and there are more to come. The drive to the 11th is blind but not unduly alarming; the 12th, with its falling fairway and long, narrow green, is a charming hole; the 14th needs a drive that must not be pulled, and clear judgment of distance for the second; the 15th fairway is invitingly wider than most, but the measure of these last three holes is a prevailing wind. If there is a wind, substantial second shots are needed. Even then the 14th may be out of range, but toil here-abouts will find recompense on the mighty 17th, which then can be reached with two good shots. With a helping

breeze behind him Nicklaus was home, using a 3-iron and a 5-iron, in the last round of his Open. Here again temptation to cut a corner must be sternly resisted. Innocent though the prospect may seem, a horrid wasteland of humps and bunkers awaits the pull. The round offers few more satisfying moments than the sight of a long second soaring over the great range of bunkers that traverse the fairway, but anyone unsure of his capacity to clear the bunkers is well advised to play short; rare is the third shot that reaches the green from their depths. The 18th has few peers as a finishing hole. The slightly angled tee shot must be held away from bunkers on the left and rough on the other side. Then a wonderfully challenging stroke remains to a green tightly embraced by bunkers, but with no trouble beyond.

This is a feature common to Muirfield: the straight, bold stroke rarely, if ever, is in any way seriously punished, but the timid, the gutless, and the wayward as rarely will escape retribution. This surely is the mark of a great golf course.

The 17th

A Crushing Blow for Jacklin

In the last round of the 1972 Open, Muirfield's 17th hole was the setting for one of the most dramatic turns of fortune in modern championship golf. Tony Jacklin and Lee Trevino were level on the tee needing, as events proved, two pars to beat Jack Nicklaus. Trevino pulled into the nearest bunker, exploded out, slashed a wood into the rough short and to the left of the green and walked after it looking a dejected and defeated man. Jacklin meanwhile had followed a fine, solid drive with another good shot into a perfect position for a chip.

When Trevino's fourth shot raced over the green into the fringe rough it seemed certain that he would fall at least one, if not two, behind. But, even before Jacklin had time to mark his ball on the green after chipping rather short, Trevino hurriedly played his chip as if heedless of the outcome. It was not an easy one against the grain of the grass on to the fast green, but all the gods were with him. It vanished into the hole, dealing a crushing blow to Jacklin, who then took three putts to fall behind.

Left: It is a hallmark of many of the great champions that not only are they very good players but they are blessed with good fortune as well. Of course the key is having the ability to capitalize on moments of good luck and no one did that more than Lee Trevino, left, in winning the 1972 Open at Muirfield.

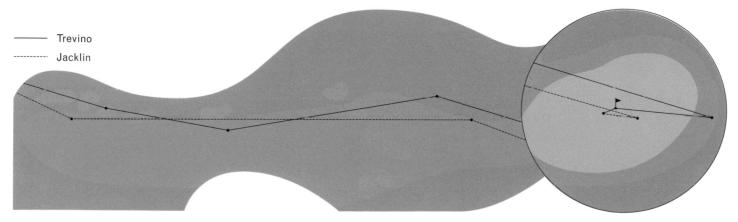

——— Trevino

---------- Jacklin

Vision and Faith
Resurrect a Compelling Course

The sun sets on another golden day at Turnberry, the symbolic lighthouse that dominates part of the course framed here behind the 14th green.

No small part of the pleasure of golf is that the game is so often played in beautiful surroundings, which can soothe anger, console frustration, and enhance joy. Such a place is Turnberry and, travel the world as he will, the golfer would be hard-pressed to find its equal. As a course it stands high in any championship company and was endowed by nature with a background that none of the others can surpass. It lies on a curve of rock-bound coast, far from the anxious turmoil of everyday, in the southern reaches of Strathclyde where the river estuary spreads forth to the sea.

Across the waters the great mass of Arran's mountains, the long curves of the Mull of Kintyre, and the lonely rock of Ailsa, rising like some primeval beast from their depths, make a scene of compelling majesty. Other courses may have sea and mountains for their setting, but none compare with those at Turnberry, which are forever changing with the whimsical moods of the weather. It can be transformed within the hour from a place haunted by mist, or savage in wind and rain, to one of entrancing beauty. On a fresh day, with the sea tranquil and deepening in its blueness as the sun rises higher, or at evening when the mountains turn black in the fading light and the sky is vivid with color, Turnberry is incomparable.

There are two courses, the gentle Arran and the nobler Ailsa—scene of many championship events, but to stage its first Open only in 1977. It may well be the most memorable, too, a duel in the sun over the last 36 holes between the two great players of the age, Tom Watson and Jack Nicklaus. Here we had the greatest strokeplay tournament effectively turned into a matchplay event, so much so that Hubert Green, who finished third, remarked: "I won my tournament." Nine years later it was the turn of Greg

The Course Card

Turnberry Hotel courses,
Turnberry, Strathclyde
Ailsa course

Record: 63, Greg Norman, The Open, 1986

Hole	Name	Yardage	Par
1	Ailsa Craig	350	4
2	Mak Siccar	430	4
3	Blaw Wearie	462	4
4	Woe-be-Tide	165	3
5	Fin' me oot	442	4
6	Tappie Toorie	231	3
7	Roon the Ben	529	5
8	Goat Fell	431	4
9	Bruce's Castle	454	4
10	Dinna Fouter	452	4
11	Maidens	174	3
12	Monument	446	4
13	Tickly Tap	412	4
14	Risk-an-Hope	449	4
15	Ca Canny	209	3
16	Wee Burn	409	4
17	Lang Whang	597	5
18	Ailsa Hame	434	4
Out		3,494	35
In		3,482	35
Total		**6,976**	**par 70**

With eight of its first eleven holes played alongside—and often over—the ocean's edge, the championship Ailsa course is no place for the golfer suffering from a hook. The outward half culminates in the spectacular Bruce's Castle, where the drive is from a spit of rock above the sea, with, for the brave, a carry of 200 yards over the sea and rocks toward a cairn on the horizon. Further inland, the shorter Arran course—unmarked here— is gentler, but still a stiff test of golfing skills.

Norman to finally win his first Major championship. In 1994 Turnberry staged its third Open, another memorable event, this time won by Nick Price. Watson had his chances that year, seventeen years after his greatest performance. Time had not been kind to his putting stroke, however. He missed a crushing series of short putts and at the end those hands that had looked so sure and steady in 1977 were shaking as badly as an old man's.

Turnberry has changed considerably in recent years. The majestic old hotel, which surveys an unparalleled vista from a hill above both courses, was modernized at considerable cost and now stands among the best in the British Isles; a new clubhouse has been erected. But the cost has been passed on. Now, to get a tee-time in high summer at Turnberry one must stay a night in the hotel and while the pleasure is considerable so is the cost. No guest can effectively expect to play the Ailsa for less than $300. Beauty certainly does not come cheap. Both courses date from the early twentieth century and both have survived mutilation through their transformation into an airfield in two world wars. The extensive wartime leveling operations, laying of runways and building, destroyed not only the courses themselves but also many natural features. Anyone seeing Turnberry in 1945 would have found it hard to imagine that a first-class course had once existed there, and harder still to believe that it ever would again. Within a few years it had been restored, involving vast movements of concrete and sand—to all intents, the creation of a new course. It remains a tribute to Mackenzie Ross, the architect, and to the vision of men like Frank Hole, who had faith in the future of its golf.

After a comparatively quiet beginning the course gathers momentum, so to speak. The 2nd and 3rd holes can be formidable, depending on the wind, and even if there is none they are still considerable. By then the coast has been reached. The tee of the short 4th is hard by the lapping waves, the line is over the edge of a sandy bay, and the slightest pull to a green cradled in the dunes will find its way onto the beach. The hole, not inaptly, is called Woe-be-Tide. A long valley contains the great curve of the 5th and, whatever the weather conditions, the stroke to the 6th, one of the longest of short holes, is always a substantial hit, often with a driver.

As on all really fine courses accurate driving is essential and never more so than on the next three holes. The carry to the narrow 7th fairway, sharply angled across the line of flight, needs a powerful stroke and then follows a long second over rolling ground to a far green. The 8th fairway leans from left to right, and unless the drive is true it will fall toward bunkers; the green is a plateau, the shelf of rock behind it a hint of glories to come. There are few more spectacular or beautifully sited tees than the 9th on its pinnacle high above the rocks, and few more forbidding

The greatest Open Championship of all? Forget Tom Watson's gaudy trousers; when he took on Jack Nicklaus for the title in 1977, everyone was too wrapped up in two days' compelling golf to worry about fashion.

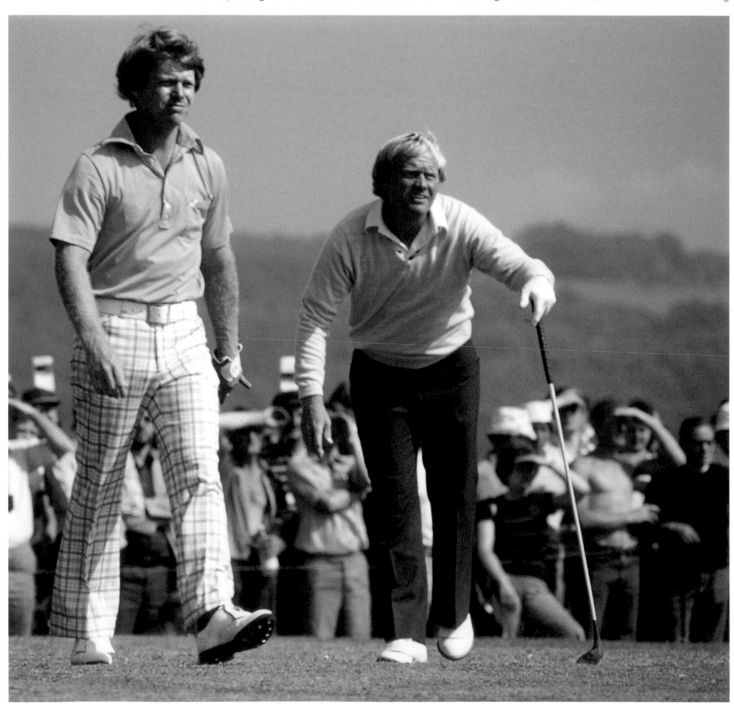

prospects to the frail in heart and swing. The carry is not enormous, but the sight of the cliffs, the abyss below, and the knowledge that a mishit will be lethal, is disturbing. The hog's-back fairway is by no means easy to hold nor, once one has arrived there, is the second shot easy to judge. This is a superb golf hole, marked for the viewer from afar by the slender white pencil of the Turnberry lighthouse. To stand on the 10th tee at the height of a summer morning is to know the full beauty of Turnberry. Past the remains of a castle, a base for some of Robert the Bruce's stirring deeds, the hole plunges down beside the rocky shore; there are few more satisfying moments than the sight of a drive arching away to the broad, crested fairway. Small wonder the golf hereabouts has stirred memories for many Americans of the great courses of Monterey.

Again on the 11th there is the feeling of being at one with the sea and the rocks, for here is another pulpit tee, though the hole is short and not overly taxing. As the course swings for home along the 12th traces can be seen of the airfield that Turnberry became on two occasions. The monument placed on the hill high above the green commemorates those who died in World War I.

The 13th, with an elusive plateau green, and the 14th, which can be reached only with two splendid shots, usually into wind, form a prong toward the hills and bring a welcome variety of direction to the long homeward trail. The 15th is a classic short hole, normally a long iron to a green with bunkers on its left to trap those who steer too safely away from a steep hollow on the right. At the 16th comes a hole decisive to the outcome of the Walker Cup match in 1963, when, but for the stream in front of the green, there might have been a British victory. After the long valley of the 17th, with its second to a green on the uplands, the last hole is not severe. The drive is testing with bunkers on the inside curve and great banks of gorse on the right, but the pitch to the broad green is inviting and a memorable round is done.

It will have tested the golfer to the limit of his skill—and beyond, if the wind was firm: its direction is of no consequence, because the holes are angled with subtlety and imagination. There is nothing of monotony. Every one is a challenge and every prospect a joy. The golfer, whether talented or humble—or simply in search of exercise and beauty—will find fulfilment in rich measure. Over the years Turnberry has had many great moments. The women golfers were the first to avail themselves of its beauty in 1912, and nine years later Cecil (Cecilia) Leitch, the strongest golfer of the period either side of World War I, beat Joyce Wethered (as she was then) in the final of the British Championship. In a sense this was a historic occasion; Leitch avenged her defeat of the previous year in the English championship in which Wethered achieved the remarkable performance of winning at the first time of entering. But the old order was changing. Wethered had ascended her throne, there to remain supreme until her abdication in 1929.

Long ago J. H. Taylor said that the best way to win a championship was to win easily—a dictum that he himself observed on many occasions and which Norman followed in winning the 1986 Open at Turnberry by five strokes. But, in the history of the game, few have proved their right to a title in more emphatic fashion than Michael Bonallack in the 1961 Amateur championship. He won eight matches and only on the morning of the 36-hole final was he called upon to play the last two holes. This was a triumph of many qualities: rare devotion to the game, boundless perseverance and determination, and a charming, natural manner. After that Bonallack won many championships before settling down to oversee both The Amateur and The Open in his role as Secretary of the Royal and Ancient Golf Club of St. Andrews. But this was the start and there could have been no more perfect setting for it.

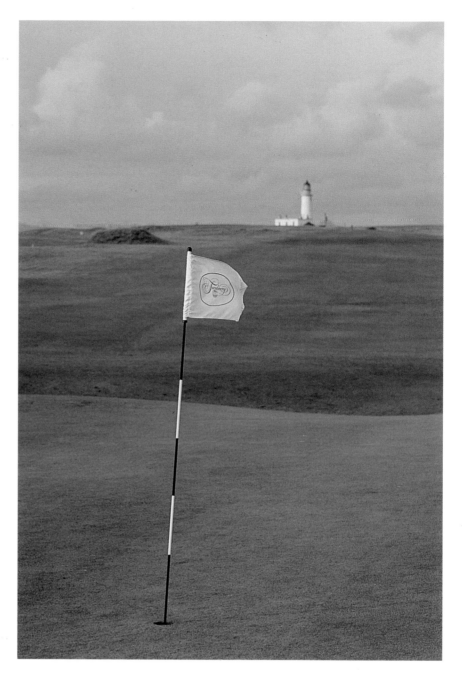

The 16th

Failure for the Faint-hearted

The 16th hole appears innocent enough but can hold considerable terrors in the wind, for the second shot over the burn always plays much longer than it looks.

The very nature of British courses, where allowance for run after pitching often has to be made, encourages underclubbing. Usually the penalty for doing so is not severe because fairways flow into greens, but there are holes where the aerial route is essential. Just such a hole is the 16th at Turnberry, where a deep, steep-sided cleft in the land, containing a little stream known as Wee Burn, winds across the fairway immediately in front of the putting surface. There is nothing subtle about the hole. In most obvious terms it warns: take enough club for the second shot.

In the 1963 Walker Cup match several experienced British golfers failed to do so when an uphill green with banks behind and the wind against begged for a bold shot. Many of them stood on the 16th fairway undecided between a 3- and a 5-iron, usually choosing the more lofted club, often with dire results.

The Modern Masterpiece of
Timeless Beauty

The course has the same grace and style that its designer brought to the game. Tom Weiskopf's gem on the banks of the legendary loch is easy on the eye and captivates both the professional and the amateur.

Since golf has been played in Scotland for over 500 years it would be asking the impossible of an architect to come up with something entirely new in golf course construction. Wherever he goes he is standing in someone's footprints. Who could hope to create a links course that could compete with the mystique of St. Andrews, the sheer terror of Carnoustie, or the remote beauty of Dornoch?

Yet in the 1990s we have seen something quite unique and magical created on the banks of legend that sit tight to the ethereal beauty of Loch Lomond. Not even Gleneagles is a rival when it comes to the majesty of setting; none of its courses comes close to the perfection of Tom Weiskopf's design. The tall American was, of course, the most elegant of players. His swing was an exquisite study in technique and had he blessed it with a temperament to match he would have won far more than his solitary Major championship suc-

cess in the 1973 Open at Royal Troon. Weiskopf's foray into golf course design has been as impressive as any former champion in this business. Together with his partner Jay Morrish, he has created an intelligent portfolio that runs counter to the belief that modern architects have precious little to contribute. His version of Troon in Arizona, for example, is worthy of carrying the name while Loch Lomond is as good an inland course as one could hope to play. It will prove his legacy to a game he has graced with elegance and style.

Loch Lomond's passage to greatness, however, was fraught with difficulty. The original developer needed almost a decade to gain planning permission. When Weiskopf was approached he needed no second invitation, for no architect sane of mind would turn down such a site; yet it took three years to complete the layout and then, just as things appeared to be falling into place, Britain was plunged into

The 14th

Tom and Jay's Chance:

The tendency in modern course architecture is to forsake subtlety for force, to measure the strengths of a hole not in terms of the demands it makes on the power of the imagination but on power, period. The 10th at The Belfry is a welcome move away from such damaging schools of thought, a short par four that cleverly uses a natural enclosure of stream and trees to create a setting that positively dares the big hitter to seek out the green. The 14th at Loch Lomond is similar in many ways, hence its name. The conventional drive leaves a pitch over Arn Burn. For those with the ability to carry the ball 230 yards through the air, however, the temptation to try for the green is overwhelming. Sanctuary lies in the long apron to the front of the putting surface.

The Course Card

Loch Lomond Championship Tees

Hole	Yards	Par
1	425	4
2	455	4
3	505	5
4	385	4
5	190	3
6	625	5
7	440	4
8	155	3
9	340	4
10	455	4
11	235	3
12	415	4
13	560	5
14	345	4
15	415	4
16	480	4
17	205	3
18	430	4
Out	3,520	36
In	3,540	35
Total	**7,060**	**71**

recession and Loch Lomond into receivership. Weiskopf's frustration was understandable. What point a masterpiece if no one could play it? Fortunately he knew a wealthy businessman in Arizona named Lyle Anderson, and persuaded him to fly to Loch Lomond. Weiskopf knew that if he could get Anderson as far as Scotland the allure of the banks would do the rest.

And he was right. Today, Lyle Anderson is the President of the Loch Lomond Golf Club. The course has not only been completed, it has been conditioned to a standard rarely found in Britain. Each year it stages the Loch Lomond World Invitational and professionals who rarely leave home without an appearance fee happily register to play for nothing. "It is as good a course as I have ever seen," said Nick Faldo, at the inaugural staging. "Would that all new courses were like this."

There is no gentle introduction to Loch Lomond. Weiskopf himself describes the 1st as a "pretty doggone tough starting hole" and if the wind is blowing off the loch and into a player's face then two good blows are needed simply to reach the green. The fairway, which runs along the edge of the water, is beautifully contoured. An old oak tree, perhaps standing in the grounds since the days when the Clan Colquhoun fought here against Robert the Bruce, provides a perfect sight line and opens up a small green that is well protected by bunkers both to the front and left-hand side. The 2nd is played into the prevailing wind and features some of the delicate touches that make Weiskopf and Morrish's courses such a delight to play. A low wall runs across the fairway some 50 yards from the green and so is not really in play. When the architects were surveying the site the wall was a sorry site, just remnants from the past. Most designers would have left it there. Weiskopf and Morrish rebuilt it, a small aesthetic that accentuates the hole.

The 3rd is a par five, complete with an architect's optical illusion. From the tee the bunker to the left of the fairway appears in play; in fact it is a carry of over 300 yards. Instead of being a hazard in the true sense of the word, therefore, it is more a sight line and helps to give the hole definition. For the long hitter the green remains reachable in two but there is marshland to avoid to the right of the putting surface. The hole is a beauty as is the 4th, played back toward Ben Lomond which frames it in a graceful idyll. The 5th plays back toward the water and is the first of Loch Lomond's four very good short holes. At 190 yards it does not lack for length, and can prove a wooden club even for a useful amateur. The key is to miss the bunkers on the left, for only a rare touch with a sand iron will lead to a par from there.

The 6th is the longest hole in Scotland, a monstrous par five measuring 625 yards. The hole is saved from being simply a grotesque slog by its setting. Its entire length it runs alongside the loch, with the snow-tipped mountains in the distance lending an eerie sense of stillness. The 7th is a beautiful par-four, a dogleg in the classic manner with a bunker on the angle at 190 yards signifying the change of direction. The short 8th is overlooked by Rossdhu House, an 18th century Georgian mansion that in the lingering years of the 20th century has become a positively palatial 19th hole. The front nine is completed by a short par four, which is driveable for the professionals from the front tee, although the green, as one would anticipate, is heavily protected by the jagged bunkers that are a trademark of the course.

The loch disappears from view at the start of the back nine but not the sumptuous surroundings. The tee shot at the 10th is an inviting one, downhill toward the hills and mountains. The long approach is then played across the Arn Burn from which the hole takes its name. The par-three 11th continues the forbidding start to the home half, 235 yards long and playing every inch of it. The 12th is Weiskopf's homage to Donald Ross, with a green that falls away sharply both to the front and right. The 13th is a fine, downhill par five, the 14th a splendid short par four with the green reachable for the professionals if the wind blows from a helpful direction.

And so we come to Loch Lomond's exceptional finish, beginning with a breathtaking tee shot from the 15th, the fairway flowing away from the plateau tee toward a narrow, deceptive green, where the yardage appears to be playing tricks with the mind's eye. The 16th is another sweeping, majestic par four before the golfer returns to the loch for the final two holes. The 17th is a daunting par three across marshland to a well-protected green. A quietness pervades the setting here, a solace allied to the surroundings that led Weiskopf to select it as his favorite hole. Most people, however, prefer the last, a 430 yard par four that sways gently around the loch. How much dare one take off the drive? Enough, certainly, to avoid crashing into the bunkers that sternly guard the right-hand side of the fairway. The approach shot is enticing, the sort that characterizes this splendid addition to the great Scottish courses. Behind the green lies the ruins of Rossdhu Castle, a gentle reminder of turbulent times past.

The 18th, below, sweeps around Loch Lomond and makes for a glorious finishing hole.

An Exercise in Fear

Hoylake is older than all but one of the English seaside golf courses (Westward Ho!, founded in 1864, is its senior by five years) and is considered among the foremost of all the links of northern England because of its traditions and infinite merits. It was responsible in 1885 for starting the Amateur Championship, the oldest event of its kind in the world. The first international of all, between England and Scotland, was played there in 1902. In the same year Alex Herd won the Open with a rubber-cored ball, and the gutty was dead for evermore. In 1921 the first men's match between the United States and Britain was played at Hoylake, inspiring George H. Walker to inaugurate his contest—the Walker Cup—the following year. In all, ten Open Championships were played there before the event grew beyond what Hoylake's confines could accommodate.

rhythmical imaginable." He was a formidable competitor with an austere approach to the game but was, nevertheless, a modest man. After he had retired to a home in the Welsh hills someone asked to see his medals; he had given them all away. In 1890 he was the first amateur and the first Englishman to win the Open; he was amateur Champion the same year, a feat equaled only by Bobby Jones in 1930. A measure of his enduring skill was that he competed in the Amateur championship of 1927, forty-nine years after his first Open appearance.

Remarkably, Ball's greatest amateur rival was also a Hoylake member. Not only did Harold Hilton win the Amateur four times and in 1911 the U.S. Amateur Championship at Apawamis, but he was Open champion twice again, an achievement that only Jones among amateurs has sur-

Long before golfers came, Hoylake was a significant place. Late in the seventeenth century the broad Dee estuary, at the mouth of which Hoylake stands, sheltered a fleet that transported the army of William of Orange to Ireland for the battle of the Boyne. In time the estuary filled with silt and at low tide it looks as if one could walk across to Wales. The importance of Hoylake diminished with the gathering sands and Robert Browning, in his scholarly *History of Golf*, wrote that the waste of dunes and links, on which the course now lies, would not then have fetched $15. In 1911 the Royal Liverpool Club bought it for $50,000.

Until 1876 the golfers shared the links with a racecourse and it cannot have been amusing, even in those days when courses were not sleek and manicured, to find one's ball in a hoof mark. Now only faint traces of racing remain; a post or two, an old saddling bell, and the names of the first and last holes, the Course and the Stand. The club soon became a lively spirit in English golf. In 1884 the honorary secretary, Thomas Owen Potter, suggested that an open amateur tournament be held the following year. At once the club was faced with the problem of what was an amateur; status was not defined in those days. An entry was received from Douglas Rolland, a Scottish stonemason who had won second prize in the previous Open championship. Rolland was ruled out—but what of Hoylake's greatest son, John Ball, who, at fifteen, had played in the Open some years before and had accepted a half-sovereign for finishing sixth? The decision in favor of him was delicate and possibly tinged with nepotism. In the long years to come Ball was amateur champion eight times, a tally that probably will never be approached.

Comparison between the ages is fruitless, but Ball was supreme in his own time. Apparently his grip was unorthodox and his stance a little stiff, but the swing was described as the "true poetry of motion, the most perfectly smooth and

passed. Hilton was said to be the most accurate wooden club player of his day, with a swing of great vigor. He also had a lively intelligence and love of experiment. He and Ball were great masters; another, Jack Graham, was almost so and it was small wonder that Hoylake worshipped these men. Hoylake is unique among British championship links because it is possible to be out-of-bounds within the confines of the course, and innumerable golfers have condemned it on this count. Until 1920 the penalty for out-of-bounds was loss of distance only and thus the golfers of old were not so harshly punished. Now, Hoylake can inflict the tortures of the damned. There is always an alternative to flirting with danger, but what an exercise in fear some of those holes can be.

The right angle of the 1st makes a forbidding opening hole. On the left from the tee is the clubhouse with its silken putting green; on the right, for the full length of the hole, is the sinister crest, a bank no more than three feet high that encloses the practice ground. A good drive will finish past the corner, but a long shot remains with the haunting thought that a slice will be fatal if one aims for the green, which is right next to the crest. Many a player has been out-of-bounds with his drive and approach; many have run out of hope of ammunition before completing the hole. Before the 3rd was changed, and a fine new short 4th created in readiness for the 1967 Open, the slightest pull would sail out-of-bounds over another crest. But now the golfer is free until the 6th. This is the famous Briars, where a high-fenced orchard is in line for the drive; against a strong prevailing wind the carry from the back tee is terrible to behold.

No hole in Britain caused more argument for decades than the 7th, named Dowie after Hoylake's founder. The narrow ellipse of green is protected on the left by yet another cop, and it is possible to hit a perfect long iron to the heart of the green and see the ball hop over the bank out-of-bounds within a few yards of the flag. Unless the green is soft, to aim at the flag is either heroic or stupid, depending on the state of the game. To play safely out to the right leaves a tricky chip through a little swale. In the last round of the Open in 1930 Jones needed two fours to be out in 35. After two long shots over the 8th fairway he was no more than 15 yards from the green but, as he wrote later, he took seven for the hole "in the most reasonable manner possible." His torment of mind is only too easy to imagine; so, too, is the enormous effort of will and control that enabled him to finish just safe from pursuit. This was the second leg of the "quadrilateral."

From the 8th the golf is of the old, true seaside character, dipping and curving along the sandhills; Hilbre Island and its myriad birds and the quiet hills of Wales are in the distance. The 9th with its bowl of a green, the superb short 11th, the Alps, its green an oblong oasis in the dunes, the lovely sweep of the 12th, and the tightest of pitches to the 13th, with its necklace of bunkers, make a splendid prelude to the long, long finish on the plain below.

Now the field comes into play again. It is possible to slice into it from the 15th tee, and its corner cuts across the direct line to the 16th. Then shorter, this hole was decisive in the last round of the 1967 Open when Jack Nicklaus and the sentimental favorite, Roberto de Vicenzo, fought a superbly entertaining duel. Nicklaus, playing ahead, scored a birdie-four, before Vicenzo struck his drive to the very edge of the field. From there he hit a soaring spoon to make sure of a birdie and the title. Of all the finishing holes at Hoylake the 17th can make the greatest play on courage and fear. A cool, firm contrary wind emphasizes the severely taxing nature of the hole where the green is angled across the line of flight, with a road flanking its far side and approaches. The slightest overhit, cut or pushed second shot can easily trickle out-of-bounds under the fence, while the cautious, playing to the left, risk deep bunkers from where the recovery must be played toward the road, a disagreeable prospect. To have a reasonable shot for the flag the drive must hold the right side of the fairway and escape the bunkers that lurk there for the shot that leaks. Although the last hole is not overly demanding, the man who has played the last five in fours is no mean golfer.

The Course Card

Royal Liverpool, Golf Club

Record: 64, Brian Waites, European Open 1981

Hole	Yards	Par
1	429	4
2	393	4
3	505	5
4	194	3
5	448	4
6	422	4
7	198	3
8	519	5
9	392	4
10	412	4
11	200	3
12	455	4
13	159	3
14	547	5
15	459	4
16	558	5
17	420	4
18	418	4
Out	3,500	36
In	3,628	36
Total	7,128	72

Few great courses combine such a searching trial of skill and courage as Royal Liverpool—or exact such a toll for loose play. The 1st, calling for a drive between clubhouse and practice field, is harrowing; it is fearsome as a matchplay tie-breaker. Short holes, like the controversial 7th, give no respite from the demand upon accuracy. And the long finish (22 strokes for the 2,402 yards of the last five holes) is a real test of endurance. With a wind blowing off the Irish Sea, the 17th is a daunting prospect for the most precise of golfers. Altogether, Royal Liverpool provides one of the greatest tests of quality golf and is a regular venue for the British Open Championship, which it has hosted ten times. In 1930 it was the scene of Bobby Jones' second leg in the unparalleled "Grand Slam."

Soft to the Eye,
Steel to the Touch

The Course Card

The Royal Lytham and St. Annes Golf Club St. Annes-on-Sea, Lancashire

Record: 65, Christy O'Connor, The Open, 1969; Brian Huggett, Bill Longmuir, Severiano Ballesteros

Hole	Yards	Par
1	180	3
2	396	4
3	433	4
4	373	4
5	163	3
6	466	5
7	544	5
8	389	4
9	144	3
10	320	4
11	460	5
12	155	3
13	324	4
14	431	4
15	450	4
16	340	4
17	395	4
18	371	4
Out	3,088	35
In	3,246	36
Total	**6,673**	**71**

Unlike some of its peers among British links, the Lytham and St. Annes course, founded in 1886, has no visual splendor. It has an urban setting, surrounded for much of the time by houses and with railroad tracks forming one boundary. No noble sandhills mark its horizons, the ground does not move in dramatic fashion, and the sea might be miles away. But don't be deceived by this apparent tranquility and smoothness. The course is a test of golf many times proven to be among the finest in Britain. The clubhouse is serene, substantial, and Victorian, similar to others in the northwest of England; it is at one with the links, which touches its very walls. There is a dormitory, a rare facility at British clubs nowadays, and its grounds have a garden atmosphere that makes a soothing background to the earnest pursuit of golf.

The club has a proud place in the championships of the past century. It was there in 1926 that Bobby Jones won the first of his three Opens in Britain. Soon afterward he won the United States Open as well, becoming the first man to hold both titles the same summer. After World War II an international parade of champions, Bobby Locke, Peter Thomson, and Bob Charles, had their hours before Tony Jacklin stopped the overseas domination. In 1974 Gary Player won one of the most emphatic victories of his generation before the course paid testament to the true genius of Severiano Ballesteros. Twice he won the Open at Lytham, first in 1979 and then in 1988 with a last round of 65 that will stand for the ages. In 1996 Tom Lehman created history by becoming the first American professional to win at Lytham, a popular triumph for a humble man. The success of that Open has led its return to Lytham after just a five-year absence, in 2001.

Lytham's tally of champions is an impressive tribute to the quality of the course, of which Bernard Darwin, the first golf writer of real distinction, wrote long ago: "If the day is calm and we are hitting fairly straight the golf seems rather easy than otherwise; and yet we must never allow ourselves to think so too pronouncedly or we shall straightaway find it becoming unpleasantly difficult." Many great golfers today would agree with him.

The short 1st hole, with its tee in a pleasing arbor, is comparatively placid, but the shots to the next two are haunted by the adjoining railroad tracks and in a flanking wind it is all too easy to slice or push out-of-bounds. Bunkers, too, are nicely set up to harass those who take an overly cautious line to the left. If a breeze helps on the opening holes it certainly does not on the 4th. It is a timely reminder of what may lie in wait on the homeward journey. Often the island of fairway between dunes and rough can seem disconcertingly remote and the green is angled to the left. An early birdie can easily be encountered here, and anything but a straight and truly judged shot to the short 5th is more likely than not to be punished. In normal summer conditions the next two holes quicken thoughts of birdie fours, given a fair stance on the crumpled 6th fairway from which to carry cross-bunkers and hold an exposed crown of green and a drive threaded down the long ribbon of the 7th. The green here is concealed by a bank between sentinel dunes, but in a helping breeze Tiger Woods and his like in power from the tees can be home with medium or even short irons.

Here the course has more the expected character of a links; the dunes are wild and owe nothing to the hand of man. High on a plateau among them is the 8th green, an exposed and deceptive target for the approach from the valley below. Many players take irons from the high tee because —with the railroad tracks taking its last look at the course—straightness is everything. The 9th is a pure target shot down to a green nestling amid bunkers and is more taxing than it looks, though numerous golfers have made light of the outward half. As long ago as 1963 Peter Thomson and Tom Haliburton turned in 29 on the first day of the Open, a record for the championship, but few such starts have not been delayed by the demands of the closing holes.

The 10th, a relic of other days with its drive blind to a tumbling fairway and its tilted little green, and the long dull plain of the 11th, where huge bunkers challenge the drive, may not be too severe. The 12th is quite another matter: it is the only short hole on the inward half, and presents the most difficult and uncompromising shot to a green of the whole round. A wood shelters the tee from the prevailing left-hand wind and the shot—long iron or even wood—must be held against it if the raised green,

Though it lays no claim to be the most attractive course in Britain, Lytham and St. Annes is certainly one of the most difficult, demanding both nerve and subtlety. It has become less of a links and more of a seaside course over the decades—softer and lusher—but nonetheless it remains essentially a testing layout and a premier championship venue.

with bunkers to the left and front right, is to be reached. If the shot slides away or is overhit, out-of-bounds is perilously close. The hole is as finely designed as any of its length on a British links and is the introduction, after a breather at the 13th, to a finish that rarely fails to influence the outcome of any event.

The 14th is straight enough, but even in a light crosswind the fairway is hard to hit and hold and so, from the rough, is the green, which falls gently away from the striker. Unless the drive to the 15th cuts off a substantial slice of the curving, rising fairway there is little hope of reaching or even getting a sight of the green. When the 15th is tough the 16th offers relief and likely birdies, but the blind tee shot must be placed to avoid bunkers, and to take advantage of the opening to the guarded green, to which

the strength of the short approach must be perfectly judged. For Ballesteros in 1979, placing the tee shot meant locating the temporary car park to the right of the fairway. He argued that it opened up the green, a line of thinking that did not hold court when judged alongside the three stentorian bunkers that guarded the side to which he took aim. Nevertheless, Seve being Seve, he got his birdie three.

Then the course attacks once more. The driving area from the 17th tee narrows between, on the left, a nest of shallow bunkers and real wilderness and, on the right, rough to an appendix of fairway that ends abruptly against a bank of sandhills. The hole then swings to the left with an inviting shot to an open green with bunkers on either hand—but it is inviting only to the man who has

The 18th

Ballesteros's Finest Hour

Only one man in the last thirty years has come close to matching Tony Jacklin for popularity with the British crowds and, oddly enough, he is Spanish. It was in Lancashire that his skills were first appreciated, at the 1976 Open at Birkdale, and twelve years later at Lytham they had matured to the point where Ballesteros' golf was an exquisite mix of talent and maturity. Two years earlier he had lost a Masters he should have won and had brooded upon his failure. Now he forgot the past to conjure an unforgettable final round of 65, one he would later describe as the sort "a player may complete only once or twice every twenty-five years." Pity Nick Price, the brave runner-up, who had lost out on the main prize as he had six years earlier at Royal Troon. But he took solace in the fact he could have done nothing else on this occasion. Six years more and his philosophy would gain its reward when he won the Open at Turnberry.

driven far enough on the right line. Ideally, the shot should be as far as possible down the right side of the fairway. If short or to the left, the green is invisible.

It most certainly was for Bobby Jones in 1926, as he faced the shot that, down through the ages, was to become a legend. Rarely has the destiny of a championship depended on one stroke and the balance between disaster and triumph been so sharply defined. Jones had come from behind in the last round and he and Al Watrous were level after seventy holes. Watrous hit a good drive into position for a clear shot to the green, but Jones pulled into one of the little bunkers just off the fairway. Between his ball and the flag, some 170 yards away, were all kinds of perdition—sandhills, thick scrub, and rough. Watrous played to the edge of the green and his feelings can be imagined as he waited for Jones to play. He must have thought that he would lead by at least a stroke going to the last tee.

Jones must have been angry with himself for what seemed likely to be a fatal drive, but when he saw the ball lying clean, hope must have stirred anew. He had to go for the green; a safe recovery to the fairway would probably cost a stroke and leave Watrous with the psychological advantage and the lead. It was all or nothing. He took his mashie iron (which remains a precious reminder in the clubhouse) and struck the deathless stroke. It finished on the green inside Watrous.

The wonder of the stroke, now marked by a plaque on the side of the bunker, was that Jones had the control of nerve, rhythm, and swing to strike the ball perfectly at such a moment; the margin of error was so slight. As later he wrote of this moment: "An eighth of an inch too deep

with your blade, off dry sand, and the shot expires right in front of your eyes. And if your blade is a thought too high ... I will dismiss this harrowing reflection." The effect on Watrous must have been fearful. Suddenly all the pressure was upon him and who would condemn him for taking three putts ? He was bunkered by the last green and Jones was safe except from Walter Hagen, who eventually had to hole his second shot to tie. Hagen, with his love of the dramatic, had the flag removed. His ball very nearly pitched into the hole but it went over the green. Jones moved nearer to Olympus.

Crisis and the 17th seem almost inseparable. In 1963, Nicklaus stood on the 17th fairway in the last round, knowing that two fours would probably be good enough to win. They would have been, but a 2-iron was a club too much for the second shot. It ran through the green into heavy rough, from where he took three more. His last drive was pulled into the left hand of the seven bunkers that make the hole so testing from the tee and he took another five. This was one of the rare occasions when Nicklaus could be said to have cast away a major championship. A few minutes later Bob Charles and Phil Rodgers made their fours on the last hole to beat him. The next day Charles became the first left-hander to win one of the world's major championships.

There was no crisis for Jacklin in 1969. He could afford to take five at the 17th and still remain two ahead of Charles. He played the last hole superbly and strode down the fairway toward a moment the likes of which even Lytham, in all its long history, had never seen before.

In 1974 the large 1.68-inch ball was made compulsory for the Open, and the elements combined to make the

With his second landing right by the wall of Lytham's Victorian clubhouse, right, on the last hole of the 1974 Open, Gary Player played left-handed with his putter. He missed his par but still won his third Open.

The 18th

Dramatic, Emotive, and Unorthodox

The Open has had few more exciting finishes than those played at Lytham, where the strength of the last two holes has heightened the drama. Bobby Locke, Peter Thomson, and Bob Charles won there after some tense moments on the 17th and 18th, but it is the manner in which four of Lytham's other Open winners have finished that is best remembered. Bobby Jones demonstrated his supreme control under pressure, Tony Jacklin's win was an emotional moment in British golf, Gary Player struck the most unorthodox final approach of any Open, and Severiano Ballesteros played the best round of his career.

Player Wins Left-handed

In the last round of the 1974 Open, Gary Player's approach to the 18th ran through the green and lodged against the side wall of the Lytham clubhouse, leaving him without room for his swing. He avoided taking an extra stroke by electing not to hit away from the green but to play the shot left-handed. He used his putter and stroked the ball to the center of the green. Player said later that he had been careful to take a short backswing and to play the shot with a long follow-through.

golf a severe test of control and patience. It confirmed Gary Player's greatness. Of his eight major championship victories it was unarguably the most commanding, and his winning margin of four was less than he deserved.

The last two holes were responsible. Player was leading Peter Oosterhuis by six shots when he pulled his second into the menacingly deep rough to the left of the bunkers guarding the green. Several minutes' frantic search followed before the ball was found; he could hardly move it at his first attempt, but chipped dead for his five. His second to the 18th was too strong and overran the green to settle close to the wall beneath the clubhouse windows. From there, the Open champion played his last, dramatic approach—left-handed, with a putter.

In 1988 there was an equally memorable shot for the members to observe, this time a deft chip from the side of the green from Ballesteros to defeat a gallant Nick Price by a stroke. The Spaniard had confirmed his brilliance eight years earlier, collecting his first major championship at Lytham at the tender age of twenty-two.

Some are born great, but Tom Lehman achieved greatness with his victory in 1996. His third round of 64 was not only a course record but created the space he needed to parry the challenges of Nick Faldo and Ernie Els. In the last round he was paired with Faldo, and his six-stroke advantage carried echoes, for some, of the similar deficit that the Englishman had wiped away three months earlier when defeating the challenge of Greg Norman at Augusta. Lehman held his nerve and the 18th green was bathed in a beautiful light as he collected his glittering reward.

The 18th

A Supreme Moment For Jacklin

In all British golf there has never been a moment to compare with that when Tony Jacklin walked onto the 18th tee in the last round of the Open at Lytham in 1969. He was two strokes ahead of Bob Charles, his partner and closest challenger, and the championship was his for the taking. It was to be the first British victory since Max Faulkner had won at Portrush in 1951, and the end of the longest span of overseas domination since Henry Cotton had arrested American supremacy at Sandwich in 1934. The vast amphitheater of stands embracing the last green was packed with thousands and the flanks of the fairways were solid with people, tense, expectant, and longing to explode with pride and acclaim for the young and popular champion. The greatness of the 18th hole, only 386 yards, lies in the tee shot. Across the fairway in the driving area are two diagonal lines of bunkers, seven in all. The farthest of these from the tee are on the left, threatening the drive pulled away from the wilderness of bushes on the right. It is the most demanding final tee shot on any British links. Watching Jacklin's swing for the drive was sufficient to know whether the shot was good because the pace of the takeaway was so smooth and deliberate. It proved to be a superb stroke far clear of any danger, and leaving him only a quiet 7-iron from the green. Tempo or rhythm had always been the key to Jacklin's best golf. In his younger years he would whip the club away from the ball too quickly, but as he pro-

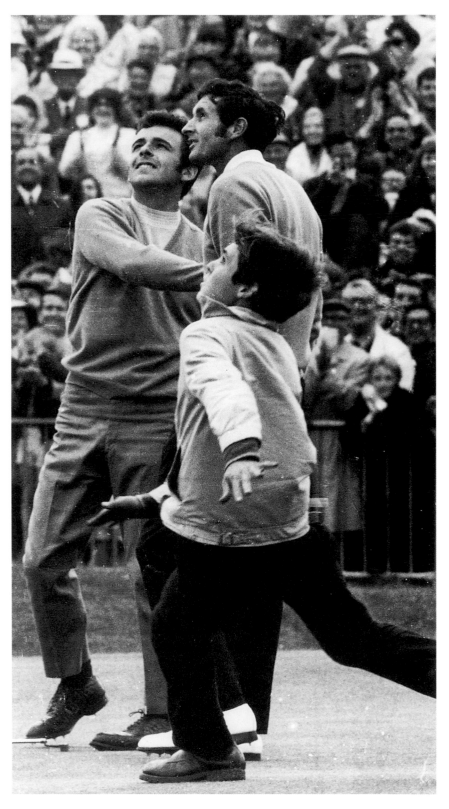

gressed toward the heights he concentrated on making his backswing much slower and thereby smoother. Throughout that Open he preserved his finest tempo, concentrating his practice each day, mostly with a 7-iron, toward the point where he felt that the slow tempo was natural to him.

Rare is the golfer who would not profit greatly from striving to find the rhythm best suited to him. It can vary considerably according to individual temperaments, but once discovered it is worth preserving, so that in moments of pressure the swing is less likely to become a nervous snatch.

Tony Jacklin throws his golf ball into the crowd after winning the Open Golf title in 1969. He was the first British player in eighteen years to win the title.

Much of Sunningdale's air of open innocence disappears when the golfer off the tee arrives to play his second shot, with tricky pitches to raised greens and well-placed bunkers to catch anything that rolls. The course starts off in unusual fashion with a very long hole, just short of 500 yards. The boundary is to the right, but the fairway is comfortably wide. However, playing to the left and too much safety can leave an awkward chip up the banked side of the plateau green and, with bunkers set into it, there is little room for error. With half the greens placed on hills, Sunningdale rewards good chipping and pitching.

The Supreme
Heathland Course

Early golf in Britain was confined to links beside the sea. Apart from a few courses in Scotland it was not until the late nineteenth century that it was played to any extent elsewhere. As the game increased in popularity, the eyes of golfers turned inland; courses were laid out on public commons and in private parks and a new conception of the game was born. The most significant development was the discovery that even rough heathland could swiftly be converted into ideal golfing ground. The outcome was a proliferation of splendid courses that, in their fashion, have become almost as distinctive an expression of British golf as the ancient links themselves.

The finest examples of heath courses lie on a stretch of country west of London. All have common features of pine, birch, heather, and wonderfully firm, smooth turf that, on account of the sandy subsoil, absorbs moisture with rare speed. Of all these courses, Sunningdale stands supreme.

The Old course owed its foundation to the enterprise of two brothers, who conceived the idea of golf on the wild heathland spreading away to Chobham Common. It was owned by St. John's College, Cambridge University, which granted leaseholds for a course and the building of houses nearby. This was one of the earliest instances in

England, if not the first, of property development with the creation of a golf course. Willie Park, son of the first Open champion, was commissioned to lay it out for $6,000, a sum that would not suffice for one of its greens today.

The club was fortunate—or inspired—in its choice of Park, for he was one of the pioneers of modern course architecture. He had the experience from being a great player, having won the Open twice, and was educated and ambitious to a degree rare in professionals of those days. In his appreciation of the classic features of the old courses, and his awareness of the changing needs of the time, he set unusual standards that, doubtless, influenced many of his successors.

Seeds were sown in the late summer of 1900 and a year later the course was ready. The soil on the heath was poor and sour and, apparently, some decried the project as foolish. Not long afterward they were claiming that anyone could make a course in such splendid, natural golf country.

The course is one of enchantment, rarely of menace; its challenge is one of subtlety rather than length. When the fairways are running in summer the longest holes, the 1st and 14th, can be reached in two shots. At no time is the Old overpowering and it offers an appealing variety of shots, not least at the short par fours The 3rd green can be driven, but the normal tee shot leaves an approach of rare delicacy to an away-sloping green. The 11th is a gem; the blind drive to a falling fairway must avoid a bunker on the left and a copse of pines on the right, but the greatness of the hole is in deciding how to play the little approach to the raised table of green.

Several tees command superb views and offer the exhilaration of driving from high places: from the 5th with its green beyond a shining pond, and the 6th mounting into the wooded distance from an island fairway; from the 10th where the driver looks down upon a promised land with, far beyond over the woods, a glimpse of the russet and white of the clubhouse; and the short 13th, with its deceptive shot from a pinnacle tee to a green part-embraced by an insidious little grassy trench.

The 15th, a taxing shot across the prevailing wind, is a noble short hole that begins a sternly beautiful finish. Unless the drive is long the approach to the 16th green must be flighted from a downhill lie over cross-bunkers on the far side of a shallow valley. Again, at the 17th—unless the drive flirts with a thicket lurking on the left—the approach must be played from a hanging stance. The gentle incline toward the home green, with a great spreading oak just beyond, makes for a fine drive and an approach that was improved by German bombs in 1940. One bomb made a crater to the right of the green which prompted the idea of converting it into bunkers. The shot can be demanding, the more so because a path marks out-of-bounds beyond bunkers flanking the left of the green and is more in play than the striker from the fairway might imagine. There never was a course that someone did not murder on occasion. In kindly weather, when the beautiful greens are at their best, the expert can readily enjoy himself. Shortly after World War II, Australian Norman Von Nida burned his way to victory with a 63 in the last round of the Dunlop Masters. Gary Player, in winning the first important event of his life in 1956, played the Old in 64. Ian Woosnam averaged 65 shots per round for 72 holes when winning the 1988 European Open. In the same event two years earlier, Nick Faldo went around in 62, the course record. In 1997, on her way to a commanding eight-stroke victory in the women's British Open, the Australian Karrie Webb shot 63; but the most

famous of all rounds were those of Bobby Jones when qualifying for the Open in 1926. The first, a 66, was often quoted as the perfect round; 33 putts, 33 other shots, every hole in three or four. The next day he did have one five and one two in a 68 and it was no wonder that he said later, "I wish I could take this golf course home with me." Other golfers must have thought likewise after playing one of the loveliest of all courses. The New course, designed by Colt in 1922, is quite different from its elegant sister. Where the Old might be feminine in its grace and wiles the New is sterner, more masculine. It is more exposed to the winds and bleaker in prospect but it has beauty in the emerald fairways curving through the heather, the broadness of the scene, and the downs rolling away in the distance. And the challenge of the golf is undeniable.

The Course Card

Sunningdale Golf Club, Berkshire Old course

Record: 62, N. Faldo

Hole	Yards	Par
1	494	5
2	484	5
3	319	4
4	161	3
5	410	4
6	415	4
7	402	4
8	192	3
9	267	4
10	478	5
11	325	4
12	451	4
13	185	3
14	509	5
15	226	3
16	438	4
17	421	4
18	432	4
Out	3,144	36
In	3,465	36
Total	**6,609**	**72**

In the 1997 British Open at Sunningdale, the runaway winner Karrie Webb from Australia gave probably the finest exhibition of golf ever seen by a woman in Britain.

A Young Course Worthy of the 100th Open

The Course Card

Royal Birkdale
Golf Club, South-
port, Merseyside

Record: 64,
Mark O'Meara

Hole	Yards	Par
1	450	4
2	418	4
3	406	4
4	200	3
5	338	4
6	484	5
7	150	3
8	410	4
9	407	4
10	384	4
11	374	4
12	181	3
13	433	4
14	197	3
15	542	5
16	347	4
17	497	5
18	472	5
Out	3,263	35
In	3,427	37
Total	**6,690**	**72**

Standing within a glorious expanse of dunes on the Lancashire coast, Royal Birkdale has been the setting for more championships and international matches than any other British course since the end of World War II—not even St. Andrews has been as richly endowed. During that time it has tested the mighty and produced a number of champions of enduring stature.

Birkdale arose from the inspiration of a handful of visionaries who rented for a mere $8 a plot of land, so plentiful on the Lancashire coast where dunes tumble in wild profusion; the first clubhouse was a dollar-a-week room in a private house, and the first professional discharged his duties for only three times that sum. The club has been extremely fortunate in its professionals. Only three have been there this century: David McEwan, Robert Halsall, and the present incumbent, Richard Bradbeer.

The course, mainly designed by George Low, did not follow the principle, beloved by architects of old, that blind shots were essential. Instead, the holes were laid out in valleys between the towering sandhills and were not the adventurous exercise they might have been. A new clubhouse was built and pulled down again when it was found to be on someone else's land. The foundation of present eminence did not really begin until 1931, when Southport Corporation bought the land and gave the club a 99-year lease. From then on it was all was progress. Fred Hawtree and J.H. Taylor redesigned the course and the clubhouse was built. Even then Birkdale was not a seaside course in the traditional sense. Many of the fairways are flat and pose no problems of stance, the greens mostly are outlined against the dunes, often in clefts between them, giving a perspective of distance to help the golfer and also some protection from the wind when putting. There is nothing of the typical old seaside green with its flag shimmering on some distant horizon, and all kinds of folding ground to make the hole look shorter than it is.

More than any other British championship course, Birkdale offers golf of a target nature. But if problems of judging distance are not so acute, others are emphasized, notably the cardinal virtue of straightness. It is enough to say that a green is a sharply defined target, like the 2nd, 10th, or 17th, but it still has to be hit. To miss the greens at Birkdale, even narrowly, can leave an infernally difficult stroke from the clinging willow scrub that abounds on the course, and often from a hanging lie at that.

When the fairways are narrowed for a championship they make a fine test of driving, and should they happen to be fast as well, accuracy is crucial and power of little significance. The Open Championship in 1965 was a fine example; it brought victory to Peter Thomson, simply by virtue of his unerring straightness, and precious little reward to Arnold Palmer and Jack Nicklaus.

In preparation for this memorable year in Birkdale's history—the Ryder Cup followed a few months after the Open—further alterations were made to the course. These involved a new 12th, a short hole cradled in the dunes, the elimination of the short 17th, and the lengthening of the finish. Birkdale became possibly the only course in the world with four of the last six holes measuring over 500 yards. By the 1991 Open, however, the 13th and the 18th had been slightly reduced to become fours, and Birkdale had a fin-

The final six holes at Royal Birkdale extend across almost two and a half miles, yet aspiring champions are rewarded more for accuracy than for power. The many well-placed fairway bunkers are a key feature, for wherever there is a stroke to be saved, by cutting a corner or stretching a fairway wood to the green, there is inevitably an abundance of traps through which the golfer must thread his way. The approach to the 13th is particularly demanding and the prevailing wind and intimidating cross-bunkers make the 15th daunting. But when pressure mounts at the finish, it is a brave player indeed who is prepared to open up among the ten bunkers of the 18th hole.

ish that was not only daunting in length but par, too. In the 1954 Open, Birkdale's first, Peter Thomson's winning score of 284 was about strict par for the event; seven years later Arnold Palmer won with the same total but in dreadful conditions.

The days were never free of wind, with a gale for the second round. Not since 1938, when wind almost wrecked an Open at Sandwich, had the golfers been as violently assaulted as that day at Birkdale. Before play began many tents were flat and the fairways were heavy with casual water but Palmer, loving the challenge of it all, was inspired to attack.

Few had ever seen iron play such as his that fearful morning; his massive hands rifling the ball under the wind made the senses reel. He was three under par for the first five holes. A magnificent round was in the making, but it was not to be. The 7th tee is high, yet protected from a sea wind, and Palmer should have forced a low shot. Instead he used a 9-iron; the ball was swept away and when he pulled from the next tee the spell was broken.

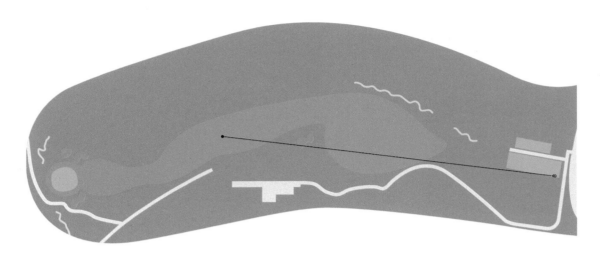

Severiano Ballesteros introduced himself to British audiences in 1976 with a drive that made a mockery of the hole's pretensions to be a double dogleg. Eschewing the caution exhibited by practically the rest of the field, the Spaniard drove over the bunker that guards the corner, leaving himself a short iron to the green.

The 1st and 18th

The Making of a Legend

It is only natural that when people think of the great times of Severiano Ballesteros they think of the courses associated with his victories: the young conquistador at Lytham in 1979; the vengeful champion of Augusta in 1980 and 1983, atoning for some hurtful remarks made by certain Americans; the smiling matador of St. Andrews, saluting the crowds on all sides after winning over the Old course in 1984; the domineering captain of Valderrama, overseeing his charges to inspire an unforgettable win in the 1997 Ryder Cup.

There are many people, however, who cannot look back over the Spaniard's career without remembering the place where it all began, where he burned his name into the consciousness. That place was Birkdale in the 1976 Open. It began at the opening hole, a double dogleg, where the perceived line from the tee in the year of that parched summer was an iron to the right of a dune to hold the fairway. Ballesteros was having none of it. He drew his driver and proceeded to carry the dune with yards to spare. The ball bounded miles down the fairway, turning a double dogleg into nothing of the sort. Over the next seventy holes Ballesteros went from unknown to local hero; only Tony Jacklin had known such acclaim in these parts. When he walked down the last the cheers were deafening. He had led after the second and third rounds but experience had caught up with the nineteen-year-old on the final day; that and a golfer named Johnny Miller near the apex of his considerable talent.

Miller recognized the genius of the man close by. When it was clear he would win he encouraged Ballesteros not to give up, that second place was still within his grasp. As he accepted the thunderous acclaim, Ballesteros knew he had to get down in two shots from a seemingly impossible place to the left of the green to tie Jack Nicklaus. The pin was cut to the left as well and there were bunkers to negotiate. Ballesteros found the stroke for the occasion; it would invariably prove thus. He threaded the ball between the bunkers and it came to rest four feet from the hole. Miller putted close and generously decided to tap in. He left the stage for Ballesteros and when he holed a bond had been established between the player and his people that lasts to this day.

The 9th is one of the more testing drives because the angled fairway is not quite visible from the tee. Birkdale tends to punish the hook rather than its opposite. The 10th and 11th certainly do so, but offer no great problem if the drive is straight. Woe to the player who hooks on the latter, however, into the scrub, as Severiano Ballesteros discovered in 1976. This was the hole that effectively ended his chances of victory, for even his remarkable powers of recovery did not alleviate matters. He ended up with a seven to Johnny Miller's four, and the American was clearly on his way to his solitary Open triumph. At the 12th there is a brief excursion into the lonely sandhills but wonderfully worthwhile for this is a short hole to rank with the finest, the green tucked intimidatingly away in the distance. The treacherous road for home has begun in earnest.

The 13th has a long diagonal carry from the tee to a fairway fringed with bunkers, and the last short hole, again from a high, sheltered tee, is over a valley to a

closely trapped green. The 15th is a superb hole, compelling a drive in the fairway if a great gathering of bunkers is to be carried with the second shot. These are angled so that the player going for the green must attempt the longest carry. The 16th green, poised on a table of rising land, can be difficult to judge. From the 17th tee a platform in an ocean of willow scrub – the line is guarded by huge dunes, Scylla and Charybdis, on either side of the fairway's entrance; it is a forbidding shot under pressure. In 1971 Lee Trevino pulled into one of these in the last round and his struggling seven enabled Lu Liang Huan (Mr. Lu) of Taiwan to challenge to the end. Trevino, however, held on to become one of five players to date who have won the British and American Opens in the same summer: the others were Bobby Jones, Gene Sarazen, and Ben Hogan before him, and Tom Watson in 1982.

Palmer, too, survived a savage break on this hole in 1961. Down the hard wind his second whistled through the green into a small bunker. Normally recovery would have been easy, but the wind moved the ball as he struck. He skimmed it into bushes beyond the green and holed out in six. On reporting to officials that he had hit a moving ball he was automatically penalized another stroke. Nevertheless, if a player has to complete the last two holes in nine strokes to collect the title, he would hope to march on to the last tee with a birdie four on his card. The 18th is now one of the great par-four finishing holes, one that captured Tom Watson in his pomp in 1983, when he struck a 2-iron second shot 213 yards to within fifteen feet of the hole to secure the fifth of his Open titles. He would later call it the best 2-iron of his life, and with good reason.

One of the strangest Opens to have been staged was at Birkdale in 1991. The greens had succumbed to disease and infuriated many of the players but they seemingly did not bother a tall, dark Australian named Ian Baker-Finch. Reaching the turn in just twenty-nine strokes on the final day, he won by a more comfortable margin than two strokes over Mike Harwood would suggest. What happened to Baker-Finch? In that summer a decade of success appeared to have dawned before him. A distinguished apprenticeship had come to a stunning close. Four years later his golf was broken, and he was unable to keep the ball on the first hole at St. Andrews. Three years later his spirit was broken too. The Open returned to Birkdale and went on without him. Baker-Finch had retired to social golf in the tranquil climes of his home state of Queensland. As on other great links—such as Lytham, Turnberry, and Westward Ho!—women were the pioneers in holding a championship at Birkdale. In 1909 Dorothy Campbell (later Mrs Hurd) won the trophy with "beautiful and deadly creek

play." She remains the only woman to have won the British and American titles more than once.

Some fifty years passed before Birkdale was host to an important men's championship. Then, in 1946, the prodigious recovery power of James Bruen was too much for Robert Sweeny's graceful golf in the final of the Amateur Championship. Bruen made light of the willow scrub, a feature of Birkdale and a fearsome hazard for ordinary mortals. He was the first of Birkdale's famous champions. Since then a host of great events have been held at Royal Birkdale, not least the 1969 Ryder Cup match, when the home side held the Americans to a tie. Remarkably, of the thirty-two games played, foursomes, four-ball, and singles, no fewer than sixteen were decided on the last green, and the last of all made an unforgettable climax. The countries were even when Jacklin, who had holed a monstrous putt on the 17th to square his game, and Nicklaus stood on the last tee in the final match—all to play for between the two finest golfers of the generation from their respective countries. The hole was halved, Nicklaus holing from 4 feet and immediately conceding Jacklin's short putt, which was by no means dead. It was a gesture totally in keeping with the man and it ensured that a proud day for Britain and Birkdale would pass into history.

The story of Birkdale came full circle in 1971 with the 100th Open Championship and victory for Lee Trevino, ultimate extrovert of golfers. This was the peak of a sustained spell of success that had rarely been matched in the game's history. Trevino played with formidable confidence, skill, and attack; his command of the championship was absolute on the last day until he took a seven on the 71st hole, which enabled Lu Liang Huan to challenge until the last putt.

Tom Watson's second shot to the 18th at Royal Birkdale in the 1983 Open was one of the finest of his career, and deservedly led to tumultuous applause for a popular champion. It was his fifth Open win.

A Monument to
Technology

A map of the Sutton Coldfield area in the 1970s would have shown a potato field lying in the region now occupied by The Belfry, one of the most successful hotel and golf course establishments in Europe. The venue is a monument to the wonders of technology, to what can be achieved with massive investment and obstinate faith.

The original design was uncompromisingly American and marked a new departure in golf course architecture in Britain. This was going to be a course that took into account the changes in technology that allowed the players to hit the ball even farther distances. This was one venue where all the par fours would not be reduced to drive and pitch holes. The early years were fraught with difficulty and many professionals disliked it, but in 2001 the Belfry will host its fourth Ryder Cup, an honor no other venue can match. The Brabazon course was closed for much of 1998 in order to amend several of the mediocre holes that dominate the front nine. They will make quite a difference. The 3rd, hitherto a straight and tedius par four with little to relieve the monotony, will now be a

The story of the Belfry illustrates that with the help of machinery and courageous investment it is possible to create a silk purse out of a sow's ear. Once a potato field, the venue is now among the most successful golf establishments in Europe.

dogleg par five, with water coming into play for the shot to the green. The big hitters will be encouraged by the sight of the putting surface within reach for their second shots but the penalties are plain. This man-made lake used to fall in front of the fourth tee and serve little purpose other than for drainage. Now it will be a focal point of the front nine and the 3rd will join the other water holes, in particular the 9th, 10th, and 18th, for which The Belfry is deservedly famous. The 4th, previously a long, straight par five with little chance of reaching the green in two because of a ditch in front of the putting surface, will now play as a difficult par four. The ditch will be more of a feature; instead of people pitching over it with a nine-iron or wedge, they will have to tackle it with a long iron.

The first two holes are straightforward par fours, the second in particular a nice hole to play at less than 350 yards. The amended 3rd gives the player a further chance to ease himself into the round before the course begins to extract its price. The 5th is often played directly into the wind and if it possesses any teeth then the ditch that runs across the fairway at the 180-yard mark can come into play.

The 6th has water patroling both the left- and right-hand sides of the fairway. The architects, Dave Thomas and Peter Alliss, have created an illusion from the tee, as the fairway is much wider than it appears. Nevertheless, most professionals will take a long iron from the tee as insurance against finding the hazards. The Belfry's great weakness has always been its three short holes, none of which possess much character. The first of them is the 7th, a mid- to long-iron shot to a green protected both fore and aft by an enormous bunker. The 8th is another good long hole, which achieved a peculiar sort of fame during its early years. The right-hand side has three bunkers to catch the pushed drive, an all too likely occurence given the far greater hazard of water down the left. In 1979, Severiano Ballesteros, going for the big drive, turned in disgust almost at the moment of impact since he knew he had violently hooked the ball. The drive was not merely in danger of finishing in the hazard but likely to find the middle of the lake. Whereupon it struck a small boat advertising wares for the sponsor and bounced back onto the fairway. It hardly needs adding that the Spaniard went on to win the tournament.

The 9th is the best hole on the outward half, a testing par four to a green shaped cleverly around the lake that also dictates play on the closing hole coming home. In the three Ryder Cups to have been played to date this area has become a splendid amphitheater. Massive stands have been erected behind the greens allowing spectators to watch the action on both the 9th and 18th holes.

The 10th is the famous short par four, its features deservedly well-known owing to the enormous influence of television. Originally designed to measure 310 yards, it was shortened to just 267 yards at the last two Ryder Cups in order to encourage more players to go for the green with their tee shots. It played to its best length at the 1985 Ryder Cup, when measuring 299 yards, and provoked an argument among the American players.

Lee Trevino, the U.S. captain, stood on the tee in practice and declared the green, its sliver tucked behind trees and protected to the front and side by water, out of range. He ordered that whatever the state of the matches, his players should take an iron and hope to make a birdie by getting their approach shots close. The strategy greatly upset attacking players. The unrest in the American camp was obvious, and played its part in the humbling five-point margin of defeat that gave the Europeans their first victory in the Ryder Cup since they were assimilated into the team in 1979.

The 11th is a dogleg par four, the green opening up to the drive that misses two bunkers that guard the fairway's left and right sides. Alterations have been made to the long par three 12th, previously the worst hole on the course. Before, it offered no option but a mighty smash with a metal wood or 1-iron.

Now the tee has been raised to establish some character and the ditch in front of the green has been widened.

The 13th is a par four that skirts the outer rim of the site and is a little too similar to the 11th to be rated highly. The 14th is the last of the short holes and in 1993 Nick Faldo holed in one against Paul Azinger in the singles matches.

So to one of the longest finishes in golf, the final four holes measuring over 2,000 yards. The 15th is a 550-yard par five where the drive has to be threaded between two bunkers. A ditch that crosses the hole at the 390-yard mark becomes a problem for anyone who has strayed from the tee, or if the wind against has any velocity. For the straight hitter, a bunker that sits imposingly in the middle of the fairway, 50 yards from the front of a three-tier green, invariably dictates the strategy for the second shot, leaving a pitch that can be anything from a half swing to a full 9-iron depending upon where the pin is positioned. This is the first of the four big greens that are a feature of the Belfry's closing holes.

The green at the par four 16th falls away dramatically to the left, and with the flag invariably positioned on the top shelf this can mean the most difficult of putts for the iron shot that has narrowly missed its target. The 17th is another par five that doglegs sharply to the right and, when downwind, is reachable in two shots. The drive, a forerunner to the strategy the player will have to adopt at the last, is one of the most intriguing on the course. Enough of the dogleg needs to be cut off to avoid running into the bunker that sits on the angle, but another bunker guards the right-hand side to ward off any greedy golfer. The green is again massive at 39 yards and slopes gently from back to front. In twenty-two years it has become one of the most famous finishing holes in British golf. Its reputation was made at the Ryder Cups in 1985 and 1989. The hole's difficulty comes in deciding how much of the severe left-hand dogleg to carry. Too little and the shot to the green, over a large expanse of water, becomes daunting; too much and the ball will not make it over the water. The green is of St. Andrews proportions, measuring 59 yards from front to back, with three tiers. Locate the wrong tier and it is all too easy to three putt. It is the sort of hole that no golfer easily forgets. Together with the 10th it leaves a warm, ruddy glow, and while the sum of all its parts might not lead to the conclusion that The Belfry is a great course, it undeniably has greatness contained within its boundaries.

The Course Card

Belfry, Brabazon, Wishaw, Warwickshire

Hole	Yards	Par
1	418	4
2	349	4
3	465	4
4	579	5
5	399	4
6	396	4
7	183	3
8	460	5
9	400	4
10	275	4
11	420	4
12	235	3
13	394	4
14	194	3
15	550	5
16	410	4
17	575	5
18	474	4
Out	3,649	37
In	3,527	36
Total	**7,176**	**73**

The 18th

The Perfect Finishing Hole

The question of why The Belfry will stage a fourth successive Ryder Cup in Britain in 2001 has little to do with merit. The first two were the *quid pro quo* to The Belfry's owners for housing the Professional Golfer's Association and charging merely a peppercorn rent. In return for a fourth contest, the PGA got its own golf course at The Belfry, called PGA National. The Belfry does have the virtue, however, of a perfect geographic location, and has shown itself capable of handling large crowds. It also has the 18th, perhaps the most demanding finishing hole in golf.

It is the perfect matchplay hole. In the three Ryder Cups to date, no less than 25 of the 36 singles matches have finished there and they form an unforgettable memorial to the range of emotions that a great finishing hole can inspire. We have seen Sam Torrance stand in the middle of the green, his arms forming a V for victory salute after taming the 18th with a perfect drive and 9-iron; witnessed Christy O'Connor Jr., equally jubilant after a daring 2-iron approach over what must have appeared a cavernous expanse of water. Naturally there have been many failures, too, many who have discovered the hole and the context in which it was framed beyond their capabilities. It will be the same in 2001. One may argue with considerable justification that the Ryder Cup should not be going once more to The Belfry; but no one can counsel against the 18th again providing scenes of unique drama.

The Course Card

Royal St. George's Golf Club, Sandwich, Kent

Record: 64,
Tony Jacklin,
Dunlop Masters 1967;
Christy O'Conr Jr.,
The Open 1985

Hole	Yards	Par
1	441	4
2	376	4
3	210	3
4	468	4
5	421	4
6	155	3
7	530	5
8	418	4
9	389	4
10	399	4
11	216	3
12	365	4
13	443	5
14	507	4
15	466	4
16	163	3
17	425	4
18	468	4
Out	3,408	35
In	3,452	35
Total	**6,860**	**70**

A Kentish Haven of History

No course is closer to the golfing heart of England than Royal St. George's at Sandwich because of its association with the growth of championship golf and its distinctive character. No other English club moved so swiftly from a quiet and pleasant beginning to a lasting place in the chronicles of the game. Since Roman times Sandwich has been a harbor. More than 1,000 years ago Wilfred, Bishop of Northumberland, arrived "pleasantly and happily in Sandwich haven"—and a haven it remains. The town, with its quaint, mysterious little streets and ancient dwellings, is snug and peaceful, and the links are wild and lonely, free to the winds and the sky as they have been since the tides withdrew countless centuries since.

The setting has changed little since one Doctor Laidlaw Purves "spied the land with a golfer's eye" from the tower of a Sandwich church. The sight must have stirred his imagination, and that of others. A syndicate was formed and in 1887 the club was founded.

That was the age of mighty amateurs, whose stature surpassed that of all the English professionals with only one notable exception. The Scottish had commanded the scene until 1894 when J. H. Taylor, a sturdy young professional from Winchester, won the first Open Championship to be played outside Scotland. His score of 326 on the desolate and windswept links seems monumental by modern standards.

In those years there was no challenge to the supremacy of British golfers until in 1904 Walter J. Travis, described by one observer as "a little man in middle age with a black cigar and a center-shafted putter," came to Sandwich from the United States to compete in the Amateur Championship. He was, it seems, a coldly determined, implacable person who played with great steadiness, winning match after match with accurate approach work and uncanny skill on the greens. His success was not popular, for the British were unaccustomed to defeat and American golf was hardly out of the embryonic stages. The chagrin that must have swept St. George's when he beat Horace Hutchinson in the semifinal and the vast hitter Ted Blackwell in the final can be imagined. The center-shafted putter was banned for years to come, but it was too late. Travis, who was born in Australia, was the first American citizen to win in Britain.

Soon after World War I, in 1922, another American came to Sandwich. He also had cigars and an enchanted putter—and more besides, for Walter Hagen was the most colorful personality that British golf had seen. He won the Open that year, the first in which native-born American supremacy was becoming established, and at its peak Hagen won again at Sandwich, in 1928. In 1930 Bobby Jones led his side to an overwhelming victory in the first Walker Cup match to be played in England. Then, four years later, the incomparable Henry Cotton stemmed the transatlantic tide not far from where King Canute had made his fruitless gesture a while earlier.

In 140 years of championships no golfer can have endured a greater agony of suspense than he did on the last day, when illness threatened to sabotage his triumph. In 1938 Cotton again played magnificently in one of the most ferocious gales that has ever beset an Open, but the yeoman figure R.A. Whitcombe just prevailed. After Bobby Locke had won the first of his four Opens at St. George's in 1949 the championship came no more to Sandwich until 1981, when a young American with a genial smile walked off with the main prize. It was to be the highlight of Bill Rogers's career. He did return later that year to Walton Heath as part of the strongest American Ryder Cup side of all time but in the team photograph he was almost hiding in the back-

Soft-sprung rolling fairways and yawning duneside bunkers make Royal St. George's a classic links course. A good score on the outward half—much improved by Frank Pennink's recent modifications—can lay the foundations for a winning total, but this can be so easily spoiled by the long parfour 13th, the daunting 14th alongside the boundary wall, and the heavily bunkered 15th. No matter what his score the golfer can take pleasure from the beauty and seclusion of verdant fairways that run along hollows between high dunes, making golf at Royal St. George's a very private pastime.

ground and it proved pertinent. When the Open came back to Sandwich just four years later he was already harboring thoughts of retirement and now he rests easy, the head professional at San Antonio Country Club in Texas with just the flag of the 18th hole at St. George's to remind him of his daring deeds of yore. In 1985 it was Sandy Lyle's year, repeating the feat of Cotton long before in ending overseas dominance. It was the first home triumph since Tony Jacklin in 1969 and it was duly celebrated with raucous scenes. No British player since Jacklin had been more popular than Lyle, an easy-going character from the heart of Shropshire. It said everything about his unassuming demeanor that three hours after winning the Open he was washing the dishes at his rented home in Sandwich. The 1993 Open at St. George's is a firm candidate for the greatest last day of all. The greens were hard, the fairways parched, and the leaderboard read like a who's who of the modern game: Norman, Faldo, Langer, Pavin. Norman triumphed, returning a 64, the lowest final round in Open history. As he walked down the 18th the wise old denizen Gene Sarazen was standing by the 18th green, ninety-two years old and bright as a button. Later he said of Norman's achievement: "I never thought I would live to see golf played like this," a statement verified by Norman's generous playing partner Langer, who called it the finest round he had witnessed.

What a glorious place Sandwich is for golf. When sunlight is dancing on the waves of Pegwell Bay, the white cliffs of Ramsgate shining in the distance, the larks singing as they always seem to sing at Sandwich, and a sea wind

The Sandwich hall of fame includes such figures as, left to right, Walter Travis, Walter Hagen, and Roger Wethered. It was there in 1904 that quiet American Travis became the first overseas player to win the British Amateur title, and where the great Hagen became America's first British Open champion in 1922. In 1930, Sandwich was the first English venue for a Walker Cup match with Wethered making the fourth of five British team appearances. But it was not enough and the Americans won for the sixth successive time.

stirring in the sand grasses, the golfer may share the famous golf writer Bernard Darwin's view that it is "as nearly my idea of heaven as is to be attained on any earthly links."

As with many another historic course, St. George's was admired in its earlier days more for its charm than the quality of its golf. It was a place of mighty dunes and blind carries, and there were those who claimed that the art of the game was not hitting a ball over a sand hill and running to the top to see where it had finished. But changes were made and the course is now a rich and varied examination of golf, owing little to guessing or fortune.

The 1st, its fairway like a stormy sea of green with a cross-bunker threatening the second shot, is a perfect opening hole; a mounting crest before the 2nd green makes the approach difficult to judge. Then comes a demanding new short hole, a long iron or more over wild country to a narrow shelf of green. This hole replaced a relic from gully days and was one of several changes by the architect Frank Pennick that came into play in 1975. Previously three short holes pursued the same direction. The 6th, alongside the

Maiden, remains, as does the 16th. The 8th is now an appealing par-four with its drive to a plateau amid the crumpled land and approach down to a green in a dell of its own. It is replaced as a short hole by the 11th.

Early in the round the golfer will be aware of frequently changing levels and stances, such as the long rise of the 4th past a mountainous bunker to a sharply contoured green high on a folding hillside, and the drive from the next tee into a valley enclosed by dunes. Only if the drive is placed right is a sight of the distant green possible, for otherwise the approach is blind. This hole is typical of the course's beauty; so, too, is the 7th with its drive to a love-

Henry Cotton had his first big success at Royal St. George's when he won the 1934 Open there, setting an Open record of 65, after which a new and now famous Dunlop ball was named. But his return there in 1938 was less happy when he lost in the gale-swept final round by going out-of-bounds at the 14th hole.

The 14th

The Low Road Home in a High Wind

The ability to maintain balance and rhythm of swing and to flight the ball truly in a strong wind is not given to many. Among modern golfers few have mastered the art to a greater degree than Sandy Lyle. His stance is so solid that it seems immovable; his hands so powerful that he can drive the club through the ball, keeping it so low that its flight is hardly affected, even by strong wind. During the final round of the 1985 Open Championship at Sandwich, Lyle had dropped a shot at the 13th hole and so when he came to the par-five 14th he knew he

needed a birdie to maintain his dream of emulating Tony Jacklin's achievement in 1969. The drive at the 14th is the most difficult on the course and Lyle's was duly hooked away from the out-of-bounds and into wild rough. He had to play short of Suez Canal, thus leaving him over 200 yards to go for his third shot. A par not a birdie now appeared the limit of his achievements for the shot was far from easy to a green lavishly protected by sand. Yet into the wind Lyle flighted the ball beautifully, keeping it low as it raced over the ground to finish 35 feet from the

Left and Far Left: Greg Norman, with the winner's spoils following his record round in the 1993 Open. Gene Sarazen, watching by the 18th green, said of Norman's final round 64: "I never thought I would live to see golf played like this."

In 1949, Royal St. George's was the scene of Bobby Locke's first Open win. It was the last Open played over the old links.

ly, hidden expanse of fairway running clear to a green that may or may not be reached according to the wind.

Thereafter the mood of the course quietens somewhat except for the approach to the 10th high on an exposed plateau, a fiercely testing shot in a wind. Around the turn pars may not be too difficult, but the 13th is the first of a great trinity. The drive is diagonal over a long shoulder of rough country toward the clubhouse of the neighboring Prince's, white and remote in the distance. The 14th can be the most fearsome tee shot on the course, with dunes to be carried and with out-of-bounds on the right all the way to the green. Then the golfer must decide whether he can carry the wide waters of the stream crossing the fairway.

A similar decision is often required at the 15th, unless the wind is helping or the fairway running fast. An array of cross-bunkers must be carried, and the narrow green is farther beyond them than it seems to be. The 16th is fringed with sand, a target shot. This is the hole that gave British television viewers their first sight of a tee shot being holed in important competition. On his way to winning the 1967 Dunlop Masters, Tony Jacklin holed out with a 7-iron. The 17th is a strong four and the approach to the 18th, from a downhill fairway, is a great finishing stroke, made by one beautifully placed greenside bunker.

Sandy Lyle 1985 Open

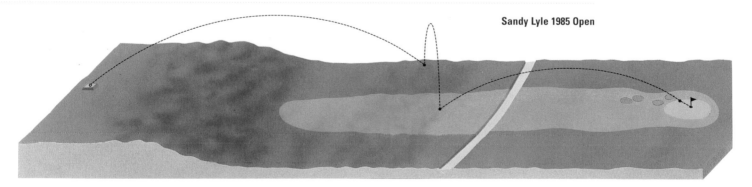

flag. It gave him sustenance at the time he most needed it and the confidence to hole the putt for a birdie that changed the face of that Open. The 15th would yield a birdie as well and Lyle could afford the bogey that resulted from missing the green at the 18th and still claim the prize—though not before a thirty-minute wait for others to finish that seemed to drag for an eternity. When asked about a turning point afterward he had no hesitation in pointing to the 2-iron that set up the unlikeliest of birdies at the 14th.

Intimacy that Belies

Quality

An odd characteristic of seaside golf in the British Isles is that many links courses permit little more than an occasional glimpse of the sea; it can be heard, but is usually invisible. A fine exception is Royal Porthcawl, on the rock-fringed southern shores of Wales.

In the strictest sense it is not a links. There are occasional sand hills, but gorse, hummocks, heather, and deep bunkers are its principal features. The land hereabouts leans down to the rocks and the smooth shining sand and from every point the golfer can look across the Bristol Channel to the long dark line of the Somerset coast. At times when wind and rain sweep in from the Atlantic he might long for the shelter of dunes, for Porthcawl is exposed to every mood of the elements, but such days are exceptional. For most of the time there are few courses as agreeable to play.

The origins of golf in Wales are by no means as ancient as those in Scotland. Most of the early clubs were formed toward the end of the last century and Porthcawl is regarded as the senior, in stature if not age; the Glamorganshire club at Penarth is a few months older. Porthcawl was founded in 1891 and started with nine holes laid out on common land near the sea. However, cattle on the greens, carriage wheels, and camping were a constant nuisance and eighteen holes were planned afresh. Many years passed before their quality was appreciated and even now a first sight of the intimate little clubhouse would not suggest the presence of a championship course. Nevertheless a more beautiful, princely beginning could hardly be imagined.

The opening holes follow the line of the coast and when surf is foaming on the rocks, and the sky fresh and clear, the urge to play is almost overwhelming. The 1st is not severe—a tempting drive into a valley and pitch to a subtle green—but the next two holes are beautifully fashioned over gently falling ground, demanding substantial approaches to greens on the shore's edge. They are classic seaside holes.

After a fine short hole the course swings inland, mounting the long 5th to a trough of green whose sides were once so steep—alas, no more—that many a wide shot would find its way unerringly and obligingly into the hole.

The golf on the uplands is more of a heathland character. Great banks of broom and gorse, a glory in early summer, threaten, but not too unkindly, the 6th and 8th. Between them is a charming little hole for which strong players hardly have a club small enough. Anyone would settle for a four at the 8th with its long second uphill over cross-bunkers, and the 9th is harder than it looks. The drive must hold a leaning fairway and huge bunkers guard a sharply sloping green that invites three putts unless a player thinks carefully before approaching it. The golfer's task thus far may not have been too severe unless there is a strong wind, and this proviso must be made for all British seaside courses; wind is as much a part of their character as the links turf, the dunes, and the gorse. They can vary enormously in difficulty and Porthcawl is as good an example as any. Professional events are rarely played there, but in 1961 Peter Thomson had to play outstanding golf in a strong wind to win the Dunlop Masters with 284. On the other hand there has been remarkable scoring in good weather. When, after many attempts, Richard Chapman won the Amateur Championship there in 1951, he produced a sequence of figures that even Charles Coe could not match. He was little over an average of threes for the last nine holes of the matchplay contest, which ended on the 14th.

In 1995 the Walker Cup was held in Wales for the first time and nowhere but Porthcawl would have been suitable. The match was a memorable one, the towering figure of Gordon Sherry, all 6 feet 8 inches of him, proving too much for an American side that contained one Tiger Woods. From the turn the levels of the holes vary constantly. The 10th dips into a valley and offers a testing pitch

At Royal Porthcawl, as is often the case with British seaside courses, a high premium is placed on a golfer's ability to play accurately in the elements. Finding the fairway from the tee is often only the beginning. At the 5th, for example, the player who manages to avoid the out-of-bounds and the pond on the Jeff has to play right up against the boundary again to find the green. At 124 yards, the 7th is one of the shortest holes in championship golf, but there are several long holes on the back nine.

The 15th and 16th are similar holes, pursuing opposite directions, with drives to island fairways far below and second shots of rare quality. The whole of the greens cannot be seen, but the distant, fluttering flags should be guide enough to the golfer who knows his course. The shot to the 16th poses the age-old problem of getting the ball airborne when there are no two ways about the need to do so. Deep cross-bunkers must be carried or a six is almost inevitable.

Whether by design or coincidence most of the famous British courses have 17th holes of great distinction. That at Porthcawl may not rank with the Road Hole at St. Andrews, the Royal at Royal Liverpool, and one or two others, but it is admirable nonetheless. As all such good holes should, it gives the golfer who is trailing a chance to recover—if he can pro-

to a narrow oblong of green. The short 11th is a target hole, while the 12th mounts a somewhat forbidding hill. Few can reach its green with their seconds, but the effort is worthwhile. From the crest of the 13th fairway the prospect is superb. The green lies at the foot of a long slope with the sea shining beyond. All around, the great basin of the course can be seen; the golfers moving out on the early holes, climbing the 5th, approaching the 10th and 11th, toiling up the nearby 12th and—it is hoped—choosing the right club at the short 14th, where nothing but a true shot is rewarded.

duce two superlative shots. Reid Jack, one of Britain's finest amateurs, did so once when playing for Scotland in a crucial match against England. His wood shot finished 6 inches from the hole, a wonderful stroke considering that the green is diagonal to the line, with bunkers on its near side.

The last hole can be very demanding, tumbling gently toward the sea and a slippery, falling green. The approach over hummocks, hollows, and heather demands a delicate touch to finish within reasonable putting distance. And, when the sun is going down and the Bristol Channel gleams like polished pewter, the shot can be close to impossible.

Royal Porthcawl
Golf Club, Glam-
organ

Hole	Yards	Par
1	327	4
2	454	4
3	421	4
4	196	3
5	515	5
6	389	4
7	124	3
8	475	5
9	384	4
10	336	4
11	186	3
12	468	5
13	441	4
14	150	3
15	464	4
16	433	4
17	511	5
18	411	4
Out	3,285	36
In	3,400	36
Total	**6,685**	**72**

The 13th

A Battle Against the Wind

Most golfers regard the 1-iron with a certain awe. Because of its slight loft and the fact that it demands greater precision of strike than any other club, it is not normally included in a set of irons. The development of the more lofted woods has rendered it superfluous for most golfers and it is generally used only by those of the highest class. Some, like Nicklaus, Player, and Miller, use the 1-iron for tee shots when position rather than length is the criterion, and when a hole is dangerously narrow. One of its greatest virtues, in the hands of an expert, is that it can give greater control in contrary winds than the fairway woods.

A heavy westerly wind gusted down the Bristol Channel throughout the final of the Amateur Championship in 1973. The golf was so demanding that the experienced Dick Siderowf of the United States soon had a clear edge over Peter Moody, his young English opponent. At one point in the afternoon he was six up, but Moody came back at him and was three down going to the 426-yard 13th. The crest of the fairway before it swings left and begins its graceful fall to the green is a high point of the course, and that day was exposed to the full force of the hammering wind.

Moody was in trouble from the tee and Siderowf, whose drive had found the fairway, had the opening to take complete command of the match. His 1-iron shot bored through the wind with an unwavering flight to the heart of the green. He said later that it was his finest shot of the week and it proved to be conclusive. The quality of his golf is revealed in the accuracy of his iron play, made possible by a splendid extension of the swing through the ball.

Royal Porthcawl, where the sea is visible on every hole, is the prince among Welsh courses.

A breathtaking backdrop of mountains and sea is reward in itself at Royal County Down, but the golfer who strays can pay devastating penalties in the fierce rough and bewildering frequency of traps that make the championship course one of Ireland's best. It is an added hazard, too, that the 2nd, 5th, 6th, 9th, and 15th holes all call for blind tee shots, and others, such as the 13th, offer only markers to guide approach shots to unseen greens.

Emerald Fairways
by a Sapphire Sea

The lasting appeal of the finest British courses is their variety. Royal County Down bears little resemblance to its great Irish companions, Portrush, Portmarnock and Ballybunion; an occasional valley hole might stir memories of Birkdale or Turnberry, but not strongly. At County Down one is, as so often, on a course with such individual character that it is among the hardest, yet most rewarding, to play anywhere in the British Isles.

It lies on a curve of Dundrum Bay, with the Mourne mountains in the background. It can be a paradise for the golfer in early summer, when sunshine turns the sea to sapphire and brings forth the golden glory of the gorse and the richness of emerald fairways, and greens with cloud shadows playing on the mountains and the quiet green hills to the west.

The club came into being in 1889 and minutes of an early meeting reveal the remarkable fact that Tom Morris was to lay out a course for a sum not exceeding $6.50. How far this princely sum availed the old man is not known, but within a decade the links were written of as the finest in Ireland. It was reconstructed later; Vardon gave it high praise in 1908 and the same year King Edward VII

bestowed the Royal title on the club. Since then the golf has changed but little. Purists might claim that there are too many blind shots—five from the tees and others where the green is all or partially concealed—but somehow they are so in keeping with the nature of the course that they cannot with any justice be condemned.

The opening holes head northward along the shores of the bay, which is screened by ranges of dunes. The long 1st resembles a trough from the tee—an inviting prospect for the straight driver—but the next tee shot is the very reverse. A high ridge must be carried and against the wind it can seem insurmountable; the second shot must be steered through a divide in another ridge to a well-guarded plateau green—not a long hole, but one that can be fierce indeed. The drive down the valley of the 3rd should be held to the left, for bunkers in a spur of dunes on the right protect the straight line to the flag.

The short 4th, a medium shot over a waste of rough heather, is followed by a great 5th. The drive must be aimed to carry as much as the striker dares of a heathery outcrop of land, around which the hole swings to the right. The approach is a fine shot to a green backed against sand hills.

The 6th is a lovely hole, blind from the tee but not harassingly so, and the 7th a tricky little pitch over a gully; part of the green is behind a hummock and its sides are closely bunkered. In the Irish Open amateur final in 1933 Eric Fiddian, playing Jack McLean, holed his tee shot there in the morning round.

In the afternoon he did likewise at the 14th, a feat without parallel on an important occasion but one that still failed to give him victory. Into a prevailing wind, the approach to the 8th green between its embracing hills can be a taxing stroke. This is the highest point. As one drives from the next tee into a valley far below, leading to a distant plateau green, the mass of Slieve Donard, highest of the Mourne mountains, can seem menacingly

The Course Card

Royal County
Down Golf Club,
Newcastle, Down
No. 1 course

Record: 66,
James Bruen, Irish
Open 1939

Hole	Yards	Par
1	506	5
2	421	4
3	474	4
4	212	3
5	438	4
6	396	4
7	145	3
8	429	4
9	486	5
10	197	3
11	438	4
12	525	5
13	443	4
14	213	3
15	464	4
16	276	4
17	427	4
18	547	5
Out	3,507	36
In	3,530	36
Total	**7037**	**72**

close, and the spires and roofs of the town at its foot almost alpine in appearance.

The turn is by the clubhouse, blessed virtue of design, and the 10th, although short, is another characteristic hole, from a raised tee along a valley to a green where bunkers abound. The 11th leads to more open country and after the falling sweep of the 12th comes a gracefully curving hole in a valley all its own. The second shot is blind and the one swinging in over the hill has the best chance of finding the green. This is a splendid hole to watch from on high, where its secrets are visible to the spectator but not to the player.

After the challenge of the 14th, a downhill shot over sand and gorse to a well-bunkered green, the course heads for home. The 15th demands two substantial strokes of anyone's game, and maybe more, but the 16th is fun. The strong can drive the green, but a charming little pool with an island lies in the fairway below. The finish on the landward side of the big dune country is not typical of the rest but a pond, just out of driving range, must be carried at the 17th, and the last hole is the longest of all.

Newcastle is an examination for any golfer whatever the elements, and how swiftly these can change. Once during an international meeting the seas were a tossing, angry turmoil and the wind so violent that eight holes could not be reached with two wooden club shots. So low were the clouds that one young golfer, forgetting that the sea was at his feet, asked, "How high are we here?" Mercifully such days are rare.

Many of the most memorable moments at County Down have involved women golfers, in particular three from France. In 1927 the tiny Simone Thion de la Chaume (later Madame Renç Lacoste) became the first Frenchwoman to win the British championship. Her daughter Catherine succeeded her, remarkably also in Northern Ireland, at Portrush in 1969. The dark, lithe grace of the Vicomtesse de Saint-Sauveur (now Madame Segard) prevailed in 1950,

and Brigitte Varangot, one of the most accomplished woman players of her time, succeeded in 1963.

The one Amateur championship to be played there was in 1970 when Michael Bonallack won for a third successive year. This was a record and also his fifth victory, a tally surpassed only by John Ball long ago. By an extraordinary coincidence, and one without precedent in a major championship, Bonallack's opponent in the final was Bill Hyndman, as it had been the previous year at Royal Liverpool.

The distant clubhouse and town of Newcastle, and the sweep of the mountains of Mourne, provide players with a diversion so magnificent as to make concentration difficult at the 4th. The hole measures 212 yards, almost all of it carry across gorse and heavy rough. The green, much longer than it is wide, is protected by no fewer than ten bunkers, most of them positioned to catch the underhit or the sliced tee shot.

Ulster's
Green Leagues of Links

The informed golfer in search of the game in Northern Ireland may head south from Belfast to Newcastle in County Down, or north to Portrush; if he is wise he will make both journeys. When Portrush is the first choice, and there is no particular haste, he should take the Antrim coast road, not only because it is one of the most beautiful in Britain but because, as an approach to a links, it has few parallels. Soon after the road passes the ancient ruins of Dunluce Castle it turns a corner, and there below, with enchanting abruptness, the whole spread of the course can be seen in a sweeping glance: green leagues of tumbling, broken links falling away to cliffs of sand—the highest near any golf course—and the shining seas. The course, much changed since it was established in 1888, winds and climbs and falls over a profusion of green hills, and within their grasses are primrose, bluebell, and dog rose. To the east and west the dark headlands of Benbane and Inishowen rise from the sea, and not far off shore the long, low sprawl of the Skerries stand patient against the tide. In the distance, the faint shadows of Islay and the Paps of Jura, remote outposts of Scotland, can be seen when the air is clear, and a few miles away lies the Giant's Causeway.

The modern version of the main course, named Dunluce after the ancestral home of the lords of Antrim, evolved from the work and imagination of many men, from one McNeill, a greenskeeper who laid the greens, to the architect, Colt, who was responsible for most of the improvements. From a purely golfing point of view the most distinctive feature is the severe driving. There are few great courses where the erratic driver can consistently escape all consequences of waywardness; at Portrush he has less chance of

doing so than on almost any other championship course, not because of particularly savage roughs or hazards but by the design of the holes. The first and last alone are straight; all the others curve, usually more than 200 yards from the tee. When the rough is allowed to grow inward for an important occasion, and the fairways are no more than the width of a street, uncommon accuracy is essential for any golfer, let alone the long hitter who tries to carry the corners.

Another unusual aspect is the comparative absence of bunkers around the greens. Mostly these are protected by natural hills and mounds, hollows and runners, and holding the greens can be difficult unless the drive has been rightly placed. If they are missed then the little shots can be a real test of touch. Neither are the greens enormous, and this accounted for Max Faulkner having so few putts when he won the Open in 1951: few champions have had fewer than four rounds. The number was said to be 108; even allowing for exaggeration it was an astonishingly low proportion of a winning total of 285.

The opening holes move along the uplands of the course. After a rise to the plateau of the 1st green, the 2nd winds down a long path through the dunes. The 4th is a lovely hole with its drive over a stream, out-of-bounds on the right and a green nestling in the sand hills, and from the next tee the whole glory of the links can be seen. The 5th fairway cascades to a green by the sea, and an inadvertent step backward would bring a long tumble down a precipice of sand to the beach. The 6th is a beautiful short hole calling for a long fade into the green; and now the stern stuff has begun.

The middle holes of the round swing back and forth, but in no way monotonously, for the angles of their approaches are alternately inclined, never unduly favoring the slice or hook. After a picturesque dropping shot to the 11th, the course takes a turn toward the sea again; and soon one stands on the tee of the 14th, as famous a short hole as there is in Ireland, with the singularly appropriate name of Calamity Corner. Between tee and green, 200 yards away, is a chasm of rough, and the prevailing wind does not help; often enough the stroke calls for wood. The merest slice can mean disaster, just as a pull from the next tee is a most unhelpful

Spread out over tumbling dune country on a beautiful stretch of the Ulster coast, Portrush offers a unique kind of links golf. All but the first and last holes curve and it is this rather than tough hazards that proves challenging. Bunkers are few, and natural mounds and hollows guard the greens. In the 1951 Open (the only British Open held in Ireland) only two players managed to beat 70 in testing, blustery conditions.

stroke. The 16th fairway leans left toward a grassy bank, and it was there, in the last round of the 1951 Open, that Tony Cerda's drive finished and, as it proved, his challenge to Faulkner expired. Nine years later the hole saw a memorable stroke in a semi-final of the Amateur Championship. Robert Cochran, an American of middle years, was two down to Gordon Huddy when he struck a 3-wood shot low under the wind to within only 12 feet of the flag to win the hole.

The last two holes, lengthy and flat, are not entirely in character, but they favor the strong as they did Joe Carr in the other semi-final against James Walker. Rarely had Carr been so pressed, though he was a different golfer the next day. All the anxiety, the straining at the leash, and the tendency to steer had vanished. He drove vast distances, usually to the heart of the winding fairways; the mood of conquest was upon him and Cochran could muster no lasting response. As a beautiful May afternoon reached its zenith, Carr became ten up and ten to play. Life could hold little more for a golfer and soon he was champion a third time.

The Amateur Championship returned to Portrush in 1993 when the Yorkshireman, Iain Pyman, defeated his fellow Englishman in a final described by Michael Bonallack as the best he could remember. It finished on the 37th and represented a considerable conquest over nerve for Pyman since on the home green he had missed from barely 2 feet for victory. A number of memorable women's championships have also been staged over the Dunluce links. In 1895, Lady Margaret Scott, a handsome figure with skirts trailing the turf, won her third successive victory in the British championship. She could hardly have done more; the championship was where Scott's family had their enduring hour, and in 1969, Catherine Lacoste, one of the greatest of all women golfers, won the British title on the way to conquering all her worlds. Another Hezlet—Charles—was an Olympian amateur golfer during the years around World War I. During these same years, in which a young caddy at Portrush, Fred Daly, was learning to become one of the longest straight drivers of his time. Daly, a great competitor, won the Open in 1947—the only Irishman ever to do so

Why No Open Since 1951?

It is a question that has often been posed, not the least by the Irish, and the sad answer lies in the fact that the Open Championship has long outgrown some of the courses with which it grew up. No one doubts that the venue is challenging enough at Portrush, just as it is at Royal Liverpool. But it is the infrastructure that goes with an Open, from trying to accommodate upwards of 40,000 people a day to ensuring their safety as they line each fairway, to housing the exhibition and hospitality tents, that causes problems. The Royal and Ancient took the Senior British Open to Portrush in 1995 to see how the event would cope with 10,000 people a day and the answer was that it was very difficult to find a spare hotel room within 30 miles of the course; it was also hard to watch several of the matches that drew sizable crowds. Imagine the problems for four times that number? Of course the years of the troubles have sadly had their effect, too. Would all the top Americans still make the effort to come over if the Open was at Portrush, knowing the event would be a security nightmare? One thing that is beyond dispute is the success of the Senior British Open, which was held there for a fourth successive summer in 1998. The first was singularly memorable. One week after the recovering alcoholic John Daly won the Open Championship at St. Andrews, his senior equivalent, Brian Barnes, triumphed at Portrush, and over the course where his father-in-law Max Faulkner had won the Open. With Faulkner among the gallery, celebrating his 79th birthday, it was a most dramatic occasion as Barnes triumphed on the third extra hole of a sudden death play-off, the 17th, by holing an eagle putt from 25 yards. His winning prize, incidentally, was $96,245. Faulkner's was $500.

There is no room for error at the aptly-named Calamity Corner, the 211-yard 14th. The tee shot can vary from a full-blooded drive to an easy mid iron, depending on the wind force and direction.

The Course Card

Royal Portrush Golf Club, Antrim Dunluce Links

Record:
66, Jack Hargreaves,
The Open 1951

Hole	Yards	Par
1	392	4
2	505	5
3	155	3
4	457	4
5	384	4
6	189	3
7	431	4
8	384	4
9	475	5
10	478	5
11	170	3
12	392	4
13	386	4
14	210	3
15	365	4
16	428	4
17	548	5
18	469	4
Out	3,372	36
In	3,446	36
Total	**6,818**	**72**

The Very Irish Hazard of
Maggie Leonard's Cow

The Course Card

Portmarnock Golf
Club, County
Dublin, Dublin

Record: 66, Christy
O'Connor, Dunlop
Masters 1959;
Gary Player, Canada
Cup 1960

Hole	Yards	Par
1	341	4
2	404	4
3	431	4
4	141	3
5	448	5
6	360	4
7	169	3
8	532	5
9	296	4
10	344	4
11	426	4
12	215	3
13	435	5
14	344	4
15	268	4
16	458	5
17	373	4
18	179	3
Out	3,122	36
In	3,042	36
Total	**6,164**	**72**

In a land where beauty, poetry, conflict, and passionate belief in the individual are constantly intermingled, the Irish have found golf to be a ready expression of their character and flair for games. The enthusiasm of the players, the variety of styles, and the quality of courses is remarkable. Ireland is not large, but it has several of the finest tests of golf to be found anywhere in Europe.

Except in the country itself, where local feelings might influence judgment, one would be hard-pressed to find agreement as to which was the greatest course—Portrush, Portmarnock, or County Down on the coast to the east and north; or Ballybunion on the far Atlantic shore. Killarney, serene on its lakeside amid the mountains; Waterville, and Rosses Point also have elements of majesty. Of all courses, few are blessed with the natural magnificence of Portmarnock. Within the fine sweep of coastline curving to an end at Howth Hill, the northern guardian of Dublin Bay, there is a long tongue of linksland between the Irish Sea and an inland tidal bay. It is thus almost enclosed by water, a private place where a man is alone with the turf, the sea, the sky, and the challenge of the wind. It is brave, splendid golfing country. Portmarnock's moods can vary from a sternness that can be savage, to wondrous peace. In summer, with a fresh breeze sparkling the bay and stirring the dune grasses, Ireland's Eye and Lambay rising sharp from the sea, there are few more tempting places for a golfer to be. On such a day, long ago, Sam Snead was at practice, pouring a stream of flawless strokes with a 1-iron into the morning distance. Watching golf could offer little more.

Like its great Irish rivals, Portmarnock often changes direction, somewhat after the fashion of Muirfield, with two distinctive and separate trails finishing by the clubhouse, a graceful white landmark from afar. The spectacular quality and unexpectedness of County Down are absent, but Portmarnock's problems are straightforward, even if considerable and often severe. There are no blind shots to the greens and few from the tees, no sharp changes of level yet no monotonous flatness, either. Several holes follow shallow valleys, but they are never as pronounced as they are at Birkdale. They might suggest, but certainly do not afford, protection from the wind.

The design of the course is natural rather than contrived. The 3rd, along a wide valley, narrow and slightly convex between sand hills on one side and the marshy fringes of the bay on the other, is an example. So, too, is the one bunker guarding the pin at the 5th. The approaches to the shorter par-fours such as the 2nd and 8th, are beautifully shaped. There are only three short holes—the 7th, into a dell, the 12th, high in the dunes, and the 15th, which can be fearsome with a wind from the sea on the right. To hold the narrow table of green, it may be necessary to swing the shot over the beach—which is out-of-bounds—and back again. Even in still air the green, shelving away on either hand, is difficult to hold. Only a true stroke here will prevail.

The three par-fives can be immense. At times the 6th, along its dimpled fairway and valleys, can be 3-woods for the strongest, yet the second shot can be as little as a medium iron when the course is running fast. The 13th has a long carry from the tee, behind which the waves pound, and there are bunkers to attract and destroy the second

shot. The 16th is of similar shape, down from the sea with the approaches swinging in from the left.

These two noble holes are part of a challenging finish, for the 14th, too, is a great hole although less than 400 yards. According to the wind, the second from a rolling fairway can be anything from a wood to a pitch and must carry huge bunkers in front of a long plateau of green in the dunes. Legend has it that Joe Carr, greatest of Irish amateurs, drove the green, the ball somehow escaping the bunkers; and that Henry Cotton once took seven strokes there—and lost an Irish Open in the process.

As a strong par-four, the

Surrounded by the sea on three sides, Portmarnock offers a genuine links course comparable with any of the great British championship links; indeed, Bobby Locke rated it among the finest in Europe. It never lacks challenge, and many of the less demanding holes become severe tests of skill and control when the wind comes in off the sea. Two in particular—the 14th and 15th—can wreck a card.

17th takes a deal of beating. Bunkers flanking the straight fairway are cause for thought on the tee and the second demands a long, accurate shot to a closely guarded green. The 18th, a fine hole, owes less to fortune than it did when the home green was right near the clubhouse. The hole has been shortened and the green moved to a position offering less of a threat to the constantly peppered building.

Portmarnock has been the setting for many great occasions, played in the wildest extremes of weather. When a tempest assailed the last round of the Irish Open in 1927, George Duncan one of the greatest of inspirational golfers—was around in 74, the only player to break 80. The weather was such that, even with this historic round, his winning score was 312. Christy O'Connor took thirty-six strokes fewer when he won the Dunlop Masters at Portmarnock thirty-two years later. The inexorable march of improvement reached its apex with Bernhard Langer's winning score of 269 in the 1987 Irish Open, an achievement that still provokes open-mouthed awe in in the vicinity of the links. Langer's victory was the second of five consecutive Irish Opens to be staged at Portmarnock. The roll call of winners reads like a who's who of European golf: Ballesteros, Langer, Woosnam (twice), and Olazabal. The oft-heard cliche, to judge a course on the quality of its champions, leaves Portmarnock to puff out its chest with justifiable pride, although more than one or two of the locals would have been happy for Woosnam to have settled for just the first of his titles. His successful defense, you see, was achieved in a play-off against Philip Walton who hails from the town of Malahide, a matter of miles away from the links. Woosnam's birdie on the first play-off hole, the 18th, doused the anticipated victory.

In 1991 the first Walker Cup to be staged in Ireland took place at Portmarnock, won by America. The only time the Amateur Championship has been played in Eire, in 1949, it was won by Max McCready. His golf had power, authority, and great confidence and it disposed of the two most formidable Americans in the field, Frank Stranahan, the defending champion, in the semifinal, and Willie Turnesa in the final.

None of this might have happened but for the inspiration in 1893 that led two men, J.W. Pickeman and George Ross, to row across the mouth of the estuary from the point where the Sutton clubhouse now stands. They visualized a

golf course on what was then a wilderness of dune and bracken inhabited only by a remote and self-sufficient community of farmers and fishermen, yet only ten miles from Dublin. The first clubhouse was a shack and the greatest hazard Maggie Leonard's cow, which devoured hundreds of balls. Golfers reached the course by crossing the estuary at low tide in a horse-drawn cart, at other times by boat. There is a road now and this delightful and very Irish way of reaching the 1st tee has gone the way of Maggie Leonard's Cow.

The 174-yard 15th is right by the sea. The tee is high in the dunes above the level of the narrow table of green, so that only a long, true shot will hold. It is the subject of many wagers.

Ireland's
Gift
to the World of Golf

The Course Card

Killarney Golf
Club,
Mahony's Point,
County Kerry
Championship
Course

Record: 70,
Ian Hutchin, Euro-
pean Amateur Golf
Team Championship
1975

Hole	Yards	Par
1	347	4
2	347	4
3	179	3
4	378	4
5	430	4
6	184	3
7	446	5
8	378	4
9	349	4
10	155	3
11	465	5
12	434	4
13	404	4
14	353	4
15	385	4
16	475	5
17	354	4
18	411	4
Out	3,038	35
In	3,436	37
Total	**6,474**	**72**

Killarney's setting exhausts

superlatives. The loom of Macgillicuddy's Reeks, the blue-black depths of its lake, the changing light and moist, Atlantic-tempered climate have conjured enough ballads to drain the repertoire of a bar-room tenor. A golf course in such a setting is bound to have a magnetism for even the most prosaic of golfers, and Killarney's championship course is worthy of its incomparable surroundings.

The success of Killarney Golf and Fishing Club stems from the untoward behavior of a land agent in 1936. For forty-five years, golf had been played at Killarney on a course in Old Deer Park, owned by the Earl of Kenmare, for a token rent of only a nickel a year. In 1936 the Earl's agent—obviously no golfer—proposed to the club that the rent should be increased to $125, an increase that horrified the club committee. They emerged to ask the Earl if they could take over another area of his land—a wild stretch of trees and scrub on sandy soil bordering Lough Leane, Killarney's lake—where they would create a new course. It was at this point that the Earl's heir, Lord Castlerosse, a larger-than-life luminary of the London social scene and a good golfer in his university days. He took an immediate interest in the project, seeing in it the chance to create on the shore of Lough Leane a course of beauty far exceeding in quality the modest attributes of the original parkland Killarney course.

Sir Guy Campbell was called in to design the new course and Castlerosse invited Henry Longhurst, a close friend, to add his views. The course was three years in the making but its completion and opening, in October 1939, was overshadowed by more momentous happenings in Europe. Once hostilities ended, the new location and the more challenging course began to attract visitors from around the world. The course, enjoyed by so many since the end of World War II, bears little resemblance to the one designed by Sir Guy Campbell, for when Castlerosse succeeded his father as Earl of Kenmare in 1939 he spent more and more time pursuing his dream of the perfect golf course.

Eventually thirteen holes substantially changed, no fewer than three new designs.

Of the three holes that bear the unmistakable stamp of Castlerosse, the 13th is perhaps the most difficult of the current thirty-six-hole layout. A modest par-five of 478 yards from the championship tee, it demands nothing of the tee shot except that it be long and straight—for even the biggest hitters need a near-perfect second shot to hold the ball on a raised green that falls away to both sides, with bunkers, trees, and a nearby road waiting for the ball that does not find its target. Even those who play short in two are faced with an extremely difficult pitch to the green. The heavy penalty extracted by this hole from good shots that are not quite good enough has led to criticism over the past thirty years, but every great course should have one hole that rewards a perfectly struck shot and consigns the often successful mediocre to the fate it deserves.

It is typical of Castlerosse that he should include such an examination in his personal contribution to the Killarney success story. His two other gems survive as the 3rd and 9th holes of the championship course, a par-three and par-four both demanding accuracy and reasonable power to achieve results. His work at Killarney was unfinished at the time of his sudden death in 1943 and his plans to plant every part of the course with extravagantly colored shrubs, as he had seen at Augusta, regrettably died with him. Castlerosse's prediction that Killarney would eventually need more than eighteen-holes of golf was borne out in the late 1960s when the Irish Tourist Board acquired enough land for a further nine holes and the club itself reclaimed a parcel of land between the existing course and the lake. The new eighteen holes were opened for play in 1971, parts of the old course being inter-mingled with the new to form two completely new courses—Mahony's Point and Killeen. Not unnaturally, the changing of the old course brought protests from many quarters. But the clearing of the land close to the lake brought the water into play at many more holes and also opened up wonderful new vistas of lake and mountains. Strangely, it is the work of the

The completion of a second eighteen holes at Killarney in 1971 brought about the creation of two new courses on which the old and new holes are cleverly intermingled. The championship layout is made up from both courses—Mahony's Point and Killeen.

The 18th

"What a Lovely Place to Die"

The whole essence of golf can be encapsulated in a fine par-three hole. It presents a challenge, a clearly defined target that allows the golfer to see instant results. In watching the ball fly from tee to green there is a special pleasure; just as there is a singular agony in seeing it miss so tantalizing and palpable a target.

At any two-shot hole the outcome of the drive is important but seldom conclusive, which is why it is unusual for a course of quality to finish with a par three as Killarney does. Two factors save this slight architectural blemish—the Mahony's Point 18th (which also serves as the closing hole on the championship course) is both tough and spectacular. Set right on the edge of Lough Leane, it measures 179 yards from the back tee and a shot at the pin must carry across the rugged shore of the lake to a narrow green angled slightly to the right. The margin for error on the right is small: trees flank this edge and the back of the green, and the waters of the

lake wait to snap up any ball that is farther off target.

The one consolation is that the prevailing wind comes off the lake, carrying the ball back toward the safe side of the green. Yet even here there is little room for error. The entire left side of the putting surface is edged by a long, thin bunker, with a road and more trees beyond. Short of the bunker on the left side lies an enormous thicket of rhododendrons. The only safe area for the shorter hitters is a small patch of grass that lies just in front of the green.

Add to this golfing challenge the magnificence of the setting, with the waters of the lake lapping beside tee and green and the backdrop of sparkling green hills and distant blue mountains, and the result is a finishing hole that will never fail to stimulate the senses. The ironic nature of the hole—its beauty and its difficulty—was perhaps summarized most succinctly by Henry Longhurst when he said of it: "What a lovely place to die."

The magnificent setting of the 18th, a par three, provides a fitting, if unconventional, ending to Killarney 's Mahony's Point and championship courses, which are among the most beautiful in the world.

1930s that best captures the imagination. In addition to the three holes designed by Castlerosse, Sir Guy Campbell's original finishing trio remain virtually untouched, bringing the championship and the Mahony's Point courses to a testing and beautiful conclusion. The par-five 16th swings gently downhill to a green set against a backdrop of Lough Leane and Tomies Mountain. There is water in front of the green and along both sides of the fairway. After the tee shot, the green is at least one club farther away than it appears.

The par-four 17th runs along the lake shore, dog legging slightly to the right, but with the safe left side of the fairway lined with trees. Bunkers are unnecessary for this green, for the lake to the right and trees behind offer suffi-

cient warning. And so to the 18th, a one-shotter across the corner of the lake to a narrow green—a fitting finish to a spectacular course. Killarney has attracted only a small number of tournaments and championships, but there was a memorable Curtis Cup triumph for Great Britain and Ireland in 1996 and the legendary Joe Carr scored the first of a trio of victories in the Irish Amateur Close championship there in 1963. Scotland's Eric Brown won the first of only two professional events to be staged at Killarney in 1955. Perhaps the most significant aspect of this event was Gary Player's first tournament appearance outside South Africa. He scored 84 and 76 and failed to qualify for the two final rounds. Gary Player and Killarney have come a long way since then.

Man-Made Beauty

at the Ocean's Edge

The Course Card

Ballybunion
County Kerry
Old Course

Record: 68,
Gary Scanlin

Hole	Yards	Par
1	392	4
2	445	4
3	220	3
4	520	5
5	524	5
6	364	4
7	432	4
8	153	3
9	454	4
10	359	4
11	453	4
12	192	3
13	484	5
14	131	3
15	216	3
16	499	5
17	385	4
18	379	4
Out	3,495	36
In	3,098	35
Total	**6,593**	**71**

Few golf courses can compete with Ballybunion when it comes to the naturalness of its setting. Located against the Atlantic shore in a remote region of County Kerry, the first surprise is that it was designed by man not evolution. Tom Watson considers it a course that all architects should live and play before they practice their art and certainly one would be hard pressed to find another venue so perfectly in tune with its surroundings.

Ballybunion is a traditional links in every sense of the word. Its configuration is delightfully eccentric with back-to-back par fives on the front nine followed by consecutive short holes on the inward half. It has several blind shots and its hard, crumpled fairways can lead to difficult stances and undeserved moments of ill fortune. But there's a rewarding feeling for a good shot perfectly executed that one rarely finds elsewhere and the sea views are extraordinary.

In common with most links courses, Ballybunion can seem straightforward on a calm day. It possesses no great length and its small greens appear inviting targets with short irons. A mild breeze is enough to change the examination and on doleful days, when the Atlantic closes in, the course can be completely merciless.

Ballybunion was founded on March 4, 1886, with George Hewson of Listowel appointed president and C. Mark Montserrat, a local real estate agent, its first secretary. The club quickly ran into financial problems and for eight years lumbered in oblivion. It might never have emerged but for Colonel Bartholemew, an Indian army man who retired to the area. He formed the present club in 1906 and contracted Lional Hewson, for many years the editor of *Irish Golf,* to lay out nine new holes (incidentally, Pat Ruddy, the editor of the leading Irish magazine today, *Golfers' Companion,* is also a distinguished architect, his work including the Irish Open venue Druid's Glen and the excellent European club in Wicklow, which he owns). The course was extended to eighteen in 1926 by a Mr. Smyth, whose employers, Carter and Sons, had become famous for laying out sports grounds.

Smyth did such a fine job that when the English architect Tom Simpson was called in eleven years later to make changes he suggested just three minor ones, the most famous being a sand hazard on what is now the first that has become known as "Mrs Simpson's bunker." The reasons for the name remain shrouded in mystery, thereby adding to the mischievous possibilities that countless clubhouse wits have suggested. Owing partly to the remoteness of its location, Ballybunion has staged few tournaments of note. Perhaps the pick came in 1957 when Harry Bradshaw collected the last of his ten Irish Professional Championships.

It is only in more recent times that Ballybunion has gained the recognition it deserves, for which ease of travel is but one explanation. Two more factors were responsible: the first, the decision to relocate the clubhouse and change the numbering of the holes. Previously the closing two holes had been a pair of mundane par fives, a severe detriment to any course with pretensions to greatness. Now these holes are the 4th and 5th. They are still not great holes but tucked away on the front nine they occupy the less pivotal place they deserve.

The second factor was the patronage of Tom Watson when at the height of his powers. Watson fell in love with links golf from the moment he made his first trip to Britain, for the 1975 Open Championship at Carnoustie, which he would go on to win. It whetted his appetite. When he got home he read up on the great courses that lay hidden along the shoreline of Great Britain and Ireland.

Before each Open he would come a week early and discover them one by one. In 1981 he made his first trip to Ballybunion and was startled by the beauty of the surroundings and the challenging nature of the links. Like many a tourist both before and after, Ballybunion was his starting point and he got no further, and for many years it became an annual pilgrimage. "The contours on the fairways and greens are what make it a great golf course," he explained. "There are uphill, downhill, and sidehill shots, uphill and downhill par threes. You must play accurate iron shots into the greens, usually to a small target with not a lot of margin for error. But there is room to roll the ball on to the greens in the true links manner and I like that style of golf best of all."

Ballybunion is not a links course that immediately captivates the player. The first six holes are modest, played against an austere background. Like Turnberry, which starts out equally slowly, it then opens out and its spectacular ocean holes again invite comparison with the Ailsa course in Ayrshire.

The opening hole is a par four of medium length, the chief feature the unusual hazard that captures stray golf balls to the right; and yes, the graveyard, for that is what it is, is out of bounds. The 2nd can be a difficult par four, with bunkers patroling both sides of the fairway followed by a second shot to a raised green that needs to be threaded through two enormous dunes. The 3rd is an example of how a hole is only as great as its setting. If the backdrop from the plateau tee to a plunging green were rocks and sea it would rank among the best on the course. Unfortunately, we are heading inland and the backdrop is a caravan site. This plainness is followed by the two tame par fives, leaving the golfer to wonder what all the fuss is about. Not for long. The 6th, a dogleg par four, plays directly toward the Shannon Estuary. Now the course asserts itself. The 7th winds its way along the cliff top, a magnificent par four that any player is happy to walk off recording a regulation figure.

The next three holes loop inland in a triangle; the pick of them is the 8th, a lovely short par three where the penalty for missing the green is severe indeed. Watson said it was one of the most demanding tee shots he had faced, and it is the severity of the punishment that makes it so intimidating. The three bunkers toward the front are huge and the hollows and mounds that surround them are equally penal.

The 9th measures 454 yards and anything less than a well-struck, arrow-straight drive leaves a player glumly confronting a green he cannot but hope to reach in two. The first hole coming home is a dogleg par four of unassuming length with a green that sits on the cliff top and on sunny days the urge to look west is irresistible. The pleasures are only starting to unfold. The 11th would feature in many people's list of the world's best 18 holes, a dramatic par four that once more runs along the perimeter of the cliff top.

The short 12th and the 484-yard, par-five 13th offer respite and the chance for a player to recover his score before the tribulations to come. First the back-to-back par threes, both of which are wonderful. The first is just 131 yards and presents torment over club selection. The 15th, at 216 yards, is less problematic in that area but presents other difficulties. It is probably the hardest of the five par threes.

The 16th and 17th holes are doglegs of quite breathtaking severity. The first bends to the left, a par-five where the drive is away from the sea to a small target area; at the par-four 17th the tee shot is back toward the Atlantic, leaving a short iron to one of the more accessible greens on the course. So to the 18th, described by one critic as merely a device to get from the 17th green to the 19th hole. The cause of the ire is the appropriately named Sahara bunker that sits grotesquely in the middle of the fairway and allows little strategy. One plays before it and then one guesses what to hit over it.

Blind shots have always caused controversy on links courses yet they are a feature of the traditional venues. They stem from a time when it was not possible to move huge amounts of earth as it is today. Nowhere is this more apparent than at Ballybunion where the huge dunes that punctuate the course both straddle it and dominate it. On a younger links like Birkdale they are used to create amphitheaters; at Ballybunion you play around them, over them, on top of them.

Perhaps it is not the finishing hole that such a course deserves, but no one will sit lingering in the bar mulling over its deficiencies. This is a course that scores highly on all counts: it lingers in the mind and long after the day's play is done, a player can mull over his score and play and recall all eighteen holes with little difficulty.

Ballybunion, situated in a remote corner of Kerry on Ireland's west coast, rewards all pilgrims who make the long trek to get there, for its ocean holes are among the best of their kind to be found anywhere in the world. Three tame holes from the 3rd may lead to some initial skepticism but no one would dispute the quality of golf offered from the 6th onward. There are fairer links courses, and more daunting ones, too. But few can compete with the sheer pleasure that playing Ballybunion offers.

Tumbling Links Amid the
Dutch Sand hills

The Course Card

Kennemer Golf &
Country Club,
Zandvoort
B/C Course

Record: 65, Sid Brews,
Dutch Open 1935;
David Thomas,
Severiano Ballesteros,
Wayne Grady,
Glenn Ralph,
José-Maria Canizares,
Gordon Brand.

Hole	Yards	Par
1	452	4
2	165	3
3	524	5
4	330	4
5	346	4
6	476	5
7	371	4
8	187	3
9	425	4
10	361	4
11	460	4
12	546	5
13	373	4
14	385	4
15	163	3
16	480	5
17	168	3
18	398	4
Out	3,276	36
In	3,334	36
Total	**6,610**	**72**

There is no finer example of seaside links on the continental mainland than the Kennemer club at Zandvoort, half an hour by car from Amsterdam. Despite the popular conception that Holland is a land of unwavering flatness, this coastal stretch is a place of wild tumbling dunes to stir the heart of any golfing architect. It must have inspired H. S. Colt when he came to create the present course in the late 1920s. The club was founded in 1910 and started elsewhere with nine holes on flat meadowland; no greater contrast to it could be imagined than this links with its glorious fairways, towering sand hills, and clusters of pine. It has no parallel in America but, at first sight, brings thoughts of problems of stance—not in a severe or arduous sense, but sufficient to test balance and control and to compel thought before striking.

One essential feature of a good course is that its attraction should be immediate. There are few more inviting prospects than the tees of the 1st and 10th holes at Kennemer; the course runs in two loops of nine, beginning and ending by the handsome thatched clubhouse poised high with a commanding view of the whole golfing scene. The 1st hole falls away to a spreading fairway, flanked by dunes with pines on their crests, the kind of drive that would appeal to the most humble performer. After an exciting short hole over a valley to a huge sloping plateau green one stands again on a high tee looking down upon another expanse fairway, gently curving to the left around a wood: a splendid hole. Even if you have not started 4, 3, 4—none too difficult down a prevailing south-westerly wind—a sense of pleasure to come and beauty all around is inescapable.

There are all the pastel shades of quiet fawns and golds and greens, and in the summertime the rough, often uncommonly tenacious, is alive with wildflowers. Buckthorn, with its savage spikes piercing the thickest trousers and vivid orange berries in the autumn is another occasional menace and delight. Pheasants nest in the long grasses and twice a year or so shoots are rewarding. Only the wild driver need fear the rough. For all normal purposes the fairways are of a generous width, but they could be narrowed, as could the entrances to the greens, to an extent that would challenge a championship field of the highest quality.

The 4th begins a fine stretch of golf. Colt considered this the one weak spot in his design and it has been converted from a par-three into a par-four. This hole aside, the course is little changed from his original concept, although it is some 400 yards longer and has a par two strokes lower. The drive from the new championship tee at the 4th through a cluster of trees, together with a tightly trapped green, makes a challenging hole. The 5th is a challenge, too, with its fairway all swales and mounds, out-of-bounds threatening the slice, and a valley before the green to confuse estimates of distance. Most of the greens are fairly large, offering a variety of pin positions; happily their undulations are slight and subtle and the surfaces of fine fescue putt swiftly and true. The carry to the next fairway, the longest outward hole, is deceptively far and the golf hereabouts can be sterner than the card suggests; the wind, more often than not, will be leaning against the line of flight. Blind shots can be a tiresome affliction, but an occasional drive to an invisible fairway is effective for contrast. The one to the 7th is welcome, for the sight from the fairway's peak is splendid with the green set against tree-crested dunes and protected by a considerable cross-bunker. The 8th presents no great problem if a long iron is hit straight. It is followed by another tempting drive to a slightly angled, crumpled fairway, and an approach to a green in a basin below the clubhouse. Here, as on many holes, the placing of the drive determines the difficulty of the second shot as much from the question of stance as of line. In this respect Colt made memorable use of the terrain's natural features.

The drive to the 10th over a wild valley to a distant unseen fairway can be infinitely satisfying or disastrous, according to contact with the ball. The course then swings away to more open country, past the tunnel entrance to the 11th green, down the long, straight 12th, turning again for a lovely 13th with its green on rising ground, outlined against a dark cluster of pines. The long hitter may reach the deep hollow of the 14th fairway and find his view of the green obscured, but not if he holds the left side of the fairway.

At first glance the tee shot to the short 15th looks formidable, for the green is on the summit of a smooth, grassy cliff, down which the underhit or underclub will roll relentlessly into one of three traps at its foot. The high ground by the green makes a superb vantage point from which to watch the play of the last five holes—the long second away to the 16th cradled in the dunes; the last turn for home with the shot over wilderness to the short 17th, and the gradual rise of a fine finishing hole, its green between two large guardian bunkers.

Perhaps the most memorable contest at Kennemer was for the 1976 Dutch Open, since it marked the first victory of a young nineteen-year-old Spaniard named Severiano Ballesteros. Three weeks earlier he had competed strongly for the Open Championship at Birkdale, conquering its parched fairways and winning over its galleries with the sort of swashbuckling play that was his trademark. At Kennemer he showed he could win. Thirteen years later, his protégé, Jose-Maria Olazabal, would win the same title over the same course. Well, parts of the same course anyway. By then nine new holes had been built and they were incorporated into the championship design. They do not compare to Colt's original, however, and it is those eighteen holes we come to praise here.

The most shining moment in the club's history did not occur in competition but when a Canadian colonel—presumably a golfer—agreed to demolish the anti-tank wall built across the course during World War II. The area had been a defense zone, and the course virtually vanished under the concrete. By 1947 golf was again being played at Kennemer and now all recognizable traces of a massive stupidity have gone from a beautiful course.

Dutch Links and the Origin of Golf

There has long been a school of thought that golf evolved from the ancient Dutch game of *kolven*, but the evidence is far from conclusive. Through the centuries many games have shared the aim of hitting a ball with a club toward a target, but researchers have failed to discover a definite link between any pursuit of the Middle Ages and the game of golf as mentioned by James II of Scotland in his famous decree of 1457. This demanded that "the futeball and golfe be utterly cryed downe and not to be used"; presumably the citizenry were neglecting the practice of archery and military training in those troubled times when England was a bitter enemy.

The precise origin of golf probably will never be known but the paintings by van der Velde, Avercamp, and others of *kolven* on ice, and not its normal form on indoor courts, stirred the imagination of historians. The indoor game was played in a walled space or court with a club and ball and involved the striking of posts at either end, but both club and ball were larger than those used for golf, as were those used on ice. The attitude of the players about to strike was the main resemblance to golf. The ancient Flemish game of chore has also been suggested as an origin because of its cross-country nature. It was played to targets often miles away but both sides used the same ball. It had little similarity to golf save in the act of striking a ball with a club. This simply fulfills a fundamental human instinct from which various games have evolved. The likelihood is that golf was the form peculiar, in the beginning, to Scotland.

The continental challenge to Scotland's outstanding claims as the birthplace of golf is led by the Dutch. This painting by Adriaen van der Velde shows seventeenth-century Dutchmen adapting their game of *kolven*, normally played on an enclosed area of sand and clay with posts as targets, to winter conditions.

At Kennemer, the challenging eighteen-hole course of H. S. Colt, described above, has now been extended by a further nine holes, and it is possible to play three variations on the 27 holes: A/B, B/C, and A/C. The old course illustrated here is essentially the new B/C course.

A Royal Course

that has Few Peers

Belgium is not one of the world's great powers in golf, but it has made a notable contribution to the European game. Nonetheless, among its courses are several of outstanding quality: Waterloo, where Henry Cotton was professional between the wars; the Royal Club de Belgique at Ravenstein, the birthplace of Flory Van Donck, one of the finest European players; the Royal Zoute, a splendid links by the sea; the Royal Club des Fagnes at Spa, a beautiful examination of golf; and Royal Antwerp at Kapellenbos, which comes close to being a masterpiece of its kind.

All those clubs are distinguished by the Royal title, bestowed upon them by Belgian kings. The choice of a single course from this excellent company is difficult but Royal Antwerp, twelve miles from the seaport, makes so favorable an impression that it takes pride of place. It is also the oldest club in the country, founded in 1888—the year that the St. Andrews club in New York became the first in the United States. Like most of the older continental courses (only Pau is its senior on the continental mainland) Antwerp was formed by a few members of the local British settlement there. The course at first was laid out on an army training ground. It cannot have been a particularly sympathetic site and soon after the turn of the century an area of woodland

was bought some seventeen miles north of the city. Willie Park was called upon to make the new course and it was in play several years before World War I. It remained as Park designed it until, in the late 1920s, Tom Simpson created what became the ten middle holes of the course. Within its confines nine shorter holes, including some of Park's original work, remain for those seeking relief from sterner pursuits.

In all Europe Antwerp has few peers for the type of course that wends its way through woods of pine and silver birch, heather, and shrubs. Its level changes hardly more than a yard or so; rarely do the trees threaten peace of mind, even that of a golfer. Yet its very flatness calls for fine judgment of distance, and the unusual disposition of some 6,700 yards makes the strict par of 73 severe even for the good player. Few courses anywhere have so high a proportion of good long par-fours. Only the 1st, with its uncommonly billowing fairway, and the 4th, where the drive must be placed for a clear shot to the pin, are drive and pitch holes. On most, even the first-class golfer will be using longish irons to the greens—or occasionally wood, depending on the strength of the wind and the pace of the fairways. For the driver of average length the course is a great test of iron play, because the greens are not large and only that of the 16th, which is the shortest hole, is in any way set up as a target.

From a purist's viewpoint the one criticism is that the par-fives are not long enough for modern conditions. The 3rd is a lovely hole with the fairway angling away to the left, a heathery crest to threaten the second shot, and a long,

The holes labeled on the map: 5, 6, 7, 8, 9, 10, 11, 12, 13, 14

Royal Antwerp has come a long way from an army training ground, and with its pine and birch forests is now more reminiscent of Sunningdale. Though the level varies by only a few feet, a combination of long par fours, doglegs, and small greens makes 73 an exacting par. The 17th, Bloody Bidet, is perhaps the most testing hole, requiring a near-perfect second to avoid trouble on all sides.

narrow green. A finely placed center bunker 50 yards short of the green makes the long, straight 5th and players can get home with an iron on the 11th. The drive must be held left center of the fairway and, unless the second is similarly placed, it will probably break from a shoulder of ground toward a bunker well short of the green.

The course is notable for its economy of bunkering—an admirable precept of the architects of old. The 7th, with a smooth hump protecting the line to the pin and ground falling toward a single right-hand bunker, is a beautiful short hole. The 12th has an extra bunker, threatening the safe way home, but the second is the stiffest of the short holes. It is a big shot, with a fold of ground making it look less than it is.

Several holes are compellingly beautiful. The 6th curves around an elbow of woods and narrows like an hour-glass where a long drive finishes. The fairway of the 8th is almost an island of heather, from where a medium iron shot should flight to the heart of a green set against a shining stand of birch. From the back tee of the 13th the carry is considerable, and the drive must be right to open up the hole around trees to a green that is for once beset by bunkers. The 14th is a real dogleg, swinging sharp left with cross-rough challenging the approach. The finish is testing enough to keep hope alive in the breast of anyone who is trailing. The 15th needs two long shots, and the championship tee of the 17th would give even Tiger Woods food for thought. Two big bunkers emphatically suggest that the approach should come in from the right, especially as a smaller bunker lies concealed beyond. This was the inspiration of a secretary wise in the ways of golf. At first it was known as Beatty's Bath, but its victims were so plentiful that it is now called Bloody Bidet. Bunkers await the slice on the last fairway and the hole is just short enough to quicken hopes of a saving three.

Then only memories remain and they will linger; every hole is so attractive. Always the silver of birches leaves the blackness of pine; rhododendrons bloom in the spring and in the late summer the heather is a purple glory—if a constant menace to those who stray from smooth fairways.

The 9th, 10th and 14th

Tackling The Doglegs

Tom Simpson, the architect of Royal Antwerp, was a great believer in the dogleg hole and seventy years ago was something of a pioneer in this form of design. It is a conspicuous feature on the course's middle holes, seven of those between the 6th and the 14th curving markedly. Five swing to the left, favoring the right-to-left player.

Doglegs provide variety and avoid the monotony of a sequence of straightaway holes. As at the 10th, with its narrow-waisted fairway, they stress the importance of placing from the tees. Occasionally, as at the 14th, the dogleg is used to restrict the length of the drive, but the player with power and skill can bend his shot around the curve.

Such holes can be a snare in that they may tempt the player into attempting too much in order to cheat the corner, either by trying to clear it or by bending his shot around it, despite the ease with which an intentional draw can become a hook and a fade become a slice. Architects often place bunkers within the inside of the curve, as at the 9th, and where position rather than length is essential one can visualize Faldo, for instance, aiming at the hazard and fading the shot gently away from it. In this way, when the shot's power is expiring, the ball is moving away from and not toward trouble, as the shots of humbler mortals are prone to do.

The Course Card

Royal Antwerp Golf Club, Kapellenbos

Record:
68. Aldo Casera

Hole	Yards	Par
1	331	4
2	203	3
3	480	5
4	381	4
5	477	5
6	424	4
7	185	3
8	418	4
9	449	4
10	416	4
11	484	5
12	179	3
13	398	4
14	478	5
15	492	5
16	147	3
17	377	4
18	394	4
Out	3,348	36
In	3,365	37
Total	**6,713**	**73**

Classic Links
in a Remote Northern Landscape

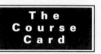

The Course Card

Falsterbo Golfk-
lubb, Fack

Record:
65, Peter Senior

Hole	Yards	Par
1	420	4
2	175	3
3	510	5
4	390	4
5	360	4
6	155	3
7	290	4
8	175	3
9	385	4
10	350	4
11	145	3
12	370	4
13	520	5
14	210	3
15	475	5
16	350	4
17	340	4
18	445	5
Out	2860	34
In	3,205	37
Total	**6,065**	**71**

True links courses are rare outside the British Isles. There is one at Le Touquet and a few nestled among the sand hills of the Low Countries, but one of the finest examples on the mainland of Europe is at Falsterbo in Sweden. It is not the oldest of Swedish courses—Hovas, near Gothenburg, came into being a few years earlier—but its very nature and its spectacular setting give Falsterbo pride of place. The course is laid out on the tip of a tiny peninsula that all but drops off the southernmost corner of Sweden—Stockholm is more than 300 miles away to the northeast, Copenhagen a mere 30, as the migrant geese and waders fly, across the ôresund.

In Sweden, golf's beginnings around the turn of the century were at best hesitant—the first eighteen-hole course was not built until 1929, and as recently as 1945 there were only twenty-two clubs. Now there are more than 200 courses and over 500,000 golfers. The explosion in recent years stems from the commendable policy to encourage junior golfers. Golf in Sweden is not just for the bourgeoisie and the reward has been a string of fine players, both men and women, who have contributed hugely to the world game over the past twenty years.

From its start, in 1909, Falsterbo has been a pace-setter. In the year it was opened it staged Sweden's first international match between clubs (against its near neighbor, the Copenhagen Golf Club) and it became, in 1930, one of the country's first eighteen-hole courses. Falsterbo incorporates all the links qualities of turf, natural hazards, and changes of wind—now from the mainland, now from the Baltic—that can present a totally different test within a matter of hours. Such is its strength that it has been altered little over the years. It is an obvious setting for a golf course. The holes blend beautifully into natural surroundings which no amount of money could ever copy or create. The vast stretch of water that gives the 4th, 5th, and 11th their menace and charm is to a measure reminiscent of the marsh holes at England's Royal West Norfolk, although only at the short 11th hole does very much of it have to be crossed.

At the excellent 4th, however, a stiff second has to skirt the water dangerously and it preys on the mind in the way that only water can. It is a feature by which players remember this links.

Falsterbo is invigorating rather than oppressively daunting, but like all good courses it commands respect, calling for unrelenting concentration, confidence, and sound technique. From the moment the golfer encounters the dogleg at the demanding 1st hole, with out-of-bounds on the right, he is confronted with the severity of Falsterbo's challenge.

The next four holes form a narrow offshoot out to the end of the marsh and back and, because of their low-lying position, they have more of an inland character than the rest. The high, marshy reed grasses readily identify the edges of water hazards—which add flavor to the short 2nd, with its well-bunkered green, divide the 3rd and 4th holes and completely surround the 5th. The 3rd is the only par-five in the outward half. It has all the hallmarks of a long hole, offering little alternative to a good drive, a good second, and a good pitch. But it is probably the 4th, with its green tucked into a little alcove by the water's edge, and the 5th, where there is no margin for error with the drive, that most players will be pleased to pass without a skirmish with the water that haunts the slice. Not that the short 6th offers any respite. It has more water in front of the tee, an artificial out-of-bounds to the right and some of Falsterbo's few trees on the left. However, the 7th, a dogleg to the left, offers the chance of a birdie and heralds the start of what the British would recognize instantly as true links golf. With the odd exception, bunkers now take the place of water and at the 8th, the third short hole, one that is particularly well sited has to be carried from the tee. The two medium par fours which follow do not present too much difficulty, but when the wind is against, the short 11th can be reached only with what is perhaps the most spectacular shot on the course. Although only 145 yards, it is death or glory, all or nothing, with water on all sides and the

The only true links among Sweden 's golf courses, Falsterbo is one of the finest of that rare breed on the continent. It has been host to many Swedish championships and, in 1963, to the European Amateur Team Championship. For those five sunny days Falsterbo was serene, but the course is exposed and when the wind blows, its numerous lakes and almost 100 bunkers assume added menace.

A Finish Fit for a King

green nestling on a peninsula that looks minute from the tee.

The 12th has its fairway split into two by bunkers and the green is generously encircled by sand, but it can be child's play compared with the 520-yard 13th, known as Tipperary. Both fairway and green are closely guarded with bunkers and a substantial carry is necessary from the tee, the drive again being threatened by out-of-bounds on the right.

The 14th is the last and longest of the five short holes. The tee shot is threatened by a large cross-bunker, but it is the setting that makes this hole memorable. Beyond the green stands the old Falsterbo lighthouse, a reminder of the remoteness of the setting and the nearness of the sea. Golf's rich variety of settings provides a powerful reason for playing and at Falsterbo there is the added delight of a vast, uninhabited stretch of shoreline, a haven for migratory birds in spring and autumn. Birds and golfers have chosen well at Falsterbo, and it is fitting that the true character of the course finds appealing expression in its finish. Shaped rather like the head of a fish, the 15th and 16th run out to the tiny peninsula's tip, where the sound and the Baltic meet, and the 17th and 18th return along the line of dunes.

The 15th and 18th are par fives and, with the 16th and 17th among the best of the par-fours, Falsterbo certainly does not use up its ammunition in its opening salvos. Varying with the wind, the finish strikes a nice balance, but the splendor of the golf and the sheer pleasure of being in this remote northern landscape are exemplified by the prospect from the 17th tee. From there the views across the sound to Denmark and along Sweden's surf-fringed southern shore are positively breathtaking, but the golfer must constantly beware of letting them slacken his concentration, for it is quite possible to slice a shot far into the Baltic. To the very end Falsterbo's golfing charms refuse to be outdone by their almost excessively scenic setting.

The uncertainty and drama of matchplay often makes it more enjoyable than strokeplay. There is something fundamentally appealing about two men dueling their way around a golf course, and it is through such encounters that many courses have become legendary.

Professionals of world class or even amateurs of international standing rarely play at Falsterbo, but in 1963 the European Team Championships brought it to the notice of golfers of many countries, and one of the matches produced a dramatic finale that can seldom have been repeated anywhere. Appropriately, the scene— as in all good matchplay plots —was the 18th. From a tee in the sand dunes, the hole doglegs to the right between fairway bunkers to a deeply bunkered green some 500 yards away. On the day that Sweden played Italy it was reachable in two. Italy's Angelo Croce was just on the fringe at the back of the green, but Sweden's Rune Karlfeldt was short and much less likely to make the four it seemed he would need to halve the match, in which he had the support of a few hundred Swedes, including King Gustav.

The celebration, the cheering and stampeding that followed the chip with a 6-iron that Karlfeldt holed for his three is therefore not hard to imagine. Victory seemed assured, the King shook his hand and Croce, who had yet to play, somehow managed to convey that he, too, was pleased. After order had been restored, Croce stepped up to a putt that, to a man having only one shot in which to save the match, must have seemed an impossibility. But Croce duly holed it for as unlikely a half as anyone could remember. Happily, he, too, was hailed by the Swedes and the celebrations and the handshakes were resumed.

The 18th: 498 yards par 5

Karlfeldt -----
Croce ———

The heavily forested 220 acres of the Club Zur Vahr holds one of the most difficult layouts in Europe. The length (well over 7,000 yards including six par fives) undulating fairways narrowing at strategic points, great patches of heather, and comparatively small greens all combine to produce a real challenge. Any wayward shots are punished by dense rough.

The 5th hole at Club Zur Vahr is a short par four that offers a reasonable chance of a birdie.

A Forest

Where Even the Caddies Get Lost

The turn of the century was a halcyon time for golf. Adherents to the game were growing in number, especially among city dwellers seeking exercise in the open air. Cities themselves were expanding rapidly, but not yet to a degree that put the availability and cost of land at a premium—as, for example, in Japan today, where enthusiasm for the game, which almost amounts to a national obsession, is stymied by shortage of space in which to indulge it.

Bremen Golf Club, one of the oldest in Germany, was founded in the last years of the nineteenth century as the Hanseatic town was beginning its years of growth. It began with a nine-hole layout and the present course is the result of a decision by the Club Zur Vahr, which embraces a number of sports and social activities, to build a course suitable for major championships. The site chosen for the new course was the Garlstedter Heath, a setting with all the natural attributes needed to echo, in the mind of the club's president, August Weyhausen, those virtues he had found when playing the great Scottish and English courses. He sought a course where players of all standards would be forced to think, to accept their personal limitations and negotiate a tough test according to their abilities. The course planned by Weyhausen and architect Bernard von Limburger occupies 220 acres in thickly forested, undulating countryside. On the premise

that nature itself is the best architect, the Bremen course was constructed with minimum change to the existing landscape. It is dominated by pine trees, tall and dense, crowding in from tee to green, controlling play on holes that bend narrowly to generally small targets. The strategic effect of the forest was such that it was necessary to construct only twenty-four bunkers. From the championship tees, the course measures 7,147 yards, with six holes of more than 500 yards.

Since its completion, the Garlstedter course has commanded respect from all who have played there and appreciated its disciplines. From the fine, modern clubhouse, three holes—the 1st, 7th and 9th—run over fairly level, pastoral parkland. Most of the others make their way through the forest, narrow and with sharp doglegs that call for clear tactical thinking, since most fairways offer a choice of routes to the green. Among the trees there is thick undergrowth, with its risk of an unplayable lie and almost certainly a lost stroke.

The pressure of the natural hazards is compounded by the fact that, to reach the ideal driving area, shots must be long as well as straight. When he was competing in the 1971 German Open, Roberto de Vicenzo was asked if it would help to have more fore-caddies. "No," he replied, "for then the fore-caddie is lost also."

The 7th hole is a good example of Bremen's thoughtful design, a 410-yard par four with two completely separate routes to the green. Here the player has to weigh up the risks and make a clear choice. The good golfer drives out to the right to a fairway that begins only after a carry of 220 yards. Accuracy is essential, since there is out-of-bounds close by and the approach can be easily blocked by a copse just before the green. The second shot would normally be a 6- or 7-iron. A much wider fairway is open to the left, following a curving route around the copse. It is an easier choice, longer and over trees, but better for the handicap player.

Bremen has been an infrequent host to the German Open, perhaps owing to the fact that the city is less accessible than Munich or Frankfurt. The last occasion was in 1985 and the tournament was something of a disaster, owing to continual rain. Eventually it was reduced to fifty-four holes and, with parts of the course flooded a half-mile was trimmed from its original length. At least the name of the winner—Bernhard Langer—bore the stamp of authenticity. Probably the best tournament to have been staged there was the 1971 German Open, which attracted a fine field from twenty-three different countries, including Peter Thomson, Roberto de Vicenzo, and Peter Oosterhuis. The winner was Neil Coles, who remembers the course well. "I would rate it as one of the best championship courses I have played in Europe," he said. "One could compare it to Augusta—it is a course with a big feel about it. The construction is very natural; there are not a lot of fairway bunkers off the tee, because they are not needed. The big thing about Club Zur Vahr is that it is a very good driving course, the penalties are tough if you are off line. Once you are among the trees which come right up to the edge of the fairway, you can only hope to come out sideways—assuming you find a playable lie.

"I think the par fives are the outstanding holes. The 2nd and 6th, both of which have two routes, are particu-larly good. To reach the green in two, you have to take a chance off the tee and drive very close to the trees. The 10th, 568 yards and almost a right-angled dogleg, is probably the best hole of all. You drive from the apex of a V, with tremendously tall trees on both sides. You must take a driver because you cannot play safe—you need the length, but with tall pines either side, it's quite a drive." The main thing about the course is that it is not only tight but long—on most holes in a tournament, you need that driver to avoid being blocked off by the doglegs. The 12th hole—509 yards, par five—is one of the narrowest, and is a good example. Even after a long drive you are still left with another long, narrow shot to the green over marshy rough and scrub. It is an easy five, but to get a four you have to take a chance.

"Another good hole is the 15th—a snaking, double dog-leg of 548 yards, lined with tall trees all the way. Again you have to keep close to the left to get the best shot in for your second. If you go right, playing safe, you really are shut out.

"Like all good courses, the finish is tough. The 16th is good, with a single, large tree plumb in the way of your drive, leaving a narrow entrance on to the fairway. The 215-yard 17th is probably the best short hole on the course. You play through a narrow avenue of tall pines to an elevated green with one large bunker front left. There is out-of-bounds just on the left; if you hit the bank, you can very easily go out. Altogether, an excellent championship test—forcing you right to the limit all the way."

Brian Huggett, another Ryder Cup player and a former German Open champion, agrees: "It is like Champions at Houston, the best course that I have played in America. If you don't drive on the correct side of the fairways, you have to hook or cut your next. There is probably no harder course in Europe, not just because of length but because there are so many holes which call for skill as well."

The Course Card

Club Zur Vahr, Bremen Garlstedter Heide Course

Record: 68, Neil Coles, Peter Thomson, German Open 1971

Hole	Yards	Par
1	366	4
2	529	5
3	206	3
4	547	5
5	320	4
6	555	5
7	410	4
8	165	3
9	420	4
10	568	5
11	183	3
12	509	5
13	401	4
14	348	4
15	548	5
16	445	4
17	215	3
18	412	4
Out	3,518	37
In	3,629	37
Total	**7,147**	**74**

A Classic Course in a

Classical Landscape

The Course Card

Circolo Golf
Olgiata, Rome

Hole	Yards	Par
1	380	4
2	213	3
3	467	4
4	401	4
5	489	5
6	427	4
7	196	3
8	380	4
9	555	5
10	398	4
11	433	4
12	429	4
13	432	4
14	170	3
15	505	5
16	203	3
17	523	5
18	429	4
Out	3,508	36
In	3,522	36
Total	**7,030**	**72**

The approach to Rome from the north pass is through a gentle, rolling landscape, the home in antiquity of the Sabines and the southernmost of Etruscan lands, and the home today of Circolo Golf Olgiata, perhaps Italy's finest course. For a long time this area has been famous for the stables of Dormello-Olgiata. Thus the course, itself a thoroughbred, is in an appropriate setting. The Olgiata courses—an eighteen and a nine hole—were designed by C.K. Cotton, one of Britain's foremost architects, and completed in 1961. The championship course frequently changes direction, moving in two loops beginning and ending at the clubhouse.

One of the greatest blessings a golf architect can have is ample room for the wanderings of his imagination. Cotton was fortunate at Olgiata and was able to plan every hole in its own spacious setting, thus ensuring that each have an individual character. There is no congestion or monotony; the holes are easily remembered long after playing them.

The strongest first impressions are of the large greens and the manner of their protection. Most of the entrances are narrow and between bunkers, but the attacking stroke is rarely punished; there is room enough behind the greens whichever pin position is used. Another feature is the changing levels; none is harsh, but all serve to tax judgment of length. The golfer is soon aware that his driving will be tested. The opening hole swings uphill to the right, and to have a clear pitch to the green the tee shot must be long and straight between the trees. The emphasis on placing is not always obvious; at the 3rd and 5th it is achieved by a single tree, and a perfectly placed bunker on the left of the 6th fairway encourages a fade toward woods, for the hole moves that way. The drive to the 8th is narrow, but the spread of fairway below is enticing—as is that of the 9th. This is the longest hole, with cross-bunkers to be carried and trees to be threaded to a favorable position for the final approach.

The drive to the 10th, like several others, is stiffened by the placing of one bunker on the opposite side of the fairway to the natural hazard of the woods that make a kind of spine to the course. Most of these bunkers are a good way out from the tees and—as Sam Snead remarked after a 72—they tend to make the course difficult for the good player. Lesser mortals can aim away from the major hazard without fear of reaching the alternative. A minor criticism is that from the 11th three successive holes are blind from the tee. Yet this matters little, for the hills are not steep and all the holes are worthwhile. The approaches to the raised plateau of the 12th are testing strokes. Once the drive has cleared the ridge of the 13th the hole is not too difficult, and the 14th is the mildest of the short holes unless the shot is short and fails to carry a pool. Thereafter the course yields nothing.

The 15th is forbidding because the fairway tilts steeply to the left toward a stream and woods, the end of which can cut into the line of a long second. Nothing less than a true, straight shot has any chance of reaching the next green. This narrow hole is the only one enclosed by trees, and a dramatic setting they make. The 17th, a great leaning curve along woods to the right, is a glorious hole and—if the final drive is not sliced—a challenging stroke remains over cross-bunkers to a green of varying levels.

All this amounts to a considerable golf course, as the players in the 1964 World Team championships for the Eisenhower Trophy discovered. Their tasks were intensified by dreadful weather, for, after an opening day when sunshine was warm on the olive hills, a strong wind gusted through the trees. The greens were, however, the real problem. Their grass was beautiful and consistent but very soft.

On the second evening a violent storm exploded over Rome; the skies were alive with wild blue light and the course was drenched. The greens were like sponges, but the British players—Michael Bonallack, Rodney Foster, Michael Lunt, and Ronnie Shade—made fewer putting errors than their immediate challengers. They began the last day five ahead but suffered awful suspense before triumph was theirs. In the dripping twilight a Canadian, Keith Alexander, slender and easy of style, could have put his side level with Britain if he had finished with five birdies. As four in succession fell to his courageous golf, British agony and Canadian joy swelled, but his second to the last fell away from the green. Olgiata was engraved on the memories of those who watched and played that day, as it will be remembered by many who have the good fortune to play there on less earnest occasions.

Balding's Eagle Takes the World Cup

The Canadians Al Balding and George Knudson won the World Cup, the trophy that once bore their country's name, in 1968. They began the last round at Olgiata two behind Julius Boros and Lee Trevino of the United States and finished two ahead. Their play of the 17th proved decisive. Throughout its length the curving fairway falls to the right toward deep woods, ever threatening the shot that drifts a little. On the left edge of the fairway a little cluster of trees, nature's contribution, ensures that those wary of perdition to the right do not hold up the second shot too much. Standing above the ball with a wooden club in hand does not make for the easiest shot in golf, especially when hoping to reach the green poised above a steep bank on the right.

For once the gifted Knudson was outshone. Balding's short game that day had a celestial touch that reached its climax on the 17th. He played his second with a wood almost perfectly, keeping his weight back and—essential with such strokes—making a good turn, but the shot was fractionally off line, not more than 5 yards, and it was bunkered some 15 yards from the flag. However, he exploded into the hole for an eagle, the ball pitching short of the pin and resting against it. Canada was ahead. The Americans still had their chances of birdies at the 17th, but Boros floated a 4-wood over the green and Trevino cut his into the trees. Finally, they needed a birdie and a par to tie. But the birdie was not forthcoming and Balding, in his graying years as a competitor, had won a memorable victory for his country. Italy, too, did remarkably well to finish in third place, only four strokes behind Canada and two behind the United States, Roberto Bernardini shooting a splendid 279.

The 17th hole at Olgiata proved decisive for Canadians Al Balding and George Knudson as they completed a surprise win in the 1968 World Cup over the strong American pairing, Julius Boros and Lee Trevino.

Completed in 1961, Olgiata has all the advantages of a course constructed from scratch. Ken Cotton was able to design a spacious. well-balanced layout of great variety, and one to test every aspect of golfing strategy and tactics—particularly the choice of club on the shorter holes. It was impressive enough to be chosen as the venue for the World Cup in 1968, only seven years after it opened, when the Italian team of Bernardini and Angelini finished a fine third.

The Course Card

Chantilly Golf
Club, Oise

Hole	Yards	Par
1	454	4
2	394	4
3	153	3
4	375	4
5	410	4
6	217	3
7	439	4
8	480	5
9	576	5
10	465	4
11	427	4
12	402	4
13	457	4
14	219	3
15	417	4
16	219	3
17	429	4
18	596	5
Out	3,498	36
In	3,631	35
Total	**7,129**	**71**

"... Nor the Slightest Glimpse of
An Alien World"

Situated in beautiful woodland in one of Europe's greatest horse-racing areas, Chantilly is an outstanding course that has hosted several French Open championships. It is a pleasure to play there—not merely because of its serene forest setting but also because of its demanding qualities. Two series of holes in particular, the 9th to 11th and the 13th to 15th, provide a stern test of power and accuracy.

More than a century has passed since golf was first played in France. In 1856, when the Duke of Hamilton and a few of his friends formed a club at Pau, in the foothills of the Pyrenees, golf was hardly known outside Scotland; there were but few courses in England and no others on the continent of Europe. In the last years of the last century clubs appeared in Biarritz, Cannes, and the hinterland of Paris; now, the game's influence is growing and numerous beautiful courses have been created.

Few would dispute that the course in the forest of Chantilly, twenty-five miles north of Paris, stands high if not paramount in France. The club was founded in 1908 under the presidency of Prince Murat, and five years later the French Open championship was played there after seven years at La Boulie, the golf course of the Racing Club de France. Few clubs other than Chantilly have longer enjoyed the blessing of two courses. In the early 1920s Tom Simpson was commissioned to lay out a new eighteen holes, and to redesign those that form the present championship course, known as the Vineuil. Much of his work was damaged during World War II and nine of the new holes were abandoned, but there is little doubt that Simpson's work on the main course, which included reducing the number of bunkers, was the foundation of its greatness. A first sight of Chantilly gives an impression of dignity, peace, and space. Nothing is confined or cramped; there is always ample room around the greens

and tees and between the holes. The course falls quietly away from the clubhouse, rather as it does at the Augusta National: all around is the great forest and nowhere is there the slightest glimpse of an alien modern world. At once the impulse to play is strong; the awareness of a beautiful and demanding course immediate. After the opening drive over a valley, a long second must avoid bunkers staggered to the right and slice traps by the green. A pull from the 2nd tee is disaster; a fade may be engulfed by a long bunker but a good shot leaves a pitch to a raised target of green. A long, flat bunker acts as a false lighthouse on the short 3rd, and the view from the 4th tee is like looking down a gun barrel. The hole is not long but the entrance to the green is tight with bunkers across and flanking the approach.

The French Open returned to Chantilly for a trio of titles from 1988. The first two were won by Nick Faldo, the third by the Irishman Philip Walton, but all three championships emphasized that the course had withstood the test of the new technological age. The respective seventy-two hole winning scores were 274, 273, and 275. The 5th is a fine hole, turning at a point from where the approach must be played through a neck of woods, with a cluster of pines by the green threatening the golfer who has driven too far to the left. Every instinct suggests a faded tee shot to the short 6th, but if it is played too safely pines again come into the reckoning. Although it might not appear so, there is room enough to pitch and hold after carrying the bunker guarding the green. A compelling feature of Chantilly is its constantly changing character and, for that matter, direction as well. The holes around the turn swing back and forth across more open country. The woods may flank—as for the full length of the 8th and the 11th, curving away from the dark forest toward a green set against a backdrop of ivy-clustered trees—but they never enclose. A whole series of bunkers, quickening memories of Muirfield, await the sliced second to the 7th. The angled curves of the 9th and 10th run parallel, but each drive and approach poses different problems. The importance of placing the tee shot is emphasized at almost every hole and is particularly true of the 12th, where no player would wish to come into the green from the right and toward the steeply falling ground beyond. At its foot lies the 14th green in a secret dell, and a golfer can enjoy a brief, if imaginary, feeling of superiority watching those putting far below. For the next three holes the golf is spectacular and testing.

A good drive to the 13th leaves a lovely second shot over a deep, grassy chasm to a green set against a fringe of trees. The 14th is the longest of the short holes, the green an oasis in its basin. Then comes a formidable drive. The championship tee is high in woods that snare the slightest hook and, on the right-hand peak of the deep valley—which must be carried to reach the fairway—is a tall cluster of oak and lime trees. The second shot is straight to a twin-level green.

The closing holes are sternly orthodox. Another target tee shot, to a green ringed with sand, is followed by a perfect-length 17th. A diagonal of hazards is meant to challenge the second shot. The green, like so many of Simpson's, has bunkers for the man who does not stay with his shot. The 18th, plunging and rising through a valley, makes a compelling climax to a noble course.

A Test of Stamina to the End

When Nick Faldo stood on the 18th tee in the last round of the 1989 French Open he knew that he needed a birdie four to retain the title he had won over the same course a year earlier. A par five would have presented the unpalatable prospect of a sudden death play-off with three other players: Bernhard Langer, Hugh Baiocchi, and Mark Roe. At 596 yards a four is not an open invitation. Furthermore the green is well protected with two bunkers on either side and when Faldo's second shot trickled into one of them, a play-off appeared likely.

This possibility was compounded by the lie. The ball was perched so near the front of the bunker on the upslope that Faldo's left foot was outside the sand. It is difficult to judge the yardage with such a shot; the temptation is not to hit the sand hard, consequently the ball flies vertically and comes up short of the target. Faldo was not fooled. The ball finished a yard from the flag and he knocked it in to complete his defense.

Unlike Faldo, Peter Oosterhuis had room to maneuver in needing a par five on the hole to win the 1974 French Open. The beauty of the hole is that the green encourages an attacking stroke because there is no trouble beyond and the ground slopes gently upwards. Oosterhuis's beautiful 3-wood approach located the middle of the green to secure a two-stroke victory over Peter Townsend.

Chantilly is perhaps the most highly regarded of all French courses, a sublime experience for amateurs and a consummate test for professionals.

The Pursuit of
Perfection

The Course Card

Valderrama
Sotogrande,
Cadiz, Spain

Record: Jose Rivero,
Volvo Masters 1990

Hole	Yards	Par
1	389	4
2	399	4
3	173	3
4	535	5
5	381	4
6	163	3
7	461	4
8	345	4
9	441	4
10	389	4
11	547	5
12	212	3
13	302	4
14	370	4
15	225	3
16	422	4
17	511	5
18	454	4
Out	**3,048**	**35**
In	**3,305**	**36**
Total	**6,353**	**71**

Valderrama stands testament to one man's dream to recreate the immaculate precision of Augusta in the Andalusian region of Spain. He has succeeded to the extent that you almost feel inclined to remove your golf shoes while walking the fairways for fear of damaging the grass. Tom Kite believes the greens to be among the best he has ever putted on, and the setting is idyllic, too. From the highest point, on the 11th green, Gibraltar's imposing rock slips easily into view, as does the faint outline of the coast of North Africa.

At 6,353 yards, Valderrama is a short course by today's standards but the bald facts do not take into account the capricious winds that swirl and bedevil club selection. Valderrama has not one prevailing wind but two: the *Poniente,* which blows warm breezes in from the west, and the *Levante,* which brings cooler air from the east. Occasionally the two appear to mingle; the weather vane perched next to the 11th green can be flapping furiously one minute and resting the next.

When Kite, the American captain at the 1997 Ryder Cup, made his first reconnaissance visit to Valderrama, the winds caused him more concern than anything else. He knew the Europeans were familiar with the course, since it was the annual venue for the Volvo Masters. His players would have no such luxury. Kite practiced on the course one day and was confronted by the *Levante;* the next by the *Poniente.* After America had lost he would remember those practice days and look back with regret that he had not been stronger with his team in persuading them to visit the course in advance of the match to experience Valderrama's moods.

The man whose dream it was to create this celestial setting was a Bolivian tin magnate named Jaime Patino, who had retired to the area. At the time of his move to Spain's Costa del Sol the courses were filling up and he was fed up with it. So he bought the second course at Sotogrande, a Robert Trent Jones layout called Las Aves, and renamed it Valderrama.

Jones was commissioned for a redesign but the course possesses as many Patino hallmarks as those of the great American architect. The waterfall protecting the 4th green is one example of his pursuit of perfection and the 17th has had more facelifts than a Hollywood actress. It is said that he spends $8 million a year in maintenance. Average American courses need around 600 sprinkler heads to maintain pristine condition. Valderrama has 4,600.

The 1st hole sets out the challenge of Valderrama. The fairway is narrow and lined with cork trees. It is a fairly modest par four at 389 yards but the reward of a short iron to a green that often lies in shadow will only follow a straight drive. The 2nd is one of several controversial holes, owing to the cork tree that splits the fairway. It stands 264 yards from the tee and many a player has strode to his ball after his drive only to be disappointed when he arrives at it, the green blocked from view by the imposing cork. Valderrama's four par-threes are fine holes, and the third is the first of them, requiring a mid-iron to a green where the punishment is severe if missed either long or to the left.

The 4th is a gorgeous par-five, the drive an inviting one from an elevated tee. The second shot provoked some early excitement in the Ryder Cup since it is clearly in range for the long hitters. The waterfall proved a diligent guardian and few players found the putting surface in two. The fifth is a dogleg par four to the left, a drive over the angle setting up a birdie opportunity to a contoured green that possesses many subtle breaks. The 6th resembles the 6th hole at Augusta, a wonderful par three from a raised tee to a green surrounded by six dazzling bunkers. The effect is intimidating, the club selection difficult as the tee is sheltered by a cluster of trees. To add to the difficulty, the green is tiered and three putts is a likely consequence of finding the wrong shelf.

The 7th is one of the hardest holes on the course, particularly if the *Levante* is blowing into a player's face. At 461 yards it has plenty of length anyway, but bunkers and cork trees at 260 yards place the emphasis on a long, straight drive to have any prospect of reaching the green in regulation. The 8th runs parallel, a fine short par four with a deceptive bunker that guards its front edge. The 9th is a par four straight into the teeth of the *Levante,* and it if possesses any ferocity the green can be unreachable in two.

The inward half opens with two holes where a professional has birdie opportunities. The par four 10th requires a short iron to the green off a drive that reaches beyond the angle of the dogleg. The 11th is a par five that is reachable in two on less windy days. The 12th might well be the hardest hole, a par three that never plays less than a long iron. The green tilts from front to rear and is hemmed in by cork trees which also offer protection down the par four 13th.

Enhancing the pleasure of Patino's beautiful course is the profusion of wildlife that garlands the course. Fluttering between the cork oaks and olive trees that line almost every fairway are twenty-two species of butterfly; when someone asked Patino whether the lake that guards the 10th green was dyed blue, as they sometimes are at Augusta, he replied haughtily: "We don't put dye in our water because it would harm the otters."

The 17th:

—————— Attacking approach

------------ Laying up short

A feature of the par four 14th is the raised green that requires one iron more than usual and the 15th tee makes use of the same high ground to create a long, plunging par-three to an angled putting surface. The 16th is called "Very Difficult," not without reason. The hole doglegs to the right and the tee shot has to be bold, toward the right side of a sloping fairway that will throw it to the left. The 17th seeks to re-create the 15th at Augusta but controversy has dogged its various re-creations. The wide band of rough across the fairway prevents a player from driving much more than half its length. Water guards the front of a green that tilts severely toward it, so the inclination is to go for the green in two is tempered by the prospect of a devilish chip back if he falls off the green at the rear. Further complicating the choice are three back bunkers. The 18th is a fine finishing hole. The drive has to be kept away from the trees on its right side but not so far that a player runs out of fairway to the left. Even so the second shot is still a long iron to a well-protected green.

At the 1997 Ryder Cup the match went to this final hole, where Colin Montgomerie proved equal to the task and Scott Hoch did not. The 18th, therefore, had shown itself to be cherished ground where the difficulties were severe enough to sort out the confident from the ill at ease. Indeed Valderrama did this as a whole, easily justifying its reputation as the Augusta of Europe. One man's dream has become reality.

The 17th

Seve's Focal Point

When it was announced that Valderrama would have the honor of being the first course to host a Ryder Cup in mainland Europe, attention immediately turned to the 17th hole. Redesigned by the European captain, Severiano Ballesteros, his team was divided as to its merits. Colin Montgomerie, somewhat hurtfully, referred to it as the worst hole in Europe. What cannot be denied is that it became the focal point of that Ryder Cup, its vast bank behind the green turned into an amphitheater where hordes of supporters gathered each day to watch what was invariably a critical hole of action. Some of the deeds witnessed there were incredible, and none more so than Ignacio Garrido's recovery from a back bunker to get down in two to force a remarkable half in his four-balls match with Jose-Maria Olazabal against Phil Mickelson and Tom Lehman. For all the fuss about the unfairness of certain aspects of the hole, there were a number of instances where players showed that the green was receptive to the perfectly struck second shot, thereby negating much of the criticism. Why should anything less than precision succeed when it is a second shot to a par five?

A Test Of Finesse
High Above the Atlantic

The Course Card

Vilamoura Golf Club, Algarve

Record: 67, Des Smyth, 1979

Hole	Yards	Par
1	310	4
2	435	4
3	324	4
4	163	3
5	485	5
6	212	3
7	393	4
8	419	4
9	265	4
10	153	3
11	390	4
12	487	5
13	348	4
14	440	5
15	150	3
16	514	5
17	353	4
18	413	4
Out	3,248	36
In	3,006	36
Total	**6,512**	**72**

Until the mid-1960s, the sunny Algarve coast in the south of Portugal—a beautiful stretch of white beaches, rugged, red cliffs, and tessellated villages—was a well-kept vacation secret enjoyed by only the few: a place apart, rich in orange, olive, and fig trees, fish and flowers. There was not a golf course to be seen. Even now, despite its popularity as a high-class resort, the Algarve retains the essential charm and character that are the legacy of its history, its location and its climate. It also now offers some outstanding golf.

All the early courses, although scenic and kept in immaculate condition, were of high championship quality and, even off the forward tees, much too difficult for the average golfer. Not that golfers have been deterred, relishing as they do a really stout challenge. And on all the Algarve coast, no course offers that challenge more surely than Vilamoura.

The umbrella pines of Vilamoura provide a beautiful backdrop and create an atmosphere of seclusion. Its taxing par threes are well known, but Vilamoura also has five par fives, four of them more than 500 yards long. Even here judiciously sited single bunkers, inconvenient trees or the fierce dogleg of the 12th put the premium on accuracy, not length.

Designed by Frank Pennink on and around a ridge of high ground as part of a 4,000-acre development, it opened in January 1969. Pennink's original brief was to create a course resembling the beautiful but testing courses of England's Berkshire, and this is what he achieved. Using the steeply sloping land as well as the more level areas, and judiciously siting his fairways through mature umbrella pines, he produced a flowing succession of fine golf holes that are reminiscent of Swinley Forest or of the Berkshire Club itself. From the outset he planned it as a championship course, but in the event it turned out to be tougher than he intended.

Although basically a vacation retreat, Vilamoura has seen many professional events, most notably the Portuguese Open, which was was staged there in 1973 and 1979. Jaime Benito won the first, following a tie with Bernard Gallacher on a score of 294. Six years later Brian Barnes lowered that total by seven shots to claim victory. From the beautifully appointed clubhouse at one end of the ridge, the course spills down either side in green ribbons between the attractive but punishing umbrella pines. Four holes occupy the high-level ground, from where there are fine views out over the rolling Algarve countryside. Vilamoura is an attractive course, with no blind shots and much variety in the holes and in the recently relaid greens. The strength of the par threes registers immediately. Each is different, each intensely visual and attractive; all require careful club selection and control for a par. For the rest, a crucial role is played by the trees that line the fairways and often encroach strategically to block off a long approach. There is little or no rough under the umbrella pines—merely sand and rocky ground. But try to play a golf shot up through one of the trees and you discover why they are such an effective hazard—the pine needles clutch at the ball and kill its flight immediately. In the trees, a player must accept the fact that the only sensible shot is a chip out sideways back to the fairway.

Despite its location at the center of a popular coastal resort, Vilamoura has a unique feeling of quiet isolation. This is partly due to its setting, high on one of the few pieces of elevated ground on this part of the coast. With holes rising, curving and dipping down through a billowing green sea of bushy-topped pines, the course has eighteen quite separate holes presenting widely varying problems. On the long holes, bunkering is minimal and strategic—the main hazards are the trees that line the narrow fairways. There is no need for semi-rough; a shot under the trees is a stroke lost.

Vilamoura is memorable for the umbrella pines that line each hole, providing a beautiful backdrop and creating an atmosphere of seclusion. Its taxing par threes are well-known, but Vilamoura also has four par fives, one of them more than 500 yards long. Even here judiciously sited single bunkers inconvenient trees or the fierce dogleg of the 12th put the premium on accuracy, not length.

Vilamoura's main defense is the umbrella pines lining each hole, but a duck-festooned water hazard presents a further dilemma.

The best long holes come in the tough back nine, a rugged, 3,006-yard par 36. The 12th is 487 yards from the back tee and curves sharply to the right around a large hill. It is an excellent hole, since a player cannot bite off too much from the tee—there are trees on the right coming into play, and he has no view of the green wherever he reaches the fairway. The hole narrows for the second shot, which is all uphill with concealed bunkers waiting to catch the errant approach. A tilted, elevated green has out-of-bounds immediately behind. The next long hole is the 514-yard 16th, a great driving hole with the ideal landing area pinched between a large bunker and some trees that lurk on the right. The hole follows a gentle curve to the right, partly downhill, requiring exact placement of each stroke and—like all good par fives—it leaves no room at all for error to the birdie-shooter. There is a duck-festooned water hazard left of the fairway, with further traps and strategic trees; the kidney-shaped green is well-bunkered, offering a narrow target, with steep fallaways on all sides. Finally, the last hole, which now measures 413 yards, was a par five. This hole, with probably the widest fairway, is made by three trees. Drive slightly left and the second shot is blocked by a large, lone umbrella pine; too far to the right and two trees on the very edge of the green deny the route to the flag. Bernard Hunt, former Ryder Cup player and a winner of the Algarve Open at Vilamoura has great respect for the layout. "It is one of the hardest courses in Portugal because there is no let-up," he con-

tends. "It is a very tight driving course, demanding mastery of all the shots in the bag, and it is the sort of course that the longer you go on the more certain you are that you will have a disaster somewhere. For me, the three short holes are outstanding. I believe a good short hole should be a test of finesse. I would criticize any course or any par three hole where you have to fire a wood to a large green with big bunkers. The modern, American style of golf tends toward this. But I think the short 4th, 10th, and 15th at Vilamoura, which are all mid-irons or less, yet still very difficult par threes, represent the ideal test. They also happen to be the most attractive holes at Vilamoura. One of the big problems at these holes is picking the correct club. The greens are not very big anywhere on the course, but this is particularly so on the short holes.

"Two of the short par fours, the 1st and 9th, are almost reachable off the tee and you are very tempted to go for a birdie because you know that somewhere out on the course you are going to drop a shot or two, so the temptation is to gamble. But they are par fours where, in going for a three, you can well end up with a six. Although they are short, they are still good holes. Two other really good holes are the 11th and 12th. I think Frank Pennink did a great job when he laid out this course—it is a very tough test indeed."

Few who have marveled at Vilamoura's beauty or tangled with its ubiquitous umbrella pines would disagree.

North America

Golf in the United States is statistically overpowering. Since the emergence of Tiger Woods in the autumn of 1996, courses are being built at a rate of 450 a year in order to cope with the game's new status as the trendiest sport on the block. In the last twenty years the numbers have practically doubled and most of the 20 million who express an interest in the game try to play at least once a month—a feast of golfing indulgence that far exceeds that of all other countries put together. There is a breathtaking diversity of settings for the game, from the Monterey Peninsula on the West Coast, where cypresses weep over the shot that is sliced into the Pacific, to the nation's capital, Washington, D.C., and the Congressional Club, which stands just a short helicopter ride from the White House. The science of agronomy has made golf possible in deserts where previously grass could never grow; and shrewd businessmen, together with brilliant architects, have bulldozed forests and drained swamps to create resort golf in the islands of the Caribbean and elsewhere. Linksland courses in the manner of the Old Country do not exist, but other true tests of golf are there in profusion. The game in the United States had its tentative beginnings in the old colonial states of the Atlantic seaboard during the latter years of the eighteenth century, but records are fragmented and discontinuous. The first authenticated club was St. Andrews at Yonkers, New York, founded in 1838 (here, the United States must give precedence to Canada, where the Royal Montreal began life fifteen years earlier). Within twelve years the United States had more then 1,000 courses—including the first outside Britain for public use, at Van Cortlandt Park in New York City (1895). From that time on, golf in the United States passed through well-defined phases. There was an early period in which the Scots still dominated all things to do with the game, from course design to the winning of championships. The free-spending, freewheeling 1920s saw considerable growth, much of it due to the luminous talents of Bobby Jones. The next dramatic boom coincided with the rise of Arnold Palmer, one of the most compelling of all sporting heroes. Now we are living in the most extraordinary period of all—the era of Tiger Woods.

1. Shinnecock Hills 2. Augusta 3. Cypress Point 4. Oakmont 5. Baltusrol 6. The Country Club 7. Olympic 8. Harbor Town 9. Winged Foot 10. Pinehurst 11. Merion 12. Seminole 13. Pine Valley 14. Firestone 15. Southern Hills 16. Medinah 17. Oakland Hills 18. Champions 19. Pebble Beach 20. Dorado Beach 21. Banff 22. Capilano 23. Royal Montreal 24. Mid Ocean 25. Club de Golf Mexico

Among the oldest (some claim the oldest) golf clubs in the
United States, Shinnecock Hills is—despite Dick Wilson's later
changes—the American course closest in style and spirit to
the links of Britain.

Golf Takes Root

Among the Burial Mounds

**The
Course
Card**

Shinnecock Hills
Golf Club,
New York

Record: 65,
Raymond Floyd and
Mark Calcavecchia
U.S. Open, 1986

Hole	Yards	Par
1	394	4
2	226	3
3	454	4
4	379	4
5	498	5
6	450	4
7	185	3
8	361	4
9	418	4
10	412	4
11	159	3
12	470	4
13	367	4
14	445	4
15	399	4
16	513	5
17	167	3
18	425	4
Out	3,365	35
In	3,357	35
Total	**6,722**	**70**

More's the pity, but it is next to impossible to find
in the U.S. the kind of pristine golfing conditions that exist on
the historic seaside links of Great Britain. There are a few
approximations, however, along the northeastern seaboard
facing the Atlantic Ocean, and of these nothing of finer quality exists than Shinnecock Hills, which has a claim to being
the first "formalized" golf club in the United States and the
first eighteen-hole course. Part of the stylish summer resort
of Southampton at the eastern end of Long Island, Shinnecock's qualities have been overshadowed by the exclusive
"social" panache that was attached to it over the years.

Because of the club's seniority, the genesis of Shinnecock Hills is of considerably more interest than that of most
other clubs, for it epitomizes the almost casual manner in
which golf planted its roots in the United States. During the
winter of 1890-91, William K. Vanderbilt, the prominent
sportsman and son of the founder of the Vanderbilt dynasty,
was traveling through southern France with a couple of his
friends. At Biarritz they came across Willie Dunn, one of the
early Scottish professionals who were then beginning to
export their native game to foreign countries. Dunn was
building a course at Biarritz, so he staged an impromptu
exhibition of his skills for the visiting Americans, who were
fascinated. Within a few months, the Americans were back
home and excitedly discussing the possibility of building a
golf course at Southampton. By the early summer of 1891
they had imported Dunn from Europe and taken him on a
tour of the Southampton area in search of an appropriate
locale. Eventually, they settled on some low-lying sandhills a
couple of miles from the seashore and within a few minutes'
drive of a small summer colony. Equally important, the land
adjoined the railroad line from New York City, giving those
golfers who would be making the two-and-a-half-hour journey from the city in future years easy access to the club.

With the help of 150 Indians from the neighboring
Shinnecock Reservation, Dunn set to work on his pioneering
project. His primitive methods are best described in his own
words. "Except for several horse-drawn road scrapers," he
said, "all the work was done by hand. The fairways were
cleaned off and the natural grass left in. The rough was very

rough with clothes-ripping blueberry bushes, large boulders,
and many small gullies. The place was dotted with Indian
burial mounds, and we left some of these intact as bunkers
in front of the greens. We scraped out some of the mounds
and made sandtraps. It was here that the Indians buried their
empty whiskey bottles, but we did not find this out until later
when playing the course. One never knew when an explosion shot in a trap would bring out a couple of firewater
flasks, or perhaps a bone or two."

Twelve holes were ready by late summer, and there is
little argument that this was then the most sophisticated golfing facility in the country. Forty-four members had already
been enrolled at several thousand dollars apiece, and the
eighty acres on which the course had been laid out were
purchased for $2,500, a sum that would today scarcely buy
a piece of turf on the same property. Stanford White, the most
fashionable architect of the day, was commissioned to build
a clubhouse in the shingled style of the region, with such
modern appurtenances as a bar and grill, lockers, and
shower-baths. Although there have been additions in subsequent years, White's original building, which was ready for
use by the summer of 1892, has essentially remained intact.
Within a year of its founding, the Shinnecock Hills course had
been enlarged to eighteen holes. Golf quickly became a fad
among the wealthy and prominent figures who summered at
Southampton, and the club became a thriving vortex of the
social whirl, the members adding to the splendor of it all with
their red blazers, monogrammed brass buttons, and white
flannel trousers.

In 1894, an attempt was made to conduct a national
championship (for amateurs, of course) at Newport, Rhode
Island. It ended in unhappy bickering, but an open championship that was appended to the Newport event was won by
Shinnecock's Willie Dunn, giving him the unofficial claim to
having been the first U.S. Open champion. As a result of the
bickering, the United States Golf Association was formed
with Shinnecock Hills as one of the five founding clubs.

The USGA's first official championship was held at
Newport in 1895, and the following July the championship was
brought to Shinnecock Hills. In the Open championship that

Only the Good Shot-maker Will Succeed

was played over thirty-six holes on the day after the Amateur championship was completed, so many of the professionals broke 80—not a commonplace feat in championship golf until the introduction of the rubber-cored ball a decade later—that some second thoughts were prevalent regarding the quality of the course. At less than 5,000 yards, it was obviously not of championship caliber, and so the first of a long series of alterations and improvements was undertaken.

It was not until 1931 that the course emerged as it now exists. Largely the work of Dick Wilson, who was to design many of the better southern courses, Shinnecock fully utilizes the outstanding features of the area—the strong prevailing winds off the Atlantic to the southwest, the sandy and rolling terrain, and the thick, reed-like grasses that border the fairways. While not truly linksland—the grass is of an inland texture—the windy bleakness of Shinnecock Hills on an average day evokes feelings of the British seaside links.

At 6,722 yards Shinnecock Hills has been lengthened to cope with the improvements made in club and ball technology, yet it remains a course that brings one's long and middle irons out of the bag quite often enough. Virtually all the shorter par fours play into the wind, and the longer ones with it. The true playing qualities of the course are never more evident than on the parallel closing holes of the front and back nines, both doglegs with the wind blowing strongly from the right and the long roughs on either side that are bound to cost a stroke or two, if the ball can be found at all. The fairways are undulating, in the Scottish tradition, so the placing of the drive is half the battle. The second shots off a good drive are in each case entirely reasonable, yet the price of a misplay is very high indeed. In fact, that might be said to be the predominant nature of Shinnecock Hills.

As Ben Hogan remarked after playing it in the early 1960s: "Each hole is different and requires a great amount of skill to play properly. You know exactly where to shoot and the distance is easy to read. All in all, I think Shinnecock is one of the finest courses I have played." His sentiments were echoed by many when Shinnecock hosted the 1986 U.S. Open, won by Ray Floyd. Lee Trevino, who finished three shots back, said, "I wish all our courses were like this."

It goes without saying that any great course (Augusta may be the only exception) is a strong test of driving. This is conspicuously true of Shinnecock. Whatever one's standard may be, to drive indifferently from either the members' or the back tees is to court unavailing struggle for the remainder of the hole; but drive solidly and the rich rewards of a glorious course are there for the playing. In one sense, although certainly not in setting, Shinnecock is reminiscent of Augusta in that the ability to carry crests on the fairways sets up the approach nicely. Otherwise, it can be most demanding. In this respect holes like the 9th, where it is essential to carry a great mound in the fairway (otherwise the second to an uphill semi-blind green is most taxing), and the 15th come immediately to mind. If the drive from the 15th tee, poised high in a wilderness of scrub, can carry into a valley, the next shot to an island target of green is comparatively easy.

But Shinnecock is far from being only a driver's course, as Corey Pavin, one of the game's shortest hitters, so splendidly proved in the centenary U.S. Open in 1995. Pavin's main rival for the title was Greg Norman, who met all the pre-tournament criteria predicting the winner would be someone who drove the ball long and straight. Pavin, however, demonstrated that, ultimately, Shinnecock is a shotmaker's course, as he shaped his strokes around the hazards and never more so than at the 72nd hole, where he rapped a 4-wood up and over the mound at the front of the green, the ball eventually coming to rest no more than 5 feet from the hole. Pavin was the only player in the 156-man field to match par over 72 holes; a testament not only to his own shotmaking skills but to a consummate test of golf.

The heavily bunkered, 399-yard 15th is typical of Shinnecock's short but difficult par fours.

Augusta National is one of the most idyllic of golf courses. It is at its best in the spring, when flowering shrubs are a blaze of color among the trees that bring seclusion to almost every hole. But the inviting width of its lush green fairways is deceptive, for it is a course on which cutting corners in a bid to beat par can bring severe trouble.

Dream Course
in a Dream Setting

Needing three birdies in the last four holes to tie the Masters, Gene Sarazen sank his 4-wood second at the 15th, then a 520-yard par five, for a double-eagle. This remarkable shot brought Augusta National and the Masters Tournament instant fame.

It was characteristic of the uncommon grace, the high intelligence, and ordinary horse sense that had marked his too-brief career that, when it came time for Bobby Jones to build his dream course, he employed a wisdom far beyond his years by enlisting the aid of a professional architect.

After all, he was certainly well-qualified in his own right to build any kind of course he wanted and people would have bowed to it. In eight Olympian years he had won more than 60 percent of the national championships he had entered, winning thirteen national titles in all. And he had won them on some of the most hallowed fields in golf—St. Andrews, Merion, Hoylake, Oakmont, Winged Foot. At the age of twenty-eight, he retired from competition. He played every note there is to play in the symphony of golf, capping it all with a Beethovian burst by winning the Open and Amateur championships of both the United States and Great Britain in the single triumphant year of 1930. It was a feat so far beyond the imagination of the public that people did not even have a name for it until months after, when a New York newspaperman tagged it the "Grand Slam," picking up the parlance of the day when contract bridge was the great indoor pastime.

Having performed his masterpiece, Jones walked off the stage of competitive golf forever. He had decided never to play professional golf, and that was that. Naturally, there was a call for an encore by the genius from Georgia, for his audience reached to every continent where grass will grow. Jones refused to leave the wings, but he did leave a legacy. This is the Augusta National Golf Club—easily the most famous American course, quite possibly the best and, for a certain period each year at least, simply the most beautiful golf acreage anywhere in

the world. Jones could not have made the course more universally appealing, and it remains so today as it has since its inception more than forty years ago—and as it undoubtedly will do a century from now. It is one of the few courses anywhere that even the tweediest of professionals will play tight-lipped and then go home and rave about. Despite the force of his personality, his golfing background, his intelligence, Bobby Jones's 365 acres did not come into being in a final, perfected form. The Augusta National as it is now is far different from the course he had visualized and—as Jones would have been the first to admit—it is far better today. The architect he chose and with whom he worked side by side was Alister Mackenzie, a Scottish-born physician who had recently emigrated to America and who abandoned medicine in order to concentrate on his first love—golf.

In Mackenzie, Jones could not have picked a more adept partner for the venture, particularly for the venue he had chosen for the course of his dreams. The site was on rolling hills ablaze with fruit-bearing trees and flowers—the kind of scene any lesser architect might have ruined by building a good golf hole at the sacrifice of its beauty, or else a bad hole in order to maintain it. Mackenzie best showed his self-discipline in this respect at the spectacular Cypress Point in California. So an architect who had an artistic bent for hewing a golf course out of exciting terrain joined forces with a designer who knew more about shot values than anyone in the history of championship golf since the great Harry Vardon.

Like many of America's great courses, Augusta National is not exactly at the center of things. The city of Augusta is hardly the crossroads of the United States or even of the southeastern part of it—or, for that matter, of

Georgia. Its history had been that of an antebellum resort that Jones, as an Atlantan, often visited. He married an Atlanta beauty named Mary Malone and it was at Augusta that he made the acquaintance of a well-to-do New Yorker, Clifford Roberts, who often wintered there. Soon after his retirement from golf, Jones had expressed to Roberts his desire to found a very private golf club that his many friends throughout the world could join, or just visit to revel in—a course that he himself would design with the master's touch clear down to the roots.

Roberts, who always had a knack for knowing when to buy and sell things, had got wind of a famous nursery in Augusta, named Fruitlands, that was for sale. It had been owned for three-quarters of a century by the family of a Belgian baron, Louis Mathieu Edouard Berckmans, whose son Prosper became a renowned horticulturist. Almost single-handedly, Prosper had popularized the azalea, now so common all over the southeastern stretches of the United States. The setting was practically perfect for Jones's wishes. It had the gentle hills he wanted for his inland "links," which would capture the spirit—but not imitate the characteristics—of the British seaside courses he loved so much. What with its almost endless flora, the property would be ablaze with the colors of so many flowers that it later became no problem at all to name each hole after a different one—dogwood, redbud, magnolia, and so on. Furthermore, it seemed to have just the right cluster of trees through which Jones would want his fairways to meander. To top it all off, the highest point on the property was dominated by a pre-Civil War mansion that could form the nucleus of a clubhouse. Bobby Jones looked no further.

Bobby Jones, one of the truly great figures of golf, achieved a unique combination of old Southern charm and pure golfing challenge at Augusta National.

The Course Card

Augusta National Golf Club, Augusta, Georgia

Record: 63, Nick Price, 1986

Hole	Name	Yardage	Par
1	Tea Olive	400	4
2	Pink Dogwood	555	5
3	Flowering Peach	360	4
4	Flowering Crab Apple	205	3
5	Maglia	435	4
6	Juniper	180	3
7	Pampas	360	4
8	Yellow Jasmine	535	5
9	Carolina Cherry	435	4
10	Camellia	485	4
11	White Dogwood	455	4
12	Golden Bell	155	3
13	Azalea	485	5
14	Chinese Fir	405	4
15	Firethorn	500	5
16	Redbud	170	3
17	Nandina	400	4
18	Holly	405	4
Out		3,465	36
In		3,460	36
Total		**6,905**	**72**

———— Ben Hogan, 1950s

- - - - - Tiger Woods, 1990s

No golfer can win the Masters without a carefully planned strategy for every hole. At the 11th Ben Hogan used to say that if he was ever on the green in two it meant he had hooked his second shot; he used to play for the right-hand side of the green to avoid any prospect of finishing in the water to the left. Tiger Woods's strategy on the hole is more explosive. He just blasts his drive as far as he can down the right-hand side before letting the fairway's slop-ing contours move it back toward the middle. This move can cause problems for ordinary mortals since it invariably means the second shot has to be played directly toward the water. Woods, however, was hitting it so far in 1997 that he had no need to worry about the water with his second shot as he had just a sand wedge to the green. As Bobby Jones intimated, any hole is a birdie hole if you have the weaponry.

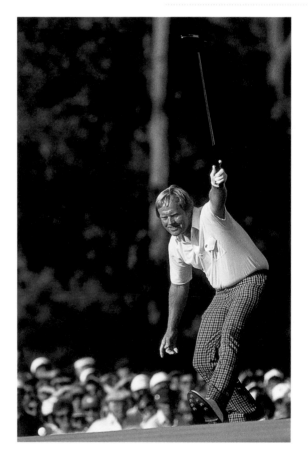

Jack Nicklaus sinks his birdie putt on the 71st hole at the 1986 Masters. The look of triumph says it all. Supposedly all washed up, he was about to become, at forty-six, the oldest winner of a green jacket.

Amen Corner— *Where Even Golfing Gods Pray*

The Masters has been won or lost so often between the 11th and the 13th that this three-hole stretch, menaced by the waters of Rae's Creek, has become known as Amen Corner. The term was first coined by Herbert Warren Wind in a 1958 *Sports Illustrated* article and years later the American professional Dave Marr took up the theme when he quipped: "It's called that because if you get around it in par you believe a little bit more in God." When Byron Nelson won in 1937 and 1942 it was mainly because of his sub-par barrages at Amen Corner, where possibly his most memorable shot was a gently chipped 3-iron for a 50-foot eagle-three at the 13th in 1937. Five years later he birdied all three holes to defeat Ben Hogan in a play-off. Hogan did the same thing many years later when, at the age of fifty-four, in one of the most emotional moments in golf, he tamed Augusta's back nine in a remarkable thirty shots. In 1954, a little-known amateur, Billy Joe Patton, blew his chance to beat the great Hogan and Snead when, after making up a five-shot deficit, he hit into the creek at the 13th and wound up with a disastrous seven. Greg Norman, six shots clear of Nick Faldo going into the final round in 1996, three putted the 11th and then pushed an 8-iron into Rae's Creek at the 12th to finally torpedo his chances.

Fruitlands would be his Augusta National. In essence, the course Jones and Mackenzie finished in 1933—with Jones playing thousands of experimental shots off every potential tee and to every possible green site—is almost the same today. The original front nine is now the back nine; Jones reversed them in 1935 because he thought that the original 9th was a far more demanding finishing hole than the old, shortish 18th, which could not be lengthened without giving the player an unconscionably difficult shot off a downhill lie to an elevated green. One thing Jones wanted Augusta National to have was flexibility, to be a course that would not overpower his 90-shooting members or be a push-over for his par-busting visitors. It remains so to this day.

By and large Augusta National remains, despite numerous changes since, what Bobby Jones wanted it to be: an elegantly flexible course with fairways so broad they seem impossible to avoid, with greens so huge they seem impossible to miss, with bunkers so sparse they seem impossible to get into. The course has a mere forty-five sandtraps, twelve of which are in the fairways. Although its tantalizingly beautiful trees are as inviting as Greek sirens, there is no rough in the ankle-deep American sense and certainly not in the knee-deep British sense.

So what makes it so great? It is great because Augusta National is a thinking man's golf course, the least obvious championship layout in America, perhaps matched nowhere in the world except by the Old Course at St. Andrews. Like all great courses, it must be played mentally from the green back to the tee before a single shot is hit. Since the greens are so fast, three-putting is a very real hazard, no matter where the flagstick is placed. A shot to the green must be finely gauged and truly struck, or else it will bounce and roll unimpeded across yards of green, making three-putting a staggering reality. Since getting close to the flagstick with approach shots is not only the easiest way of getting a par but very often the only way, the angle at which the green is approached is a constantly critical problem. It requires the player to spot his tee shot judiciously—not an easy task to discipline himself to, when the fairways are so prosaically wide and so free of hazards. In other words, Augusta National has made many a mere ball-hitter look and feel a fool. For the first time he discovers that a golf course can hit him back. All these subtleties, all this foresight and golfing technicality, might have gone for nothing. Augusta National might very sadly but easily have remained one of the great but rarely tested championship courses in the United States—such as Shinnecock Hills on outer Long Island or Prairie Dunes

The 12th

No Place to Gamble

No man is better qualified to assess the problems of Amen Corner than Jack Nicklaus, who has won a record six Masters titles. In his estimation the short 12th, only 155 yards long, is "the most demanding tournament hole in the world." The target is a mere sliver, with bunkers both fore and aft. The real problem comes in trying to judge the wind from a sheltered tee. In the final round in 1992 Fred Couples got it wrong. His tee shot pitched into the sharply sloping bank in front of the green and 99 times out of 100 that translates into the ball rolling back into Rae's Creek. But this was the one time fate put an arm around Couples's shoulder. The ball stopped before the water and Couples was able to make par. A certain five became a three and he won by two shots. Amen indeed.

The 13th

Safety in Distance

The 13th, a par five measuring 485 yards, provides a classic illustration of the advantages enjoyed by the game's long hitters. Here the average golfer's only chance of reaching the green in two is to hit his drive dangerously close to the creek at the left corner of the fairway. A big hitter can hit his ball well around the corner and make it home in two. The difference was emphasized by Tiger Woods during his runaway victory in 1997. For most players the green was reachable only with a long iron off their best drives. Woods, by contrast, had a 7-iron. It is impossible to stop the ball on either of the green's tiers with a long iron. A 7-iron is a different matter, a point Woods demonstrated in the second round with an eagle three.

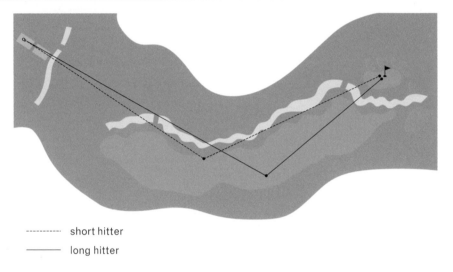

---------- short hitter
———— long hitter

in deepest Kansas—were it not for the almost incidental invention of the Masters Tournament.

Soon after the course was finished, Jones decided to hold an informal get-together, a tournament of sorts, with all his amateur and professional friends. He agreed to play himself, but only under the condition that he was participating as host. Even though he had lost his amateur standing, he refused to accept any prize money: that, he said, belonged to the "pros." Despite the fact that for eight years he had handled them on the course like yo-yos, off the course he deeply admired them. And they, in turn, revered him. Bobby Jones was probably the most genuinely loved golfer who ever lived.

This get-together would be by invitation only, he decided, and without anyone giving it much thought it was tagged the Augusta National Invitation. The title did not last past the four days it took to play it. Newspapermen almost immediately began calling it the Masters. Among all the reasons behind the evergreen success of the Masters as a golfing saga, none approaches that of its gift for supplying the unexpected. Like all larger-than-life stories, the history of the Masters has always been strong on character, from the improbable sixth triumph of Jack Nicklaus at the age of forty-six in 1986 to the stirring first victory for Tiger Woods in his first appearance in a major championship as a professional in 1997. But its greatest strength lies in its plot, in its unique ability to supply each year another chapter of almost

unendurable suspense, bordering on the impossible and stopping just short of the implausible. Each year it is invariably the most dramatic of the four Major championships; even when a relative journeyman such as Larry Mize triumphs it is in the most incredible circumstances imaginable, holing a 30-yard chip on the 11th in a play-off against Greg Norman that he could not hole again if he had 100 chances.

Since the tournament began in 1934, there remains not a hole that hasn't been eagled. Two of its four par fives have seen albatrosses, and three of its four par threes have been scored in one. The eclectic score for the event is a fantastic 35—37 strokes under par. But back in 1935, professional Frank Walsh needed twelve strokes to play the uphill, par-five 8th. Herman Barron, another professional, took an eleven on the par-three 16th in 1950, and the following year Dow Finsterwald took twelve on the par-three 12th. In 1951, again, Sam Snead started the last round tied for the lead and, after having shot a 68 the day before, took 80. That same day, William "Dynamite" Goodloe, leading the amateur field after a third-round 72, completed the course in 88.

In 1935 Craig Wood was in the clubhouse, the apparent winner. Out on the par-five 15th Gene Sarazen gambled on carrying across the water that fronts the green. He knew he needed three birdies to catch Wood and he hadn't much to lose. He chose a 4-wood for the 220-yard shot he had left,

Top: Most people know only the Augusta of the Masters, with its vast crowds. Then the 12th green, scene of this leisurely play, becomes the focus of world attention as the heart of Amen Corner, the scene of so much drama.

The 16th

Lovely but Lethal

In Mackenzie's original design the key to the 16th hole—then 150 yards, now 170—was a tall pine at the edge of a narrow creek. The green lay directly to the left of it and had two steeply terraced levels. It was approached from two different tees, one to the left and one to the right of the 15th green. In 1947 the hole was completely redesigned by Robert Trent Jones. He kept the tee on the left but, along with the original green, abandoned the other. He then turned the innocuous creek into a lake that runs virtually the entire length of the hole, thus forming a classic hazard. A new green, to the right of the pine and about 25 yards beyond the original, was constructed.

Trent Jones made the green kidney-shaped, the length of it facing the player. To the right front he placed a smallish bunker, a large one along the right side, and a strip trap back on the left. The green has no distinct terrace, but it slopes sharply from right to left and from front to back, the lowest points being the left front and left rear. As a final bit of dash, he placed two grassy mounds directly behind the green.

"All these revisions," says Trent Jones, "give the

The lovely 16th hole, set in a verdant glen epitomizes the elegant tranquillity of Augusta. The tee is set back in the shadows of tall pines and in April, at the time of the Masters, pink azaleas bloom among the trees and sunlight sparkles on the long lake. Finding the green from the tee is no guarantee of a par. Three putts here sealed Ben Hogan's fate when he went down to Sam Snead in the 1954 play-off.

caught the ball flush and watched it soar over the water. To the astonishment of Walter Hagen, his playing partner, and Bobby Jones, who had wandered down from the clubhouse to see what was going on, the ball rolled slowly onto the putting surface and trickled into the hole for what is known in America as a double-eagle. In one shot he had caught Wood, and he won the play-off the next day. It remains one of the most famous golf shots of all time. It is difficult to name a hole at Augusta on which something spectacular hasn't happened. Take the 400-yard 1st hole, a slight dogleg to the right. (There are eleven doglegs at Augusta National, but only the first and the last bend to the right.) In 1968, after a booming tee shot, Roberto de Vicenzo holed a 9-iron for an eagle to catch the lead—which he later tragically lost by signing an incorrect scorecard.

In 1966 Jack Nicklaus engaged in a play-off with Tommy Jacobs and Gay Brewer. On the 2nd hole a 555-yard downhill par five—neither Jacobs nor Brewer could reach the green with their drivers and their best fairway woods. Nicklaus hit a 3-wood off the tee to give himself a level lie. Then, again using his 3-wood, he hit the flagstick on the fly! He won the play-off handily for his third Masters. The second shot to the par-four 3rd can be a devil if the pin is back on the left. It helps, however, if your name is Tiger Woods and you drive the ball to the brink of the putting surface.

During one particularly windy tournament, Cary

Middlecoff elected to use a driver on the par-three 4th, the tee-markers set only a shade over 200 yards since the hole was playing into the teeth of the near-gale. At the instant Middlecoff struck the ball, the wind died. His ball was a hundred feet in the air when it reached the green, carried clear over the gallery standing behind it, and sailed off the confines of the golf course.

The 5th hole—a 435-yard par four, with an uphill second shot—has a two-level green that is lightning fast. Sam Snead once left himself on the lower level 55 feet from the flagstick, which was on the upper level. His approach putt just barely made the crest of the upper level, turned left, and then rolled down the crest leaving him 65 feet away from the hole. He then proceeded to sink that one!

In 1991 Jose-Maria Olazabal finished one shot off Ian Woosnam's winning score and while the immediate temztation was to critically analyze his bogey at the last, what about the quadruple bogey seven he had run up at the par-three 6th, the highest score ever recorded on that hole? And so it goes through the gorgeous 10th—485 yards, par four—where Severiano Ballesteros once cried his way back up the hill after falling out of the 1987 play-off with Norman and Mize at the first extra hole. Then there is Amen Corner—the deviously treacherous 11th, 12th, and 13th holes. And finally the exciting finishing holes where all sorts of drama has taken place. Art Wall won in 1959 by making birdies on six of the last seven holes. On the 18th, in 1961, Arnold Palmer needed a par for his second successive title and a bogey to play-off against Gary Player. As he was walking up the hill to play his approach a member of his gallery cried out and Palmer walked over. "Congratulations on winning the title again," came the

hole more definition. It now has a more receptive landing area for the shots required to carry the water." He
might have added that his revisions gave the 16th infinitely more beauty, the spectators a million new thrills,
and some of the contestants cause for a heart attack.

Yet the 16th is symptomatic of Augusta, a perfect
example of a hole that can be relatively straightforward
or terrifying depending simply on where the greenskeeper happens to have placed the flag that day. Even though
the experienced competitors who return year after year
know where the pins will be placed they still struggle for
an answer to at least two of the options. Easily the most
difficult is the one perched almost on the fringe of the
green in the back right quarter. It is possible to be 8 feet
beyond the flag here and, if too aggressive, be putting for
par from 35 feet away, as Tom Watson was in 1996.
Watson, incidentally, went on to five putt. It will come as
no surprise to learn that this is often the pin position for
the final round, although another is back left, tucked
behind the bunker. Although it sounds perilous, it is the
easier of the back pin positions, since the green's natural
contours will shape a well-struck tee shot toward the target. The easiest pin position of all is the one to the front
and right, and usually offers up a number of birdies.

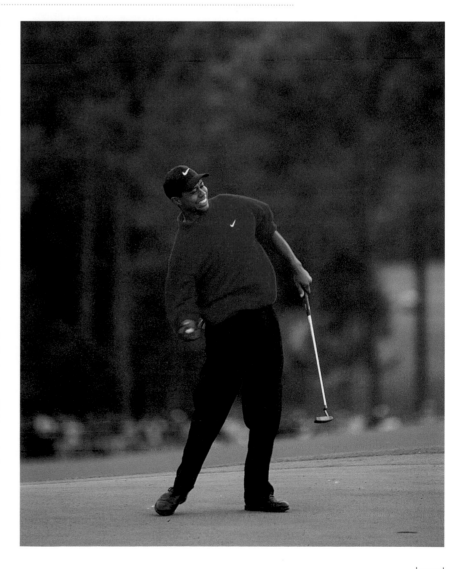

**The three pin positions
of Augusta's 16th that
offer a diversity of pos-
sibilities. From a
potential birdie at the
front right of the green
to the bogey-vending
back positions.**

words of wisdom. "Thank you," said Palmer. Moments later
he hit his second shot into a bunker, took two to get out,
and lost by a shot to the South African.

Doug Ford won in 1957 by holing out of a bunker at
the last, a stroke that was equaled for drama and quality
by Sandy Lyle in 1988 when he plucked a fairway sand
shot with a 7-iron to 10 feet from the flag and holed the putt
to defeat Mark Calcavecchia by one.

In 1956 Jack Burke won over Ken Venturi by picking
up a clear nine strokes in the last round. In 1997 Tiger
Woods had nine shots to spare coming into the final day.
It led some to believe that perhaps the course had
become too easy, but Woods's effort fitted effortlessly into
the philosophy espoused by Bobby Jones, who once
declared: "I have always said that this can be a very easy
course or a very tough one. There isn't a hole out there that
can't be birdied if you just think. But there isn't one that
can't be double-bogeyed if you stop thinking. A lot of the
difference has to do with the weather."

Proof of this had been established in 1965 and 1966,
when Nicklaus first shot the tournament record of 271
(which stood until Woods broke it in 1997), winning by
nine strokes from Palmer in near-perfect weather. The following year he ballooned to 288, even par, under less
than ideal conditions. He still won. In 1976 conditions
were again perfect and Ray Floyd managed to equal
Nicklaus's record 271, but only eight players beat par and
Floyd's closest pursuer, Ben Crenshaw, finished eight
shots back. In 1997 it was a similar tale. Woods might
have shot eighteen under par but no one else could
improve on six under. It was hardly the conclusive evidence claimed in some hysterical quarters that Woods
had rendered Augusta obsolete.

**Tiger Woods, right, on the final green at the 1997 Masters. He
had not only become the youngest winner of the event but had
achieved it by a record 12-stroke margin.**

The terrain of Cypress Point on the Monterey Peninsula varies in the most exciting way. The 8th and 9th are typically inland in character; the 5th, 6th, 7th, and 10th are of the wooded hillside type; the 1st, 12th, 13th, 14th, and 18th are seaside holes; and the 15th, 16th, and 17th are grand examples of the spectacular oceanside, cliff-top hole.

The Course Card

Cypress Point Club, Pebble Beach, California

Hole	Yards	Par
1	421	4
2	548	5
3	162	3
4	384	4
5	493	5
6	518	3
7	168	3
8	363	4
9	292	4
10	480	5
11	437	4
12	404	4
13	365	4
14	388	4
15	143	3
16	231	3
17	393	4
18	346	4
Out	3,349	37
In	3,187	35
Total	**6,536**	**72**

"The Best
Seventeen-hole Course in the World"

Cypress Point, it has often been claimed, is perhaps the loveliest golf course ever built. If anything, that is an understatement. Cypress Point is not just lovely; it is dazzling. Situated on the palisades of the Pacific at the tip of the Monterey Peninsula, it is 100 miles or so south of San Francisco and barely a mile from its more famous neighbor, Pebble Beach. "Pebble," Julius Boros once claimed, "has six great holes—all those that lie on the coastline. Cypress has eighteen of them, whether they lie on the coast or not."

For a championship course, and nobody would deny that it is, Cypress Point has several anachronisms. For one thing it has never staged a Major championship, indeed it does not hold any event of national prominence at all these days, since it backed down from hosting the U.S. Tour event, the AT&T pro-am. For another, it has two par threes and two par fives back to back, an architectural anomaly it shares with Ballybunion. To top everything off, the course is only 6,536 yards long, the length you would expect of a public links. Cypress Point, however, is anything but: its clubhouse, one of the most conservative in America, is barred to all but its small number of members, even during tournaments.

One thing the great architects have all understood is the dictum best expressed by "Nipper" Campbell, the pioneering Scottish architect who helped establish golf in America: "The best golf course is built into the landscape you've got." Consider, then, the landscape Alister Mackenzie, Cypress Point's architect, got when given the job by the promoter, Marion Hollins, the 1921 Women's Amateur Champion.

Cypress Point sits at the foothills of the Santa Lucia mountains where, when the tide is out, the land drops 60 feet or more straight down into the Pacific. When the seas are high they batter the edge of the course with the immense waves and awesome roar you would expect to see or hear only in the North Atlantic. Just offshore, sealions bask in the sun atop gigantic rocks. The ocean is dotted with fishing boats plying between the nearby fishing grounds and the canneries of Monterey. And the course itself is set within the Del Monte Forest, 5,200 acres of private land developed by the late Samuel Morse into one of the world's most stunning seaside resorts—complete with deer that roam freely across the course.

The turf at Cypress Point is rather special—springy and sparkling. In the dusk or in the light of dawn, when the deer

The Ultimate in Water Hazards

come out of the woods to romp upon the fairways, the dew gives the grass an emerald brilliance that contrasts vividly with the chalky sand of the dunes and bunkers. Bordering the fairways and many of the greens are Monterey cypress, bewilderingly picturesque trees. To O.B. Keeler, the Atlanta newspaperman who was Bobby Jones's Boswell, they were "the crystallization of the dream of an artist who had been drinking gin and sobering up on absinthe." The real wonder of Cypress Point is how anybody can keep his mind on golf.

Given the spectacular site, Dr. Mackenzie's design at Cypress Point was a monumental work of conservatism. There are a hundred places where he might have sacrificed the principles of sound golf course architecture to show off the natural beauties of the property—to make a hole badly in order to make it look good. The miracle is that not once did he succumb to such a temptation, although it usually takes several rounds to realize that you are playing a traditional, marvelously strategic course as well as a thrilling one, and not just moving within a playground of the gods.

The 1st hole at Cypress Point starts from atop a hill and drops into a valley with a turn to the right that cannot truly be called a dogleg; you can see the green quite easily from the tee. The hole goes inland, so there is no sight of the sea. Just a glimpse of it comes into view on the magnificent 2nd—a par five that is 548 yards long—and over the next three holes. From there on, the course winds its way through eight holes of sandy dunes and sylvan glades and past Fanshell Beach until, at the 15th, it reaches the point from which it derives its name. Now the golfer faces the first of the back-to-back par threes. It is a mere niblick shot across the booming surf of a deep rocky inlet; a lovelier 9-iron has never been called upon. Then comes the 16th, 231 yards long from the championship tee. The carry is again across the water, but this time it holds real menace and a large bunker may temper the pleasure of those relieved at just making across.

The 17th is the hole most admired by the professionals. It measures a mere 393 yards. The drive from the elevated tee high above the steep cliffs behind the 16th green carries across the Pacific to a wide fairway. This is only the beginning. The second shot must bypass a strategic pine to the right front of the green, not in itself the least tricky but backed and flanked by massive bunkers and a tangle of cypresses.

If there is a weak hole at Cypress Point it is the 18th, which should be the strongest hole on any golf course. It is a par-four dogleg going right and uphill to a green where it is hard to know where the flagstick must be faced. However, a long iron off the tee will still leave only a 9-iron. Over this hole alone Jimmy Demaret takes issue with Julius Boros's assessment of Cypress Point. In Demaret's view, "Cypress Point is the best seventeen-hole course in the world."

The 16th at Cypress Point is quite possibly the most beautiful golf hole in the world. Both tee and green are perched above the ocean and the roar of the surf drowns all other sounds. The green is lush and circled by sprawling traps of white sand and beyond to the horizon, is the blue Pacific.

Officially, the 16th has a par of three. But everybody who has ever made a par feels he has made a birdie. It should be a par four, it can be a par eight. In the seventy years since it was designed, only a few holes in one have been made on it. Amazingly, one of them was by Bing Crosby, a longtime member and mentor of the National Pro-Amateur, that used to be played annually over Cypress Point and neighboring Pebble Beach and Spyglass Hill (the tournament is now sponsored by AT&T and Cypress, of its own volition, has been replaced by Poppy Hills).

This hole stretches 231 yards from the back tees. Every inch of that distance is complete carry. To fall short means disaster. The dangers of the hole are obvious and members and even some of the professionals use the alternative route to the left settling for a drive and a pitch for a bogey-four. In this way they avoid the possibility of picking up. Against the wind—and it usually is—the hole calls for a full driver. Even with the wind, only hitters with the power of Jack Nicklaus would use an iron. To compound the problems of this devilish hole, going over the green can present worse trouble—more rocks, or the ultimate in water hazards, the swift tides of the Pacific.

Requiring a full driver off the back tee and carry all the way, the 16th at Cypress Point strikes fear into the hearts of the greatest golfers, and even pros play safely to the left.

The Toughest
Golf Course in the World?

Oakmont is torn in two by highway and railroad and scarred by nearly 200 bunkers. It can be a cruelly punishing course, boasting as it does such fearsome hazards as the mammoth Church Pews bunker separating the vast 3rd and 4th fairways. For those who succeed off the tee, torment and anguish can be found on the lightning-fast greens. The strength of any golfer will be sapped by the 12th, a huge par five of 605 yards that ends in a typically treacherous green.

The Pennsylvania Turnpike is America's oldest super-highway. It wends its way westward from Philadelphia, connecting the heavily industrialized eastern coast with Pittsburgh, the coal and steel capital of the nation. It bends across the northern section of the city and through the suburb of Oakmont, a lovely stretch of flatlands that lies at the foothills of the Alleghenies.

When the turnpike was being constructed it had to go directly across a dream of a golf course that had been fathered by a steel magnate, Henry C. Fownes, in 1904. Luckily for Fownes and the rest of the golfing world the course had already been sliced in two by a railroad whose tracks formed a gorge. The Pennsylvania Turnpike was also laid through the gorge, leaving the Oakmont Country Club course practically intact. Bobby Jones, Tommy Armour, Sam Parks, Ben Hogan, Jack Nicklaus, Johnny Miller, and Larry Nelson might have given their heartfelt

thanks, for it was there that all seven wrote some of the finest chapters in America's golf history. But perhaps no professional expressed more gratitude than Arnold Palmer, who was brought up in the same state at Latrobe and who has been a member at Oakmont for nearly half a century. The course's eminence was further recognized in 1987 when designated a National Historic Landmark.

Oakmont might well be the toughest golf course in the world, barring the weather as a factor. It is a course that will humble a golfer like no other, even on a lazy day in May. Bobby Jones played there in the 1927 U.S. Open and never broke 76. That year Armour won over 898 entries, without even breaking par. In 1935 Sam Parks—who knew every blade of grass on the course was the only player to break 300 on the way to his surprising U.S. Open victory. Hogan won the U.S. Open there in 1953 with ridiculous ease by breaking par—by one stroke. Nine years later, Nicklaus tied Arnold Palmer with an identical score—283—and then won the play-off simply by matching the scorecard. In contrast Johnny Miller won the Open at Oakmont in 1973 by playing the last round in 63. It has been said that it was the finest round of golf ever played. A decade later, Nelson won with 280, rallying from four strokes back. Even in the '90s, a decade where architecture has strayed toward the machismo, the course retains its reputation. On the eve of the 1994 U.S. Open Nick Faldo declared it the toughest course he had seen. The event was won by Ernie Els after a play-off that went to twenty holes. After recording totals of 279, five under par, Els, Loren Roberts, and Colin Montgomerie went out the next day for a scheduled eighteen holes. Montgomerie ballooned to a 78 and even Els and Roberts could do no better than 74, three over par. Els eventually prevailed with a par at the second extra hole.

What makes Oakmont so tough? To begin with, it once had 220 bunkers (it now has some thirty fewer, five times more than Augusta National). Each was raked in furrows two inches deep and two inches apart, a process carried out with a rake specially designed by Henry Fownes. "You could have combed North Africa with it," the 1950s golfing wit Jimmy Demaret used to say, "and Rommel wouldn't have got past Casablanca."

Then there are the greens, originally rolled with barrels of sand weighing a quarter of a ton each. After that was done, they were cut to a sixteenth of an inch and an area within six feet of the cup to one thirty-second of an inch. They were not watered in any way, by sprinklers or otherwise, during the early years. In 1935 Jimmy Thomson drove, on the fly, the par-four 17th. Thomson was then justifiably known as America's longest hitter, though not as one of its best putters. Tied with Sam Parks at that point, he proceeded to four-putt the green. Thomson recalls, "I could have six-putted. When the ball got to two feet from the hole, I thought I had an eagle.

The famous Church Pews bunker, which will catch any hooked drive at the 3rd and 4th holes, has come to epitomize the terrors of Oakmont. The tapering trap, almost 40 yards wide at its broadest point, takes its name from the seven grassy ridges that run across its 60-yard length.

Then it took off again. I had to hole a three-footer for my bogey. On the 5th green I had spotted my ball with a dime so Parks could putt out. When I got back to the ball, the dime was gone. It had slid off the green!"

Under championship play no other course has more big greens or more narrow fairways than Oakmont. "I only had six three putts in nine holes," Tom Watson said ruefully during practice for the 1994 U.S. Open. "If this course were a woman it would never say 'I do.'"

The Course Card

Oakmont
Country Club,
Oakmont,
Pennsylvania

Record: 63, Johnny
Miller, U.S. Open 1973

Hole	Yards	Par
1	467	4
2	346	4
3	425	4
4	564	5
5	382	4
6	199	3
7	435	4
8	253	3
9	478	5
10	462	4
11	382	4
12	602	5
13	185	3
14	371	4
15	471	4
16	232	3
17	319	4
18	456	4
Out	3,549	36
In	3,469	35
Total	**7,018**	**71**

Above: The green at the par-three 16th as it was when Hogan played his memorable 4-wood to the very center, 25 feet from the pin, which was placed on the extreme right. For the 1973 Open a bunker was added to the front right-hand corner and this has made the flighting of a high fade over the left corner even more crucial than it was for Hogan.

Above: At 382 yards the 5th is, for Oakmont, a relatively short par four. The three fairway traps, positioned to catch the hooked drive, are matched by a series of four on the right side. But, like the ditches running diagonally across the front of the green, they should not present too much of a problem. The real difficulty in this hole is in mastering the heavily trapped and severely undulating green. In the final of the 1951 PGA championship Sam Snead managed to circumvent any putting problems by sinking his wedge shot from the hillside rough above the green. His birdie-three gave him the hole and helped him defeat Walter Burkemo 7 and 6.

All that has been said about Oakmont might seem as though it were some sort of tricked-up golf course. The opposite is true. Oakmont has character, the quality that separates the men from the boys, the players from the ball-hitters. A player can have the time of his life—or hours of torture. The par-five 9th is so short that a professional can easily reach the green in two shots. The problem is that he might have a putt more than 100 feet long. The 9th green is not the biggest in the world but it comes mighty close. In 1919 Bobby Jones, then a lad of seventeen, lost to an Oakmont member named Davey Herron by the lopsided margin of 5 and 4. Six years later he returned for the U.S. Amateur and won his matches 11 and 10, 6 and 5, 7 and 6, and in the final, 8 up. All this was done with hickory shafts, iron heads that were drop-forged, a driver that had a hole in the center of the sweet spot, and a putter—later to become famous as "Calamity Jane"—that looked like a toy. Now, as the years have passed, the tools of golf have improved immeasurably. Had Jones played out the last four holes of the 1925 Amateur final against a better match, he would probably have gone around Oakmont in 66, hickory clubs and all. It was a performance to be surpassed only by Johnny Miller's in 1973.

Palmer's Paradise

It all began for Arnold Palmer at Oakmont in 1953 and, as far as the U.S. Open was concerned, it ended there as well in 1994. The local member had come home to hang up his spikes. It was one of the most emotional occasions golf has seen. The fact he missed the cut mattered not; his was still the biggest gallery by miles and when he walked up the 18th that Friday afternoon half of Pennsylvania appeared to have turned up to watch. Palmer first played at Oakmont when he was just twelve years old. "I came with a member called Harry Saxman and it was one of the great thrills of my life," he recalled. "I thought the locker room was just the most elegant thing I had ever seen. The wooden lockers are the same as they are today." In his press conference that day fifty-two years later, Palmer was asked one question but for a long while did not answer, his face buried in a white towel. Eventually he composed his thoughts sufficiently to speak in sentences fractured by a catch in his voice. He said: "I have not won all that much... I have won a few Majors I suppose... the most important thing is the fact that it has been as good as it has to me... ." The silence in the room was complete as Palmer tried to come to terms with his feelings, to speak further. Eventually he gave up and wizened old hacks who thought they had seen everything stood as one and applauded him as he made his gentle farewell through a small gap at the back of the tent.

Oakmont's Finish Fails to Humble Hogan

All great courses have great finishing holes. Sometimes it may only be the last, sometimes the last two. Oakmont has four and they are positively heroic, The 15th—a par four—is a back-breaking 471 yards. There are two key bunkers, the first lying to the right of the landing area to catch the errant drive, the other guarding the left side of the green. The par-three 16th is 232 yards, which is just about as long as a par three can be without becoming ridiculous. The 17th is a short par four of 319 yards—but every inch of it goes uphill and bunkers are everywhere, the key one guarding the right front of the green. The 18th is a 456-yard par four. The tee is elevated, but the second shot plays uphill. How these four holes play is best illustrated by the way they were tackled by Ben Hogan in 1953, the year he won the Masters, the Open at Carnoustie, and the United States Open at Oakmont. Hogan's closing round 71 gave him a winning margin of six strokes.

During the last round Hogan came to Oakmont's 15th tee with a slender lead over Sam Snead, playing a few holes behind him. Hogan, who often played an intentional fade to offset an earlier tendency to hook, this time let his fade get away from him. The ball bounded into that key fairway bunker. He had to choose between pitching out sideways into the fairway, or going backwards into the rough, which was not a very exciting prospect. He shook his head, plucked out his wedge, and then almost nonchalantly played a light sandshot on to the fairway. He then hit a soaring long iron 20 feet from the flag, and holed the putt.

On the 16th he elected to use his 4-wood. He wanted height on the shot so the ball would drop, which it did—about 25 feet to the left of the flagstick. Two putts. The 17th in those days was 30 yards shorter than it is now. Hogan slashed a drive that landed a few yards short of the green and bounded on, leaving him about 35 feet away. Two more putts, this time for a birdie three. At the 18th he hit a towering drive that left him with only a 6-iron to the flagstick, which was situated toward the rear of the putting surface. Hogan struck the shot 6 feet to the right of the hole. The championship was over, because in the meantime Snead had faltered badly and, as it turned out, Hogan could have taken five putts and still won. He took one, for his third straight three.

Above: Curtis Strange said of Ernie Els after partnering him in the early rounds of the 1994 U.S. Open: "I've just played with the next golfing god." They were to prove prophetic words. Above, Els is on the 72nd hole after securing his place in the following day's play-off against Loren Roberts and Colin Montgomerie. It was one he would win to collect his first major championship at the age of twenty-four.

The 15th to the 18th

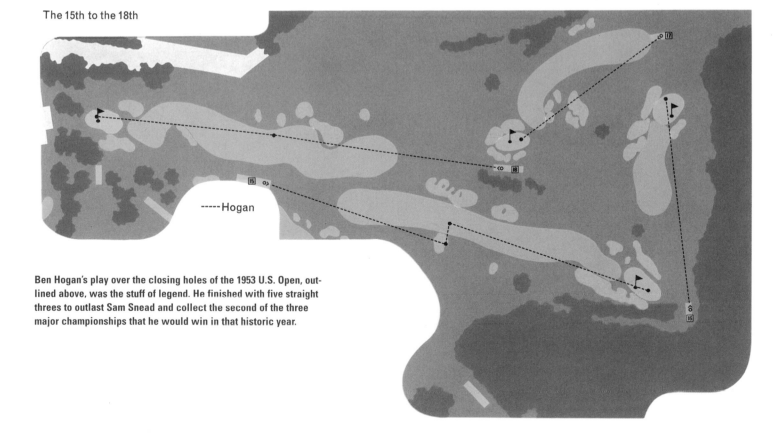

-----Hogan

Ben Hogan's play over the closing holes of the 1953 U.S. Open, outlined above, was the stuff of legend. He finished with five straight threes to outlast Sam Snead and collect the second of the three major championships that he would win in that historic year.

The Reluctant Legacy of

Mr Baltus Roll

The Course Card

Baltusrol Golf Club, Springfield, New Jersey

Record: 63,
Jack Nicklaus and
Tom Weiskopf
U.S. Open 1980

Hole	Yards	Par
1	478	5
2	381	4
3	466	4
4	194	3
5	413	4
6	470	4
7	505	5
8	374	4
9	205	3
10	454	4
11	428	4
12	193	3
13	401	4
14	415	4
15	430	4
16	216	3
17	630	5
18	542	5
Out	3,486	36
In	3,709	36
Total	**7,076**	**70**

The curious distinction of having won a major championship—the U.S. Open—by playing two different courses in his winning round belongs to Ed Furgol, a consistent if until then not markedly successful competitor on the American circuit. Furgol's never-to-be-forgotten year was 1954, the course—or courses—Baltusrol, located just forty minutes south of New York City in New Jersey. Named oddly after a local farmer, one Baltus Roll, whose life was brought to an untimely end by a murderer in 1825, Baltusrol has two courses, the Upper and Lower. The Lower course was chosen for the 1954 championship and for, the most part, was used by Furgol.

At the end of the third round Furgol was four under par, leading Dick Mayer by a stroke. Not far behind were Lloyd Mangrum and Gene Littler, at that time the boy wonder of the American circuit. Baltusrol is an architectural oddity in that the last two holes are both par fives. The 17th is a 630-yard monstrosity that is half sand—a lot of which is left unraked—and with a green as high as a house. The 18th is much shorter—542 yards—with a downhill tee shot that can be hit so far that reaching the green in two is foremost in the mind of any professional player as he stands on the tee.

Playing in front of Furgol, Mayer hit himself out of the championship with a wild push to the right into some Jersey jungle to finish with a horrendous eight. Furgol, in his turn, hit a darting hook off the tee into the woods which line the fairway to the bottom of the hill where he had hoped to land. He had a nasty lie with no possible access back to the fairway. Looking to his left, he found an opening, no bigger than a doorway, to a patch of fairway on the Upper course. He

called for an official, and asked if he could play to it. Baffled, the official called another official, who in turn called for another. Finally, they decided that, since the fairway of the Upper course had not been staked off as out-of-bounds, Furgol could play there if he wished. He took his 8-iron, punched the ball through the doorway, used the same club to leave the ball 8 feet past the flagstick, and holed the putt.

Golf first came to Baltusrol when the land once owned by the ill-fated Baltus Roll eventually found its way into the hands of a New York socialite, Louis Keller, the owner and publisher of the *New York Social Register*. He had been one of the first enthusiastic golfers when the game hit America in the 1890s, playing it in Newport and Southampton, where the rich spent their summers. In the early nineties he laid out a nine-hole course of his own and formed a club of friends that was soon 200-strong. Keller then added on another nine holes and gained 200 more members. For a professional he hired a transplanted Scotsman, Willie Anderson, the first man to win four U.S. Opens (a record since matched only by Bobby Jones and Ben Hogan).

The courses today bear no resemblance to the original. They were both laid out by the ubiquitous A.W. Tillinghast during the Roaring Twenties, when everybody was getting rich and when Bobby Jones and Walter Hagen were converting golfers out of fast-talking opportunists who didn't know the difference between a bunker and a brassie. The Lower course has a great deal of variety, playing to what would seem a monotonously long 7,076 yards and a par of just 70 for the U.S. Open, 72 for members. The 1st hole is a very short par five, only 478 yards (for the Open it

Thirteen national championships have been staged at Baltusrol, where every hole presents a unique challenge. For championship play on the Lower course, the par five 1st and 7th are shortened to long par fours, leaving only two par fives, both at the finish. The shorter holes offer no refuge; the difficult 4th is well protected by water and at the 12th the tee shot is aimed toward a semi-blind green sheltering behind an expanse of sand.

is played as a par four). It is followed by a slightly uphill par four 381 yards long and out-of-bounds guards the left of both holes. Now there is another fairly sharp right turn to face a longer par four of 466 yards, downhill off the tee.

Then all hell breaks loose. The 4th is 194 yards long, every inch over water, to one of the most diabolical greens

The 630-yard 17th, the longest par five in the history of the U.S. Open. The drive has to be threaded between two towering banks of trees; should a player find trouble off the tee he may not be able to carry the Sahara Desert, which splits the fairway at the 375-yard mark.

ever made. The 5th is a relatively short par four, but requires a very exacting drive. Then comes a long par four followed by a short par five (both played in the Open as par fours of the maximum length of 470 yards), a short par four and a long par three.

The course varies as much on the back nine as on the front nine: a teasingly short hole here, an agonizingly long one there. The cloth of the course has been so cut that it seems to have no pattern at all, which may account for a golfer wanting to come back again and again. Like the whole course itself, the bunkers have the variety of shapes and sizes, flatness and depth that can put a frown on a brow or a smile on a face. Tillinghast did some of his finest bunkering at Baltusrol. There are not too many and each one seems always to be in just the right place.

The contours of his greens were masterpieces of restraint. There are no steep terraces to drive a putt up to or, on the other hand, feather a putt down from. There are no ninety-foot putts across half an acre of putting surface and no six-footers with three feet of break. To be sure, a player has to borrow something here and something there, for the greens are not just eighteen pancakes. But they are, in a word, subtle.

In keeping with the greens and bunkers, Tillinghast's fairways are just as decorous. They do not bend in those ridiculous right-angled doglegs to which contemporary architects are so prone, thus creating more home sites for the real estate developers who underwrite them. There are no downhill lies where the right foot is as high as the left knee. Nor are there sidehill lies where the ball seems to be up to the waist, or a yard below the feet. Tillinghast's fairways just roll along, like miniature Mississippis, with just a slight bend every now and then. Baltusrol, in the final analysis, is simply aristocratic.

Nicklaus's Finest Moment

It seems ridiculous in hindsight, but when the U.S. Open returned to Baltusrol in 1980, Jack Nicklaus was not so much considered an outsider but written off altogether. He was thirty-nine and the previous year had been his first without a victory since he began his professional career. "Forget Nicklaus," opined one newspaperman, who better remain nameless. To say that Nicklaus was a Golden Bear with a sore paw when he read these press cuttings is not putting too fine a point on it. He was also returning to the course where he won the 1967 U.S. Open, when he smashed Ben Hogan's nineteen-year-old record 72-hole total. Then he had been imperious but still unloved, the thuggish usurper to Arnold Palmer's matinee idol. In 1980 it was a completely different matter. In the first round he matched Tom Weiskopf's new course record of 63; and that despite not birdieing either of the last two par fives. The final round was an emotional cliffhanger with Isao Aoki trying to become the first Japanese to win a Major. The 17th was the crucial hole. Aoki, two adrift, was certain of a birdie; Nicklaus, 20ft away in three was not, and desperately did not want to go down the last clinging to a one-stroke lead.

Consequently, he took forever over that 20 foot birdie putt but, as so often during his illustrious career when it mattered, he found a way of willing it into the hole. The 18th duly became a lap of honor as the New Yorkers saluted the man they had derided thirteen years earlier. Years later, Nicklaus would declare it his finest moment, unlike the aforementioned newspaperman.

Right: The 4th hole at Baltusrol, above and left, was redesigned for the 1954 U.S. Open by Robert Trent Jones and is now considered one of the finest on the course.

The 4th

A Heroic Hole Made by an Ace

When golfers start choosing the greatest holes they have ever played, their minds invariably turn to par-threes and, in the United States, almost inevitably to the 4th at Baltusrol. It is not a strategic hole in the sense that there are a dozen different ways to play it. It is more along heroic lines, meaning that it takes one good shot to get anywhere near the flagstick and then the courage to try to do it. It also means that if a player does not bring the shot off, he just has to grit his teeth and reload.

The 4th at Baltusrol is simply a water hole, water hazards being almost a trademark of U.S. courses for a variety of reasons, not the least of which is that they feed the sprinkler systems when Artesian wells cannot be found or when piped water is simply too expensive. The shot to the green can be anywhere from 150 yards to almost 200, depending upon where the tee markers are set. It must be all carry, because the entire front edge of the putting surface is faced with a stone wall. The green itself is about four times wider than it is deep. It slopes down from left to right and from back to front. To the left, guarding the high side, is a fair-sized bunker guarding the entire rear are three other bunkers side by side. Thus if you over-club you end up in one of those, thereby facing a delicate sand shot to that down slope which might well take you back into the very water you were trying to avoid.

The hole was redesigned over Tillinghast's original by Robert Trent Jones for the 1954 U.S. Open. When Jones got through with the job, the members protested that it was too tough. Jones disagreed. He offered to pay for any necessary changes out of his own pocket and to settle the issue he, Johnny Farrell, the club's famous pro, the club president, and the chairman of the Open Committee went to play the 4th. Jones stood by while each of the others played their shots. Now it was his turn. He struck a lovely shot that hit short of the flagstick, bit the green, and gently rolled into the cup for a hole-in-one. Jones shrugged. "As you can see, gentlemen," he said, "this hole is not too tough."

The 4th, a 194-yard par three, is a daunting prospect for the amateur golfer: the water awaits the less powerful, the bunkers the over ambitious, and trees and more water await any slice or hook. The shot must be from tee to green with no detours. In the background is the clubhouse, which has admirably lived up to the aims of its founders who, in Article II of their original constitution, declared: "The object of this club shall be the playing, cultivation, and advancement of the royal and ancient game of golf."

The Definite Article

Despite its Extra Hole

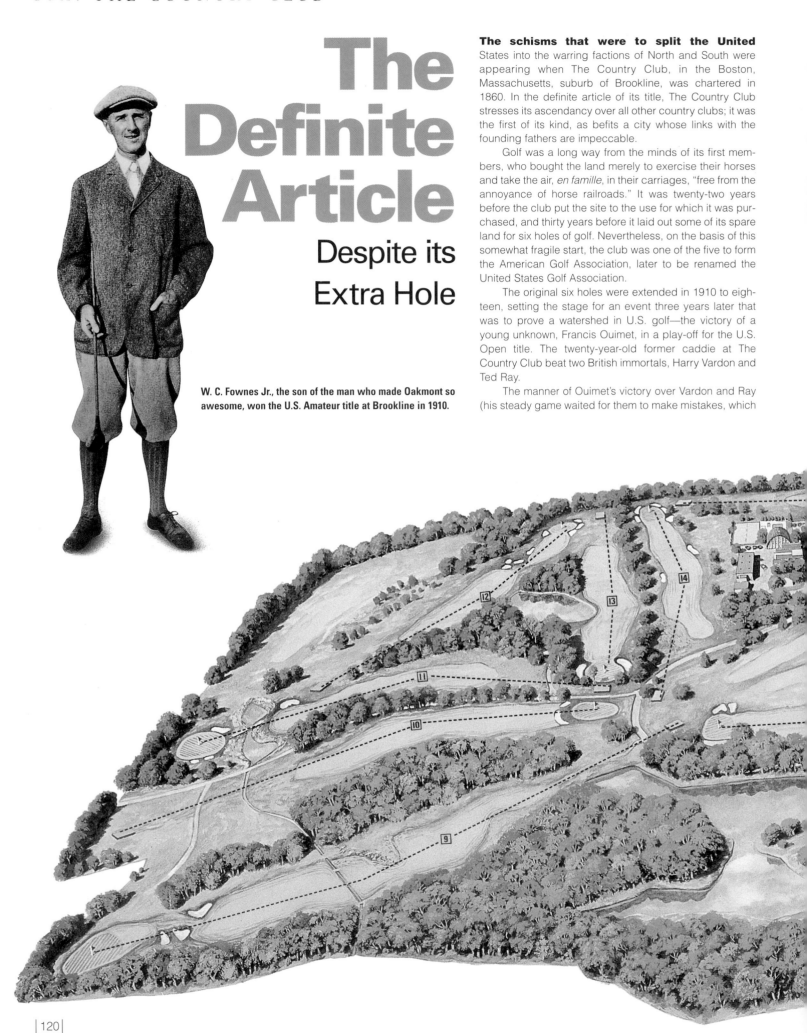

W. C. Fownes Jr., the son of the man who made Oakmont so awesome, won the U.S. Amateur title at Brookline in 1910.

The schisms that were to split the United States into the warring factions of North and South were appearing when The Country Club, in the Boston, Massachusetts, suburb of Brookline, was chartered in 1860. In the definite article of its title, The Country Club stresses its ascendancy over all other country clubs; it was the first of its kind, as befits a city whose links with the founding fathers are impeccable.

Golf was a long way from the minds of its first members, who bought the land merely to exercise their horses and take the air, *en famille*, in their carriages, "free from the annoyance of horse railroads." It was twenty-two years before the club put the site to the use for which it was purchased, and thirty years before it laid out some of its spare land for six holes of golf. Nevertheless, on the basis of this somewhat fragile start, the club was one of the five to form the American Golf Association, later to be renamed the United States Golf Association.

The original six holes were extended in 1910 to eighteen, setting the stage for an event three years later that was to prove a watershed in U.S. golf—the victory of a young unknown, Francis Ouimet, in a play-off for the U.S. Open title. The twenty-year-old former caddie at The Country Club beat two British immortals, Harry Vardon and Ted Ray.

The manner of Ouimet's victory over Vardon and Ray (his steady game waited for them to make mistakes, which they duly did) is enshrined in the histories of golf. Ouimet's subsequent career as one of golf's outstanding amateurs and best-loved characters received unique recognition in 1951, when he became the first non-Briton to be elected captain of the Royal and Ancient.

The value to American golf of his win was inestimable. It marked the first real loosening of the grip which players from the British Isles had seized upon the game in the New World. More, it showed Americans that success was not limited to those with a high and esoteric talent, or to those with deep pockets.

Francis Ouimet is not the only champion that The Country Club has produced. The club has an ice rink, and six members—one of them Tenley Albright, an Olympic gold medalist—have won a total of forty-one United States figure-skating championships. Its world-class tennis players have included Hazel Wightman, winner of fifty-three national tennis titles and donor of the now disbanded Wightman Cup.

The golf course over which Ouimet played and won was later the scene of a U.S. Women's Amateur Championship, and three Men's championships. In 1927, a third nine holes was added "for ladies, children, and beginners." The championship course now draws holes from all three nines, one of them, the 11th, is composed of two holes ordinarily used by members—a short par four and a par three over water. Combined, they make a brute

of a par four, particularly since the golfer must drive through an avenue of oaks and maples.

There are probably 300 golf courses in the United States that are tougher to play than The Country Club and perhaps fifty that are more artistically designed. Neither is it excessively bunkered nor severely doglegged and its greens average about 6,000 square feet, about half that of most modern greens. Wind is only an occasional factor and while there are a number of trees, the course was certainly not hacked from a forest; all in all, playing it is rather like playing through a park.

If these seem modest credentials, they are deceptive. When the U.S. Open was played there in 1963 to commemorate the fiftieth anniversary of Ouimet's famous victory, it produced the highest winning score for eighteen years, Julius Boros's nine-over-par 293. The previous highest was Sam Parks's eleven-over-par 299 at Oakmont, which was then more of an obstacle course than a golf course. The Country Club's greens are of bent grass and are feathery-fast. If the golfer misses them he is bound to chip—or, more likely, pitch – out of ankle-deep rough of rye grass. At tournament time the fairways are like ribbons in a schoolgirl's hair and the 19 holes that are chosen from the twenty-seven available (remembering that two holes form one for championship purposes) are certainly not the easiest. Accordingly, it will be a most worthy venue when the United States take on Europe in 1999 to try to reclaim the Ryder Cup.

The Country Club, Brookline, Massachusetts

Hole	Yards	Par
1	452	4
2	185	3
3	448	4
4	338	4
5	439	4
6	312	4
7	201	3
8	385	4
9	510	5
10	439	4
11	453	4
12	450	4
13	433	4
14	527	5
15	434	4
16	185	3
17	381	4
18	438	4
Out	3,270	35
In	3,740	36
Total	**7,010**	**71**

Already drenched in tradition as the first-ever country club, Brookline became even more famous with tantalizing finishes in the two U.S. Opens held there, won by Francis Ouimet in 1913 and Julius Boros half a century later. Narrow, tree-lined fairways and exceptionally small greens make accuracy off the tees and fine chipping essential for a low score.

The 1988 U.S. Open, in hindsight, could almost be seen as a dry run for those matches. Oddly enough, another Championship at Brookline ended in a play-off, this time between the best American player of the day, Curtis Strange, and the leading European, Nick Faldo, who had tied on a 72-hole score of 278. It was Strange who prevailed in the 18-hole play-off the following day, 71 to 75, to become the first player since Ben Hogan in 1950-51 to successfully defend the U.S. Open.

The 1st hole runs right down an old polo field with a stretch of The Country Club's old racecourse on the right. It is a routine par four of 452 yards; the 2nd, an uphill par three of 185 yards to an ample green, is also unremarkable. The 3rd becomes demanding, for the rough intrudes on the fairway at about 260 yards, leaving a long iron to a green overshadowed by ancient oaks and guarded from every conceivable angle by sand.

From the 3rd to the 8th, the course is again nondescript—no more demanding than a thousand other holes in the U.S.: the 9th is where the golfer really has to start to play. If he is not under par at that point his chances of finishing in par are remote. The 9th measures 505 yards, nothing to speak of as par fives go, which probably explains why it is slightly shortened for the U.S. Open and converted to a par four. Drives off the elevated tee must be hit comfortably short to avoid rolling into a stone-filled cliff, or hit hugely long to carry it. It is a do-or-die hole—an easy par or a muscular birdie, the decision has to be made on the tee. For the professionals there is no such option, of course. From the front tee, they have to carry the cliff to hope to record a par.

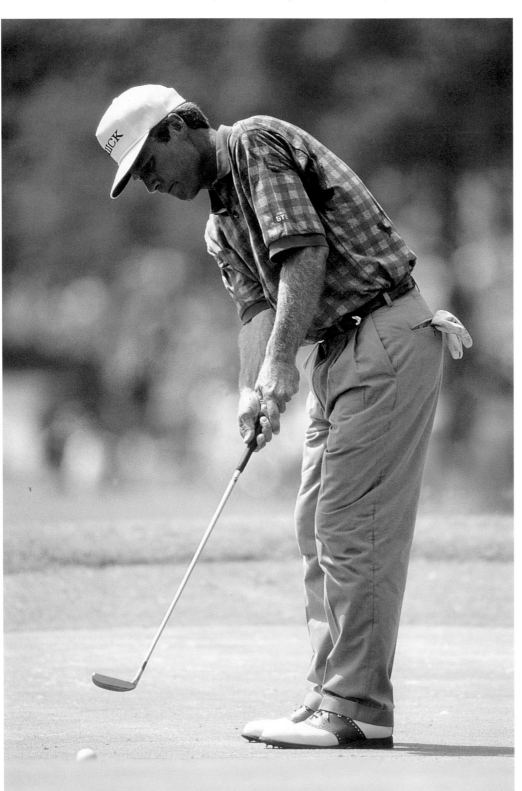

Now the course narrows. The 10th, 11th, and 12th are long and hazardous par-fours, 439, 453, and 450 yards in turn—and the 12th is one of the most rugged par fours anywhere. Even a long hitter must use a wickedly long iron or a wood shot to reach the green, which is not only elevated but hidden from view. All access to the green is cut off by five bunkers in front of it, and too much club lands the ball in either of two bunkers behind.

The remainder of the course is deceptively simple, even the 18th, which is straight to an elevated green guarded by an enormous and very obvious bunker and shadowed by a similarly imposing oak that was something to be avoided even in Ouimet's day. In its lifetime, The Country Club has been host to more than a dozen international events, including the Walker Cup (twice), and the forthcoming Ryder Cup; its members, too, have a special international distinction—their annual contest with Royal Montreal, first played in 1898, was the world's first golf match between teams from different countries. Added to Ouimet's famous victory, they give The Country Club a pedigree of which it is justly proud.

In 1999 Ben Crenshaw, left, will be the American captain accorded the responsibility of trying to reclaim the Ryder Cup at The Country Club.

The Hole That Influenced Three U.S. Opens

Apart from the geography of the course itself there were quite a number of reasons for the stratospherically high scores of the 1963 U.S. Open, played at The Country Club to commemorate Francis Ouimet's famous victory there fifty years earlier. They were so high that even Jack Nicklaus failed to qualify for the last thirty-six holes.

The championship was staged, as usual, in June, but the weather was unseasonably cold—so cold that two sweaters were the order of the day and, for those who had the uncommon foresight to bring them, windbreakers. The cause of all this was a freakish storm blowing from the northeast off the North Atlantic, and the winds made the greens like slate. Sitting as it does so far inland and protected by its numerous ancient trees, the course is not ordinarily a windy one. But that week it was more like the Open in Britain than the Open in the United States.

However, the wind brought into the reckoning two holes in particular—the 1st and the 17th, which had been redesigned by the New England architect Geoffrey Cornish. The 1st hole, already 452 yards, now played in to the teeth of the wind. But it was the 17th, regarded for years as one of the pushover holes, that had the decisive influence. It turned out to be the most difficult hole to par. The 17th, only 381 yards long and slightly doglegged to the left, had already influenced the result of one Open. In the crook of that dogleg was a small but deep bunker—the key hazard to the hole—and it was there that the 1913 Open was effectively won by Francis Ouimet or, more accurately, lost by Harry Vardon. In the fourth round, Ouimet hit a fine drive safely to the right of that bunker, hit a jigger 20 feet past the hole on a green that is long and extremely narrow, and made the birdie-putt that enabled him to tie with Vardon and Ted Ray. In the play-off the next day Ouimet came to that same hole with only a stroke advantage over the seemingly invincible Vardon who, realizing he had to make a birdie quickly, bit off too much of the dogleg and landed in the bunker. He took a bogey-five. Ouimet played the hole precisely as he had the day before, including another downhill putt for a birdie. Fifty years later Geoffrey Cornish enlarged that bunker, added two more to the left of the green, and re-

Francis Ouimet and caddie Eddie Lowry in the 1913 U.S. Open at The Country Club. A former caddie himself, the 20-year-old Ouimet snatched the title from Vardon and Ray.

contoured the putting surface, giving it multitudinous breaks. The hole still required no more than a 3-wood off the tee (as against Ouimet's hickory-shafted driver) and a niblick pitch to the green (against Ouimet's jigger) but, half a century later, it was still baffling. The late Tony Lema bogeyed it to lose the chance of a tie and Arnold Palmer's bogey cost him the opportunity to win the championship outright. And Jacky Cupit, needing only a par and a bogey to win, took a double-bogey six. Julius Boros took only one putt at the 17th to join Cupit and Palmer in a play-off. He won handily with a one-under-par 70.

In 1988 it was Rees Jones who was called in by the USGA to look at the course and he added nearly 300 yards to its length, taking it above the 7,000 mark that now seems to be mandatory for most Major championships. At the 17th during scheduled play Curtis Strange three putted to fall back into a tie with Nick Faldo. Then, in the play-off the following day, Faldo overshot the green and the resultant bogey cost him any prospect of winning the title. Once again the 17th had been instrumental in deciding a U.S. Open.

The 17th: 365 yards par 4

Old   New

—— Vardon
----- Ouimet

The old 17th showing Vardon's bunker shot and Vardon's precision. Right: How the hole has been changed since then.

A Course that was
Built in Reverse

The Course Card

The Olympic
Club,
San Francisco,
California
Lakeside course

Hole	Yards	Par
1	530	5
2	400	4
3	220	3
4	428	4
5	456	4
6	434	4
7	288	4
8	135	3
9	424	4
10	412	4
11	427	4
12	386	4
13	185	3
14	417	4
15	147	3
16	604	5
17	517	5
18	338	4
Out	3,315	35
In	3,433	36
Total	**6,748**	***71**

*Reduced to 70 for the US
Open by changing 17th to
a par-four of 443 yards

San Francisco's reputation for beauty and charm is so widespread one tends to forget many of its less celebrated assets: the great University of California just across the bay; the influence it has had on the literature of the Far West; and, by no means least, the fine sportsmen and athletes who have been sent out from time to time to spread fame in foreign lands. The first of the international-class golfers was Lawson Little, and a generation later came Harvie Ward, winner of U.S. and British amateur titles in the 1950s, and Ken Venturi, the 1964 U.S. Open champ-ion. It is appropriate and perhaps significant that Venturi played much of his junior golf at a course known far and wide as Lakeside, although that is not its formal and proper name. Actually, it is the Lakeside course of the Olympic Club Country Club, a clumsy designation deriving from Lakeside's rather untidy and varied history.

Almost all U.S. cities of any size contain some organization akin to San Francisco's Olympic Club. These are athletic clubs with a membership numbering many hundreds, and their facilities usually include a sizable clubhouse in the downtown area with a swimming pool, gymnasium, squash and handball courts, Turkish baths, and pleasant common rooms in which to dine and drink or just read and relax. The Olympic Club, whose origins go back more than a century, is such a place. It fosters teams in almost every sport that Americans enjoy, and just after World War I it expanded into golf.

In 1922, the Olympic Club bought a golf course on the western edge of San Francisco alongside the Pacific Ocean. The course had been built by the then floundering Lakeside Country Club and, as its name implied, it bordered a lake—Lake Merced, which is a small fresh-water lake less than a mile long and separated from the sea by

a spine of low sandhills. The course had been built on the bare inland side of the hill, and its principal feature was the canted topography of practically all its holes as they sloped abruptly from the crest of the hill to the lake. The Olympic Club promptly planted a mass of eucalyptus, pine, and cypress trees to frame all eighteen of the holes in a veritable forest as the trees reached full maturity some twenty or twenty-five years later.

Thus the course was, in a sense, built in reverse. For it is the towering trees that now give Lakeside its unique character and make it so different from the club's other eighteen holes, the Ocean course, which is built on the seaward side of the hill. The nearby Pacific and its enormous dunes play no part in the personality of Lakeside except for the prevailing wind that blows off the sea most afternoons throughout the year and the fog that comes rolling in from the ocean most evenings to wrap the course in its silent, cottony moisture, keeping it soft and damp and green even during the hot, dry months of early autumn. When the winter rains begin around December, Lakeside tends to become much too heavy for real enjoyment, and it stays that way during the wetter winters until the early springtime of northern California begins to dry it out in March and April.

By June, the course is almost always in its ideal playing condition, a lovely and noble-looking arboreal parkland. It is not surprising that the USGA has four times chosen Lakeside as the site of its Open (including the summer of 1998), always a mid-June affair, and so made it one of the only three courses in all of sports-minded California ever to play host to its premier championship, Riviera and Pebble Beach being the others.

Lakeside plays long—very long. During the 1955 Open, with the 17th hole reduced from a par five to a par

Some critics claim that the 3rd's fame rests on the view from the tee, but it is a trying par three with a green that is difficult to hold.

four only six rounds were played in sub-par figures, the lowest being Jack Fleck's closing 67 that brought him a 72-hole tie with Ben Hogan. The second Open to be played at Olympic was eleven years later and this also resulted in a tie and a horrendous turn of fortune for Arnold Palmer: he lost a seven-stroke lead in eight holes to Billy Casper, who then beat him in the play-off by four strokes. In the 1987 Open, only winner Scott Simpson and runner-up Tom Watson broke par.

Except for the short holes there is no such thing as a straight line at Lakeside. The course winds and bends its way through the trees in such a way that the second shot on at least half its holes is dictated entirely by the terrain and little, if any, advantage is to be gained by the big drive. It is, in addition, a course that plays havoc with the hooker, or with the player who likes to draw big, long drives from right to left for added roll. Those who would take a shortcut on the bent and crooked holes find their route frustrated by the towering trees that close in on both sides

of every fairway. Off many of the tees, the shot must be played as out of a chute because of overhanging branches at the front edge of the tee or just beyond, thus further confining the leeway available on the drive. Finally, Lakeside's use of the sloping fairways and the dogleg has been so artfully contrived that the very shot designed to defeat the purpose of the hole will bring on the most severe penalty; for example, if a golfer tries to cut the corner on the right with a fade and misses the trees, he will probably find his shot slipping downhill off the fairway and into the scrubby rough, with his next shot a rather humiliating little recovery into a playable area.

The course starts out docilely enough with a par five that can be reached comfortably in three strokes while one is untying the kinks. The 2nd hole, however, abruptly indicates the sort of trouble ahead. The hole feels as if it moves leftward, and the fairway slopes sharply to the left toward the lake, yet the two big shots must be moved from left to right—against the contour of the land. The 3rd

Although short by modern U.S. standards, Olympic's Lakeside plays long because the moist San Francisco climate limits roll and carry. Narrow fairways and small greens strengthen its challenge.

is a longish par three, with bunkering that is typical of Lakeside. It is a very sparsely bunkered course, with only three holes, two of them short, in which there is no opening to the green for the player who prefers to run the ball on to the putting surface rather than hit directly for the pins and hope to hold the green. This is just as well, for the greens are relatively small by today's standards, averaging approximately 5,000 square feet or so, and in many instances it is foolhardy to hit long irons directly at them.

It is at the 4th hole that one first confronts the problems of hitting a drive out of a chute. The exit from the tee is extremely narrow because of the overhanging branches from the tall trees on either side, and there is no choice but to drive the ball straight to the target area on the fairway, some 220 to 250 yards distant. From there, a long, uphill iron or fairway wood is the proper shot. As is so often the case on this course the trouble is on the high side of the fairway, forcing one to favor the side that will bounce the ball into the rough and the trees. This same problem exists in reverse on the 5th hole, where the trouble is on the right, and the fairway slopes to the left.

The 6th hole, a slight dogleg left, is one more longish par four, but it is notable because it provides the only fairway bunker on the entire course—a large sandtrap on the left—that will catch any shot trying to shave some distance off. The 7th is an unusually short par four; again a drive out

of a chute to a small fairway from which there is just a little flip of a pitch shot to a green that falls away if one plays the shot too boldly to the back portion. The 8th would be a rather easy par three were it not for the overhanging branches again, not only in front of the tee but also overhanging the entrance to the green on the right.

The 9th through the 12th are all longish par fours, the last three directly into the prevailing wind, and in all of them there is the problem of the precisely hit drive between the trees and the carefully hit second shot into greens that offer only a minimum target. The turn for home really begins at the 13th, where two par threes and a par four now border a deep culvert on the left that is played as out-of-bounds, except in major tournaments such as the Open. However, anything hit into the impenetrable foliage of this culvert is virtually unplayable and might just as well be out-of-bounds.

The 16th is extremely long—more than 600 yards—and played with the prevailing wind at one's back. Despite this, few players have putted for eagle, although Bobby Jones was one of them. The trees on the left were smaller then and no doubt he took a shortcut over them, for the hole bends in a seemingly endless crescent to the left. The drive needs to be played to the center of the fairway, with a long iron for the second shot to the right side, avoiding a large tree on the left. Then a short iron is needed for the approach.

The 15th to the 18th
—— Palmer
----- Casper
•••••• Hogan

The 15th to the 18th

Hogan, Palmer, and Watson Fail

Late one June afternoon in 1955 all the world was convinced that Ben Hogan was assured of a record fifth Open victory; one radio broadcast actually announced it as a fact. But as a weary Hogan waited in the locker room, his task complete, the news came that Jack Fleck, up until then quite unknown, needed a birdie-three on the last hole to tie. Hogan dreaded the prospect of a play-off. Since the accident that nearly destroyed him in 1949, he had to husband his resources with great care. His strategy for a championship was confined to 72 holes and as he waited he said he hoped Fleck would make two or four. Fleck did neither. He holed from seven feet for the tie. Even then nobody dreamed that he could beat the almost invincible Hogan the following day. But Fleck was in an exalted state of confidence, seemingly unafraid of the implacable

It is at the 17th hole that a good deal of the excitement usually develops at the US Open, for it is shortened for that tournament from a 517-yard par five to a 443-yard par four simply by using a shorter tee. It is uphill all the way, the fairway slopes sharply to the right, and even at the distance used for the Open the very biggest hitters among the professionals can seldom reach the green in two shots playing directly into the teeth of the prevailing wind. The 18th hole, a very short par four at 338 yards, is a driving problem. The trouble is on the left, but again the fairway slopes so sharply to the right that one is always tempted to flirt with the left rough. On the other hand, if the ball carries to the right side of the fairway, the pine trees and their overhanging branches completely cut off any entrance to the green, which leans steeply forward and seldom offers a simple, straight putt. Hogan had to sink a 30-foot putt for a six here in his play-off with Jack Fleck for the 1955 Open, and that was the *coup de grace* to any chance he had for an unprecedented five U.S. Open championships. Nobody who hits the ball straight and can play a well-controlled left-to-right fade should have any large problems at Lakeside, but the hooker would be well advised to take a long look at it, drink in its arboreal, park-like beauty, and then go find somewhere else to play.

Lakeside's Upset Finish

Rarely in the history of championship golf has expectation been as thoroughly confounded as in the first three U.S. Opens to be staged at Olympic's Lakeside course. All three ended in startlingly similar fashion. Each time they had apparently been won by the emotional crowd favorite—Ben Hogan in 1955, Arnold Palmer in 1966, and Tom Watson in 1987—when a sudden change of fortune let in the unfancied outsider. The first two produced play-off wins for, respectively, Jack Fleck and Billy Casper, with the third claimed by Scott Simpson for his only Major championship success.

The climax of two great chases, and ties, in U.S. Opens—Jack Fleck after Ben Hogan in 1955 and Billy Casper after Arnold Palmer in 1966—the short par-four 18th at Olympic has tempted many players to flirt with the rough on the left. Most wish they had gone for accuracy and safety—the golden rule of the course.

presence beside him or of the prospect of victory, and he was playing the golf of his life.

After seventeen holes he was one ahead. Then, on the last tee, Hogan's foot slipped, he hooked into a patch of vicious rough from which he needed three strokes to recover and Fleck had achieved the seemingly impossible.

If ever there was an instance of a golfer being betrayed by the very qualities that made him the most compelling sporting figure of his time it was Arnold Palmer's failure to win the 1966 Open. For all that Billy Casper played one of the great last rounds, Palmer should never have allowed him to tie. On the 10th tee he was seven strokes ahead and surging to victory. Casper was forgotten and Palmer was intent on beating Hogan's record score of 276, but Casper was playing superb golf and had regained two strokes by the time they reached the short 15th. The flag was close to a bunker that Palmer's shot, just failing to hold the green, found. He took four while Casper holed for a two. On the huge 16th Palmer strove for length after driving into heavy rough and "the finest six I ever made" was of no avail. Casper's flawless

birdie gained him two more strokes. When Palmer again pulled his drive into the rough from the next tee Casper had drawn level. One of the greatest of attacking golfers had attacked when it seemed that prudence decreed a conservative approach, but had Palmer been a prudent golfer he would never have been the idol of millions. Again in the play-off Casper came from behind, two strokes at the turn, and even Palmer's resistance was spent.

When Tom Watson rolled in a 20-foot putt at the 14th on the final day in 1988 to draw level with Scott Simpson, once more convention dictated a win for the favorite; in this case a ninth Major championship. How could Simpson hope to compete against the dominant player of the age? He found a way, just like Fleck and Casper before him, to stifle a legend. From the 14th he managed three birdies in a row, a credible achievement at Olympic, and then surpassed each of them with a save from a greenside bunker at the 17th that can scarcely have been bettered by anyone who has ever played the hole. When Watson misjudged his second shot to the 18th, the Lakeside course had maintained its reputation for the unexpected.

Behind the 18th green the lighthouse at Harbor Town makes for a picturesque backdrop.

Only a week after Harbor Town Golf Links was opened its name was known around the world. Before even a round had been played there, it was chosen as the site for the 1969 Heritage Classic. That tournament was won by Arnold Palmer, his first victory in fourteen months, and all the world heard the news.

Harbor Town's fame has proved to be lasting. The course is spread out among the trees and along the inland coast of Hilton Head Island, in South Carolina. The nearest city is Savannah, Georgia, which is twenty-five miles away. It is one of the most beautiful golf courses in America, but it owes its reputation not so much to its undoubted scenic attractions as to its genuine quality. Each year the Heritage falls after the Masters and usually the week following a major championship is a tough one to attract the top players. It proves no such problem in this instance, the allure of the venue and an alluringly docile part of the southern states weaving its charm. Harbor Town measures 6,916 yards from its extreme back tees and possesses a par of 71. The course has only fifty-six bunkers, eight of which are off the fairways. Every bunker lies absolutely flat; not one is banked, so it is almost impossible to get a buried ball. Fully a third of the bunkers are set up behind or to one side of a green, simply to make the green a better target. There are a dozen bunkers at Harbor Town that nobody has ever been in. The greens are small and so lacking in undulations that three-putting is more a matter of incompetence than a geographic survey that went awry. For

every long par four there is a short par four. For every dog-leg left there is one to the right, and only two of them are so bent that you cannot see the green from the tee. There are no uphill or downhill lies on the course because of the nature of the land, which is so flat that the highest point on the course is only six feet above the lowest.

The course was bulldozed and chain-sawed through sub-tropical vegetation, but Pete Dye, the designer, and Jack Nicklaus, Dye's consultant, went to extraordinary pains to leave trees just where they could come into play: palmettos, towering pines, magnificent magnolias and oaks draped in Spanish moss, thick as tinsel on a Christmas tree. Where the trees stand in groves, they encroach upon the fairways so closely that they make the landing areas look much smaller than they really are.

The 1st hole is a straightforward par four, calling for a mid-iron to the green. The 2nd is typical of the par fives, short but reachable only by two very exacting shots. It calls for a drive down the extreme left side of the fairway, flirting with a bunker on the way. Only from this position is it possible to hit the green with the second shot, for a long bunker and a gigantic oak stand sentinel over the right side.

The 3rd is like the 1st, a drive and mid-iron. Although the fairway is wide, the green is very small. The 4th is one of the most diabolically beautiful par threes a golfer is ever likely to face. It is 198 yards of pure carry, because water fronts the green and lies to the left and to the rear. A flurry of pampas grass lies to the right and, to make matters

America's Oldest Club
Finds a Fine New Home

worse, the green is banked right to the edges with railroad ties between the pampas grass and the water. It is impossible to roll the ball on to the green. Like the 2nd, the par-five 5th can also be reached in two, and again both shots have to be played down the left-hand side to bypass trees near the green—which, to make the second shot even tougher, banks from left to right. Two of the more interesting holes on the front nine are the 7th and the 9th. At the 7th, a 180-yard par three, the green is surrounded by sand except for a spit of land to the rear which provides access. The 9th is one of the shortest of par fours, a mere 337 yards. A long bunker protects the front of the horseshoe-shaped green, which is wrapped around yet another bunker; land on the wrong side and the golfer will have to three-putt purposely to find a way around it.

The 10th and the 11th bend to the left away from the clubhouse, and the 12th makes a quick dogleg to the right with, unusually on an American course, a double green. It is impossible for any golfer to putt from one part to the other in two without holing at least a 30-footer for his second.

The 13th is a fascinating hole. It is not a long par four and it is wise to leave the driver in the bag. Unless the narrow fairway is hit, there is no shot to the green because oak trees narrow the approach. The green itself is Y-shaped, with the stem protected by a bunker that seems to be half an acre in size. More, the elevated green is banked with boards.

The 165-yard 14th, like the 4th, is a par three that is water from tee to green—all of it banked with railroad ties and sawn-off telegraph poles. The four finishing holes then present some of the most thoughtful shot-making a golfer will ever be asked to countenance. The par five 15th is the longest hole on the course. Although the tee shot is straightaway, close to the tiny green the fairway doglegs around a small lake. Consequently, even touring pros often lay up with their second shots.

The 16th is a shortish par four, sharply doglegged to the left. The tee shot must avoid three lonesome pines scattered down the middle of the fairway and the start of a mammoth bunker, fully 130 yards long, on the left. The narrow 17th green widens to the rear, but a strip-trap about 80 yards long skirts the left side and becomes, at the rear, a huge basket trap. For two-thirds of its flight the tee shot must carry water, which continues close along the left side all the way to the green. A par four of 478 yards, the 18th is unforgettable. Both shots must carry the tidal saltmarsh along the shores of Calibogue Sound. Played bravely the hole is absolutely straight, with the tee, the fairway landing area and the green jutting out into the marsh. It is one of the great finishing holes in golf, as events in the Heritage have proved.

This tournament was so named in recognition of the fact that the South Carolina Golf Club—whose home Harbor Town became—is the oldest golf club in North America, having been founded in 1786 at Charleston. In turn the Heritage has been won by some truly gifted golfers, testimony to the worthiness of the course over which it is played. Among the victors have been Johnny Miller, Hale Irwin, Arnold Palmer, Tom Watson, Greg Norman, Nick Faldo, and Jack Nicklaus, who calls it "a thinking man's golf course."

The Course Card

Harbor Town Golf Links, Hilton Head Island. South Carolina

Record: 63,
Jack Nicklaus, 1975;
Dennis Watson, 1984

Hole	Yards	Par
1	414	4
2	505	5
3	411	4
4	198	3
5	535	5
6	419	4
7	180	3
8	466	4
9	337	4
10	436	4
11	438	4
12	413	4
13	378	4
14	165	3
15	575	5
16	376	4
17	192	3
18	478	4
Out	3,465	36
In	3,451	35
Total	**6,916**	**71**

At a time when the trend in U.S. course design was very definitely toward length and large greens, architect Pete Dye, working closely with Jack Nicklaus, created a refreshingly different course at Harbor Town. The greens are smaller than usual, the bunkers fewer but more thoughtfully placed and designed. The premium is on accuracy and a thoughtful approach to a short, subtle course.

"Give us a
Man-sized
Course "...

In the vast Manhattan bedroom known as Westchester County, golf courses are almost as numerous as gas stations. Many of them are undeniably of championship caliber, like Westchester itself and Quaker Ridge. But Winged Foot, across the street from the latter in the town of Mamaroneck, is undoubtedly the best. It has two courses, the East and the West, both designed in 1923 by an eccentric but highly imaginative architect named A.W. Tillinghast. He was one of America's truly great designers, whose creations include Baltusrol, San Francisco Golf Club, the aforementioned Quaker Ridge, Ridgewood, Five Farms, and Fresh Meadow. The winged foot from which the club takes its name is from the emblem of the New York Athletic Club, Manhattan, a number of whose members banded

together to form the suburban golf club. Later, the affiliation between the two was severed but the emblem stayed.

It has long been a locker-room debate among the members as to which course is better. But most professionals who have played both would probably agree on the longer, somewhat more treacherous West, particularly since in 1972-73 it was toughened up in some places for the 1974 U.S. Open. Normally, par for a tournament is dropped from 72 to 70 as it was for that Open, which Hale Irwin won with 287, seven over par. In 1959 Billy Casper had won the same championship with 282, one-putting 31 greens in the process. And way back in 1929 Bobby Jones and Al Espinosa tied at fourteen over, Jones winning a 36-hole play-off by the humiliating margin of 23 strokes. It is not difficult to see why these scores came close to being stratospheric even by U.S. Open standards. The reason lies in the par fours, as everybody learns to their dismay when they first play the course. There are eleven of them, fully nine measuring more than 400 yards. This means that even the good amateur club player capable of hitting a drive 220 yards straight down the middle of the fairway is faced with a second wood shot on all ten, on seven of which he won't be able to reach the green at all. And even the other three are doubtful, for all the greens are elevated and each is protected by bunkers that are not only big but very deep. Tillinghast once explained his design philosophy on bunkers: "I think that I always will adhere to my old theory that a controlled shot to a closely guarded green is the surest test of any man's golf."

In all, Winged Foot has sixty bunkers and every one of its greens has at least two of those deep bunkers

Tillinghast's stunningly tight West course unfolds along two distinct, parallel arms. The lower front nine includes a deceptively easy looking, long par three, the 3rd, which caused so much trouble in the 1959 U.S. Open. The inward half starts with another impressive short hole, the 10th, which precedes a succession of seven doglegs and concludes with the infamous 18th, where the narrow fairway leads into a fiendishly undulating green.

The Course Card

Winged Foot Golf Club, Mamaroneck, New York West course

Record: 64, Jug McSpaden, Goodall Tournament 1946

Hole	Yards	Par
1	446	4
2	411	4
3	216	3
4	453	4
5	515	5
6	324	4
7	166	3
8	442	4
9	471	4
10	190	3
11	386	4
12	535	5
13	212	3
14	418	4
15	417	4
16	457	4
17	449	4
18	448	4
Out	3,444	34
In	3,512	36
Total	**6,956**	**70**

carved out about as close to the putting surface as you can get without actually being on it. Claude Harmon, an astute teacher who was a professional there for over thirty years, once claimed there was not a low-handicap member there who was not an excellent bunker player. It is impossible to chip from them or even to pitch out. A sand iron must be used with a finely timed swing for an explosion shot or, if one has the nerve, a semi-explosion. Alternatively, if the ball is buried in the sand, an outright blast with plenty of muscle is called for.

Many of the finer players among the members have learned from Harmon and other professionals a good way of dealing with a ball buried in sand. They leave their sand-iron in their bag and instead use a pitching wedge or even a 9-iron. The flange on the sand-iron more often than not will not permit the clubhead to cut through the sand. The club just bounces off, thereby moving the ball only a few feet. The thinner flange of the pitching wedge or 9-iron will cut through the sand like a knife. One thing more: they suggest closing the face slightly, for the force of the blow will almost surely open it out to a square position at impact.

The Winged Foot membership list has always been something to talk about, as have the professionals who have worked there. At one time the club had both the Open and Amateur champions of America. Member Dick Chapman won the Amateur in the autumn of 1940 and the following spring the head professional, Craig Wood, won the Open. Harmon, who became head professional six years later, won the Masters in 1948 and three years later member Joe Gagliardi (later Judge Gagliardi) was runner-up in the Amateur. Among the former assistants to Harmon were Jack Burke, who won both the Masters and the PGA Championship in 1956, Dave Marr, winner of the PGA in 1965, and Mike Souchak, a star on the tournament circuit who long-shared the record for the low round on tour at 61. Dick Mayer, who won the U.S. Open in 1957, was a member at Winged Foot before turning professional. Harmon's son Butch, a former assistant pro at Winged Foot, has become one of the game's most renowned teachers, his pupils including Greg Norman and Tiger Woods. It is certainly no accident that so many fine exponents have emerged from Winged Foot or have chosen to work there.

The course perfectly exemplifies the design philosophy of Tillinghast, which he himself succinctly sums up this way: "In planning holes there are thousands of combinations, each offering a mute appeal for recognition. It is necessary to decide on the collection which will work out economically and satisfactorily from many angles. But this is sure: every hole must have individuality and must be sound. Often it is necessary to get from one section to another over ground which is not suited to easy construction, but that troublesome hole must be made to stand right up with the others. If it has not got anything about it that might make it respectable, it has got to have quality knocked into it until it can hold its head up in polite society."

There can be no doubts about Winged Foot's social standing or of Tillinghast's confidence in his own workmanship, as his assessment of the course shows: "As the various holes came to life they were of a sturdy breed. The contouring of the greens places a premium on the placement of the drives, but never is there the necessity of facing a prodigious carry of the sink-or-swim sort. It is only the knowledge that the next shot must be played with rifle accuracy that brings the realization that the drive must be placed. The holes are like men, all rather similar from foot to neck, but with the greens showing the same varying characters as human faces."

Looking at those lush, velvet greens and emerald fairways, it is difficult to believe that Tillinghast had to move 7,200 tons of rock and cut down 7,800 trees to create them. The magnitude of his task was in stark contrast to the brevity of the instructions he received from the gentlemen of the New York Athletic Club: "Give us a man-sized course," they said. Tillinghast's response was a Herculean achievement.

The beautifully manicured fairways are a feature of Winged Foot, one of the most difficult tests of golf in America.

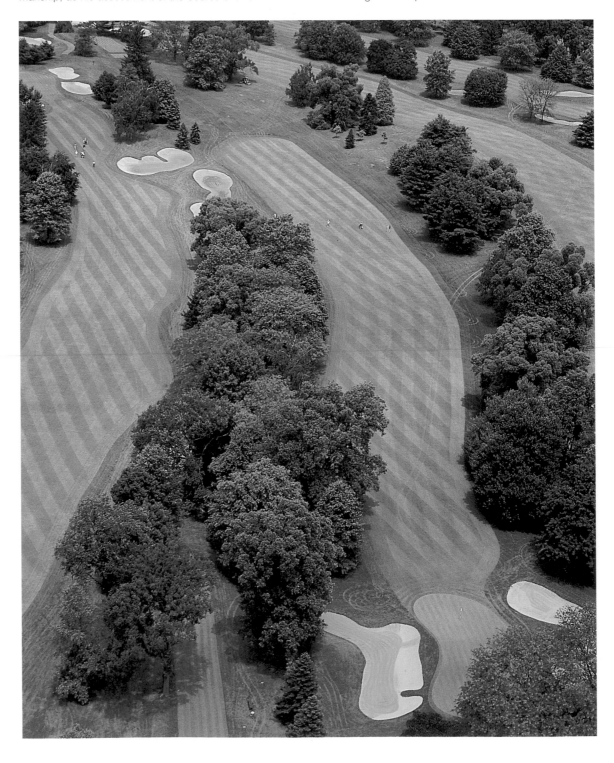

Love Conquers All

It was the sort of performance that the hugely talented Davis Love had threatened throughout his career and, for a true traditionalist, it could not have come at a better place than Winged Foot.

Love's father was a teaching professional whose best finish in the USPGA Championship was 55th in 1967. In 1988 he died in a plane crash and for two years or more Love would find his mind wandering when he should have been concentrating on his golf. Thirty years after his father's career-best in the USPGA, however, he put together the sort of performance in the same tournament that players can only dream of achieving once or twice in a career. His winning score of 11 under was scarcely believable around a course so penal; in three of the four rounds he shot 66, including the last two, which gave him a five-shot winning margin over Justin Leonard, who had won the Open Championship at Royal Troon a month previously. One of the more unusual occurrences in a Major championship also happened at Winged Foot in the 1984 U.S. Open. The protagonists were Fuzzy Zoeller and Greg Norman, who were level playing the final hole. Norman, one group in front, holed from 45 feet on the home green and set off after the ball with a jubilant spring to his stride. Back in the fairway, Zoeller waved a white towel in mock surrender. What Zoeller did not know was that Norman's putt was for a par not birdie, the Australian having missed the green with his approach. Someone in the crowd alerted him and he made the par which secured a play-off. They were the only players under par that year and the following day, only Zoeller could manage the feat, shooting 67 to Norman's 75. They walked off the last green arm in arm.

The 10th and 17th

Tillinghast's Finest

Two holes, the 10th and the 17th, stand out at Winged Foot. Jack Nicklaus describes the 444-yard 17th as "one of those text-book tests of golf—a hole that really pits the player against the designer." The hole is a slight dogleg to the right, the crook of which contains four huge bunkers. On either side of a slim, curving green are long, well-like bunkers. In Nicklaus's words: "A straight tee shot is a definite necessity. The second shot requires a long iron, which again must be hit with great accuracy to a well-trapped, extremely narrow green."

Two of Winged Foot's four short holes are at least two club lengths longer than the 10th, but it is a superior hole. Seen from the tee, the hole is not all that imposing. At 190 yards it cannot be called short. The broad, deep green tilts invitingly toward the tee. Directly in front is an opening between the two flanking kidney-shaped bunkers. The third bunker, on the left center of the fairway, is so short of the green as to be practically out of play, although the handicap golfer must be conscious that it has to be carried.

It is only at the green itself that the hole becomes imposing. One look at its smooth, subtle undulations brings worries not of two-putting but of three-putting. With the flagstick at the front of the green and the ball well behind it, comes the possibility of a chip back or, worse, playing from one of those bunkers, both of which are deeper than a man is tall. A shot out of either of

The 17th: 444 yards par 4

these, played not quite tenderly enough, can easily see the ball back into the other one. When the flagstick is to the rear of the green, a club too many could result in hitting into the out-of-bounds area, which is no more than thirty feet behind the putting surface. The hooked shot will land in a pack of trees on the left.

The hole requires precise judgment in club selection, the shot must be hit truly after that and then the putt must be stroked, not jabbed. All the hazards and other trouble are in plain view from the tee. There is nothing tricky about the 10th. The greatest endorsement the hole ever received came from A.W. Tillinghast himself. He considered it the finest par three he had ever built.

Pinehurst was the first resort to offer 72 holes of golf, but it was Donald Ross's Number 2 course that brought it world renown. Ross created a masterpiece, blending visual harmony with a balanced array of hazards: mounds guarding the greens, wire grass and pine needles waiting off the fairways, and greens falling away on all sides. As Sam Snead put it after one North and South Open: "You've got to hit every shot on old Number 2. "

Donald Ross Creates his

Masterpiece

There is no resort in the United States that is quite so saturated with golf as Pinehurst, a charming little New England-style village located in North Carolina some three hours east of Augusta. Quite fortuitously, and long before anyone had golf in mind, a pharmacist from Boston named James W. Tufts conceived the notion of starting a modest winter resort in the South so that other New Englanders of modest means and advancing years could escape the bitter winter weather. He finally chose the Sandhills of North Carolina because of the mild climate and the reasonable price of $1 an acre then being asked for this rather barren, cutover timberland. Nobody but an incorrigible optimist or an oaken-hearted New Englander would ever have had the temerity to think he could create anything habitable and attractive on such desolate land.

The North Carolina Sandhills are a geological phenomenon dating back to the ice age. They reach a hundred miles inland from the Atlantic and, except for the thick stands of pine forest, they provide much the same sort of terrain as is found on the linksland of Great Britain. Thus, when James W. Tufts and his pioneering neighbors of Pinehurst suddenly found themselves intrigued by this peculiar new game of golf somewhere around 1897-98, they had the ideal landscape on which to build an experimental course.

The year 1900, however, provided the two events that shaped Pinehurst's future. In March, Harry Vardon stopped by and played four rounds over the rather primitive eighteen holes of Pinehurst Country Club's Number 1 course. Just watching the great Vardon was enough to whet the appetites of the locals for this game. In December Donald J. Ross arrived in Pinehurst to assume the duties of resident professional. At the time of his arrival in Pinehurst, Donald Ross was a young man, a Scot from Dornoch who had taken his apprenticeship under Old Tom Morris at St. Andrews and then served a few years as professional and greenkeeper at Royal Dornoch. His youthful enthusiasm and natural gift for the "feel" of the game were just what the budding new resort needed. Within his first year at Pinehurst, Ross started to build the first nine holes of what is now the justly famous Pinehurst Number 2 course, and he completed the original eighteen holes in 1907. So great was the artistic triumph of Pinehurst Number 2, even in those Paleolithic times of sand greens, scruffy fairways and only 5,860 yards, that Ross eventually became the doyen of American golf architecture. All these years on, we can pronounce with complete certainty that it is a grotesque oversight on the part of the United States Golf Association that no U.S. Open has been played there, though 1999 will thankfully bring such dereliction of profound good sense to an end. Through the years, Ross was continually altering and improving Pinehurst Number 2 as equipment and technique required until he arrived at the course we know today, one of the masterpieces of golfing architecture of its particular genre. That is to say, Pinehurst Number 2 is a kind of idealization of the old-fashioned parkland courses that characterized American golf architecture until World War II—tree-lined, following the natural terrain, with small greens and ample but not profligate use of bunkers. It is the kind of course that puts the emphasis on the planning and precision of the golf shot rather than the great strength that the more recent courses demand, although, as it stands today, Number 2 measures an imposing 7,020 yards and calls forth the use of every club in the bag during the progress of a round. In addition to these qualities, Number 2 has the added advantage of being located on the Sandhills, thus giving it something of the playing qualities of a linksland course.

In the seventy-one years since James W. Tufts first began to develop his resort, the timberlands of Pinehurst have grown back to their full maturity. As a result, nearly every one of the eighteen holes of Number 2 is a separate aesthetic entity unto itself, completely surrounded by the tall pines and shut off from the rest of the course. Except for those who may be engaged on the same hole, a player has the feeling of being entirely isolated from the rest of the world, golfing or otherwise. Aside from whatever one's problems may be on the golf course and at Number 2 they can often be most humiliating—there is an atmosphere of peace and solitude that is seldom found in golf or any other social game. The course opens with a rather uncomplicated hole of 396 yards, which places no great premium on distance and with plenty of fairway space on which to unlimber. The only really serious trouble is the boundary fence that runs the length of the 1st and 2nd holes on the left but not unduly close to the line of play. At the 2nd the distance begins to build, and here is a hole requiring a strong second shot. At the 3rd, a shortish two-shotter, finesse suddenly comes into play, and the emphasis is on strategy, with a birdie awaiting those who have their shots

The Course Card

Pinehurst Country Club, North Carolina Number 2

Record: 62, Gibby Gilbert, World Open 1973

Hole	Yards	Par
1	396	4
2	441	4
3	335	4
4	547	5
5	445	4
6	212	3
7	401	4
8	487	5
9	166	3
10	578	5
11	433	4
12	415	4
13	374	4
14	436	4
15	201	3
16	531	5
17	190	3
18	432	4
Out	3,430	36
In	3,590	36
Total	**7,020**	**72**

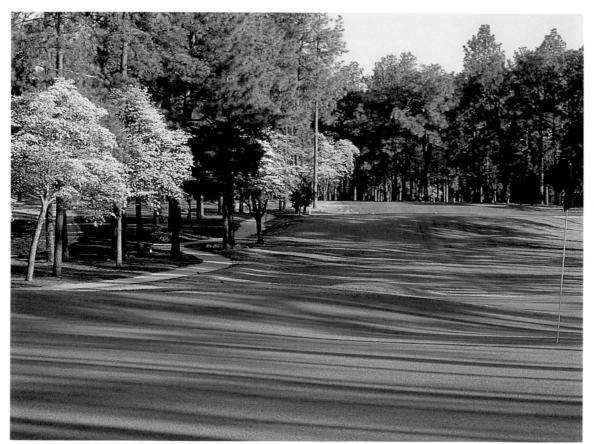

A superb hole, lined with trees and with a green falling away to bunkers at the sides and back, the 187-yard 17th is typical of Pinehurst Number 2.

Patty Berg, right, and "Babe" Zaharias were the first women elected to the World Golf Hall of Fame. Four times world champion, Berg has been a leading figure in women's golf ever since she first reached the final of the U.S. Amateur in 1935 at the age of seventeen. Glenna Collette Vare and Joyce Wethered were elected in 1975. The World Golf Hall of Fame closed in 1994, and moved to the newly opened World Golf Village in St. Augustine, Florida.

The 5th and 8th

Fairest of the Fair

Although the 445-yard 5th is not the longest par four on the course, the player is probably more aware of distance there than at the longer 8th, and it is certainly more demanding. The drive, over a quietly rising crest of fairway toward a gentle valley beyond, is the only blind one on the course, but is in no way distracting because of it. According to the length of the tee shot the second can be anything from wood to medium iron and is a most exacting stroke. The green, which leans toward the player, is angled away to the left on rising ground with large bunkers on either hand. Unless the approach is played from the right side of the fairway there is no clear entrance to the green, and the shot must carry the forward of the left-hand bunkers. The 5th is a truly beautiful hole, as indeed are all the par fours, not one of which is similar to the others.

The 8th hole, a par four of 487 yards from the championship tee, plunges into a longvalley from where the fairway rises smoothly to a green which, because of

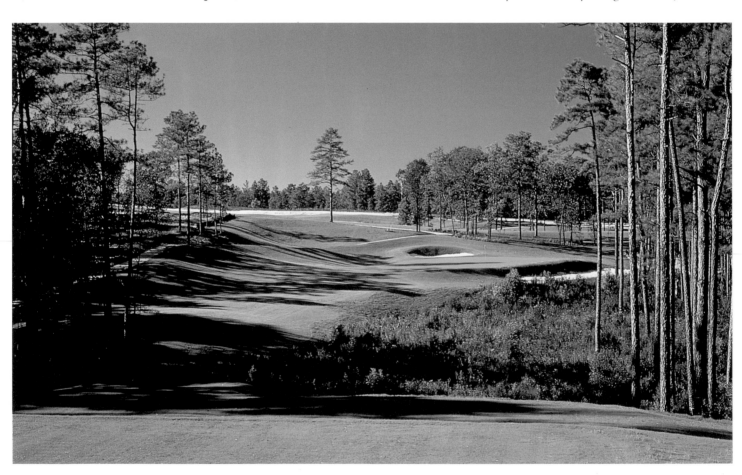

The drive at the 5th is blind, but should be long because of the exacting second into an angled green.

under control. The 4th and 5th are played over the only hilly portion of the course, the 4th providing the first of three par fives that can be reached in two with a couple of very well-executed shots. In fact, the 10th is the only one of the four three-shotters that the big player cannot expect to reach in two if he is on his mettle. The length of Number 2 is not to be found in the par fours nor even in unusually long par threes (the longest of these is 212 yards) but in the two-shotters, most of them calling for a big drive and a powerful second. Unlike so many of the better U.S. parkland courses, Pinehurst is virtually without water. The only

water hole is the 16th, where a small pond in front of the tee requires a carry of no more than 180 yards on the proper line of play, yet the water does serve to fashion the tee shot and increase the problems of mound and bunker beyond. This is the second of a stretch of four closing holes that make Number 2 one of the most exciting courses for tournament play that exists in America.

Probably because it is somewhat off the beaten path it has not entertained nearly the amount of national championship and international golf that it deserves. The 1999 U.S. Open will be the second Major championship—the

Left: The fifth hole at Pinehurst No 2 is a truly wonderful par four, where a drive to a tilting fairway needs to be followed by a raking long iron to an extravagantly protected green. Par is always a good score on this hole.

its slight elevation above the surrounding land, will hold only a truly struck shot. Such greens are a notable feature of Donald Ross's design. His intention was that a good shot should always be rewarded but that the fractionally erring one, leaking a little either way, would tend to slip off the putting surface. Punishment for missing his greens usually is not too severe but recovery can involve a variety of shots and decisions as to the most effective one to use—chips, little throw-up pitches, even

bumbles with a putter. Ross had no call to protect his greens with thick fringes, common to many U.S. courses, which can harshly penalize a good shot that is no more than a matter of inches too strong or too wide.

Pinehurst Number 2 is a monument to the genius of Ross, who spoke of it as being "the fairest test of championship golf I have ever designed." Even the most carping of professional golfers could hardly disagree, and the 5th and 8th holes are striking examples of Ross's skill.

first was the 1936 USPGA, which was a matchplay event in those days—to be played at Pinehurst. The Ryder Cup matches brought international golf in 1951, and in 1962 the U.S. Amateur championship was played there for the first time.

Since 1901, however, the North and South championship, an amateur tournament ranking in prestige only just below the national Amateur championship itself, has been played annually at Pinehurst, first on the rather short Number 1 course but since 1909 on Number 2. In 1903, the North and South Open was inaugurated there, too, but as the purses and galleries of professional golf became the paramount concern following World War II, the latter event was abandoned. It will be remembered in the record books largely for the 1940 renewal, which was the first professional tournament won by Ben Hogan at the start of his fabulous string of victories that were to extend for the succeeding fourteen years.

The World Open was played there for the first time in 1973 and for it the par-five 8th hole was shortened by some twenty yards to make it a par four of 464 yards. Gibby Gilbert set the record of 62 for this par-71 course. His score was equaled by Tom Watson, the eventual winner. The Tour Championship, the annual end of season extravaganza for the leading thirty players on the PGA Tour, was played in consecutive years at Pinehurst in 1991 and 1992, the winners being two noted shot-makers, Craig Stadler and Paul Azinger. In 1994 the U.S. Senior Open was played there and won by the South African Simon Hobday.

Nowadays the golf at Pinehurst is largely social. Particularly in the fall and spring when the Carolina climate is propitious, groups of friends will travel to Pinehurst from all over the eastern and southern part of the country to spend a few days in the soothing environs of Pinehurst's peaceful little village, living quietly in one of the numerous little inns or the large and stately Pinehurst Hotel, playing golf by day and talking golf well into the evening. For aside from the splendid testing qualities of Number 2, there are currently seven other excellent eighteen-hole courses of considerably less rigor fanning out from the pleasant clubhouse on the hill. Since James W. Tufts first conceived this semi-paradisical retreat for winter-bound New Englanders, four generations of the Tufts family have taken an active part in the development of the community. To the world of golf, the best-known of these is James W.'s grandson, Richard S. Tufts, a man who served the USGA selflessly for several decades in numerous capacities, including the presidency. Among his many great services to amateur golf was his contribution to the unification and standardization of the USGA and Royal and Ancient versions of the Rules of Golf and the inauguration of the World Amateur Team Championship, known as the Eisenhower Trophy. In 1948 the Pinehurst Resort was purchased by the Club Corporation of America, a large company that is the owner and operator of private country clubs, city clubs, and athletic clubs. The resort continues to be developed—in 1995 an eighth course was opened to mark the club's centenary and, a year later, opened to general acclaim—but its character has not been altered.

When the World Golf Hall of Fame was opened at Pinehurst in 1974 Walter Hagen was an automatic choice by the Golf Writers of America as one of the thirteen initial members. Winner of four British Opens, two U.S. Opens, and five USPGA titles, the extrovert Hagen was without peer in the ranks of professional golf in the 1920s.

There could be no more enduring tribute to the quality of his design than the United States Open at Merion in 1971. After seventy-two holes Jack Nicklaus and Lee Trevino, two of the greatest of all golfers, alone had matched the par of 280 in conditions that were uniformly fair throughout. For that Open, Merion measured 6,482 yards, only 12 yards longer than the shortest course used for the championship since World War I, and hundreds shorter than most of the others. Out of that length, 1,135 yards were contained in the only two par fives, the 2nd and the 4th. It is this lack of length with seemingly no way of remedying it, that has prevented the United States Golf Association from returning to the course since David Graham's victory in 1981. It is an acute loss.

At 6,482 yards Merion is the shortest course used for the U.S. Open since World War II. Yet the leading scores—Hogan's 287 in 1950 and the even-par 280 of Trevino and Nicklaus in 1971—reflect just how difficult Hugh Wilson's course is to master. Narrow par fours, 120 telling bunkers and tight, fast greens make it one of America's great golfing trials. It was ironic that it took a virtual unknown, Lee Mackey, to humble Merion with a record 64, including seven birdies and one bogey, in the opening round of the 1950 Open.

A Flawless Setting for
High Drama

Tommy Armour, the "Silver Scot," is one of many pros to have suffered at Merion. He sliced his tee shot out-of-bounds on the 6th in every round of the 1934 Open, ending with 314.

Some years ago an informal poll was taken among three of America's leading golf architects: Robert Trent Jones, Pete Dye, and George Fazio. They were asked to pick the finest examples of United States course design in which they had not themselves been involved. Between them they named some two dozen courses, but agreed unanimously on only six: Pine Valley, Augusta National, Seminole, Pebble Beach, Pinehurst Number 2, and Merion.

Ironically enough, four of those six had been designed by complete architectural amateurs. Fourteen of Pine Valley's eighteen holes were designed by a Philadelphia businessman named George Crump; Augusta National was Bobby Jones's first try at architecture (although with the inestimable counsel of Alister Mackenzie); Pebble Beach was designed by Jack Neville and Douglas Grant, two amateur players from California; and Merion was the first effort of a transplanted Scot, Hugh Wilson, a member of the old West course when it was affiliated to the Merion Cricket Club, whose members at the time wanted a championship layout. They dispatched young Wilson to Scotland and England to take a postgraduate course in British linksland before transforming a section of Philadelphia's Main Line—the long stretch of the city's socially elite suburbs—into a "golf links" no proper Philadelphian would be ashamed of. It remains the only complete course that Wilson was to write his name to, for he died at the relatively young age of forty-six and was never able to pursue his newly found vocation.

Bobby Jones played in his first Amateur championship at Merion, leading the field after the first of the two qualifying rounds. This happened in the autumn of 1916 when Jones was a lad of fourteen standing all of 5 feet 4 inches but weighing a chunky 165 pounds (in contrast to the spindly, sickly boy who had been practically pushed on to his neighborhood golf course—East Lake near Atlanta). He shot a 74, ridiculously high by today's standards, but it was good enough. He was playing speedy bent grass greens, not the coarse and harsh Bermuda green of his native south, for the first time in his life.

The 6th of the West was a short par four, which Jones hit with a drive and a mere pitch with his wedge. The ball ended 30 feet past the flagstick. Forgetting that he was no longer playing on his home greens, Jones hit a horrifying putt that sailed back past the cup, over the green, and into a brook in front of it. That afternoon, the "Kid from Dixie" had to play the newer East course. Suffering from stagefright, he shot 89, with every golf fan in Philadelphia and every sportswriter in America peering over his shoulder at every stroke. But he still qualified, eventually going out of the competition to Bob Gardner, the defending champion, in the quarter-final. Eight years later, again at Merion, he won the first of his record five U.S. Amateur titles and in 1930 the last of them, achieving the Grand Slam in the process. If the years of Jones were enough for any course to achieve immortality, 1950 brought a new drama when an unknown, Lee Mackey, broke the U.S. Open record with a first round of 64. But a colossus, Ben Hogan, was to bestride the stage that year like some golfing Caesar, casting Mackey's moment of glory into deep shadow.

Little more than a year before, Hogan had been badly hurt when the car in which he and his wife were traveling collided head-on with a bus. Only a man of indomitable fortitude could have returned to golf as quickly as Hogan did and he was still in considerable pain when the Open began at Merion in 1950.

He played through the competition in great discomfort, at one time stopping the car taking him back to the hotel because he felt so ill. On the final day, the Open reached its climax and Hogan reached for his astonishing reserves of courage. There were two rounds left, thirty-six holes. Hogan managed the first round with a 72, suffering no ill effects. As a precautionary measure during the afternoon round, he had his caddie pick the ball out of the cup for him so he would not have to aggravate the pain in his legs by bending over. He made the turn in 36; par on the back nine would give him a winning score of 282, four under the 286 which he had anticipated would be enough to triumph. As he started the final nine he was seized by an extreme cramp in his left leg. By the time he reached the 18th green near the clubhouse, the pain had become so acute that he thought about withdrawing—not because he did not think he could win, but because he didn't think he could walk, much less play.

That he did not withdraw is now history, and he stumbled home with a total of 287, level with George Fazio and Lloyd Mangrum. When he won the play-off the next day it was an anticlimax, the denouement taking place on the 16th green when Mangrum was penalized two strokes for blowing a bug off his ball. Hogan then scored a birdie-two on the 230-yard par-three 17th with a 4-wood and a 60-foot putt, for the second and greatest of his four Open wins.

Ten years later Jack Nicklaus, then a young amateur, shot 269 for four rounds, eighteen strokes better than Hogan had scored in 1950. American golf history has marched on at Merion.

In a sense the course is old-fashioned. It covers no more than 110 acres, compared with the 250 acres most U.S. courses take in order to accommodate the trappings now needed to back a golf course project financially. There are 120 bunkers, which may seem a lot until compared with the 280 that Oakmont once had and to those on the Old course at St. Andrews. Hugh Wilson placed each one

The Course Card

Merion Golf Club, Ardmore East course

Hole	Yards	Par
1	362	4
2	536	5
3	181	3
4	600	5
5	418	4
6	420	4
7	350	4
8	360	4
9	193	3
10	310	4
11	369	4
12	371	4
13	127	3
14	408	4
15	366	4
16	428	4
17	220	3
18	463	4
Out	3,420	36
In	3,062	34
Total	**6,482**	**70**

Olin Dutra (left) made up eight shots over the last thirty-six holes to win the 1934 Open at Merion.

Chick Evans followed his 1916 Open win with the Amateur title when he coined the phrase, the "white faces of Merion" for Hugh Wilson's traps.

exactly where it ought to be. When Chick Evans won the U.S. Amateur there in 1916, he nicknamed them the "white faces of Merion" after the glaring sand from a nearby quarry with which they had been filled.

Merion straddles Ardmore Avenue, and the 1st hole goes directly toward it. Eleven holes—the 2nd to the 12th—lie on the other side. There are only two holes at Merion, the 2nd and the 4th, that play to a par of five. On the back nine there are none—hence the par of 70. The first hole is a short par four—as an opening hole should be—bending slightly to the right but not quite enough to be classified as a dogleg. The green is clearly visible from the tee, but so are nine bunkers, most of them on the right side of the fairway to snare a slice. Once they are bypassed only a pitch to the green is left. Across Ardmore Avenue there is a completely different style of hole: a skinny, 536-yard par five uphill, with out-of-bounds all the way along the right side. Then follows a fairly long par three—not quite 200 yards—to a large green that is hard to miss. This, in turn, is followed by the longest hole on the course, a par five of 600 yards. It is straight and bunkered only for the most errant shot—two pleasant, straight woods followed by a 6- or 7-iron across a thin stream to a very deep green. It is guarded to the rear and on both sides by six bunkers to trap the foolhardy who try to reach the green in two. Four par fours follow. All are of medium length, the longest being the 5th, 418 yards but with very little bunkering, and the shortest the 7th, a mere 350 yards. The 6th and 7th present no sand problems off the tee, but they are very strategically trapped around the greens. Hugh Wilson never put a single extraneous bunker into Merion; despite the fact that there are 120 of them, every single one is for play, not display.

The 8th hole is a perfect example of his use of sand-traps. There is a bunker short to the right of the fairway for the slicer and another far to the left for the hooker. In other words, the short hitter has to be aware of the first trap and the long hitter, ignoring the first, has to be aware of the second. If both are avoided only a short iron is left, since the hole is just 360 yards long. Here, Wilson formed a snake-like trap to protect the entire front of the panhandle green, the handle of which faces the player. If the pin is on the handle, it is one of the most challenging and nerve-racking par fours to be found anywhere. The par-three 9th is some 195 yards long, but the tee shot is from a hill to a green in a small valley so it requires less club than that distance usually calls for. A brook, and a lagoon that spurs off it, have to be carried; but they lie well short of the huge green, which is guarded by six bunkers to the left, right and rear.

From the 9th green there is a walk up a hill to the 10th tee. At 310 yards and a par of four, it falls just short of being a joke until played. Big hitters have often driven nearly hole-high, only to find themselves with a pitch as delicate as picking up a teacup filled to the brim. Both sides of the green are edged by sand, and the oblong green has a dozen varieties of pin positions.

The golfer now faces the 11th, which is played in the opposite direction and, at 369 yards, is really not much longer than the 10th. The tee shot is into a slight valley and the pitch, although not overly long, is across a creek to a green banked with rocks. In 1930 Bobby Jones—having won the British Amateur at St. Andrews, the British Open at Hoylake and the U.S. Open at Interlachen—then stood dormie-eight on Eugene Homans, needing only a niblick shot to the green to be the first and only man to have won all four championships in a single season. He flicked the ball upon the green, took two putts to halve with Homans and so won, 8 and 7, to ensure himself a place in golf history. It took a body of marines to protect him from the slaps on the back and the handshakes of the immense gallery.

Right: The 9th is typical of Wilson's tight greens guarded by a brook, lagoon, and several bunkers.

The 11th was also the scene of a moment of comedy during the U.S. Open four years later. Bobby Cruickshank—the "Wee Scot," as he affectionately came to be known in America—was very much in contention. After a good drive into the valley he had to carry the brook in front of the green. He hit his approach to the green a little "fat"; the ball plopped into the water.

To everyone's astonishment it hit a rock in the brook and bounded onto the green. Cruickshank was so elated that he threw his niblick into the air and turned to the gallery in disbelief. As everybody cheered the club fell and hit him squarely on the head, knocking him to his knees. "Aye," said Bobby as he rubbed his head, "that's the first time I've made a par hitting two rocks on the same hole." The 12th is again a drive off a high tee, with no drastic situations for the moderately straight driver. There are bunkers to the left but they are of no concern to the long hitter—mainly because they serve as hazards for the short hitter off the parallel 11th. The hole is a dogleg to the right where there are trees that cannot be carried and which therefore dictate the placing of the drive. The second shot is uphill, thus compensating for the downhill tee shot, and the long green now facing the golfer is bounded everywhere except in front by bunkers, all of which drop off quickly into rough.

The green sits alongside Ardmore Avenue and may be unique in that it is probably the only putting surface that lies not two feet from out-of-bounds. Walter Hagen, one of the most delicate putters who ever lived, once overhit his putt and rolled it into the street—thus leaving him with another improbable record: the first important player in a major contest to hit a putt out-of-bounds! Next to the 7th at Pebble Beach, where the wind is always a major consideration, the 13th at Merion—only 127 yards long—may be the most stringent par three in America. It is a mere pitch to the green, but it has to be perfect because there is no margin for error whatsoever. Directly in front of the green is one of those "white faces" and to the left and behind it are three more, staring like ghosts. The putting surface is wide but not deep, and a misjudged shot or mis-hit is certain to find one of them. Since the first is deep and the others slanted, getting out and on to the green presents an even more tender shot than that which has to be played off the tee.

The next two holes, both par fours, are tightened by a road down the left side which is out-of-bounds. For the 1971 U.S. Open the 14th played at 408 yards, some 30 yards shorter than its full length. The hole doglegs left and from the back of the tee the trees on the left emphasize the need to draw the ball around the corner and clear of the traps on the right. The second shot requires only a mid-iron to an oval green, protected by three sprawling traps. The 15th is another drive and a mid-iron. It doglegs to the right and the well-placed drive has to carry two traps on that side to open up the green, which is angled diagonally across the line. Two traps flank the left side and a large bunker eats into the front, making it very difficult to go for the pin when it is placed anywhere on the right side.

The last three holes at Merion provide a great championship finish. The "quarry hole"—the 16th—is 428 yards long off an elevated tee through a valley that stops at an old overgrown quarry which, fortunately, cannot be reached with the drive; the second is the worrying shot with anything from a 4-iron to a 4-wood needed and the golfer has to succeed in carrying the green on the fly.

The 17th, played in the reverse direction, is the 220-yard par three where Hogan made a momentous two in the play-off for the 1950 U.S. Open. The quarry lies at the foot of the tee, but does not have to be taken into account any more than it does at the 18th, which again comes back across it. The 18th is 463 yards long, calling for a wood shot—or at least a long iron—to the green. It is immortalized in a photograph of Hogan making his second shot to the green with a 1-iron. It was the last time he used the club, for as he signed his card it was carried off by a souvenir hunter. One of the men Hogan beat in 1950 was George Fazio, now a golf architect and adviser to the United States Golf Association. Nobody is more qualified than he to assess Merion, which he rates alongside Pine Valley as the kind of course he most admires. Why? "It has character," he says. "It is challenging, without being backbreaking."

The 1st

An Elusive Touch of Poetry

Almost anyone can design a par five or a par four that can be reached in regulation figures only by the supremely long hitters and seldom by the average player. The same holds true for a par-three that will accept only one shot. But it takes a touch of the poet to lay out a short par four like the 1st at Merion, a mere 363 yards long but one of the great opening holes in golf.

It is a dogleg to the right, in which the only problem for the average golfer lies in his tendency to slice. The hole has no fewer than nine bunkers, only three of which are on the left, two alongside the fairway and one beside the green. A solitary trap lies in the middle of the fairway, but it is far out of reach of the amateur. All the others line the right side of the fairway clear to the green, which is so exquisitely contoured that it contains half a dozen different pin positions. The putting surface is pear shaped and slopes gently from right to left and from the front to the back, where there is a tiny, shallow trap. Thus, while the second shot may be nothing more than a mere pitch, it must be very exact. For the professional the problems from the tee are somewhat different. He must see that he does not drive into the two bunkers on the left, since he is more prone to hook, or right through the very broad fairway into the rough, which contains a series of mounds from which it is a near impossibility to pitch anywhere near the flagstick. Many of the holes at Merion have more instant appeal but the golfer who plays there regularly finds that he appreciates more and more the subtleties of the 1st. It combines the two most difficult objectives sought by a master architect: a great opening hole, and a great short par four. That achievement alone shows why Hugh Wilson was able to build such intricate poetry into the design of the Merion course.

Touches that Mold Tradition

In his determination to make Merion East a course apart, Hugh Wilson concerned himself with the kind of detail that so many other architects ignore. Over the years these touches have conspired with momentous golfing events to create a tradition at Merion that is rare among U.S. courses. One of Wilson's ideas, which he picked up from Sunningdale in Berkshire during his long pilgrimage to Britain, was to do away with flags and to mark the holes with wicker baskets atop the usual flagsticks. For many years the baskets were woven in the maintenance shop at Merion.

Although now out of favor elsewhere, wicker baskets were once widely used in Britain because they could be seen from any angle and did not aid a player in judging wind direction and strength. In the unlikely, but not entirely inconceivable, event of a ball lodging in a basket, the Rules of Golf permitted a player to remove the ball and, without penalty, place it on the edge of the hole.

The Deepest South

Gets its First Great Course

The Course Card

Seminole Golf
Club, North Palm
Beach, Florida

Record: 60,
Claude Harmon, 1948

Hole	Yards	Par
1	370	4
2	387	4
3	501	5
4	450	4
5	195	3
6	383	4
7	432	4
8	235	3
9	494	5
10	382	4
11	403	4
12	367	4
13	168	3
14	499	5
15	495	5
16	399	4
17	175	3
18	417	4
Out	3,447	36
In	3,305	36
Total	6,752	72

Golf in the tropical climate of southern Florida is a seasonal thing except to those stalwarts who will forsake their air-conditioning for the Turkish-bath atmosphere of the months from May through October. During the dead months, when their members are in the northern states or the spas of Europe, clubs like Seminole tend their courses only just enough to prevent them from running to seed. It is, then, something of a miracle that the best of these courses—and there is none better than Seminole—can be brought to such a peak of perfection during the winter.

For many years, Seminole was so pampered by a singularly devoted golfer, Christopher J. Dunphy, who had been a close friend of and uncompromising competitor against just about all the leading amateurs and professionals of his time. In fact, when one thought of Seminole, one thought of Chris Dunphy. Dunphy's love affair with golf began in earnest soon after World War I. He was employed at the time by Mr. Edward B. McLean, a wealthy Cincinnati newspaper publisher who was himself a golfing enthusiast, so in his younger days Dunphy was able to spend a good deal of his leisure on the famous courses of America and Europe in company with his employer. After McLean's death, Dunphy and his wife settled down in Palm Beach, and Dunphy began to spend more and more of his time playing at Seminole.

The club had been built in the 1920s during that prosperous period in American life. The course was laid out by Donald Ross, who was the architect for so many of the outstanding courses on the East Coast of the United States. With assistance from a former Tennessee mountaineer, T. Claiborn Watson, Ross designed a true linksland course over the Florida sand ridges adjacent to the Atlantic Ocean some fifteen miles north of the exclusive Palm Beach winter colony. At the time, the club was no more than a half-hour drive from the colony over an uncrowded highway. Ross and Watson's course was the first truly fine test of golf in that southernmost part of America, but the exclusive and expensive nature of the club meant only a few of the very rich ever had a chance to play it. From the back tees it was a long course, but its principal feature was its profligate use of large bunkers covered with snow-white sand. Even today, the bunkers, which have grown to more than 200 in number, are the most conspicuous feature of the course. As was the case with so many of the enterprises of America's wealthy businessmen, the fortunes of Seminole declined during the great Depression, but the club survived through the attention of a few deeply devoted members. When World War II left it with virtually no patronage, there was some question whether it would survive. It was at the end of this bleak period that Dunphy arrived and restored the Seminole course and club to its former glory.

The war over, members began to drift back to Palm Beach, and a new generation of the rich discovered the area as a winter playground. It was then that Dunphy assumed the role of Seminole's *ex officio* ringmaster. He spent countless hours with Watson, who had remained on as greenskeeper ever since the course was first built, restoring and improving Seminole. New hybrid grasses of the Bermuda strain were added to the fairways and greens to give them firmness and depth and to keep them in first-class playing condition during the latter part of the season when the less hardy grasses begin to die out. As a result, the ball sits up on the Seminole fairways as if it had been ever so gently placed on a soft cushion. The greens, with their Bermuda base, are large with subtle borrows, averaging around 7,500 to 8,000 square feet, and they are as true as any greens can be in that humid region with its constant spray of salty mist from the ocean. The club's annual professional-amateur tournament was discontinued in 1960 and had the largest pool connected to any U.S. tournament during its time, reaching several hundred thousand dollars. It was always interesting, however, to see the professionals struggling with Seminole's complex design of sand and water, and it should be noted that few of them ever dominated it. Nonetheless, Claude Harmon, who was for many years the distinguished resident professional at Seminole in the winter months, once scored a course record 60. A map of his remarkable round hangs on the clubhouse wall. The sight of the Seminole course on a balmy day with a brisk wind blowing in off the Atlantic is one to be cherished. The sweep of the rolling green fairways, punctuated by the multitude of dazzling white bunkers and the tall palms leaning with the breeze, is one of the most spectacular vistas to be found in this flat, tropical country, the highest point of which is only 65 feet above sea-level. It is a wide open course with little of the scrubby underbrush that characterizes so many Florida courses.

Finally, there is an unforgettable pair of closing holes running alongside the dunes that separate the course from the sea. The 17th, a par three, plays almost always into the wind from an elevated tee to an elevated green with a vast amount of sand falling away on three sides and the thick tangle of sea-grape bushes on the ocean side. As Dunphy once put it, "It is a rare sight to see all four balls of a match on the green at once." The 18th is a very long shot from an elevated tee to the elbow of the fairway below, and then a long iron or fairway wood uphill to a splendid green nestling against the sea-grapes atop the dune. A par is dearly bought here, too. The strength of Seminole and its fascination to dedicated golfers was summed up by Ben Hogan when he said: "If you can play well there, you can play well anywhere." Every golfer finds that kind of challenge irresistible.

Dominated by 200-odd bunkers and traps, a large central lake and swaying palms, Seminole is one of the most attractive of America's courses. It is also one of the most exclusive and it is unfortunate that the claims made for it by regular visitors like Armour and Hogan have never been really tested in tournament conditions.

George Crump's
184-Acre Bunker

Pine Valley is the perfect example of penal architecture, the ultimate test for the giants of golf. It lies on the New Jersey side of Philadelphia and it is hard to believe that what is reputed to be the toughest course in the world could be located in such nondescript countryside: desolate enough in itself, and a wasteland of gas stations and billboards, dusty and tawdry and almost treeless —an environmentalist's nightmare. Pine Valley may not be as tough to play as some British championship courses in a forty-knot wind, nor tougher than Pebble Beach in the near-gales that so often sweep that seaside course in winter. Yet it is assuredly the world's most challenging inland course—perhaps inevitably, when it was fashioned from such a landscape as this.

Each hole is a separate and distinct entity. No hole parallels another, and each is protected by huge tracts of pines, bushes, shrubs, and jungle-like undergrowth. During the 1936 Walker Cup a member of the British squad—P. B. "Laddie" Lucas, then only twenty-one years old—hit a wild slice directly into the woods.

"Watch it! Watch it!" he yelled at his caddie.

"You don't have to watch 'em here," the caddie replied. "Just listen for 'em."

Few championships are played at Pine Valley, because it cannot accommodate spectators, but the Walker Cup did return in 1985, resulting in the then customary victory for the home side, although, at 13–11, not the normal one-sided affair.

Uniquely, Pine Valley has no fairways, no rough, no chipping surfaces, and no sandtraps in the accepted sense. The course itself is in effect one huge, 184-acre bunker. Since the whole Chinese Army couldn't keep it raked—even if it was available for a task of such capitalist decadence—nobody bothers to. On it are 18 tees and 18 greens, the more distant sets reached via islands of immaculate fair-green. Once off these verdant oases the player is either in the trees or inside a part of that apparently endless sand that has been designated a trap. The par threes have nothing between the tees and the greens; the greens are hit on the fly—or else. Surrounding the greens and running right up against the putting surfaces are countless little potholes of sand, some so steeply faced that it is often necessary to play away from the green in order eventually to get on to it. Pine Valley took seven years to build. It was the brainchild of a Philadelphia hotelier, George Crump, who died in 1918 with only fourteen holes finished and the remaining four only roughly sketched out. It was completed in 1919. Notwithstanding its appalling penalties, it is not as tough a course as its reputation would suggest. Although the official course record has stood for many years at 67, one pro has shot it twice in 66. He did not mention the scores to any of the members for fear of not being invited back.

The chief reason most golfers fail at Pine Valley to score within ten or even twenty strokes of their regular game is psychological—the course simply terrifies them. For years they have heard of its fiendish hazards. After a few holes they discover they are even more frightening than they had been led to believe and desperation enters their play—backswings became as fast as a snap of the fingers, and follow-throughs do not pass the hip. One story

Pine Valley's reputation as the toughest inland course in the world has not often been tested in a major professional tournament, since there is virtually no room for spectators. But the evidence of visiting players is there: all testify to the constant pressure, the severe penalties, the unique challenge of every hole. One pro after a disastrous encounter in its sandy soil, called it "a 184-acre bunker."

Pine Valley members have been telling for years illustrates how easy, and yet how terrifying, the course can be. The late Woody Platt, a gifted local amateur who knew Pine Valley well, started off the 1st hole with a birdie-three, no easy task since the hole bends sharply to the right after the tee shot to a green that drops steeply into trouble on both sides and to the rear. Platt had hit a 4-iron for his second stroke.

The 2nd hole, which changes direction sharply to the left, is not long—only 367 yards. But the tee shot—no topped shots here—must carry over 180 yards of sand peppered with flash traps completely along its right side. The green is highly elevated and, being almost completely surrounded by a wasteland of sand, it resembles a miniature Mount Suribachi. Platt hit a 7-iron into the hole for an eagle two.

The par-three 3rd is, like all the short holes at Pine Valley, strictly a one-shotter. There is nothing between the player and the green but sand. The green lies below the level of the tee and tilts sharply from right to left downhill. Missing the green may mean six more shots to get back on to it. Platt solved the problem by the simple expedient of a hole in one.

The 4th hole is very long for a par four: 444 yards. The tee shot is blind and the hole swerves slightly to the right. Sand is everywhere, as on every hole at Pine Valley, but it is not much of a factor here, lying just in front of the tee and way short of the green. Platt hit a driver and a 4-wood, and then holed a 30-footer for a birdie. He was now six under par after only four holes of the roughest test of golf in the world.

The first four holes make a full circle back to the clubhouse. Platt now faced the prospect of playing the 5th, which juts out from behind the clubhouse and is easily one of the most stringent par threes in golf. A huge bunker lies well short of the green, falling steeply to the right into saplings and undergrowth. If Platt's ball had bounced there, his main problem would have been in trying to find

it. Since the hole is 232 yards long, the problem was compounded by the fact that he would have had to play a wood—probably a driver—off the tee.

Before facing the task, he decided to bolster his spirit with a drink in the clubhouse while he contemplated the dual problem of maintaining a pace of six under par and tackling the devilish 5th.

He never came out of the clubhouse.

At Pine Valley, golfers find their games falling apart with absolutely nothing at stake. People who are used to playing golf for hundreds of dollars find at Pine Valley that they cannot get their games in gear playing for matchsticks. The pines and oaks, firs and birches—which are actually well away from the trajectory of anything but a completely uncontrolled shot now seem to form a corridor. The patches of fair-green, which will accept any moderately hit drive, now look as though they could not contain a 9-iron. And the greens, most of which cover a third of an acre, begin to look like watch crystals.

On precisely which hole this terror begins to strike the heart nobody ever knows. But it happens, almost invariably. Knowing this so well, the members at Pine Valley have a standing bet that nobody can break 80 on his first try at the course. One man who did was Arnold Palmer, in 1954, when he was U.S. Amateur Champion. "I was desperate for money at the time," Palmer recalls. "I was about to be married. So I collected all the bets I could find. I don't know what I would have done if I had lost—it was far more money than I could afford. But everything turned out all right. I shot a 68." One more record for the spectacular Palmer. But there are few Arnold Palmers. Not many really good players can get around the course without a few triple-bogeys, or worse. Many rounds that might have otherwise been under par have been marred along the line by a nine or a ten—or worse. For this reason, Pine Valley is in a class by itself as a test of matchplay. A golfer can be three down and four to play and win easily, simply by watching his opponent suddenly discover that he has

Pine Valley Golf Club, Clementon, New Jersey

Record: 64, Robert Lewis, Jr., 1981

Hole	Yards	Par
1	427	4
2	367	4
3	181	3
4	444	4
5	232	3
6	388	4
7	567	5
8	319	4
9	427	4
10	146	3
11	392	4
12	344	4
13	448	4
14	184	3
15	591	5
16	433	4
17	338	4
18	428	4
Out	3,352	35
In	3,304	35
Total	**6,656**	**70**

The 7th: 585 yards par 5

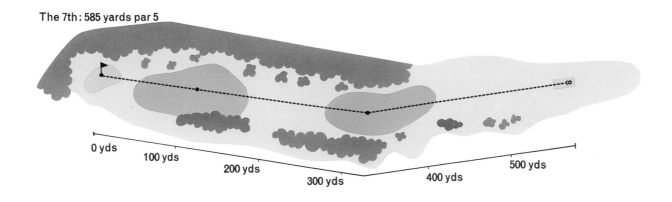

0 yds 100 yds 200 yds 300 yds 400 yds 500 yds

The 7th

The Evils of Hell's Half-Acre

George Crump was not the only architect to work on Pine Valley, for he had had the experienced guidance of the British architect H. S. Colt, whose most famous course in England was Sunningdale, near London. But it was Crump who drew up the first basic outline and the master plan, not to mention pouring $250,000 of his own money into it. Colt simply added the final touches that made it into a masterpiece of the macabre. When he died, Crump had not finished his outlines for the 10th to the 15th holes; that was done by Hugh Wilson—whose own masterpiece had been Merion—with the help of his brother Allen.

Nobody can be sure if there is even one hole that was Crump's work alone, but there is little doubt that the 7th is the hole of which he would be most proud. It may be the most exacting par five in the world. Absolutely no mistakes may be made if that par is to be equaled, and it takes a minor miracle to score a birdie. At 567 yards, there are plenty of par fives that are much longer. There are many that are much trickier. But there

are none that require the three shots of the difficulty of those needed to reach Pine Valley's 7th green in regulation figures. The length of the drive is limited by an area of sand and scrub so diabolical in nature and of such frightening dimension that it is known as Hell's Half-Acre. It begins some 285 yards from the tee and does not end for more than a hundred yards. This means that the drive and the second shot must travel at least 385 yards, the last hundred yards on the fly, just to be clear of trouble. In other words, if the tee shot is missed it leaves the golfer with no choice but to play short of Hell's Half-Acre. If he hits a good drive and a poor second shot, he's had it. Nobody can make a par from there. Even after two perfect wood shots the golfer is faced with an equally difficult problem for his third shot, which could very easily be a mid-iron. The fairway comes to an end some 20 yards short of the green, which virtually sits in a huge bunker. The green, not overly large and crowded by trees on both sides, falls away steeply at the rear.

Is it any wonder nobody hits that green in two?

The 18th hole at Pine Valley, below, is perhaps not as heroic as some that have gone before. Nevertheless, an iron shot will need to be truly struck to clear both the brook and the greenside bunkers.

been walking on water. Woody Platt made his discovery at the 5th, but Pine Valley offers no respite and even if he had completed the 5th in respectable fashion he would then have been faced with a crucial decision on the tee of the 6th. This hole is a medium-length par four, 388 yards. The pay-off shot is the drive, for an enormous bank of sand runs along the bias of the fairway as it turns right. The player is therefore faced with deciding how much of the sand he wants to bite off. Just the right amount and he will have only a pitch to the green, but too much and he will be shooting uphill off a mountainside of sand. Now comes the "Sahara," a horror of sand all along its 567 yards, with much lying around the green. It is practically impossible to smite in two shots because of the huge belt of sand (from which the hole derives its name) which crosses the fairway and stifles all hope of a really long drive.

By contrast, the 8th is only a drive and a pitch, being a mere 319 yards downhill. But what a pitch! Many a player has hit what he thought was a perfect wedge to within a foot of the flagstick, only to watch in disbelief as the backspin on the ball started it creeping down the steep slope to end up in the deep bunker in front of the putting surface.

The 9th is a long par four—427 yards—with two greens. Behind the left one is a cliff, not just a slope. The man brave enough to even attempt finding a ball down there would need to climb down a rope to do so. The 10th

The 13th

Where a Par is a Triumph

The 13th, a par four, is one of the four holes finished off by Hugh and Allen Wilson after George Crump's death. It follows his basic plan and may very well have exceeded his grand ideas of what a hole at Pine Valley ought to be. The 13th is the epitome of the heroic hole in golf, though it also incorporates elements of the penal and strategic styles of architecture.

It takes the heart of a heavyweight to play the hole successfully. It can be punishing to the point where a player might not be able to finish it. And yet, it can be played strategically if it is viewed as a par four-and-a-half.

At 448 yards it is, by the card, a par four. It is a single dogleg to the left if it is played bravely. It is a double dogleg if the player is content to seek only a bogey. There are two tees, but the difficulty of the drive and the length of the hole remain the same from both. A forest of pines obscures all view of the green from the tee. But the patch of fairway you are supposed to hit is in plain view. It

begins about 175 yards from the tee. Providing the drive is not short and to the right, the green can be seen from the fairway. However, also in full view is a bunker lining the entire left side of a second patch of fairway which leads into the green from the right.

The second shot, most certainly a wood, must carry the full length of that bunker, hit the green on the fly, and hold. Running downhill to the left of the bunker is that forest of pines, and behind the green lies yet another bunker. Those who prefer discretion to valor can play the second shot short and to the right of the green with an iron. From there it is a simple pitch and, with two putts, a bogey-five.

Of course, there is always the possibility of a par. Most players are more than content to complete the 13th in the regulation four.

The 439-yard 13th is yet another hole that gives the impression that Pine Valley is a great bunker with fairways appearing at all too infrequent intervals. The drive must land on the first patch of fairway; the second must carry a huge sandy area on the left of a curving fairway. Par is a major achievement, and many players prefer to play safe with a short second leaving a simple pitch.

The 13th: 446 yards par 4

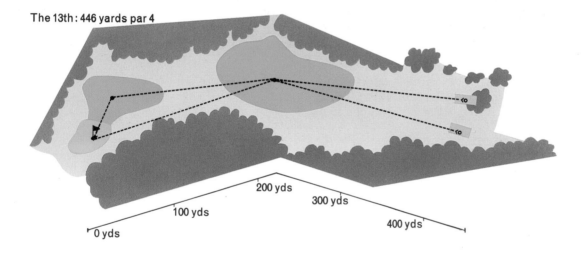

0 yds   100 yds   200 yds   300 yds   400 yds

is just an 8- or possibly a 7-iron, but the green is protected all around with what can best be described as sandpits, one of which is cone-shaped and is nicknamed after an unprintable part of the Devil's anatomy. The 11th is a fine two-shotter, at 392 yards one of those rarities in golf architecture: a great short par four. It is followed by another four, so short that the player can drive hole-high then pitch to the green from the fairway as it turns sharply to the left.

The par-four 13th is another story altogether. It requires a tremendous drive and, because the 448-yard hole is a dogleg, almost certainly another wood, all of it sheer carry, to get home. At 184 yards, the par-three 14th does not play that long because the green lies well below the tee. But, again, it is a hit-or-miss one-shotter. Fifty feet of water lies directly in front of the green and a bunker to the left of it.

The 15th hole, which sits at right angles to the 14th green, carries over this same body of water, but any fair tee shot will easily carry it. At 591 yards it is the longest hole at Pine Valley and, to make matters worse, it goes straight uphill into a narrowing fairway. Like the 7th, nobody hits this green in two shots. The par-four 16th—433 yards—plays long although it travels downhill. It has a tiny patch of fairway, guarded in front by a minor desert, and then plays over more sandy wasteland to a green strategically bunkered on the left and guarded by water on

the right. The 17th is a shortish par four, only 338 yards, but it is uphill all the way. By Pine Valley standards the green is small but it is protected all around by sandtraps, which begin a full fifty yards in front of it. Oddly, the final hole is not as heroic as might be expected at the Pine Valley finish. At 428 yards it is not short, but a drive off the high tee can easily carry the 180 yards or so of sand which lies in front of it, and this to a very wide patch of fairway. The second can easily carry a brook lying well short of the green, provided it can be truly struck from a downhill lie. But the green is mammoth and the key here lies in the choice of the correct club for the approach. The route is uphill, so it is difficult to see where the cup is, and if the wrong club is chosen avoiding three putts presents a real problem.

Despite its unprepossessing environs, Pine Valley is one of the most beautiful golf courses in the world. It has no backdrop of mountains, no craggy coastlines with waves lapping at its shores. It is simply gorgeous in its own right. Trent Jones likes to tell the story of Lowell Thomas, an avid golfer and traveler for many years. After playing his tee shot safely across the water at the 15th, he turned to admire the scenery around him. "In all my travels," he said to Jones, "I do not think I have seen a more beautiful landscape. This is as thrilling as Versailles or Fontainebleau."

Completely redesigned by Robert Trent Jones for the 1960 USPGA tournament, Firestone is now the longest championship course in America. It is especially notable for its succession of tough par fours (particularly the 4th and 9th, which proved the most testing over eleven years of World Series play) and for the 625-yard 16th, named "The Monster" by Arnold Palmer after his triple-bogey eight there in the 1960 USPGA competition.

A Rubber Man's
Long, Long Stretch

The Course Card

Firestone Country Club, Akron, Ohio South course

Record: 61, Jose-Maria Olazabal, 1990

Hole	Yards	Par
1	400	4
2	500	5
3	450	4
4	465	4
5	200	3
6	465	4
7	225	3
8	450	4
9	465	4
10	405	4
11	365	4
12	180	3
13	460	4
14	410	4
15	230	3
16	625	5
17	390	4
18	465	4
Out	3,620	35
In	3,530	35
Total	7,150	70

They are fortunate sportsmen indeed whose employer provides that ultimate in off-duty amenities—a golf course for their own use. Firestone Country Club, at Akron, Ohio, began in this way, the gift to his workforce in 1928 of Harvey Firestone, the millionaire industrialist. In the seventy years that have passed, it has become much more than an amenity for Firestone people; it is a challenge to the best in golf, rated as one of the toughest courses on the American tour.

The first of the club's two courses, Firestone South now bears little resemblance to its original plan, having been altered beyond all recognition by Robert Trent Jones in 1959. As a result of his work it is one of the longest championship courses in America: 7,150 yards, to a par of only 70. Despite its extreme length, even medium-hitting professionals regard it as Trent Jones's finest piece of work. Firestone is also a golf course with which American enthusiasts are most familiar; it has been the site of more televised tournaments than perhaps any other course. Its television exposure began with the 1960 USPGA Championship, for which Trent Jones carried out his drastic surgery—to say merely that he redesigned it would be an understatement. He added fifty bunkers, two ponds, and two greens; the remaining sixteen greens were vastly enlarged. Although always formidable, the greens were redesigned in 1985 by a Jack Nicklaus company to make them even more challenging.

This is never more typified than at the 17th—at 390 yards one of the shortest par fours on the course where there is a ripple running right through the spine of the green. Getting down in two putts is never easy. Bobby Nichols, once Firestone's head professional and a former winner of the USPGA title, believes it takes a subtle blend of strength and accuracy to win at Firestone. "You don't use 9-irons and 8-irons out here, as a pro can expect on at least a few courses on the tour. At Firestone almost all your approaches to the par fours and par threes call for long irons."

Even so, Firestone has been humbled, most notably by Jose-Maria Olazabal when he won the 1990 World Series of Golf, the annual tour event played there. In the first round Olazabal was simply in what the professionals refer to as "the zone," that blessed state when fairways appear the size of football fields and the hole a bucket. Olazabal shot 61, eventually finishing 12 shots clear of the field. Only three players broke par that year; one of them, Olazabal, was 18 under. Next to winning the Masters four years later, the Spaniard regards it as his finest achievement to date.

The 1st is a modest opening par four of 400 yards to a narrow fairway. It is followed by one that has been described as a "gambler's hole," a 500-yard par five uphill, with deep woods on the left and a heavily bunkered green. Two woods will give the chance of a birdie, but those who want to play safe will hit short and wedge it into the green.

Now begins the first of the lengthy par fours, one of five on the front nine and measuring 450 yards. After a 270-yard drive, the second must carry 180 yards on the fly over a pond in front of the green. The 4th is a par four dropping just short of a par five. There are only three bunkers: one to the right of the fairway, the others on either side of the green. Despite a prosaically easy green to putt, the 4th remains the most bogeyed hole on the course. Olazabal, meanwhile, during his round of rounds, was five under par to this point having started birdie-eagle-birdie-birdie. The 5th—a 200-yard par-three—is particularly well protected at its front by one large and one small bunker. There follows a 465-yard par four, bunkered only around the green; a 225-yard par three, bunkered broadly to both the right and left; the downhill 450-yard, par-four 8th, severely trapped around the green; and the magnificently bunkered 9th, first downhill and then uphill for 465 yards to the green. It is considered by many to be the second-toughest hole on the course and tournament statistics back them.

The 10th is a bit of a breather. Only 405 yards, it nevertheless calls for a nearly perfect tee shot to split the fairway between two finely placed bunkers. The 11th is perhaps the easiest hole on the course, a good drive to a trapless fairway and a pitch to a well-bunkered but broad green.

The 12th is the shortest par three on the course, 180 yards and nothing to speak of by Trent Jones's standards. Yet it is, as has been pointed out, "fickle." The green is elevated, guarded to the front and on both sides by big bunkers and with lots of trees, the most intrusive of which is a gigantic oak to the rear. The 13th is another 460-yard hole, but Tommy Bolt once scored an eagle-two on it—using a 3-wood for his second shot.

Television has made the last five holes at Firestone the most familiar. The 14th is just 410 yards, but the tee shot is made difficult by two deep bunkers on the right and another on the left which very much tighten the landing area. Most pros choose to lay up off the tee and then play a mid-iron for their second shot, which is slightly uphill, to a relatively flat green. If there are such things as birdie holes at Firestone, the 14th is one. But that is the last.

The 15th does not look an exciting hole, because although it is the highest on the course it is long and flat. Club selection is all important because of the winds that swirl off the flatlands of Ohio and around the elevated green, from which the ground drops away sharply on both sides. The two large bunkers on both the left and right and a much smaller one to the front-right help to make this the most disturbing one-shotter on the course. Many tournaments played at Firestone have been won with a birdie at the 15th.

The 16th is not the longest par five in the world, though it is all of 625 yards. That length seems impossible in print but the hole is entirely downhill. The second shot is the crucial one, because in all probability the left foot will be below the right for a shot into a spit of fairway. The pitch from there is into a wide green directly fronted by a pond. Only a very limited number of players have carried that pond in two shots and hit the green. Even Nicklaus, not trying to reach the green in two, has found his third shot in the water. This happened during the World Series one year,

but, ever the great competitor, Nicklaus calmly removed a shoe and played his fourth where it lay. He found the green and sank his putt for a miraculous par. The 17th, only 390 yards, is the last of the shortish par fours, but it is uphill and four bunkers—two of them on either side—dictate such a tight tee shot that most long-hitters use an iron off the tee. This leaves them with a medium iron shot to the green with its notorious rippled surface.

The 18th is another of those long par fours that have given Firestone its reputation. It is 464 yards long from an elevated tee, from which you must play to the right of the fairway to open up the tightly bunkered green. The drive is threatened on the left by a thick grove of trees and on the right by two huge bunkers that will catch any slice or push. The second shot is yet another long iron to a huge green virtually surrounded by bunkers. Three putts are not unusual here. The 18th is the signature hole for the entire Firestone layout—long and tough, but truly great.

The reshaped 18th green has four pin positions of varying difficulty, the central one being the easiest, the front one the toughest.

Rough Like Steel Wool,

Sand Like Talcum Powder

Set in gently undulating parkland, Perry Maxwell's Southern Hills course is one of the great driving tests in American golf. The figures of the first major competition played there (the 1958 Open) illustrate difficulties: only three men, winner Tommy Bolt, Gary Player, and Julius Boros, broke 290.

The
Course
Card

Southern Hills
Country Club,
Tulsa, Oklahoma

Hole	Yards	Par
1	454	4
2	440	4
3	405	4
4	366	4
5	589	5
6	178	3
7	384	4
8	217	3
9	374	4
10	376	4
11	163	3
12	445	4
13	497	4
14	207	3
15	405	4
16	567	5
17	349	4
18	430	4
Out	3,407	35
In	3,439	35
Total	6,846	70

Southern Hills Country Club, at Tulsa, Oklahoma, was built in 1935. It was an act of enlightened self-interest by a group of wealthy Tulsans at a time when one in five of the nation's workforce was unemployed.

Tulsa had made its money from oil, and its better-off citizens put up the money for a club of which the state could be proud—and one which, in its construction, would provide employment. In any event, course and clubhouse cost no more than a new locker room at today's prices. For their architect Southern Hills chose Perry Maxwell, and their choice could not have been wiser. Although he lived in Oklahoma his golf knowledge was universal: examples of his work are to be found all over the Midwest. The excellence of his work has been carried on by his son, J. Press Maxwell.

Southern Hills is fundamentally a driver's course and thus the key to it is the tee shot. While an accurate drive is a necessity for any course with championship pretensions, it is absolutely crucial at Southern Hills. Nobody ever won anything there who did not drive the ball with extreme accuracy and plenty of length. The reason is that Southern Hills, while not particularly long these days at 6,962 yards par 70, plays every inch of that measurement and more. Most of the holes are flat—the club's name is misleading, for there is no help from nature, such as a downhill roll, in driving. The only holes with any real elevation are the 9th and the 18th, and they go uphill to the clubhouse sitting majestically at the top of a hill that is, on the plains of Oklahoma, a minor mountain.

Adding to these difficulties is the tough Bermuda grass with which the entire course is planted; any other type of grass could not survive the sizzling heat in which matches at Tulsa are often played. When the USGA holds one of its championships at Southern Hills—there have been a number, including the U.S. Open for a second time in 1977 (the course has also hosted two USPGA Championships, the most recent in 1994)—the Bermuda grass is allowed to grow in the rough to an ankle-height of almost three inches. It is

like playing from a surface of steel wool so tough that Ben Hogan had to withdraw from the 1958 U.S. Open after hurting his wrist trying to extricate a ball from it. Because of the baking sun and long dry periods, the sprinkler system at Southern Hills works night and day in the summer, and even while a tournament is in progress. In the course of one day Southern Hills may use up to 400,000 gallons of water. Its greens (most of them are steeply banked from back to front and are rife with undulations) often have to be syringed twice a day. All this works back to the tee, for without an excellent drive through Southern Hills' thick trees it is impossible to get in position for a second shot that leaves any kind of putt.

The bunkers add yet another premium to the drives. While they are numerous, they are not over-abundant along the fairways. They are filled with a sand called "Number Six Wash" culled from the nearby Arkansas River. It is not unlike talcum powder, and buried lies are common enough.

The most heavily publicized championship ever held at Southern Hills was the 1958 U.S. Open. It was played in heat that would have made a camel faint and was won by Tommy Bolt, a temperamental man famed more for throwing clubs. Bolt won by a comfortable four strokes from Gary Player, who admitted afterward that he had played some of the best golf of his career. Bolt missed only thirteen of the seventy-two greens in regulation figures, yet he was three over par; Player was seven over. Asked what had won the Championship for him, Bolt just pointed to his driver.

For the 1994 USPGA Championship the weather was far more clement, and Nick Price turned in his career best performance to win a second successive Major championship. The winning margin was six strokes as Price compiled a new record PGA Championship winning total of 269, 11 under par. Southern Hills has an extremely long opening hole, a par four of 454 yards. It is off an elevated tee near the clubhouse and doglegs to the left with deep bunkers to the right of the green. At the next two holes, both par fours, a stream must be carried. Along with two bunkers across the fairway it affects the drive at the 440-yard 2nd, but presents no real problem for the approach at the shorter 3rd. The 4th, a shortish par four of 366 yards to a slightly elevated green, provides some respite before the rigors of the long par-five 5th—a full 589 yards, with a heavily bunkered green backed by trees as thick as they are high. The 6th is a fairly easy par three and the 7th little more than a 3-wood, for position, and a short iron. The 8th can be unnerving. At 217 yards it is a long par three with three bunkers, two of them large, protecting the green, the back part of which cannot be seen from the tee. The uphill 9th is a mere 374 yards.

From the elevated tee of the 10th the course descends, playing through flatlands until it hits the 16th tee, just about the lowest point on the course. In that stretch are two particularly tough holes—the 12th, once described by Ben Hogan as the "greatest par-four 12th hole in the United States," and the 13th. Trees, rough, and a big bunker strategically placed in the crook of the dogleg make the tee shot especially demanding at the 12th. The long second shot is complicated by a blind water hazard in front of the green and down its right side, and by bunkers and trees to the back and along the left side. The 13th is the only par five on the inward nine, measuring 497 yards over two lakes to a smallish green surrounded by five bunkers. A late dogleg to a green heavily trapped in front imparts difficulty to the 17th, at 349 yards the shortest par four on the course. The drive at the 18th, complicated by water on both sides of the fairway, has to be precisely positioned to open the way uphill to the last green. This is a strong finishing hole, and a tough one by any standards.

A Tough One to Finish

The 18th at Southern Hills is not the most technically perfect finishing hole in golf. It may not even be technically the best hole at Southern Hills, but it is certainly the toughest.

It has the trees, the curves, the bunkers, and the insufferable rough which all make par difficult to break at Southern Hills. From the championship tees, the hole is 430 yards long, which, while not an excessive length, could hardly be considered short. The drive goes down a slight slope avenue of trees, the thicker grove being on the right, the direction in which the hole bends. There is a narrow pond at the crook of the dogleg and two fairway bunkers lie just around the corner, which means that anybody who tries to cut it might well rue his ambition. A stream and another bunker lie ahead, and accuracy is absolutely vital.

If the hole has any flaw, it is the lie that results from a perfectly safe and sane tee shot. It is downhill. As if that were not enough of a problem, from it one has to hit uphill to the green. That is not the sort of shot any golfer, amateur or professional, wants to face.

The green is very wide and full of borrows. A huge, banked bunker lies to the left front of the green and another, for the slice, lies to the right. The gap between them is wide enough but, regardless of pin position, if the prize is the U.S. Open that must rank as one of the most difficult final approaches on any championship course.

Nick Price, in his imperishable year of 1994, when he won both the Open Championship and, above, the USPGA at Southern Hills.

Originally built as a private course for members of the Shriner organization, Medinah was the venue for the U.S. Opens of 1949 and 1975. It has violent doglegs and dense woods, crowding right to the fairway edge, bordering all but the first and last holes, and making the course seem narrower than it really is. Of all the U.S. Open courses, Medinah probably inspires the most controversy.

Chicago's Controversial
Golfing Shrine

Medinah, 20 miles from downtown Chicago, is an American country club in the most dramatic sense of the term. Its clubhouse, built by the Shriners—members of the Ancient Arabic Order of Nobles of the Mystic Shrine, an association not unlike Freemasonry—is a mock-Moorish structure at once imposing and lavish. Today, its No. 3 course is considered by many golfers to be the finest in the Chicago area and by its more dogmatic partisans to be the finest in the United States. It is not known how Bendelow came to serve the big-spending Shriners. He arrived in the United States to work as a typesetter for the *New York Herald*, but in 1895 joined Spaldings as an architectural consultant. From then on, he laid out some of the most abominable examples of golf landscaping ever seen, some of which he designed in a day for twenty-five dollars.

Medinah Number 3 has been changed out of all recognition from Bendelow's original conception. The process of change was sparked off by Harry Cooper, who shot the course record, 63, on his way to winning the 1930 Medinah Open. Five new holes were built immediately and in 1935 Cooper won there again, this time with a less spectacular 289. Since that time, the course has been revamped many times, including by George Fazio in time for the 1975 United States Open. This contest was won by Lou Graham with 287, three over par, which for the Open was 71, a stroke less than usual. For the 1990 U.S. Open, there was another extensive redesign. Two new holes were added to the course and another was rebuilt. The course became the longest ever for a U.S. Open—a mammoth 7,195 yards—and the par reverted to 72. Now Medinah has six par fours that measure over 440 yards and none of

the par fives measure under 520 yards. Furthermore, the shortest par three is a shade under 170 yards. Yet it produced the oldest winner of a U.S. Open, the evergreen Hale Irwin prevailing after a play-off with Mike Donald.

Much of the course is in sight of Lake Kadijah (named after Mohammed's wife) and four holes, the 2nd, the 13th, the 14th, and the 17th, are played across it. For the rest, the course has nine doglegs, two of which swing through a full 90 degrees.

The first hole is dead straight and on the short side, as an opening par four ought to be. There then follows a first trip across the Lake, a 180-yard par three, followed by the slight dogleg of the 3rd, to an elevated green protected on both sides by bunkers. Like the 3rd, the trees on both sides of the 4th fairway are the principal difficulties, although its contoured green is not easy. At 526 yards, the par-five 5th is a birdie hole, although there are two fairway traps, one to the right for the slicers and the other in the middle for the bit hitters. The second shot must then carry over two gaping traps on both sides of the green. What might have been gained on the 5th could very well be lost on the 445-yard 6th, which has five bunkers, one of which lies to the left-middle of the fairway, in the landing area. Out of bounds is behind the green. Then comes the formidable 7th, a dogleg par five playing to just under 600 yards. Since the hole bends right, the tee shot should stay left but it must be carefully positioned to avoid an inconveniently placed bunker. The second must carry through groves of trees on both sides and miss another bunker on the left. The third goes to a pear-shaped green, heavily bunkered, with an almost infinite number of pin positions.

At this stage the golfer begins to wonder when Medinah is going to show any mercy. As he makes the turn —from the 8th to the 11th—he finds out that it doesn't. The 462 yard 12th is considered by some to be the most difficult hole on the course and then comes the famous par three 13th over Lake Kadijah, a hole that has caused heartbreak to many and cost Sam Snead a U.S. Open.

At the 14th the players drive back over the lake, a par five of 545 yards to a green heavily bunkered to ward off any big hitter trying to find it in two. The 15th offers some respite in terms of length; at 384 yards, believe it or not, it is the shortest par four on the course. The 16th is where Irwin began his move in the 1990 U.S. Open play-off. He trailed Donald by two at this point but a birdie here enabled him to put pressure on his inexperienced opponent.

The 17th again makes use of the lake, a par three that extracted from Ian Woosnam a triple bogey. Afterward, the Welshman was in no doubt: "It is a crap hole," he said. Swiftly on to the 18th, a sweeping dogleg to the left that plays its full 440 yards. In 1990 Nick Faldo, the winner of that year's Masters, needed a birdie here to get into the play-off and keep alive his Grand Slam hopes. A wonderful 4-iron approach, to 18 feet, appeared to have given him his chance. The putt looked in the hole all the way, but at the last it dived to the right and lipped out, finishing 18 inches away. Faldo grimaced in agony; by such fine margins are Major championships frequently won and lost and why it seems inconceivable today that any pro, even Tiger Woods, will win all four majors in the same year.

Fronted by an eight-foot-deep bunker and with another one to the rear, the 17th green demands a perfectly judged shot.

The 18th

Irwin's Moment of Glory

Hale Irwin was always considered among the most austere of professionals. He did not kill them with length but with formidably straight hitting and imperious course management. It was hardly a coincidence that his favorite tournament was the U.S. Open, one that most lends itself to such strategically sound players. However, in 1990, a new Irwin presented himself. The glasses were gone, replaced by contact lenses. And then came the extraordinary scenes at the 72nd hole of that year's U.S. Open at Medinah.

In truth, Irwin had not played the hole well, given that this was a man who needed to be aggressive for a birdie. His second shot pulled up 45 feet from the hole. However, the putt that followed made up for any deficiencies. It traveled for fully seven seconds, borrowing this way and that before dropping into the hole. Pandemonium followed and the roar would have shaken elephants. What did Irwin do? If Irwin had followed the habits of a lifetime he would have raised a hand into the air, tugged at his visor, and thanked spectators for their reaction to his good fortune. What did this Irwin do? For a start there was no visor. He set off on a run that brought back reminders that here was a man who was a good college football player. But he did not stop his run at the green; he then went along the front row of spectators and high-fived them each in turn; he high-fived the stewards and then he high-fived his caddie.

When he returned the following day one had the feeling that fate was on his side, although not when he walked to the 16th tee, trailing Donald by two shots. A birdie at the 16th, though, halved the deficit and then the 18th once more came to his rescue, Donald missing the green with his approach and recording a bogey.

Irwin needed no more invitations. He birdied the first sudden death play-off hole for the most dramatic of his three U.S. Open titles. At 45 he was the oldest winner in the history of the Championship. Given his shenannigans on the 18th it would appear one of the sprightliest, too.

The Course Card

Medinah Country Club,
Medinah, Illinois
Number 3

Hole	Yards	Par
1	385	4
2	180	3
3	412	4
4	434	4
5	526	5
6	445	4
7	581	5
8	190	3
9	429	4
10	577	5
11	402	4
12	462	4
13	199	3
14	545	5
15	384	4
16	436	4
17	168	3
18	440	4
Out	3,582	36
In	3,613	36
Total	**7,195**	**72**

A Course More
Mellow than Monstrous

The Course Card

Oakland Hills
Country Club,
Birmingham.
Michigan
South course

Hole	Yards	Par
1	436	4
2	527	5
3	199	3
4	433	4
5	457	4
6	359	4
7	405	4
8	439	4
9	217	3
10	454	4
11	411	4
12	560	5
13	172	3
14	465	4
15	399	4
16	409	4
17	201	3
18	453	4
Out	3,472	35
In	3,524	35
Total	**6,996**	**70**

The most overworked nickname for a U.S. golf course is "The Monster." Press agents use it weekly (and weakly) to describe any course where the touring professionals happen to be setting up their nomadic camp, and more often than not it is applied to some harmless sequence of eighteen holes that are as drab as they are undistinguished. The original and authentic "Monster," however, is Oakland Hills, so christened by Ben Hogan after winning the U.S. Open there in 1951.

Prior to that championship, Oakland Hills had twice before played host to the tournament—in 1924, when it was won by an obscure little golfer named Cyril Walker, and again in 1937, when Ralph Guldahl was a surprise winner over Sam Snead. That was quite a different course, though, than the one on which Hogan scored his third U.S. Open victory. It had been designed in 1917 by Donald Ross, the George Washington of American golf architecture, who said of the rolling woodland when he first saw it, "The Lord intended this for a golf course."

When the time for the 1951 Open approached, the USGA hired Robert Trent Jones to modernize the work of the Lord and Donald Ross. "The game had outrun architecture," Jones has since explained in describing his work at Oakland Hills, and he set out to give the world's best players what he called "the shock treatment." The philoso-

phy behind his rebuilding program was to create two target areas on each of the par-four and par-five holes, one on the fairway for the tee shot, and another at the green. The result was a series of wasp-waisted fairways, formed by bunkers on either side, and greens surrounded by wide and deep bunkers and overhanging lips—a total of 120 bunkers in all containing some 400 tons of so-called medium-sharp sand. On his first round of the 1951 Open, Hogan spent a great deal of his time in this sand, and bogeyed five of the first nine holes to bring in a 76 that apparently spoiled any chance he might have had to win the Championship twice in a row. The next day was a slight improvement—a 73 that left him five shots behind Bobby Locke, the leader at the half-way point. Despite three bogeys and a double-bogey in his morning round on Saturday, Hogan was able to wring four birdies out of the course for a one-over-par 71, leaving him two strokes behind Locke and Jimmy Demaret, who were now tied for the lead.

There are those who still call Hogan's final round on Saturday afternoon "the finest eighteen holes of golf ever played by anyone." To escape the trouble on the fairways that had bothered him so much in his early round, Hogan often used his 3-wood off the tee and once even his 4-wood. He played the first nine holes in an even par 35. At

English-born Cyril Walker held off defending champion Bobby Jones to win the U.S. Open at Oakland Hills in 1924—the first championship in which steel-shafted putters were permitted.

the then 448-yard 10th, Hogan hit a 2-iron to the green, a shot that traveled more than 200 yards and stopped five feet from the pin. "It was one shot that went exactly as I played it every inch of the way," Hogan said afterward. He sank the putt for his birdie-three and a few minutes later a fifteen-foot putt for a birdie-two at the 13th hole. A bogey-five at the long 14th cost him a stroke when his second went over the green, but he got it back with a birdie-three at the 15th. Standing on the 18th tee, Hogan knew he had at least a two-stroke lead over the field, but he still refused to play safe. He hit a drive that even today is held in wonder by those who saw it—well over the bunkers guarding the elbow of this 459-yard dogleg right, leaving him only a 6-iron uphill to the green. He played his second shot perfectly to within four feet of the hole and sank the putt for his fourth birdie in the final nine holes and at that time a competitive course record of 67. "I'm glad that I brought this course, this monster, to its knees," he is said to have remarked at the presentation ceremony. Thus, the Monster was born. Locke, incidentally, finished with a 73 to drop into third place behind Clayton Heafner, whose closing 69 was the only other sub-par round of the entire tournament.

The U.S. Open returned to Oakland Hills ten years later to be won by smooth swinging Gene Littler, but the Monster had lost a great deal of its bite. "The course has matured," explained Al Watrous, the club professional. But the USGA had mellowed, too. The rough was not nearly as severe as it had been during the Hogan victory, and architect Jones had even removed seven of the 1951 bunkers while preparing the course for the Championship. Still, the large, undulating greens were there and are today, somewhat reminiscent of the North Atlantic during a mid-winter

storm. Littler's winning score was 281, and eleven players finished with 287 or better, the score that had won for Hogan. There were a number of sub-par rounds during the tournament, and on the second day three players tied Hogan's. During the first Carling World championship in 1964, much the same kind of field scored even better. Even so, and taking into account the understandable pride of the designer, it is only a slight exaggeration when Jones calls it "the greatest test of professional tournament championship golf in the world. The player with the best shots, swing, and nerve control has the best chance to win. "For all that, Oakland Hills has produced a bizarre set of U.S. Open Champions. In 1985 it was Andy North, who won only three tournaments during his career but two of them happened to be U.S. Opens. However the tournament is remembered as much for the joint runners-up as North, belying the old belief that the man who finishes second is quickly forgotten. One of them was the South African Denis Watson, who made an error in the opening round that probably still haunts him. At the 8th his putt stopped on the brim of the hole—and he waited twenty-five seconds before it toppled in, so contravening the rules of golf. He was penalized two strokes for unduly delaying play. He lost by one to North. Even more poignant was TC Chen's story. He was trying to become the first Asian to win a Major championship and with fourteen holes to play he had a four-stroke lead. In attempting a delicate

In winning the first of his two consecutive U.S. Open titles at Oakland Hills in 1937, Ralph Guldahl became the first player never to go over par in any round of the championship.

Though no longer the frightening specter it was for the famous Open in 1951, when Ben Hogan battled with Robert Trent Jones's changes, Oakland Hills remains a stern test with awkward doglegs, plentiful bunkers and notoriously undulating greens. Gary Player, who won the PGA title there in 1972, claims only Carnoustie rivals it as the world's toughest.

The 4th hole at Oakland Hills is characteristic of the course, a long and arduous par four where a regulation figure is always welcome.

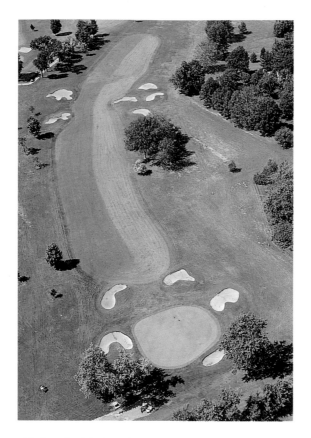

chip from beside the 5th green the clubface got caught in the thick grass and then, when it freed itself, struck the ball while it was in flight. The double chip meant a one-stroke penalty and an eight on his card. Greatly disturbed, he bogeyed each of the next three holes. He would finish with a 77 and again, one stroke adrift of the winning score.

When the championship returned in 1996 it was a qualifier of all people who prevailed. At the start of the week the extent of Steve Jones's ambitions lay in making the cut. But he showed tremendous courage on the closing hole to emerge a winner from the company of such skilled protagonists as Tom Lehman and Davis Love. Lying as it does in a Detroit suburb and less than an hour's drive from the heart of that great city, it is fitting that Oakland Hills should be an offspring of the auto industry. The property belonged originally to a printer and an accountant who were connected with the Ford Motor Co. They played golf together at the nearby Bloomfield Hills Country Club, which even then was a gathering-place for carmakers, and eventually decided to see if Ross could fashion an exciting course on their land. They opened for business in a modest way during the summer of 1918, and Walter Hagen, who lived nearby, was their first professional.

In due course, it was decided to build a clubhouse for the rather impressive sum of $275,000. The result was the huge neo-colonial structure that now dominates the entire course from the crest of the hill overlooking the 1st, 9th, 10th, and 18th holes, certainly one of the most spacious clubhouses to be found anywhere and a marvelous spot from which to watch the golf unfold at the start and finish of each nine holes. The clubhouse presented only one problem at the time it was built, however: due to innumerable changes and modifications during its construction, it cost $650,000 instead of the anything-but-modest amount that was originally budgeted for it.

Oakland Hills maintained a long relationship with Robert Trent Jones, who as a consultant kept the basic character of the course intact during his 1951 Open revamp. Although its yardage is not excessive by modern standards, Oakland

Hills concentrates a great deal on its more hazardous yards and more trying problems in the closing holes where they test the nerves as well as the ability. The 14th at 468 yards requires two very long shots. The 15th, all 396 yards, is uphill all the way with a large bunker in the middle of the fairway just where it turns left toward the green. The second shot at the 16th is a medium iron across a large pond that cuts right into the middle of the green. The 17th, with the deeply undulating green in a plateau some 30 feet above the tee, allows no margin for error since the green is completely surrounded by yawning bunkers. The 18th hole, the aforementioned dogleg, with its bunkers to the right to guard against the shortcut and rough to the left to inhibit the long approach and a hump-backed green that has only the smallest entrance between protecting bunkers in front, is the kind of hole where tournaments are far more often lost than won—as many know to their cost.

Two of these are Love and Lehman who both came to the 18th tied with Steve Jones in 1996. Love was first, finding the green with two wonderful shots. The putt he had left however, from 18 feet, was downhill and exceedingly slippery. He did the one thing he did not want to do—he left it 30 inches short. Moments later he had completed the saddest of three putts. Lehman's undoing was the left-hand bunker that guards the far angle of the dogleg. His drive was too straight, running into it and from there he had no hope of reaching the green.

Oakland Hills has undergone some drastic changes in character. It started out merely as a good course, falling short of greatness. It was then transformed by Trent Jones into a course too severe even for the elite among professional golfers. It has now mellowed with age into one of America's finest and fairest tests of golf.

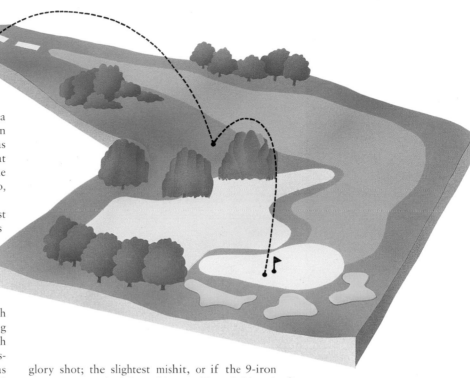

The 16th

Player Goes for Glory

Every great champion has had the capacity to make a telling stroke in the heart of crisis, but few more so than Gary Player. Three instances come to mind. There was the 4-wood shot to within two feet of the 14th hole at Carnoustie in the last round of the 1968 Open. The superb eagle stayed the challenge of Jack Nicklaus who, strive as he did, could not catch the little man.

Then there was a 9-iron shot stone dead on the 71st hole at Augusta that nearly ensured his second Masters victory in 1974, and two years earlier he played an even more remarkable stroke with the same club at Oakland Hills. Player was pursuing his second USPGA Championship with all his intense tenacity and with three holes to play was level with Jim Jamieson, who was on the 18th. The 16th curves elegantly but sharply to the right around a long lake with the green set so close to it that any approach has to cross it. Weeping willows on the near side discourage those who think of trying to cut the corner, as Player discovered when he sliced from the tee. His ball lay well in rough trampled by spectators, but he faced a blind shot of 150 yards, the willows and the lake between him and the flag. The carry was huge for a 9-iron but Player felt he needed that much loft to clear the trees. A seat stick left on the ground under the trees helped him decide the line. It was a carefully calculated death-or-glory shot; the slightest mishit, or if the 9-iron were not enough club, and he would probably take five or even six. He struck it perfectly and the ball came to rest only four feet from the hole. Down went the putt and, as Jamieson had missed a short one on the last green, Player had an insurance stroke in hand. He did not need it, thanks to a consummate blow delivered under pressure.

The 16th: 408 yards par 4
- - - - - Player

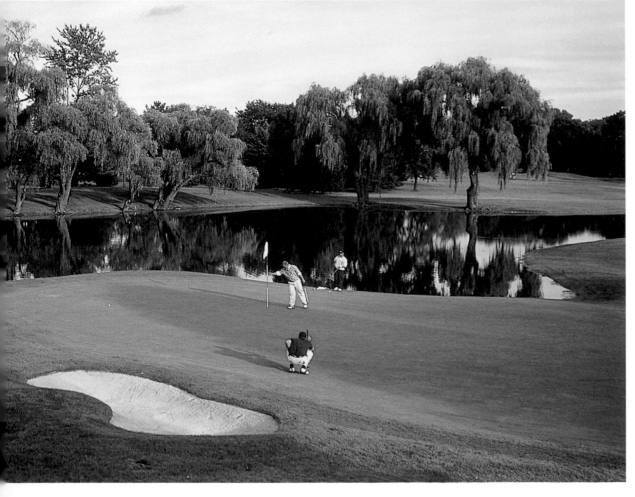

The par-four 16th hole curves elegantly around a lake, which is a factor for the approach shot.

The brainchild of two of America's finest golfers, Jimmy Demaret and Jackie Burke, Champions can claim to be one of the best courses in Texas. More than 70,000 trees dominate Ralph Plummer's layout, which has quickly become a regular venue for major events.

The Largest and Finest—

Of Course!

Right: There was no sand at the Champions club when the course opened but that has changed and shallow sand traps are now prevalent. The event was an impressive host to the Tour Championship in 1997, so much so the tournament will return there in 1999.

A golf club like Champions could really only be found in the state of Texas, where superlatives are not only commonplace but also, as often as not, quite justified as well. It has not just one but two championship courses, Cypress Creek and Jack Rabbit, a clubhouse that has almost every amenity imaginable, and a membership roll that even includes several astronauts.

The men responsible for the idea were champions, too. Jimmy Demaret, winner of more than fifty tournaments, was the first to conquer the U.S. Masters three times. When he died in 1983, his partner, Jackie Burke, operated the club. He took the Masters and the USPGA Championship in 1956, two years after being the first to take four consecutive PGA Tour events.

Slighter qualifications might not have sufficed for Houston, where, it is claimed, millionaires are more numerous than policemen. Many Texans have made their mark in golf. Apart from Demaret and Burke, Texas has produced Ben Hogan, Byron Nelson, Lloyd Mangrum, Ralph Guldahl, Babe Didrikson Zaharias, Harry Cooper, Lee Trevino, Mickey Wright, Don January, Charles Coody, Miller Barber, Ben Crenshaw, Tom Kite, Justin Leonard … the roll of honor is seemingly endless. Considering the size of Texas (it is twice as big as the British Isles, for instance) and the number of great golfers it has produced, it is surprising that it should have so few really memorable golf courses. Texas does, of course, have a number of good courses, among them Colonial at Fort Worth, Pecan Valley, Preston Trail at Dallas, and the Dallas Athletic Club. But none has the charisma of Champions, as those who have played in tournaments there —the 1967 Ryder Cup was one, the 1969 U.S. Open another —will readily testify. Today its merits have been brought to

an appreciative new audience as it held the season-ending PGA Tour event, the Tour Championship, in 1997.

When Demaret and Burke decided to build Champions in 1957, they not uncharacteristically announced that it would be "the world's largest and finest" course. "When you do something in this town, you have to do it on a grand scale," said Demaret. "So we decided to model our holes after the world's classics. We weren't going to imitate them; rather, we were going to blend their characteristics into the terrain we had. We wanted a golf club right here in our home town that would become to Houston and Texas what Augusta National is to Georgia, or Pinehurst to North Carolina, or St. Andrews to Scotland."

Burke added: "While we wanted an ample clubhouse, we wanted it strictly for golfers. We didn't want to build some barn of a place and then put the course on what was left over, meanwhile going broke with a lot of idle waiters standing around an empty ballroom. Furthermore, Jimmy and I decided we would run the club our way. You can't run a club smoothly through a board of directors, however brilliant each member may be in his own field. One wants a swimming pool, one some tennis courts, while another wants to fix up a couple of holes. So everything suffers."

The only concession they made was to construct a

swimming pool, because most of Champions' members were successful men in their thirties and forties, with children. The site Demaret and Burke decided to buy was 500 acres, heavily wooded with oaks, pines, and sweet-gums in an otherwise threadbare northern section of the town. Later, members bought a further 1,500 acres around the course for future home sites. Although the course is 20 miles from downtown Houston, it can be reached by one of the city's network of freeways in twenty minutes. Knowing their architectural limitations (as few professional golfers do), Demaret and Burke hired Ralph Plummer to lay out a master plan. Two of Plummer's most successful previous efforts had been the Dallas Athletic Club course and Shady Oaks, near Forth Worth, where Ben Hogan had localized his golf activities after retiring. After Plummer had finished, he would indicate the possible location of a tee or green to Demaret and Burke, who would then hit hundreds of balls to make sure the shots would play as projected.

At first, no bunkers were built. Instead, grass-covered mounds were bulldozed into shapes that could eventually be removed if unwanted, or converted into carefully shaped bunkers. Most bunkers are on the shallow side, especially those on the fairways. "We felt," Burke explained, "that if a player hits into a bunker, he should still be able to scramble his way to a par if necessary. There is no prettier shot in golf than a well-executed stroke out of sand, particularly a long shot."

While the Jack Rabbit course, designed later by George Fazio, is just as stringent as the Cypress Creek, it is utterly different. It has narrower fairways, smaller greens and deeper and more numerous bunkers. Cypress Creek, on the other hand, has wide fairways, tremendous greens, and bunkers that are more strategically placed. Both are about the same length, around 7,200 yards. Choosing the best hole at Cypress Creek is not easy, but two stretches of holes have impressed the professionals particularly: the 6th through the 8th, and the 12th through the 14th

The 6th and 7th are both medium-length par fours with big, inviting greens. Gay Brewer said of the 424-yard 6th that "the drive is the key shot. The hole is wooded both right and left. Under normal conditions, I'll play a 6- or 7-iron at the big green, which is guarded on the left by a sandtrap.

The great fear and problem on this hole is hooking the drive, for then the player is going to have to try to recover by hooking his ball out over the big lake which guards the right side of the green. It can turn into a disastrous hole." The 7th, only ten yards longer, can be difficult if the wind is against because hugging the right side of the fairway can be dangerous and aiming to the left makes the hole play longer. The green is large and has a big dip, and this invites three-putting. If you don't select the right club for your second shot, you can leave yourself a 100-foot putt. Another reason for avoiding the trees on the right is that a ditch comes into play in front of the green, although it is well short of the putting surface. The 8th, a par three of 185 yards, resembles the 12th at Augusta National.

The second group of holes makes no great demands on length but they come at a vital time in a round. Scoring well here can give the lift that every golfer needs to finish in style. The three-hole stretch starts with a par three and a par five back to back. The 12th is 213 yards long and, believed Jackie Burke, "a good player will use anything from a 3-iron to a 4-wood, depending on the wind. The green is rather large, well-guarded on the right by sand and in front by a lake that runs practically from tee to green. We call it Bob Hope Lake because he was the first person to hit a ball into it. He's hit a whole lot more since then." The 13th, a par five of 530 yards, proved pivotal for David Duval in the 1997 Tour Championship. The American hit a drive and 3-iron here to 50 feet and holed the putt for an eagle. Five pars to finish gave him his one stroke victory over Jim Furyk.

The 14th is a par four of 431 yards. "This is the hole that has been consistently the toughest to par," says Jack Nicklaus. "The oddly shaped green is bunkered tightly to the left, right, and rear, and a small lake directly in front of the green must be carried. Arnie Palmer says this is the finest 14th hole he has ever played. I'm inclined to agree with him."

After everything has been said about Champions, what gave it its special character were the two ebullient men who founded it. During his time on the tour the good-humored Jackie Burke was one of the most popular players among his fellow professionals and Bob Hope, adhering to the principle that only a superlative is adequate to describe a Texan, called Demaret the funniest amateur comedian he has met.

The Course Card

Champions Golf Club, Houston, Texas Cypress Creek course

Record: 64, Bob Rosburg, Champions International 1968

Hole	Yards	Par
1	453	4
2	450	4
3	388	4
4	230	3
5	514	5
6	424	4
7	431	4
8	185	3
9	506	5
10	453	4
11	460	4
12	213	3
13	530	5
14	431	4
15	416	4
16	181	3
17	442	4
18	440	4
Out	3,581	36
In	3,566	35
Total	**7,147**	**71**

Where the Old-fashioned Still

Reigns Supreme

The
Course
Card

Pebble Beach Golf
Links, Pebble
Beach, California

Hole	Yards	Par
1	373	4
2	502	5
3	388	4
4	327	4
5	166	3
6	516	5
7	107	3
8	431	4
9	464	4
10	426	4
11	384	4
12	202	3
13	392	4
14	565	5
15	397	4
16	402	4
17	209	3
18	548	5
Out	3,274	36
In	3,525	36
Total	**6,799**	**72**

Without any argument, the supreme golf course in the western United States is Pebble Beach, three times the site of the U.S. Open and again in 2000, despite the reluctance of the USGA to hold its Championship so far from a major city. Stretching for several miles alongside the rocky shore and steep cliffs of Carmel Bay, some 120 miles south of San Francisco, Pebble Beach has gained, thanks to television, a fame—indeed, even a notoriety—far beyond the immediate world of golf. Each January it is the remarkable scene of the closing round of the AT&T pro-am, a tournament that attracts a larger television audience than virtually any other event on the golfing calendar. It is almost axiomatic that once it goes on the air, the climate of the Monterey Peninsula goes into a frenzy, and Pebble Beach becomes a ruffian that intimidates and manhandles the world's finest professional golfers. Not in 1997, mind. Then Tiger Woods closed with three successive birdies for a 64 and the world learned that a special talent was about to emerge.

By American standards Pebble Beach is an old-fashioned course. At only just under 6,800 yards it is not particularly long; nor is it heavily bunkered. But the greens are small by present-day standards; many of them are well contoured, and when the course is in its best playing condition they can be as slick as any in the world—including the notoriously speedy Oakmont. The unique quality of Pebble Beach, however, is to be found on its stretch of seaside holes. Beginning at the 6th, a par five reachable in two, and continuing through the 10th, it presents one of the loveliest and probably the most severe succession of seaside holes to be found on any U.S. course of championship caliber. The vista of these holes, particularly as viewed from the upper part of the 6th fairway and looking down the shoreline to the 10th green, is one of the loveliest sights of a sport that is by no means short of beauty. More than that, the last three of these holes, even on the

balmiest of days, are enough to unsettle the strongest players and take the momentum from a round that seems on its way to something memorable. Gil Morgan certainly discovered this at the 1992 U.S. Open. One minute, during the third round, he had created history and become the first man to reach double digits under par at any stage in any U.S. Open. The birdies kept coming; he reached a scarcely credible 12-under. Then he stepped on the 8th tee. He played the next three holes in five over par; indeed he went on to play the last twenty-nine holes in 17 over. Clearly Pebble Beach was not happy with its earlier humbling.

The 8th, the first of the vicious triumvirate, is 431 yards on the card and begins with a blind drive from a slightly depressed tee perched on the side of a cliff that falls away some 50 feet to the sea below. The well-hit uphill drive of some 200 yards to the middle of the fairway leaves an awesome shot across an elbow of the bay that cuts into the fairway approximately 250 yards from the tee. There is an absolute carry of 180 yards across the bay to a small green that is liberally trapped on three sides. A scrubby bank rises up on the left side of the green to catch the overhit shot, and one would prefer not to be there either. Probably half the pars achieved here during a major tournament are made with one putt. The 9th has been described by more than one tournament professional as the toughest par four in golf. That could be an overstatement, but not by much. The hole runs downhill all the way to the green, and the fairway slopes toward the sea, so the tendency is to keep the ball to the left and thus lengthen the hole beyond the 464 yards it measures on a straight line. With the wind blowing in from the sea, as it so often does, only the very strongest hitters are going to reach this green in two. The 10th, although a little shorter at 426 yards, still poses the same forbidding problems—the sea on the right

Jack Neville was hired by Sam Morse in 1918 to lay out Pebble Beach, and with Douglas Grant and H. Chandler Egan as consultants, he produced one of the most magnificent and testing of all courses.

A magnificent course perfect for television—two dozen well-placed cameras can cover virtually the entire layout—Pebble Beach staged the U.S. Open in 1972 and in 1982. After three relatively easy holes the craggy coast comes into play, and from then on the course is a tortuous test of skill.

Bing Crosby started his pro-am tournament at Pebble Beach in 1936. It is now sponsored by AT&T and continues to attract both the best players of the day and the glamor of Hollywood. Here, Crosby is with Bob Hope and Frank Sinatra.

and the green tucked up against the side of the cliff. On a day when the winds are on the rampage, anyone who can go par-par-par along this stretch is playing virtually perfect golf.

Pebble Beach turns inland from there, but it returns to the sea at the 17th and 18th, two holes where tournaments are frequently won and lost. It was at the 17th, a 209-yard tee shot—usually into the wind—to a large, two-level green with the sea to the left and behind, that Tom Watson completed one of the great shots of his illustrious career. It was like the Open Championship at Turnberry all over again as he and Jack Nicklaus dueled for supremacy over the clos-

ing holes in the 1982 U.S. Open. When Watson missed the green on the left at the 17th, it appeared that Nicklaus would triumph this time. Watson's chip was from clinging rough and he appeared to have no chance of stopping the ball close to the pin, which had been positioned on the left side of the green. Unless, of course, he hit the pin. "I'm going to hole this," he said to his sceptical caddie. But hole it he did, in one of the great prophecies the game has witnessed. Watson birdied the last for good measure, to win by two shots. As he came out of the scorer's tent there to greet him was the great sportsman himself, Nicklaus. He put an arm around Watson's shoulders and said: "You son of a bitch, you're something else. I'm very proud of you."

At the 1992 U.S. Open Nicklaus was in the commentary box when Colin Montgomerie finished his round. "Congratulations, you are the champion," he told the Scot, who had finished a full two hours before the leaders out on the course. Nicklaus's reasoning was sound. The strong wind was becoming a gale and Montgomerie had reached sanctuary with a score of level par, 288. Tom Kite was four under but had only played seven and had the tempest to handle. He did, however. Indeed Kite, never before a Major Champion, played the back nine in one under to finish at five under and make a mockery of Nicklaus's prediction. It was some performance.

Until 1966, Pebble Beach was, for all intents and purposes, a public golf course designed for the use of visitors to the Lodge at Pebble Beach, the large resort hotel overlooking the 18th green and the sea. It was built during 1919 as part of the Del Monte Properties (now Pebble Beach

Co.), which undertook to develop a remote and exclusive resort community in the wild pine forests of the Monterey Peninsula. Until World War II few but the very rich were attracted to the Pebble Beach area. For the most part it was the weekend and summer playground of the corporation presidents and their wives from Los Angeles and San Francisco, with a sprinkling of just enough Middle Westerners and Easterners to give the area and its expensive houses an aura of eastern sophistication. The Pebble Beach course was too splendid to go unnoticed, however. California state championships were played there, and its reputation grew to the point where the USGA finally brought the Amateur championship there in 1929—the first national championship ever played west of the Mississippi. The tournament is remembered nowadays largely because it was the only Amateur championship during the last seven years of his active career in which Bobby Jones failed to reach the final round. On five of the other six occasions he was the winner, but at Pebble Beach he lost his first-round match to unknown Johnny Goodman, probably the biggest sports upset of the entire year. The impact on American

golfers can be imagined. As an amateur Jones was supreme to an extent that no other has ever been, and who on earth was Goodman? Although he lost to Lawson Little later in that championship, he was soon to make an enduring mark. In 1933 he was the last amateur to win either the U.S. or Open Championships, but that morning at Pebble Beach the great crowd was stunned. The words Pebble Beach are engraved on the heart of Nicklaus, and not just for what happened in the 1982 U.S. Open. He has often said it is his favorite golf course and it must be quite a thrill for him to redesign the short 5th hole, which was going ahead as this book went to publication. Now a par three heading inland, it will be transformed into another ocean hole, a perfect foil for the spectacular short holes, the 7th and 17th. As for his on-course exploits, in 1961 progress to his second U.S. Amateur title was little short of a massacre. Eleven years later he walked in triumph up the last long fairway by the ocean toward his third U.S. Open victory. In all golf there can be no more beautiful walk for a champion about to be crowned. His victory was assured when a magnificent 1-iron shot, drawn into the strong breeze, almost

Right and below: At 107 yards Pebble Beach's 7th is one of the shortest holes in golf but one of the most difficult, particularly in a wind, when it may take as much as a 3-iron to hit the tiny green only 8 yards wide and tightly trapped. After a punched 7-iron Nicklaus holed a birdie putt of 25 feet here in the final round of the 1972 Open.

The 7th: 120 yards par 3

8yds

The 7th

An Eloquent Plea for Delicacy

When, in the 1973 Open, Gene Sarazen holed his tee shot at Troon's 13th hole, the famous Postage Stamp, only 126 yards long, it was seen by millions and commanded welcome attention to the virtues of the short short hole. There is no finer, or more beautiful, example of this than the 7th at Pebble Beach. After mounting the crest of the 6th the golfer turns toward the ocean. There below him on a promontory, bounded with rocks where the surf spills silver, lies a tiny green of 2,000 square feet embraced by sand. The hole measures only 107 yards and is downhill. In calm air a wedge or 9-iron is the club, but when the wind is strong from the Pacific golfers may be fingering medium irons to keep the ball low on line. Normally the shot offers

no problem to the expert, but the distance is not all that easy to judge and there are no marks for being too bold. The heaving tumult of the waves awaits. Short the hole may be, but the shot requires the utmost precision because the green lies directly along the line of approach and offers a target of no more than 8 yards in width. In the 1992 U.S. Open, the 7th proved pivotal for the eventual winner Tom Kite. Having overshot the green in the wild and windy conditions with his 6-iron, Kite then chipped in from a seemingly impossible position to turn a bogey into a birdie—a momentum builder if ever there was one.

The 7th must be the shortest hole on any Major Championship course in the United States, but nobody went into the 17th hole, gently hitting the pin and finishing inches away. He became the first and most probably the last, American golfer to have won both U.S. Open and Amateur championships on the same course. In Britain, Jones alone has accomplished the feat with his victories at St. Andrews in 1927 and 1930.

In addition to his Amateur and Open, Nicklaus had won the pro-am tournament three times and a fourth seemed likely in 1976 when he was sharing the lead after the last turn. Then suddenly it was revealed that Nicklaus could be as human a golfer as any humble hacker. On the 13th, after a big drive, he hit an inexcusably bad iron shot and made seven on the par-four hole. A good tee shot to the 17th was harshly bunkered and led to another triple-bogey and, in trying to get home in two at the last, he pulled into what Bing Crosby nicknamed the "mollusc country" and took seven. Nicklaus, smiling disbelief, was back in 45 for an 82 and golfers everywhere were comforted by the thought that even the mightiest of the age, if not of all the ages, could be as vulnerable as they.

The post-World War II prosperity and the jet age drasti-

cally changed the character of the Monterey Peninsula and, in turn, brought Pebble Beach to its present fame. The new-rich built houses in the area by the hundreds, and the nation's growing population of golfers could afford to fly there from anywhere on the continent in a matter of hours. Almost adjacent to Pebble Beach was the small and exclusive Cypress Point Club with its lovely links-like course built in 1930, and it was there that most of the better-connected golfers played, if they could arrange it, leaving Pebble Beach to the general public and the visitors at The Lodge. Bing Crosby moved the National Pro-Am tournament (now sponsored by AT&T) to the area in 1947, and as it grew in size he used not only Pebble Beach and Cypress Point but a third course farther along the beach belonging to the Monterey Peninsula Country Club. By 1966, a fourth course called Spyglass Hill, designed by the eminent Robert Trent Jones, was in operation, assuming the burden of the public play; and Pebble Beach became private, yet still available to the guests at the Lodge.

No description of Pebble Beach would be complete without some mention of the professional who ran the course with as autocratic a hand as any medieval monarch's. A Scotsman whose powerful voice and style seemed never to have left the heath and heather, Peter Hay was as much a part of Pebble Beach as the misty rain that blows in from the Pacific. Some claimed they built the course around him. Peter Hay may be long gone but his stern commands remain as relevant as ever, not the least of which was "Play your shots quickly and don't complain." If only it was the clarion call of all golfers.

scorns it because of that. For the player seeking a birdie it demands a more sensitive touch than most shots of similar length from the fairway. Rightly, therefore, it commands its place in the heart of the most compelling stretch of seaside golf in the world. Pebble Beach has become the yardstick against which all new seaside courses are measured. It is a matter of regret that more architects have not been inspired by this short but memorable 7th hole.

Sadly, though, such holes are rare. The increased power of golfers in recent decades has led to short holes being made longer and longer. Often the average player is blinding away with wood or long iron, concerned mainly with making the distance and not finessing the shot to the most favorable part of the green. Every course should have at least one truly short hole, where delicacy rather than strength is of the essence. No architectural genius is needed to make it extremely testing—and hugely enjoyable.

The 9th And 10th

A Classic Test of Technique

Never were golf architects more richly blessed in a setting than were Jack Neville and Douglas Grant when they came to create Pebble Beach. With scarcely a second glance they must have visualized the great sequence of holes along the coast. By right of its place in the round the 18th is the most famous; the 7th is the most beautiful and the 8th the most spectacular but, in pure golfing terms, there cannot be two successive par fours anywhere of greater quality than the 9th and 10th. Both are classics of their kind, rolling along the jagged coast, their greens right against it and the land leaning toward the ocean all the way. If ever holes reward, indeed demand, true striking, these do. Few shots test a golfer's technique more precisely than those that compel him to hold a true line when the elements are from left to right, whether they be wind or, as on these holes, falling ground. The man who fears the slice or push toward the ocean and holds his shot too much to the left may be bunkered or, at best, face a fearsomely long approach to the green with all the perils that lie beyond. In the final round of the 1972 U.S. Open Jack Nicklaus twice found the beach at the 10th to wind up with a six that almost cost him the title.

The 9th hole at Pebble Beach is not only the most picturesque of par fours, but demanding as well.

The Course Card

Dorado Beach
Hotel Golf and
Tennis Club,
Puerto Rico
East course

Record: 64, John
Buczek, International
Pro-Am 1975

Hole	Yards	Par
1	360	4
2	530	5
3	175	3
4	370	4
5	570	5
6	370	4
7	410	4
8	195	3
9	440	4
10	520	5
11	215	3
12	390	4
13	540	5
14	205	3
15	430	4
16	455	4
17	415	4
18	415	4
Out	3,420	36
In	3,585	36
Total	**7,005**	**72**

The luxurious sprawl of Dorado Beach, its hotels and golf courses conjured out of fruit plantations and mangrove swamps on the Puerto Rican seashore, offers the apparent incongruity of a resort only the wealthiest can afford in a place where it can do some good for a poor society.

Dorado Beach was built in the late 1950s and early 1960s by Laurance Rockefeller, who retained Robert Trent Jones to design the four golf courses that it now has. His singular talent for creating resort golf could not have found a better canvas on which to work, nor one that would require more landscape engineering. Tens of thousands of tons of earth and rock were shifted to create lagoons, well stocked with fish—and, by the same token, to drain the swampy ground. The spoil was used to contour the course.

Dorado Beach is well away from the mainstream of golf and as a consequence has not staged many important contests. It has, however, staged the World Cup on two occasions, the first in 1961 when it was called the Canada Cup. This was won by Sam Snead and Jimmy Demaret, whose combined ages were then ninety-nine years. These matches were staged over a composite course, for only nine holes of the East course had then been completed. Major events are now played over the East course, which is considered tougher. Not tough enough for Davis Love and Fred Couples in the 1994 World Cup, who took advantage of humid conditions and little wind. In perhaps the greatest performance in the tournament's long history, the American pair finished a mind-boggling 40 under par to win by no less than 14 shots. Couples won the individual honors with a total of 265.

The first four holes are pleasantly challenging, the sea sparkling away to the golfer's left as he drives from the first tee. The par-five 5th, 570 yards, is the longest hole on the course. Trees flank either side of the hole from tee to green and the tee shot is threatened by a glaring trio of bunkers and one large mango tree. The second is no easier, with three more bunkers standing sentinel on the left and a fourth on the right. The third shot is to an elevated green, from the rear of which the player is faced with a harrowing putt. One bunker lies to the left of the green, another directly in front.

There follow two par fours of moderate length and then the 195-yard, par-three 8th, where the chief difficulty lies not in hitting its immense green but in getting down in two putts. The 9th is another matter; it is the most demanding par four on the course, although at 440 yards its length is not back-breaking. Three bunkers demand accuracy from the tee and the second shot is menaced by trees on either side. It is almost certain to be a long iron and the green, which is hemmed in by two giant bunkers, is deep and narrow.

The 10th is a shortish par five, the beach keeping it company on the left. The 11th is only 215 yards long, but it is moated about by water and the green is not one to miss. The short par-four 12th plays longer than it looks because the prevailing wind is in the player's teeth and the two lakes of the 13th, 540 yards, pose a fascinating dilemma for both long and short hitters. The 14th, a par three going away from the ocean, presents no special problem if the golfer does not slice or push his tee shot. Four bunkers embrace the green and water comes into the reckoning on the right.

The last four holes are all par fours, only the long 16th calling for real power hitting. The 15th requires extreme authority off the tee and in the approach to the green. The fairway is narrow and the elevated green has two tiers, with traps lying to the left, right and front. At 455 yards the 16th is the longest par four on the course, but the wind is now

Trent Jones Transforms
a Swamp

Over a million cubic yards of earth was moved to fashion the East course at Dorado Beach, the best of five fine courses situated just east of San Juan. Shortly after it opened it was host to the 1961 World Cup, when Sam Snead won the individual title with a sixteen-under-par 272.

following. The long, narrow green rises to the rear and is surrounded by bunkers. The dogleg 17th is made more difficult by two bunkers just beyond the corner. Double bunkers guard the front of the green. The finishing hole provides a challenging finale, with two large fairway traps to be side-stepped and two more barricading the green. A strong breeze gusting in from the ocean stiffens the challenge.

When the late Ed Dudley first went to Dorado Beach as head professional in 1958, from the Augusta National, he called the original eighteen holes "the toughest test for the top professionals of any course I have played." On paper, as Couples and Love so eloquently proved, the course is more attractive than tough. The secret of Dorado Beach lies in the Atlantic winds. Thus it is a perfect resort course, offering a tough challenge to the handicap player and, at the same time, giving little away to the professional.

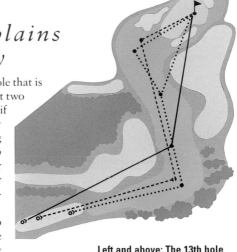

Trent Jones Explains His Strategy

Robert Trent Jones likes to design a golf hole that is not only beautiful but can be played at least two different ways, and preferably more—ten, if he can manage it. He wants the hole to play heroically for the professional who is going for a birdie, daringly for the low-handicap amateur who must go all out for his par with the possibility of a birdie, safely for the high handicapper to whom par is a victory, and not overly long for the ladies.

In this respect, the 13th at Dorado Beach is one of his favorites. It is a double dogleg par five that twice bends sharply around a wafer hazard, first to the left and then, near the green, to the right. The green is elevated and, in addition to the protection of the 75-yard-wide lake, is surrounded by traps. Behind the green, about 30 yards away, is the Atlantic. The courageous and capable golfer can reach the green, but he will have made two thoroughly superb shots. The hole embraces four possibilities. The confident golfer can hit over both lakes to reach the green in two strokes, thereby cutting off a hundred yards of the hole's 540-yard length through the fairway. Or he can elect to play to the right of the first lake and to the left of the second, leaving himself a short pitch to the length of the green. The hand-

Left and above: The 13th hole on the East course at Dorado Beach, left, with the characteristic palm trees swaying in the breeze.

icap golfer also has two choices. He may drive safely to the right of the first lake and follow this with a straight second before deciding on whether to gamble by going for the green with his third or settling for the fourth alternative, the safe four-shot route to the green. The ladies have the same options. In the words of its designer, the hole is "fair to all, demanding to be sure, but it demonstrates clearly the rewards and penalties that should be innate to all great golf holes."

Mind the Bunkers

and the Bear Cubs!

If the greatness of golf courses was determined by their setting then Banff Springs, nestling a mile up in the Canadian Rockies, would certainly make the world's top ten. Though not a venue for major championships, it is a first-rate course where the towering mountains make distances seem shorter causing many players to over-club. The most famous holes are the 8th (Devil's Cauldron), the taxing 16th (Big Bow), and the 18th (Wampum), which harbors 28 of Banff's 144 bunkers.

It was once suggested to no less qualified a judge of golf course beauty than Bobby Locke that Banff Springs occupied one of the most spectacular settings in the world. To which Locke replied: "Not really. It's out of this world." So striking is the setting of Banff Springs, in the Canadian Rockies, that few visitors can concentrate only on their golf.

Banff's first course, of only nine holes, was created by the Canadian Pacific Railway Company in 1911 as an added attraction for its huge, turreted Banff Springs Hotel. During World War I a further nine holes were built by German prisoners of war. Stanley Thompson, the Canadian architect with whom Robert Trent Jones served his apprenticeship, was commissioned to redesign the course in 1927. He was assisted by Casper McCullough, a turf expert who became the course superintendent for the next forty-four years.

Maintenance problems remain legion. Golf course greenmasters in southern Alberta wage an endless battle with the ravages of alternate freezing and thawing, caused by sub-zero temperatures and mild Chinook winds of winter, and by the warm, sunny days and sub-zero nights of spring.

Measured against the exacting standards of today's top players, Banff Springs remains a true championship test. Yet its 6,729-yard challenge has never been used for a major competition, perhaps because of its remoteness. The course is a maze of bunkers—144 in all. Twenty-eight of them come into play at the 18th, an imperious finishing hole running parallel to the Bow River and only a few hundred feet from thundering Bow Falls.

The 1st tee, immediately below the clubhouse pavilion overlooking the often torrential confluence of the Bow and Spray rivers, presents a breathtaking vista. A precipice drops to the Spray tributary directly in front of the tee and, although the carry across it is less than a hun-

The imposing sight of the Banff Springs Hotel would look over-the-top in a less sublime setting.

dred yards, the churning river has been known to unnerve the most composed of scratch players. The green opens up after a mound on the right, but accuracy is essential for a safe par, as six narrow traps crowd around the sides and rear. The 2nd and 3rd are both short, undemanding par fours. They contrast sharply with the 4th, the course's longest hole, where mounds and bunkers are neatly stacked on the fairway. The drive must clear a cavernous bunker snaking from the

left; a sound second, across a nest of mounds and traps, leaves a fairly open avenue home. From a straightforward par four of undemanding length, the route swings south toward the steep face of Mount Rundle, which so dominates the course. The short 6th is conventional, requiring an iron shot to a raised green imprisoned by traps, but the par-five 7th, aptly named Gibraltar, is unusual. The tee gazes out on a rather lean strip of greensward, bounded on the right by the rising cliffs of Mount Rundle and on the left by a series of traps. A precise shot is required to reach the green in two, for it is tucked away to the right, partially hidden, and the approach must thread between the precipice on the right and the sand that lies to the left. An easy climb to a high lookout affords a heart-stopping view of the par-three 8th, known as the Devil's

Cauldron. This famous hole calls for a most difficult shot, complicated by swirling wind, from an elevated tee across a lake to a tiny, heavily bunkered green. The 9th, a dogleg par four is sliced out of dense woods. The fairway curves and slopes left, guiding hooked shots into bunkers that lie beyond an awkward trough. A prodigious second shot is required to reach the green, trapped heavily to the right. The relatively routine 10th, straight but to an elevated and well-trapped green, leaves one at the farthest point from the clubhouse as the course angles north toward the Bow River and a cliffs beyond, webbed with pillars of clay, sand, and gravel known as the Hoodoos. A network of bunkers surrounds the green on the downhill par-five 11th, which, if the two cross bunkers are avoided, offers birdie chances.

The course now turns back along the Bow River toward the distant battlements of the hotel. The drive at the tree sheltered 12th, the 138-yard Papoose, carries a long strip of tee and a backwash of the river. The 13th green, hidden from the tee, is accessible in two with an exacting drive that will stand some pull out of a chute of trees to the more elevated left side of the fairway.

An arm of the river severs the 14th, which is lengthy for a par three: the temptation is to use a wood to reach the green, but the fairway banks sharply in the direction of the water and any slight fade or short shot is doomed. It makes the 14th a score-wrecking hole. Two cross-bunkers and nine greenside traps make the 15th tough, yet it is the 16th, another par four, that boasts the toughest rating at Banff. It is a slight dogleg to the right with a series of bunkers off the tee and a fairway that rolls and heaves, pinching in to the right and trees and sand to the left. The green is long and narrow. Accuracy with the middle irons is vital.

The shadow of nearby Tunnel Mountain looms directly above the 17th, a flat, long par three with severe traps flanking the green. The 18th, another slight dogleg right, has two massive clusters of bunkers, one of which must be carried. The fairway traps, which stretch to 185 yards off the tee, can only be avoided by courting the trees down the narrow right side, but this only makes for an extremely difficult shot across the second nest of traps.

The Banff Springs course lies within a National Park; deer and even the odd bear cub can be seen from time to time. Banff Springs calls for thoughtfulness and accuracy and is indeed out of this world.

The Course Card

Banff Springs Hotel, Alberta

Hole	Name	Yardage	Par
1	Spray	479	4
2	Goat	382	4
3	Sarcee	376	4
4	Windy	570	5
5	Prettie	438	4
6	Rundle	178	3
7	Gibraltar	513	5
8	Devil's Cauldron	175	3
9	Trough	432	4
10	Fairholm	349	4
11	Hoodoo	525	5
12	Papoose	138	3
13	Jinx	484	5
14	Little Bow	210	3
15	Magpie	400	4
16	Big Bow	430	4
17	Sulphur	225	3
18	Wampum	425	4
Out		3,543	36
In		3,186	35
Total		**6,729**	**71**

The 8th
Devil's Cauldron

Famous the world over for its splendid site in an amphitheater beneath a soaring rock face of the massive Mount Rundle, Banff's 8th hole, known as the Devil's Cauldron, is universally recognized as one of the great holes of golf. It is a par-three that calls for the drop-shot which was so popular among golfers in the 1920s and 1930s. A natural miniature glacial lake is the hole's chief hazard, but there are others—notably scattered bunkers encircling a green set on an oval terrace sloping slightly toward the water. The green is separated from the lake by a narrow ribbon of lower terrace and rimmed on three sides by more pronounced grass slopes, which rise through trees to the base of cliffs. The mountain wall had to be blasted to clear the site when the course was reconstructed in 1927.

Accuracy from the tee is vital and it is a matter of precision—an ideal example of Stanley Thompson's uncanny knack for producing marvelous holes in rugged terrain.

A Course Worthy of its
Glorious Setting

The Course Card

Capilano Golf and Country Club, British Columbia

Hole	Yards	Par
1	472	5
2	404	4
3	459	5
4	161	3
5	517	5
6	399	4
7	433	4
8	370	4
9	175	3
10	424	5
11	164	3
12	362	4
13	395	4
14	136	3
15	424	4
16	219	4
17	425	4
18	556	5
Out	3,390	37
In	3,105	35
Total	**6,495**	**72**

The visitor's first impression of Capilano is of its almost Olympian setting. Buttressed to the north and east by the coastal mountains of British Columbia, it overlooks the not unpleasing sprawl of urban Vancouver with Mount Baker beyond, south of the 49th Parallel; to the west is a misty Vancouver Island, across the Strait of Georgia. It is a vista decidedly distracting to the concentration of the visiting golfer and even to those club members most used to it.

A glorious setting does not in itself make a great golf course. But while the views at Capilano may distract, they do not detract from the course's true golfing qualities. This course, in which no two holes are remotely similar, would be outstanding wherever it were set down. Capilano is exceptional in this part of the world as one of the few courses—if not the only one—that has not been drastically remodeled since it was opened. It was designed and constructed in 1937 by Stanley Thompson, the well-known Canadian golf course architect and creator of many other exquisite courses, among them Banff Springs. The course was part of a huge project embarked upon in the early 1930s by Guinness Estates. The plan was for a high-class residential development and golf course at West Vancouver, isolated from the city proper by the Burrard Inlet but to be linked to it by a mile-long bridge. It was a huge undertaking by anybody's standards, not least in the construction of the course itself.

Capilano had to be shaped from a hillside tangled with the stumps of Douglas firs, cedar, and hemlock, a forest of second-growth trees, and massive outcrops of rock. The result, nevertheless, is a gem. It is not difficult for the player of average ability who keeps his drives in the fairways. The championship course measures 6,578 yards but it can be stretched by more than 300 yards for special events.

The 1st is downhill all the way—472 yards, but closer to 500 from a seldom used championship tee, within a stone's throw of the men's bar. It is a hole where the par of five feels more like a bogey to the scratch player. The par-four 2nd, a drive and medium iron, is followed by a blind uphill tee shot at the 459-yard 3rd, a par five that is littered with bunkers. Sprayed wood shots here create problems in reaching the relatively small and well-guarded green in regulation figures. A mid-iron will suffice to carry a pond safely to the double-tiered green of the par-three 4th, though insufficient club leaves a nasty putt if the pin placement is on the upper level.

Then comes yet another par five, a dogleg right over more water which, from one of the upper tees, demands a flush and perfectly placed drive. The second shot, hit downhill toward the city, must also be accurate to the vicinity of an undulating, treacherously fast green. The stroll down the 6th is a divine pleasure; the spectacle below of the Lions Gate Bridge, linking Vancouver with the North Shore across the sparkling waters of Burrard Inlet, is simply entrancing. By the time the golfer is putting on the 6th green he has descended almost 300 feet from the 1st tee, 672 feet above sea level. Many handicap players have negotiated these first six holes well under par figures. But there are pitfalls ahead, for now the course flattens out and Capilano begins to catch up on the careless golfer. The next two holes are both fine par fours. The climb back toward clubhouse level begins from the 9th tee. The hole is a troublesome, 175-yard par three on which club selection varies according to the weather. It usually requires a low iron or spoon to reach the elongated green guarded by gaping bunkers, from which only the top of the flagstick is visible.

The beginning of the second nine offers a possible birdie at the par-five 10th. It is less than 430 yards long, a dogleg left calling for accuracy with the second shot to an elevated, narrow-necked entrance to the green. The next hole is quite simply a sheer delight. From the elevated tee it is nothing more than a 6- or 7-iron over a man-made pond, but the slick green undulates like an oily sea in a swell. On the last seven holes birdies are all too rare and pars require considerably more finesse and thought than has previously been necessary. The exception, perhaps, is the short 14th, a pitch over the main driveway from another elevated tee. The 12th and 13th, both par fours, call for well-placed drives followed by precise shots over a stream at the 12th and a gully at the longer 13th.

The 15th, like the 7th, cannot be manipulated without two exceptional shots. It is an ominous 424-yarder, directly into the face of the mountains and slightly uphill to the green. The best that short hitters can hope to do is chip and single putt to achieve a well-earned par here. At the 16th a par three, even on the calmest of days, is a sheer victory. From the back tee it is 219 yards to the green, which sits immediately beneath the clubhouse. With any kind of opposing wind it is nothing less than a full wood.

At the 17th, slightly over 400 yards long, the main difficulties lie in club selection and in avoiding an awkward lie among the fairway mounds while steering clear of a long bunker and the obtrusive trees on the left. The green is in a beautiful setting, softened by the shadows of tall trees and the mountains.

The home hole is a classic, 556 yards long and uphill all the way to a green set on the side of a hill scattered with a network of bunkers. The safe way to approach this monster is to lay up short of the three diagonal bunkers fronting the green, leaving a mid-iron approach over the inviting sand to the elevated but reasonably flat green. Few long hitters have ever reached this green in two. It is a feat requiring a "Sunday best" drive and a gambling 3-wood over the narrow, upper portion of the fairway, which is flanked by the bunkers and out of bounds stakes. The elevation and the nearness of the mountains make Capilano vulnerable to rain, and umbrellas are an essential item throughout the winter and spring. But few golfers—no matter what the weather or their final scores—have ever left Capilano without singing the praises of this truly magnificent course.

The 4th and 11th

Thompson At His Fiercest

Stanley Thompson, Capilano's Scottish-born architect, made something of a speciality of creating fascinating short holes. Among the more celebrated are the Devil's Cauldron at Banff Springs and, at nearby Jasper, the 150-yard Bad Baby and the slightly longer Colin's Clout. At Capilano Thompson maintained his tradition of colorfully named, tough par threes.

Two of them, the 4th and 11th, are across stretches of water after which they have been named. Paradoxically these names imply a certain ease and benevolence on the part of the architect. Indeed, the water at the 4th, known as Lily Pond, is intimidating only to the handicap golfer who might otherwise find the hole relatively easy. It is only from the extended championship tees, which can stretch the hole to almost

200 yards, that the 4th becomes in any way fierce. Then, because of three huge traps that guard the front half of the smallish, two-tiered green, the drive must be absolutely accurate, particularly when the pin is on the farther, upper level.

The 11th, called Wishing Well, is an entirely different proposition. It embodies all the characteristics that have made Thompson's short holes so feared. Typically, it is only 164 yards long but the green, wonderfully sited among stately pine trees, is fast and heavily undulated and tightly enclosed by hazards. Immediately in front is a small lake and around the back and sides are four long, sprawling bunkers. Anything other than the most precise medium iron shot will find severe trouble. Fittingly, this beautiful hole became the architect's favorite.

Splendidly set beneath the mountains of the Coastal Range and high above the city and harbor of Vancouver, Capilano is challenging without being awesome. The large firs from which the course was carved make the fairways seem narrower than they really are. However, the last four holes, where architect Stanley Thompson's bunkering is especially astute, provide a stern finishing stretch.

Fit for the Next
Fifty Years

The Course Card

The Royal
Montreal Golf
Club, Ile Bizard,
Quebec
Blue course

Hole	Yards	Par
1	434	4
2	375	4
3	364	4
4	440	4
5	179	3
6	570	5
7	143	3
8	397	4
9	423	4
10	452	4
11	438	4
12	193	3
13	533	5
14	361	4
15	420	4
16	433	4
17	133	3
18	450	4
Out	3,205	35
In	3,282	35
Total	**6,487**	**70**

Whatever insubstantial traces of golf there are to be found in the history of North America before the late 19th century, pride of place in seniority must go to Canada and in particular to the Royal Montreal Club, which celebrated its centenary in 1973. It was the first properly constituted club on the continent, predating the first in the United States—St. Andrews at Yonkers, New York—by fifteen years.

Golf in Canada is older than in the United States probably because Canada attracted the larger proportion of Scottish immigrants. Toronto Golf Club, Royal Quebec, and Brantford Golf and Country Club, Ontario, though marginally younger than Montreal, are older than any of their counterparts across the border.

Royal Montreal's beginnings were similar to those of countless clubs throughout the world—a group of Scotsmen getting together to re-create, in alien surroundings, their national sport. They were led by a bearded giant, Alexander Dennistoun, whose name was proof enough of his antecedents. The medal he gave for competition (upon which, by means of a little Scottish finagling, he managed to have his name the first to be engraved) is still played for to this day as the symbol of the club's championship.

Fletcher's Field, a public park on the slopes of Mount Royal, was the club's first site. The joining fee was five dollars, the annual dues half as much; a wooden club would set a member back two dollars. The site was adequate to begin with, but in time the game attracted more players and, moreover, Montreal was growing rapidly. In 1896 a new site was found at Dixie, ten miles to the west of the city, and here the club was to remain for the next sixty-three years.

The par-four 15th hole at Royal Montreal, once the scene of a memorable play-off victory in the Canadian Open for Tom Weiskopf over Jack Nicklaus.

Though rarely used for major competitions, the Blue course at Royal Montreal is regarded by many experts as the finest in Canada. It became better known after the 1975 Canadian Open, when Tom Weiskopf and Jack Nicklaus broke the record by three shots in the opening round. The most notable feature of this beautiful course is the size of the greens—averaging 12,000 square feet, almost twice the usual size.

The Dixie course saw the first Canadian national championships, the women's amateur in 1901 and the men's a year later. The club also staged the world's first "international," the first of an annual series between Royal Montreal and The Country Club of Brookline, Massachusetts. The contest predates by four years the England-Scotland series, which began in 1902, and is still played.

Dixie was to be the venue for five Canadian Opens, won by J. H. Oke (1904), Albert Murray (1908 and 1913), Macdonald Smith (1926), and Jim Ferrier (1950). It was played by those legends of the links Harry Vardon and Ted Ray; and by the Prince of Wales (later King Edward VIII) and Lloyd George. The tentacles of the urban octopus that had squeezed the club from its first home reached out again in the 1950s. A site was found on Ile Bizard in the Lake of Two Mountains, and the late Dick Wilson was fetched from Florida to design the course.

Wilson, an outstanding golf architect, was the second choice. The Royal Montreal had first sought the services of Robert Trent Jones but he was otherwise committed. Trent Jones and Wilson made much of their professional rivalry and were never slow to damn each other's work with faint praise. The two were as different as a driver and a sand-iron. Trent Jones brings to his work a background that is almost academically perfect for the job of golf course design. At Cornell he successively studied engineering, architecture and agriculture, taking in the essential disciplines of surveying, hydraulics, and landscape architecture, among other things. He is an urbane man and his courses reflect this.

Dick Wilson, a down-to-earth, blunt-spoken man, was a fully fledged civil engineer who went to college on a football scholarship. To him, a Jones course was too contrived, paying too little attention to the nature of the land on which it was built; he believed that it took a better man to build a course than to lay one out. Trent Jones is equally succinct: the heart of a good golf course is its design, he believes—any good engineer can do the rest. How Royal Montreal's Ile Bizard courses—two of eighteen holes, the Red and the Blue, and a nine hole—would have differed had Jones and not Wilson designed them is mere speculation. They certainly needed Wilson's constructional talents. There were rocks, boulders, tree stumps to be removed, swamp to be drained, and lakes to be created, all in a climate in which snow and ice put an end to any work for months on end.

The par-four 18th hole, complete with its dominating features: the sand protecting its left side, and the magnificent and imposing clubhouse in the background.

All forty-five holes were completed for play in just over two years, finishing in May 1959. Wilson was proud of his creation. On a visit to the club before his untimely death he remarked: "There is a sweep and dimension to this layout which can only be described as exciting. That vista of the Lake of Two Mountains is the perfect backdrop to these courses. Don't ever shut off the view with too many trees. I have designed these courses for the present and the future. With the improvement in players' abilities and training and with better equipment, older courses will become old-fashioned and inadequate in the next fifteen years. The Red and the Blue courses will remain modern and can be made even more challenging for the next fifty years."

Wilson's words have held true. In 1997 the Canadian Open returned to Royal Montreal after an absence of many years. It developed into an exciting duel over the Blue course between Steve Jones and Greg Norman, with the latter claiming the title by just a stroke on a five under par total of 275. In all, only seven players managed to break par for 72 holes and one of them, Davis Love, said: "It is a very trying course, just like a Major Championship venue. The rough is very penalizing and the greens are fast. It is a tough course to score on." The event achieved one other small historical footnote: it was the first tournament since he turned professional at which Tiger Woods missed the 36-hole cut.

Both Red and Blue courses are formidable assignments and are distinctive in that they are among the few in Quebec that, for handicap purposes, are rated higher than their par. Both courses have a par of 70 but are rated at 72 (Red) and 73 (Blue). It is accepted that a Royal player can play to his handicap anywhere.

The greens—to which Dick Wilson paid particular attention—are enormous, averaging 12,000 square feet in size, nearly double the conventional size in North America. It means that from the same patch of fairway, under comparable wind conditions, the approach might call for anything from a 3-iron to a 5-iron, depending on where the pin is placed.

Putts of extraordinary length are often called for, up to 120 feet in extreme cases. Pat Fletcher, who was for many years the professional at Montreal said: "The secret is to hit your approaches a little longer rather than a little shorter. While some of the entrances are narrow, they all widen out considerably toward the back. The greens also putt deceptively."

Unlike many challenging courses, Royal Montreal is not renowned for its fairway bunkering; there are only eleven on the Blue course. But closer to the scoring areas, no fewer than forty-eight traps—deep gouges filled with heavy sand and with diabolical contours—guard the greens themselves.

The thoughtfully placed and artistically molded bunkers are typical of Dick Wilson's design. Indeed, Royal Montreal could well be described as the archetypal Wilson course. It has the bunkers, the gently contoured greens,

Determination Gains Immortality

The 16th on the Blue course at Royal Montreal is one of the most intimidating par fours in Canada. At about 415 yards from the regular tee markers and slightly over 430 yards from the very back, it is not inordinately long. It has only one sand trap—but that is all it needs.

The challenge is that the normal flight of the ball between tee and green is almost wholly over water. The drive is across a lake which the approach has to recross to reach an elevated pear-shaped green. The wind is almost always against and the second shot is invariably a long iron shot or even a wood hit low.

The lake is contoured so that the safer the line a player takes from the tee—in other words the farther to the right—the more difficult his approach becomes, because the carry over the water in front of the green is lengthened.

It is not uncommon for a proficient player to pump two or even three balls into the lake from the tee and then follow them with two or three more negotiating the approach. Scores in the low 20s have been recorded on the hole. In one tournament played by Canada's premier senior players, flooding made the hole unplayable and it was assigned an arbitrary rating of 5.5, the figure being added to everybody's card.

The hole was also the setting for a memorable par four by an intense young tour regular named Pat Fitzsimons in the 1975 Canadian Open. In the second round his drive was struck off line to the left, straight toward the water. Fitzsimons was preparing to reload when the ball came down on a raft-sized island some 10 yards from the shore. The ball was plainly visible but seemingly inaccessible. Or was it?

Nobody had ever tried it before, but there was nothing in the rules of golf to stop Fitzsimons from attempting to reach the island. He climbed on to his caddie's back but proved to be too much of a load and the two of them tottered and nearly went under. Fitzsimons then ventured out alone. The water turned out to be no more than waist deep.

He completed the crossing, lofted a 4-iron to the green, made the return trip without incident, partially dried himself, and two-putted from 30 feet for his par. The inconsequential island now has been named after Fitzsimons.

and the winding fairways, softly mounded to blend superbly with their surroundings. The hand of man is unobtrusive, the beauty of the course is muted and, despite the changes in the landscape wrought by Wilson, there is not jarring artificiality, only a serene naturalness.

Regular players regard the Red course with more respect as a test of all-around golfing skills. The "Blue Monster" is far more celebrated, largely because of the four finishing holes that throw out a direct challenge to the player, daring him to take on their vast expanses of water. Nobody in tournament play was able to peel more than two strokes from par before the 1975 Canadian Open, when both Nicklaus and Weiskopf opened with 65s. Nicklaus let the title slip from his grasp when he hooked his tee shot into the water on the dogleg of the finishing hole, and was forced into a play-off.

The tie-breaker started on the 15th, then a 410-yarder distinguished by a lake that bites into the fairway and protects the green. Because of the water, both Nicklaus and Weiskopf had to hold back off the tee, but both were left with only 7-iron approaches. Weiskopf's stopped two feet from the pin, Nicklaus's almost hit his rival's ball, but was carried back eight feet by the backspin. Nicklaus missed the putt, Weiskopf did not.

Nicklaus had come face to face with the realities of the philosophy espoused by both Trent Jones and Dick Wilson: "A golf hole should be a hard par and an easy bogey." At Royal Montreal that is true of all the holes.

Golf with a
Mid-Atlantic Accent

The Course Card

The Mid Ocean Club, Bermuda

Hole	Yards	Par
1	404	4
2	465	5
3	190	3
4	350	4
5	433	4
6	360	4
7	164	3
8	339	4
9	406	4
10	404	4
11	487	5
12	437	4
13	238	3
14	357	4
15	496	5
16	376	4
17	220	3
18	421	4
Out	3,111	35
In	3,436	36
Total	**6,547**	**71**

The name of Mid Ocean has a faraway, compelling sound. It is one of the remotest of all the Commonwealth of Nations courses in the northern hemisphere, yet it is still a very famous course. It lies on the southern shores of Bermuda, that entrancing island in the western reaches of the Atlantic, and has become familiar to legions of Americans; New York is only ninety minutes away by plane.

Mid Ocean has no close parallel; in some aspects it might resemble Cypress Point, because while the ocean plays little part in its design, it provides a glorious background to the beginning and the end. The greater part of the course is laid over beautiful inland country of rolling hills and crests, gentle vales and valleys, coursing through deep woods of casuarina and innumerable flowering shrubs. One might be miles from the sea, but no point is more than a few substantial golf shots from the coast.

The course was designed in 1924 by the great pioneer of American golf Charles Blair Macdonald, who had matriculated at St. Andrews yet it bears no resemblance to any course in Scotland. In 1953 the course was revised in some measure by Robert Trent Jones.

The impact of a wondrous setting does not diminish respect for the quality of the golf. It begins with a magnificent par four, curving to the left and rightly called Atlantic; it is simple enough to pull the second away from the raised green down to the rocks below. The 2nd swings down into the woods and up again to make a hole that is harder the longer one looks at it. From tee to green the short 3rd is a perfectly straight offering; it seems no greater problem than a thousand others of its length, until suddenly one is aware of the long fall to the ocean on the left and the garden on the right.

The 4th is another plunge-and-rise affair, narrow between trees and not altogether appealing. But what rewards await the climb; the 5th is one of the world's unforgettable holes. Far beneath a gun platform of a tee spreads the shining expanse of Mangrove Lake and, in a manner of speaking, one sips as much of it as one can swallow. There is a way to the right for the frail of heart, but any carry over the water is considerable. The next three holes are a quiet interlude before the stern tasks really begin. Solid drives to the 6th and 8th leave only pitches, but these are to greens above eye level. This is a feature of Mid Ocean, making distances—even of little shots—difficult to judge precisely. The greens are not too small, but the slopes protecting them are often steep and recovery of an erring approach can be difficult. The greens are not watered artificially, but the ample rain and sunshine permit two growths each year—Bermuda in the summer, rye and bent for the winter. Thus, the greens are good the year round, although their pace and contours need knowing.

The 7th is a medium pitch over a pool and so far par has not been too exacting; the golfer, on his first visit, may wonder whether the course is as demanding as he has been led to expect. But the hard part is at hand. From the back tee of the 9th the carry is disturbingly long, with no easy alternative, over a wilderness of rushes that would not be out of place at Westward Ho! on the north Devon coast. The drive down the 10th, after ice has tinkled in glasses at the turn, seems spacious enough, but only one of exact placing will leave a clear shot to the green. A huge bunker guards its right side, and usually the pin. This is a splendid hole except that the over-bold shot is likely to be punished too severely. After a drive over a crest the 11th is a fair par five, the 12th nobody's easy four with the tee shot across a leaning shoulder of hillside, and the 13th a long short hole to a green ringed with traps. The bunkers on the left of the 14th are suggestive of Muirfield in their clustered insistence on trapping a pull to the fairway that tilts in their direction. Two good hits to the 15th should leave an easy pitch over rising ground to the green. Then follows a menacing uphill drive between trouble on the left and a great green basin, into which anything but the truly struck drive will roll. From there the second, naturally enough, is blind; but even from the fairway—and

The Atlantic plays little part in the design of Mid Ocean, but it provides a magnificent backdrop to a course that is given something of a cathedral-like atmosphere by tall, elegant pines. Although length is important at Mid Ocean (the par-three 13th is 238 yards long, and five of the par fours measure more than 400 yards), there is some compensation in the size of the greens. The course is the best of four excellent ones on an island 21 miles long.

the hole is not long—the green on its high place, free to all the wind's force, can be elusive. And now the ocean is in sight again and a splendid 17th awaits. It was named Redan —presumably after the famous 15th at North Berwick, although there the similarity ceases. The shot is downhill, but into wind many golfers will be feeling for a wooden club.

The 18th pursues the line of the beach and the tee is situated high above it. Behind are the cliffs with pink and white houses clustered about their edges; ahead the handsome white mass of the clubhouse, where Churchill and Eisenhower once conversed of matters other than golf. The long driver must beware here because the fairway narrows abruptly. But the hole is beautifully shaped, and as one holes out there is a feeling that an enduring memory has been made. Beyond the green is the little practice ground where Archie Compston, so long the professional at Mid Ocean, gave his lessons; a memorial to him stands nearby.

Golf in Bermuda is not confined to Mid Ocean; far from it. There are four other eighteen-hole courses, two of nine holes and a par three—remarkable riches for an island of only some 22 square miles. Castle Harbor, with the most beautiful 1st tee imaginable, and an abundance of hills and valleys, is quite an experience to play. Belmont Manor is of a quieter undulating kind, and Riddell's Bay is charming. It flows along a green tongue of land with inlets of the Great Sound, where the ships glide by to Hamilton, testing the golfers from time to time. It is all gentle and appealing after the splendors of Mid Ocean. Finally, Port Royal is another Trent Jones creation. It makes fine strategic use of water and sand; the land is sharply contoured and some 200,000 trees and shrubs were planted over a period of about seven years. There are also some challenging holes, not least the 16th, right by the ocean. Everywhere there is stunning beauty, that precious part of the golfer's legacy; and the island, a minute speck in the northern Sargasso Sea, makes a background for the game that very few places on earth can match.

The 5th

A Play Upon Courage, Fear, And Greed

Feel for a shot is vital, as any golfer standing on Mid Ocean's 5th tee preparing to play across Mangrove Lake will tell you. The hole, 433 yards long, is a perfect example of how an architect can play upon courage, fear, and greed. The fairway curves around a lake that is at its widest on the direct line to the green. The timid can play safely to the right, from where there is little or no hope of reaching the green with the next shot; the alternative is to attempt to drive over as much of the lake as he can or dares. The longer the carry made, the shorter and easier the approach. From the tee high above the lake the distance across to the fairway looks shorter than it is, as distances invariably do over water. And so, until the golfer knows the limits of his skill and nerve, usually from the chastening experience of seeing a well-struck drive splash from sight forever, short of where he thought it would finish, discretion is advised.

The principle of being invited to bite off as much as one can reasonably hope to do is a basic of good design, and not by any means confined to water holes. The drive to the 6th at Pine Valley, where a wilderness slants across the line to the fairway, has deceived many into thinking they were stronger than they were, or has taught them not to be greedy. But then water is the classic hazard for such purposes. It has a dreadful finality.

The 5th hole at Mid Ocean is a perfect example of how an architect can play upon courage, fear, and greed.

High-Altitude Golf

Among the Cedars

Golf is a long, long way from replacing the *fiesta brava* or *futbol* in the hearts of Latin Americans, but it is making good progress as a sport for the privileged minority. This is especially true in Mexico, which affords a great many more opportunities to play than most of its Pan-American neighbors to the south. It was not until the late 1940s that the Club de Golf Mexico was formed, giving the country its first course of international caliber. Since its fairways were opened in 1951, the club has played host to many of the world's leading golfers and several international events, including the World Cup in 1958 and 1967 and the World Amateur Team Championship in 1966. Perhaps the most memorable of these was the first of the two World Cups, which featured a splendid win for Christy O'Connor and Harry Bradshaw. Their winning score of 579 illustrates the course's difficulties; indeed, only one winning score in the 45-year history of the World Cup has ever been higher.

Club de Golf Mexico emerged from the imagination and

determination of Percy J. Clifford, six-time amateur champion of Mexico and six-time runner-up. With the sponsorship of President Aleman, Clifford found just the terrain he wanted at a place called El Cedtal, a lovely grove of cedar, pine, eucalyptus, and cypress trees on the outskirts of the town of Tlalpan, an hour's drive south of Mexico City. Through the heart of the grove runs a deep, usually dry, creek that comes into play in varying ways on nearly half the holes.

Designed by Clifford and American architect Laurence Hughes, Club de Golf has a par of 72 and plays at an imposing 7,250 yards from the back tees. However, Mexico City's altitude of 7,500 feet lends a great deal of distance to the longer shots. A drive of 230 to 250 yards at sea level will travel anywhere from 10 to 20 percent farther in this rarefied atmosphere depending on the temperature and climatic conditions, a circumstance that makes the proper selection of clubs a distinct problem to the golfer who plays here for the first time. While he may be agreeably surprised at the new distance he has acquired off the tee, he may similarly find that his well-hit 7-iron to the green ends up in serious trouble ten or twenty yards past the target.

Flanked by a dormant volcano and a magnificent river valley, the Club de Golf Mexico is unique in having hosted two World Cups, won in 1958 for Ireland by Harry Bradshaw and Christy O'Connor, and retained in 1967 for the USA by Jack Nicklaus and Arnold Palmer.

Due largely to the thousands of trees guarding its fairways, Club de Golf Mexico is principally a driving course with a secondary premium on long irons and fairway woods. While not heavily bunkered like so many of the newer courses north of the border, the target areas off the tees are generally narrowed and confined by at least one strategically placed sandtrap. The real punishment for the stray drive is, however, the trees themselves. From among them, it is seldom possible to do more than nudge the ball back to the center of the fairway. Even the sides of the fairways are apt to cost a stroke now and then, for the overhanging branches will quite often block a straight route to the green.

The second shot problem is easily grasped by a glance at the yardage figures for the individual holes. Only four of the par fours measure less than 425 yards, and one of them

is a full 470 yards. All four of the par fives extend over more than 550 yards, and two—the 11th and the 15th—offer but a minimal entrance to the green for even the finest second shot. Only one of the short holes is less than 200 yards and all four are extremely tight, due to the crowding trees, the enclosing bunkers, or the confining boundary of the club property. Of medium size in terms of the newer golf courses, the greens have only the subtlest borrows, but they are well protected by bunkers without being unduly surrounded. In short, Club de Golf is a course where the straight golfer will be rewarded by pars, while the birdies are bought at peril.

As with all fine courses of championship quality, Club de Golf offers an imposing sequence of finishing holes that test not only the skill but the nerves of a player. The 15th is a dauntingly long par five down an avenue of trees to a green protected by two bunkers. The 16th is either a long iron or a wood off the tee with no margin for error; the 17th and 18th are both par fours, the latter featuring a creek that plays a fundamental part in both holes that close the front and back nines. Considering it has been played often by the best professionals, the record of 66 indicates how difficult it is to bring this course to its knees.

The Course Card

Club de Golf Mexico, Mexico City

Hole	Yards	Par
1	390	4
2	563	5
3	175	3
4	470	4
5	230	3
6	580	5
7	376	4
8	425	4
9	437	4
10	431	4
11	573	5
12	427	4
13	377	4
14	200	3
15	442	4
16	225	3
17	570	5
18	359	4
Out	3,646	36
In	3,604	36
Total	**7,250**	**72**

The 6th to the 8th

High Drama in Thin Air

At the 6th hole at Club de Golf Mexico, the advantage of extra distance that the atmosphere of this mile-high city adds to a shot is suddenly taken away. Out-of-bounds to the right is a feature on all the four finishing holes to the outward half, and the trees that so effectively screen out the wind line to the left. The golfer can forget about those 20-odd extra yards and concentrate on accuracy. Thus Latin Americans, who glorify length, learn that the second shot is just as important as the first.

The 6th, a par four, is very demanding off the tee. The 7th offers no room for error all the way from tee to green. And then comes the 8th. Stretching 562 yards, it is a mighty par five even in this rarefied atmosphere. For once the golfer finds a bonus in a thick grove of trees—they prevent him from hitting out-of-bounds.

Topographically, the hole is a lot more difficult than it looks. A cluster of traps lies just short of the green to catch those who drive to the right of the fairway, but what makes the hole really tough is that the second shot is entirely uphill. Rarefied atmosphere or not, you must bust the second shot in order to reach the green.

In the 1967 World Cup, the American team of Arnold Palmer and Jack Nicklaus was so far in front of the rest of the field (at 19 under par) that the championship looked a formality. They won by 13 strokes over New Zealand. Palmer won the individual title with a 12 under par score of 276, and Nicklaus, driving poorly for once, ended up seven under. But together they played that 8th hole (then the 17th, for the two nines were the other way around) for four rounds in a total score of five under par.

Asia

Golf arrived in Asia in the early nineteenth century, its vectors the garrisons and administrators of the British Empire. Far and away the oldest golf club in the world outside the British Isles—far older, even, than most of them there—is the Royal Calcutta, founded in 1829. In course of time golf spread to all the countries of the East where the European presence was strong—even into China, where there were courses adjoining the now-vanished European cantonments. For more than a century, golf was essentially a game for the representatives of colonial power, and a club of any standing rigorously excluded even the most important locals from membership. Colonialism and its trappings have now vanished, but the game has survived. It flourishes in India and southeast Asia generally, in the Philippines and Taiwan (thanks to American influence), and countries like Thailand where the sport has been boosted by the emergence of Tiger Woods, whose mother is Thai. The Omega Asian Tour did not begin life until 1994 but just three years later encompassed more than twenty-three events in sixteen different countries.

It is in Japan, however—ironically the one country that did not come under the colonial influence—where the game has taken hold to an astonishing degree. The number of golfers there so outstrips capacity that there are six times more Japanese wanting to play the game than there are registered golfers in the whole of Europe. There are 12 million actual golfers in Japan (playing on 1,800 courses), 16 million who use the driving ranges, and it is estimated that a further 8 million would like to do either or both if they had the time. New courses continue to be built despite the fact that land is at a premium, and strong opposition has grown against the use of what land there is for the pleasure of a few. Entrepreneurs and course designers have been literally driven to the hills in order to find sites for which permission will be granted—some so hilly that players travel by escalator from one hole to another. Near the cities, a player may have to give six months' notice to play a round, and even then consider himself lucky. Fees to play an average public course are over $300. And still the obsession goes on. The game is wholeheartedly embraced in the continent where it first took tenuous root so long ago.

1. Hirono 2. Kasumigaseki 3. Fujioka 4. Royal Calcutta 5. Royal Hong Kong 6. Singapore Island
7. Royal Selangor 8. Bali Handara

With subtle bunkering and a delightfully varied use of water, Charles Alison created Japan's best test of golf at Hirono. The pine trees that flank the fairways do not intrude into play but provide instead a decorous frame for the rolling terrain broken by strategically placed natural gullies. The water comes effectively into play at the short holes—the 5th, 13th, and 17th—and at the long 12th, a 550-yard par five where the drive must carry an awesome combination of rough and water to gain the safety of the fairway.

Alison's Restrained but

Inspired Architecture

The Course Card

Hirono Golf Club, Shijimi, Hyogo

Hole	Yards	Par
1	500	5
2	430	4
3	440	4
4	425	4
5	150	3
6	430	4
7	200	3
8	350	4
9	525	5
10	355	4
11	440	4
12	550	5
13	185	3
14	360	4
15	560	5
16	395	4
17	230	3
18	455	4
Out	3,450	36
In	3,530	36
Total	**6,980**	**72**

The Westernization of Japan, a breakneck process during the early decades of this century, was most marked in and around the great maritime cities like Tokyo and—farther west on the island of Honshu—the port of Kobe. It was within these cosmopolitan communities that the game of golf first took root and at Kobe, Japan, was to acquire one of the world's great courses—Hirono. It set the standard by which oriental courses are measured.

The site chosen for Hirono was in every way ideal. Twelve miles to the northwest of the port it was, in a contemporary description, "dotted with many pretty ponds, winding streams, running rivulets, pine woodlands, ravines, and gentle undulations." The materials were at hand for an architectural artist, the Englishman Charles Alison. And the course he designed in 1930 remains unaltered to this day.

At Hirono Alison took advantage of the terrain to arrange, as at Sunningdale and St. George's Hill (where he had worked with Harry Colt), several splendid carries from the tees. He planned intriguing greens at the end of generous fairways and sprinkled the course with bunkers of the type that in Japan bear his name to this day. In every way it was a piece of Berkshire transplanted to the Orient.

Charles Alison was a skillful draftsman; it was a talent that would have appealed to the Japanese. The holes, hazards, and greens in Alison's drawings were produced with amazing accuracy after he departed, a tribute to his skill in designing and to the high esteem in which he must have been held by all those with whom he came into contact.

Hirono measures 6,980 yards from the back tees and 6,100 yards from the forward ones; Alison gave it all the length a championship course should need. Nowadays too much importance is attached to playing a course of 7,000 yards or more, especially in Japan. There is generally thought to be some inadequacy in a layout that measures less. More monstrosities have been constructed in the name of length than would be thought possible; a look at Hirono provides an answer to the argument, for 6,980 yards of this kind of architecture is worth 7,400 yards of most other kinds.

Few courses outside Britain have the striking difference and variety in each hole that Hirono possesses. Each is named after its peculiarity—Lake End, Fiord, Wee-Wood, Devil's Divot, Boulevard, and Quo Vadis? We can assume that Alison had a hand in the naming, which is thoroughly appropriate. In playing or just walking the course, the titles immediately strike home. Devil's Divot, for example, is a par three across a huge gouge in the earth, in the shape of a giant divot. Fiord is another par three, across an inlet of a lake resembling a small Norwegian harbor. Some of the names commemorate people associated with the club's founding, but most announce a hole's feature or situation.

At first the greens were all of creeping bent grass but it was soon found that the ten times more virile Japanese Bermuda grass encroached and took over, in spite of all efforts to stem its advance. A fine variety of korai grass—of the same family as the fairways—was substituted, and properly maintained and mown short. It is a suitable enough putting grass even though it browns off in winter and goes dormant. It does, however, have a wiry texture that baffles nearly all golfers who are new to its acquaintance. Varieties of American seed grasses make up the rough grass together with some local flora. The trees are almost entirely pines indigenous to the area, and they are lovingly cared for.

The whole is a vista of beauty and naturalness that changes color through the seasons. In summer it is a rich green with only the sandtraps offering a contrast to the softness mirrored in the lakes and ponds, while in autumn and winter it changes to the light brown of hibernation. At all times it is an inviting golf course of outstanding dignity and class.

Like Sunningdale, which in many ways it resembles, Hirono starts off with a par-five hole. It is straight, narrow, and flat and clear of obstacles all the way to the flagstick, which can be clearly seen from the tee though 500 yards away. Two shallow depressions cross the fairway at the 100-yard and

400-yard marks. Alison placed his traps for the wayward drive at the 200-yard range on the right and at 220 yards on the left, a pattern that has been almost universally adopted by all students of his work in Japan. Two plain and modest bunkers guard the green, which inclines enough to drain itself. Here, as throughout the course, natural features are used to their best effect. Two man-sized par fours follow, the blank spots of which are filled with large-scale moundwork that suggests something of a linksland course. The 4th hole requires a spectacularly long tee shot and the green is raised high behind a typical Alison sandtrap. The 5th hole is a picture postcard par three of outstanding merit high across a large lake. Fearsome-looking sandtraps guard a modest-sized green so that even at 150 yards length the hole is a difficult one for golfers of all classes and experience.

The course turns inland then by way of another first-class par three of 200 yards. A natural, well-cleared ravine courses diagonally across it and, against a wind, it is farther than most people can hit, but the regular tee is set at 170 yards so that from this distance it is a pleasure for all golfers to play. The 8th hole uses a small pond by the green to effect. The second shot must skirt or carry the pond to an interestingly shaped green. For club golfers it is fun and a terror, the choice of shot never easy.

The 9th takes the route straight to the clubhouse. A par five of 525 yards, the tee shot is all carry across brush and pathways to a generous fairway that disappears into a natural grassed and cut hollow in front of the green. The 10th and 11th holes are two pleasant fours that take the golfer out to the lake again. The 12th hole is one of the course's best —and also one of the best par fives in Japan. Its tee shot is across an inlet of the lake, beyond which there is a small natural ditch, reminiscent of Carnoustie, to worry about. The shot is fearsome for lesser players, and difficult enough for professionals. To all except the very longest and straightest hitters the green is still two shots away. The tee shots at the 13th and 14th holes both have to carry water of marvelous proportion and beauty, giving pleasure to the player who makes it but no offense to those who don't. These two shorter holes lead to another outstanding par five in the 15th, at 560 yards, Alison's longest hole. The 16th climbs farther away from the lake to a high plateau green seemingly set against the sky. From the back tee, the 17th is a 230-yard par three across the margin

of another lake with plenty of open space to be aimed at by those who are not ambitious or strong enough. Here Alison could have made the mistake of duplicating his 5th and 13th holes but sensibly he offered something different; water plays a lesser part but sheer length is used to compensate.

The 455-yard 18th is in every way a rewarding final hole. First there is the carry across a gully to the fairway. Then the fairway turns left for the long slog to the green. Again there is an area of mounds and hollows and sand-traps off to the right, more to distract than to impede, but the greenside traps have been sited in earnest. Eighteenth greens are almost always given the best attention, by constructor and maintainer alike, and this one is no exception. Alison never even dreamed of television but made a marvelously spectacular finish.

Hirono was host to the Japan Amateur championship in 1933 and the Japan Open in 1939, but since then there has been nothing of national or international importance staged there. This is to be regretted because there is much to show off and, as far as champion golfers are concerned, much to test them.

Hirono is the course of the straight-hitter. Nearly every hole is tree-lined with mainly conifers to catch the wayward shot.

Bunkers Gain an Englishman

Immortality in Japan

A Charles Alison course, marked by restrained bunkering and superb grooming, Kasumigaseki came to the fore in 1957 when the World Cup was played there. Japan's success in team and individual competitions sparked off an astonishing golf boom there. It later spread through much of Asia.

As a game that has more than its share of ritual and etiquette, golf might be expected to appeal to the Japanese. There has been an explosion of interest in recent years—too big an explosion, in fact, for the good of the Japanese themselves, for there are far too few courses for the army of enthusiasts who would dearly love to play eighteen holes or any number of holes, for that matter—on a real course. There may well be many a Nipponese Nicklaus condemned to play out a lifetime of golf on one of Japan's proliferating practice ranges. And for those who are club members fees are hideously high.

Tokyo, one of the world's greatest conurbations, has a number of the country's principal clubs within its immediate area. One is Kasumigaseki, the country's most famous club. The course was built in a matter of months by a group of enthusiasts and opened in October 1929. The design was by a talented local player, Kinya Fujita, but it soon became clear that the possibilities of the site had not been exploited to the full. The English architect Charles Alison was called in and in his subsequent work at Kasumigaseki he was to achieve a curious immortality.

Alison was drawn particularly to the par-three 10th, a medium-length pitch across a deep ravine. He introduced several deep sandtraps into the side of a steep slope leading up to the green, and their depth was an innovation to the Japanese. Since that time, every deep sandtrap on a Japanese course has been known as an Alison.

The English architect stamped his personality on other holes also, and although some innovations have since been added the championship course is fundamentally his work. Alison was an outstanding golf course designer and his ideas place him among the giants of the profession. His simple principle was that hazards should be offset to catch the wayward stroke and that the path to the hole along the straight and narrow should be smooth and unencumbered. Alison's pattern of design has been adopted almost everywhere in Japan, but it has also given birth to some very dull and stereotyped reproduction.

The climate of Japan is one of extremes and at Kasumigaseki, as elsewhere in Japan, the soft English bent grasses recommended for putting greens could not survive the heat and oppressive humidity of summer; the grass just expired. The Japanese solution was to build two greens, one sown with conventional bents regrown each year, and the other with the hardiest grass they could find—a species from Korea called, appropriately enough, *korai*. It survives harsh winter conditions and although it turns light brown in its dormancy, it revives to a rich greenness in the spring. Finely developed strains make adequate putting greens, while the stouter grades make fairways of firm bristle.

The use of korai as a second green inevitably distorted the architecture by adding a considerable space to the green area. It also influenced the bunkering around the greens, the standard pattern being to have one trap to the extreme left, one to the right, and another at the rear. This arrangement became the safe method of design and few local planners dared depart from it.

Kasumigaseki has the well-kept, well-prepared look about it that has become customary in Japan. A ground staff of more than 200, many of them women, ensure that no weeds grow anywhere and not a dead leaf can be seen. Trees are wrapped in hessian and twine to protect them from the cold of winter; many have stays or cables to hold them upright in the wind. Paths and bridges are guttered and well drained, like miniature avenues. Flower beds around the clubhouse would do justice to the Chelsea Flower Show. On the course, the flora and the grasses receive the same meticulous attention, with the same impressive results. The

The 18th

Sophistication Brings Joy

Kasumigaseki's planner arranged a layout of outstanding variety, a feature of which is a sterling finish in the modern manner. A par five of sporting length with enough dogleg to make the best of golfers draw on his brain and brawn, the 18th makes a perfect finale to an exciting round. The drive is straightforward enough, sensibly trapped, and yet wide enough to invite overstretching. There is, of course, every temptation to do so, for the green, some 483 yards away, can be reached in two shots. Thus when Sam Snead, Roberto de Vicenzo, and others of the same power stood on this last tee in the 1957 World Cup with an eagle in mind, it made for enthralling viewing.

The second shot, though, is the spectacular one. From the perfect drive, the direct line is across the deepest part of a valley and over the large, deep traps that guard the entrance from that angle. If the traps were not smoothed with a toothless rake, the whole exercise

The Course Card

Kasumigaseki
Country Club,
Kasahata,
Saitama
East course

Hole	Yards	Par
1	388	4
2	374	4
3	422	4
4	158	3
5	532	5
6	372	4
7	220	3
8	474	4
9	532	5
10	180	3
11	433	4
12	468	4
13	375	4
14	593	5
15	433	4
16	173	3
17	349	4
18	483	5
Out	3,472	36
In	3,487	36
Total	**6,959**	**72**

expensive white river sand of the bunkers, prepared to an exemplary smoothness, as elsewhere in Japan, with toothless wooden rakes, has a tidiness that defeats its purpose. This fact first came to light in the 1957 Canada Cup (now the World Cup), when the Japanese winners demonstrated a hitherto unknown skill of escaping from the sand after poor shots had trapped them. Torakichi "Pete" Nakamura, individual winner by a convincing seven-shot margin, proved particularly adept. In the four days of the event he holed out from the sand four times, and never failed to get down in two when he was caught—as he often was.

The success of Nakamura and his partner, Koichi Ono, sparked the golf boom in Japan that shows no sign yet of collapse. At that time there were seventy-nine courses in Japan. Today there are about 1,800, with applications before the authorities for many more.

Because the demand for courses quickly outstripped the availability of suitable land, golf took to the mountains. Consequently, most modern Japanese courses are hilly, even mountainous. Some border on the absurd. Fairways shoot up one hill to tumble down the next. Greens are often placed out of sight over the brow so that only the flagstick is visible, and fairways are sometimes laid through ridiculously narrow cuts on the hillside. Yet such courses are popular because in Japan sport, and golf in particular, is a physical exercise. Kasumigaseki has no such architectural absurdities. Its standing in Japan was assured by Alison's masterly creation and consolidated by Fujita and Seichi Inoue, who collaborated on a second excellent course, completed in 1931. They faithfully followed Alison's lead.

Despite Charles Alison's marvelous creations and the desire of Japan's golf founders to produce courses with all the classic features, sandtrap design and maintenance in Japan make them vastly different from the less-manicured courses they seek to emulate. Nevertheless they are much to be admired in every other respect, and Kasumigaseki, which combines something of the ruggedness of a golf course with the beauty of a Japanese garden, sets the standard. Few can match it.

would take even more courage. The same sand left footmarked and unraked would make for an extremely punitive hazard of real championship caliber but unfortunately only Pine Valley among the world's great courses maintains this principle. This last hole at Kasumigaseki would be fearsome indeed if the penalty for falling into one of the traps was two or even three strokes. At present, because of the invariably immaculate condition of the greenside bunkers, the penalty is most often only one, and, in a significant percentage of cases, none at all. Nevertheless, this hole is a marvelous example of sophisticated architecture and a joy to play.

The 18th hole on the East course at Kasumigaseki, above, provides the perfect finale to an exciting round.

Golfing Innovations in
A Land of Traditions

Fujioka came into being in 1971 and is one of the more successful manifestations of the golf fever that reached plague proportions throughout the country—a plague that eventually resulted in legislation to check the rape of open land by speculative golfing developments.

Fujioka was the brainchild of Mr. Furukawa, the owner of land to the north of Nagoya. He set out to build a course in the established traditions of Kasumigaseki and Hirono, of modern design and to international standards, but with its membership strictly limited to a manageable 520.

The great Australian, Peter Thomson, was invited to become the course's architect, which was built by Tameshi Yamada. The practice of having a player of international repute associated with a new course had become commonplace in Japan—lucrative enough, but not without its risks for the player's reputation if the course should prove a failure.

The site was 180 acres of moderately hilly land made up of tea plantations, a large lake, and a pine forest. The layout used all the lower-lying land and valleys, leaving the higher pines intact. Drainage to and from the lake and beneath the fairways was used with great imagination by Yamada. Pipes beneath the fairways were a yard in diameter, an extravagant size that was to prove its worth a year after the course was completed: a typhoon devastated and flooded the region, but the course was left intact.

A feature of Fujioka is its lakes, reminiscent of those at Augusta National. At the time they were a radical departure in Japan, where lakes are usually used only timidly as hazards. Greens are hardly ever placed right against the water, as at Augusta, although on most Japanese courses, with their abundance of water, the golfer is invited to hit over it.

A double green was made for the 4th, a long climbing par four, and the 7th, a par three played at right angles to it. This was the first double green in Japan. At Fujioka it was not built simply to be distinctive, but to solve a construction problem and conserve valuable space in a tight corner.

At one point there was some disagreement over whether the 12th green should be flush against a small lake or higher up and well away from the water. In the end, a compromise was reached: both were built. The one beside the lake, which makes the hole into a dogleg, resembles the 11th at Augusta in its setting, and the other is straight ahead. The lakeside green sits slightly below the fairway driving spot, from which the flag placement and the water surrounding the green can be seen. The alternative is blind; only the top of the flagstick and surrounding traps can be seen.

Alison-type bunkers were included at various holes, although Yamada modified their depths, knowing from experience that among his countrymen deep bunkers with straight faces are not universally popular. The sandtraps are flexible in their depth—for ordinary club play they can be shallow and not particularly penal, but they can be deepened to suit the more prestigious occasion. Thus Fujioka, like all great courses, is flexible enough to be enjoyed not only by champions but by golfers of all abilities.

The course has a one-green system along modern lines, with modern trappings. The grass is a fine variety of korai, the safest type for the climate and the most familiar to Japanese golfers, although there are more suitable hybrids available. The fairways are of a coarser and tougher variety of korai, grown on turf farms and transported to Fujioka in two-foot squares, the standard method of turf culture in the southern and western parts of Japan. The squares are laid and pegged in with small bamboo stakes to frustrate the crows which otherwise lift them, looking for worms, before they settle down. The turfing of Fujioka took about five months and kept almost 6,000 workers fully employed during that time.

The 16th

A Man-Sized Par Five

The huge par-five 16th is a real monster, playing every inch of its 605-yard length. The back tee is never used in club golf because the first shot involves a drive uphill—always a difficult task for a golfer of little experience. Although the fairway is not generously wide, every encouragement is left for the sliced drive to hit the bank on the right side and bounce back to the fairway, even though this cuts length from the shot. The left side plunges down to an out-of-bounds fence and hooking is something to be avoided. From the top of the hill, where a good drive will finish, it is still not possible to see the green, though the second shot is framed by some pines on either side and the V-shaped fairway makes the direction unmistakable.

It is really only with the third shot that the hole's true worth is revealed, for the task before the player is below him in the shape of a massive green curving along the side of a small lake, with a steep forested hill as a backdrop. A large sandtrap guards the entrance without blocking it off, but such is the large scale of everything, including green and trap, that the distance is deceptively long. When the flag is cut in the championship position at the far back of the green, a player can be faced with a putt of some 35 yards. The green becomes progressively narrower as it recedes and there are two smaller traps at the back to catch those who—mindful

of the water on the left—overshoot. The shot into the green varies according to the wind; when there is none, and when play is from the back tee, the third shot must be a 7-iron at best for most people. The 16th is a man-sized par five.

The 16th hole at Fujioka is one of the relatively few par fives in the world to measure over 600 yards.

The whole construction took less than a year and most of it was completed in only nine months. Fujioka Country Club is now acknowledged as one of Japan's outstanding courses, modern but nevertheless reflecting architectural links with older more venerable courses. Other modern courses in Japan are following the same lines and Japanese golfers are learning to enjoy what are to them wholly new challenges in the way they play their game.

As befitted a course that looked to Japan's golfing future, Fujioka's last three holes were designed with television in mind. Each is spectacular and in the way in which they bring into play a large, attractive lake they rival even the famous water holes of Augusta, both in their beauty and in their difficulty. For the members, many good scores are ruined over this final run-in, yet there is much pride in their existence, just as there is in the way that Fujioka pioneered a golfing challenge that was new to Japan.

Fujioka, with its gently hilly fairways, is one of the finer courses to emerge from the almost frenzied Japanese interest in golf. The course, unusually for Japan, is rarely busy, the club membership being strictly limited. Water is the dominant feature of a layout that winds sedately through groves of pine trees.

The Course Card

Fujioka Country Club, Nagoya

Hole	Yards	Par
1	400	4
2	190	3
3	540	5
4	420	4
5	350	4
6	445	4
7	195	3
8	500	5
9	385	4
10	400	4
11	165	3
12	440	4
13	550	5
14	370	4
15	190	3
16	605	5
17	395	4
18	430	4
Out	3,425	36
In	3,545	36
Total	**6,970**	**72**

The Course Card

Royal Calcutta Golf Club, Calcutta

Hole	Name	Yardage	Par
1	Island	366	4
2	Tank Ahead	436	4
3	Bull's Eye	156	3
4	The Long One	525	5
5	Madras Thorns	415	4
6	The Fields	418	4
7	The Jheels	455	4
8	Ditchers	401	4
9	Dhobi Ghat	404	4
10	Long Pal	448	4
11	The Nullahs	508	5
12	Dog-Leg	359	4
13	Chota	187	3
14	Right of Way	431	4
15	Far and Sure	493	5
16	Mutt and Jeff	364	4
17	Thomson's Tank	374	4
18	Pimples	437	4
Out		3,576	36
In		3,601	37
Total		**7,177**	**73**

Vintage Legacy

of the British Raj

Right: The clubhouse at Royal Calcutta, right, the oldest club in the world outside the British Isles.

Older than any club in the world beyond the British Isles—older, indeed, than most of those in Britain itself—the Royal Calcutta has antecedents stretching back to the days when the power of the British Raj was gaining strength, beyond the beginnings of Victoria's reign. The Royal Calcutta was founded in 1829 and first used a site at Dum Dum, where the city's international airport now stands. After a series of moves the Dum Dum Golfing Club, as the Royal Calcutta was originally called, settled finally toward the end of the century in the southern suburbs.

The eighteen holes making up the present course are all that survive of the thirty-six the club once possessed but could not afford to keep up. The land farthest from the clubhouse was sold to the Bengal government to provide some much-needed recreational space for the refugees who have crowded the club's boundaries since the division of Bengal in 1947.

The refugees still pass through the confines of the course, giving it a color and atmosphere found nowhere else in the world. They walk single-file along the well-worn track that crosses the course. The women wash their saris and their children in the ponds formed where fill was taken to build the tees and greens, which are the highest points on a course that is never more than six feet above the level of the River Ganges. Small boys swim in each pond and wait for a wayward ball, for which they will dive to hand back to the owner in return for a few coins. The golfers are often clad in white shorts and frequently in colorful turbans. They pause under umbrellas held by caddies dressed in khaki. And above everything are the birds—squawking ravens, buzzards gliding in the hot air,

and the vultures that circle monotonously or peer balefully down from their nests in trees by the 3rd.

Despite the distractions, golf continues to thrive in Calcutta. Some of the more august clubs died with the Raj, others have been created, enjoying a particular popularity among members of the armed forces, where the affectations of the old English—particularly their phraseology—linger in an odd post-colonial twilight.

Almost until independence, Indians were rigorously excluded from membership of Calcutta. A Sikh, Sardar I. S. Malik, was the first, and the first Indian to play in the all-India Amateur Championship. Years later, his son Ashok won the title five times and with his partner, P.G. Sethi, represented India in every Eisenhower Trophy event from 1958 to 1968. "Billoo" Sethi, the outstanding Indian golfer of his generation, made history when he won the Indian Open in 1956, twice equaling his own course record of 68 in the process.

From the tees the flat Royal Calcutta looks easy, but good medium and long irons are needed for a low score, and water hazards affect most holes.

Royal Calcutta is immensely proud of its origins, its connections with the Royal and Ancient, and with its influence on the game in India, where, until lately, it was the champion of the rules and etiquette of golf. Perhaps more importantly, there is another way in which this ancient club has exercised an influence on the game. Golf as a worldwide sport and, particularly as a game played in tropical and subtropical climes, owes a debt to Royal Calcutta for a special reason. It was the first course to be built in the tropics and as such had to make use of whatever indigenous grasses there were available. The most suitable, if not indeed the only one, was dhoob.

Dhoob grass covered Calcutta's first fairways, and golf on grass became a reality in the tropics. Since then, in all probability because of the Indian experience, dhoob and related grasses such as hariali, Bermuda, Australian couch, and creeping dog's-tooth, have become the standard grasses, in pure, dwarfed, or hybrid form, on thousands of golf courses all over the world. Without it, golf in all but the temperate zones would be played on sand.

The eighteen holes that now make up the championship course are each a solid par of modern length and difficulty, in a flat parkland setting, with gorgeous trees and innumerable lakes or ponds (known, because they are used to store water, as tanks), drainage channels and gutters. The course can justifiably claim to be the best in the subcontinent.

The profusion of water hazards removes the need for many bunkers and, since they are below ground-level, the course at first glance gives the impression of being easy and wide open. Nothing is further from the truth.

Its best holes are the 2nd and 14th, neither of which has a sandtrap. The stiff 2nd is a gentle dogleg of 436 yards, curving around huge trees of thick, shady foliage. The boundary wall runs along the left side and against it,

at the 230-yard mark, is a lotus-filled tank that acts like a magnet. A drive that strays too far to the right lands behind the trees and so the placement of the tee shot is critical. The 14th follows the same pattern, but in reverse. It is a little shorter at 431 yards, but requires big hitting when the fairways are soft after the monsoon.

The 448-yard 10th is also a testing hole. Two large tanks split the fairway, and an out-of-bounds wall lines the entire left side. From the tee the bold line is straight over the first tank, a shot that must carry a full 230 yards. The safe shot down the right side leaves a long second over the other tank, which is all of 100 yards wide, to a small, heavily trapped green. Other first-class holes are the par-three 3rd and 13th, both of which are entirely flexible in length: they can be played from 230 yards down to 150 yards. On both there are daunting water hazards, worrying to the golfer but a never-ending source of fun and funds for the small boys.

The Calcutta club has always enjoyed close ties with the Royal and Ancient, thanks no doubt to the many Scots who served in the Indian Army and Civil Service. In 1882, a group of members presented the Royal and Ancient with what is known as the Cashmere Cup, as a gesture of goodwill. To take advantage of their handsome new silver trophy, the Royal and Ancient introduced a new form of competition, the world's first handicap event. It was to revolutionize club golf everywhere, although the first Silver Cashmere Cup (now known as the Calcutta Cup) tournament stayed with the traditional form of play, matchplay, with the handicaps in the form of "hole" starts.

In return for their new trophy the Royal and Ancient gave a silver tankard to the Calcutta club. This is still played for and it provides a reminder of the club's origins and, now that the gospel of golf has been spread worldwide, Royal Calcutta's status as the first mission established overseas.

Fairways Haunted By

Chinese Ancestors

The Course Card		

Royal Hong Kong
Golf Club,
Fanling
Championship
course

Hole	Yards	Par
1	439	4
2	155	3
3	520	5
4	295	4
5	198	3
6	425	4
7	375	4
8	192	3
9	497	5
10	377	4
11	469	4
12	525	5
13	400	4
14	426	4
15	191	3
16	409	4
17	412	4
18	417	4
Out	3,096	35
In	3,626	36
Total	**6,722**	**71**

In the years after World War I there were six golf clubs in China, at Amoy, Hankow, Shanghai, Tientsin, Canton, and Hong Kong. Today only the Royal Hong Kong Golf Club survives. It has three full-size courses sharing the same clubhouse at Fanling, close to the frontier with mainland China, as well as a nine-hole course at Happy Valley, on Hong Kong Island, where the club began in 1889. Here a handful of enthusiasts were forced to share the only flat and open space with other sports, including polo, with the result that the course's architect, Captain H. N. Dumbleton of the Royal Engineers, was not allowed to construct bunkers or holes. Instead, when golfers had the run of the land, close mesh netting was used for bunkers and small granite paving stones as holes—they had to be hit by the ball to "hole out."

It was effective enough, and popular. In May 1890, a six-a-side match was played between the club and the Argyll and Sutherland Highlanders, which the club won easily. The match attracted a number of spectators and the membership reached 100 the following year.

The first course that was more or less for the exclusive use of golfers was sited at Deep Water Bay on the eastern side of Hong Kong Island, where a tiny 16½-acre triangle of flat land by a beach became available. It was reached from the city by circumnavigating the island in a launch, and had only to be shared with some occasional cricketers.

The links was a criss-cross affair, but enough to serve the membership. A modest single-story clubhouse was built and, five years later, another story was added. In time, the popularity of the game and a growing membership led to further expansion and the acquisition of a piece of land large enough to accommodate a full-size course, or even two. It was found at Fanling, on the mainland near the Chinese border. Fanling and its neighboring villages were at the time beyond the reach of the Kowloon railway, and the journey to the course entailed a two-man rickshaw ride into the hills

above Kowloon and then a walk down the other side to Shatin, where a police launch could take you to the other end of the bay at Taipo. From Taipo to Fanling the journey was completed by pony, chair, or rickshaw, depending on the weather. Mercifully the railway was completed to the border in 1911. The first course at Fanling, now the Old, sufficed until 1923, when the membership reached 800. Permission was sought to build the second course, but the members rejected this and voted instead for a bigger clubhouse.

Whether the clubhouse or the courses should be improved is a debate that has raged in most clubs at one time or another. In the case of the Royal Hong Kong, the committee blandly ignored the rank and file and went ahead with the New course. It was opened in November, 1931, by the Governor of the Colony, Sir William Peel. In time it was to become the more popular of the two and a credit to its designer and supervisor, L.S. Greenhill.

The courses suffered from general neglect and dilapidation during the Japanese occupation from 1941 to 1945, and it required a huge effort and an equally large bank loan to put them back into working order. It was not until 1953 that all the holes of the Old and New courses and the club's third course, the Relief, were restored. Early in the 1960s it again became apparent that the two larger courses at Fanling were bursting at the seams. The answer was to upgrade the Relief course and add more land, to turn it into a course of modern dimensions and difficulty.

Land was acquired from the Royal Hong Kong Jockey Club and, under the creative supervision of Michael Wolveridge—who, along with John Harris, conceived the design—began to take shape. Numerous lakes and other water hazards were constructed to drain areas subject to flooding, and these became such strong features of the course that it could quite felicitously be called "The Lake" —as one entrant in the naming competition suggested.

Royal Hong Kong's championship course is formed from holes on the
New course, built in 1931, and the Eden course completed forty
years late. The result is a stiff and interesting test.

The 3rd

A Par Five That Is a Revelation

Rare is the par five that reveals all its secrets from the tee. The 3rd hole on Royal Hong Kong's championship course does, and it is a gem. At the 250-yard range, still short of the foot of the slope, is a large white expanse of sand with a high, thin tree standing sentinel beside it. This is the first obstacle to avoid and it dominates the scene. But there is more trouble on both sides. Down the left flank is a dense wood, on the right a pond and open ditches. Driving from a high tee is exhilarating but, because curved shots have considerably farther to fly before they hit the ground, fairway widths are effectively reduced.

The second shot runs a gauntlet of sand and water. The sand is on the right, a large lake beckons on the left. Shirking the challenge and playing short leaves a near-impossible third shot because the green is small and angled to the right. Because the green is built up in table-top style the difficulty of the pitch is increased. Avoidance of traps is achieved by approaching from the right at an angle of some 45 degrees, which is possible with the second shot.

For its entire length this hole is carefully carved out and constructed to be of championship caliber. Sixes and sevens are not uncommon and a par is well-earned.

As with the construction of earlier courses at Fanling, numerous old and forgotten Chinese graves were unearthed and compensation had to be paid to the families whose ancestors were disturbed. Ancestors continue to lurk in the hillsides around the course and on Ancestor Worship Day the golf course is crowded with people of all ages visiting their now long-departed forebears.

On completion, the new course was named the Eden —the name of the third course at St. Andrews. Of necessity it was squeezed into the corners of the last available land, which gives it some tightness. But this limitation comes where it serves a good purpose—when holes are unavoidably short for par fours. This applies to the 10th and 11th holes, which are at the point farthest from the clubhouse. The rest of the course rolls smoothly, with adequate width and stretch, and includes some holes of undoubted world class, notably the 3rd and 18th. To counter the severe monsoon rains the greens are mostly built up off the ground. Hitting to these raised targets is an additional test of enterprise and skill, making the Eden course quite different from the other two courses.

The Hong Kong Open and other championships are played on a composite course of the New and Eden, choosing the convenient best of each to form a course that provides very nearly the ultimate in challenge for the competitors of many nations. One who certainly likes it is the German, Bernhard Langer, who won the 1996 Asian Masters there; it was a victory that saw him emerge from a wilderness of bad form, and his first win achieved with the long putter that ever since has been his salvation.

**The weather was wet at
Royal Hong Kong during the
Far East qualifier for the
1992 Alfred Dunhill Cup.**

The Course Card

Singapore Island
Country Club,
Singapore
Bukit course

Hole	Yards	Par
1	407	4
2	205	3
3	408	4
4	537	5
5	175	3
6	449	4
7	450	4
8	366	4
9	364	4
10	380	4
11	426	4
12	223	3
13	563	5
14	191	3
15	501	5
16	429	4
17	132	3
18	488	5
Out	3,361	35
In	3,333	36
Total	6,694	71

A Cool
Oasis
of Peace

There is no more cosmopolitan meeting place, outside the United Nations building in New York, than the Singapore Island Golf Club. Once the exclusive preserve of colonial administrators—the city was founded by a giant among empire builders, Sir Stamford Raffles—the club now reflects the island-state itself, an international entrepôt set at the heart of all eastern trade.

There are four courses: the Bukit (6,694 yards), the Island (6,365 yards), the New (6,874 yards), and the Sime (6,314 yards). They are grouped attractively around the Pierce and MacRitchie reservoirs, which help, in a humid climate, to generate refreshing breezes. All four courses are exceptionally beautiful, by any standards. The green fairways twist and turn their way across the hills and dales of the catchment slopes, between the huge native trees that were left in place when the course was made. In the background are the reservoirs and beyond them the jungle.

Each of the four courses has its own personality and qualities. Bukit is the parent course, built by the Royal Singapore club in 1924 after thirty-three years at a site on the old racecourse. It is the most popular, as well as the most important, of the present four courses. It is an undeniably hilly course, so some of its holes either plunge awkwardly downhill or else climb steeply. Yet each hole is a worthy challenge; the par threes are especially difficult, even for champions. The fours are all strong, featuring either length, narrowness, or canny trapping, and sometimes all three. The par fives are an invitation to disaster, two of them being near the end of the round when the legs are apt to be wobbly.

The greens, built on local clay, are hard for the approach shot and fast for the putt, a combination that provides the most difficult of all championship conditions. The Bermuda grass in use can reduce the most stolid of golfers to a nervous wreck.

The Bukit course was chosen as the venue for the World Cup when it was first played in Southeast Asia in 1969. Improvements were made by the English architect, Frank Pennink. The United States team of Lee Trevino and Orville Moody predictably won the team prize. Trevino just beat the smallest of the competitors, Sukree Oncham of Thailand, for the individual honors although Oncham won the popularity contest. In 1993 the course again had a chance to show it could cope with the best, staging a Johnnie Walker Classic that is still talked about at the club. It featured Nick Faldo at

A recreational haven among the bustle of Singapore, the Island Country Club boasts four good eighteen-hole courses. The best, Bukit, was chosen as the venue for the first World Cup held in Southeast Asia.

holes across the valley below the clubhouse. It is a frightening prospect when results of matches—and a lot of money—depend on the final effort.

The merger of the two clubs in 1963 brought a boom in membership and resulted in the building of the fourth course, the New, starting from the old Island clubhouse and taking the last space along the shores of the reservoirs. It was originally designed by the English partnership of John Harris and Frank Pennink and is a massive and imaginative layout, with many fine and memorable holes on modern length lines. It makes a splendid course for the professionals who follow the Asian circuit through March and April.

The original layout was adjusted to accommodate changes in the lake level, but little was lost and the New course, with its tiny clubhouse, is outstanding in its own right. The Sime course is the shortest and hence is regarded as being the most appropriate for women, although it is not theirs exclusively. It occupies a section of the Bukit, using up, as it were, the ground the bigger course does not need. The first nine holes rush over hilly ground, while the second nine is a longer excursion with even more ups and downs, following more or less in tandem with the inward nine of the Bukit.

The Sime is an enjoyable and more than usually scenic club course. Nothing more is claimed for it. But the Singapore Island Club's members are proud of the strength of their championship course, the Bukit—and they have every reason to be.

his finest, putting together four rounds in the 60s to defeat Colin Montgomerie by a stroke.

The Island course was that originally occupied by the old Royal Island Club, whose membership took in those golfers excluded by the Royal Singapore. It was built in 1927, three years after the Bukit course, and gathered the cosmopolitan membership enjoyed by the present club, which was formed when the two clubs merged in 1963.

The Island course is on the short side and some of its fairways are rather hilly on the transverse, making driving extremely difficult in dry weather. Its first nine holes wander around the reservoir shore and return to the foot of the clubhouse. The inward half is farther inland and uphill, but it is wider and longer. Both nines finish with attractive par-three

The 18th

Faldo Reigns Supreme

The best of finishing holes are made to provide drama and the ultimate hurdle. The Bukit course's 18th hole has few equals in that respect. It is a par five, but it makes an excellent end to a round because it has awkwardness and, at 484 yards, length. The well-struck tee shot carries across a huge valley into a fairly steep uphill slope. It is from this slope that the most awkward of second shots—with wooden club if shooting at the green—must be executed. When swinging hard on a steep slope it is all too easy to forget about balance while altering the plane of the swing to a flatter one. The ball is considerably higher than the feet and this means that full power in the execution of the stroke is not possible because the club's full length must be curtailed to accommodate the lie.

Yet the target of the green seems tantalizingly within range and, given the golfer's usual optimism, it is tempting to try. A line of massive trees blocks out the left side so that more often than not the shot must be bent around them with a long draw. The slope actually helps this but disaster is always possible. At the green are deep traps and a small out-of-bounds wall, over which most

tour regulars have sailed at one time or another. A slice of any magnitude can end in the locker room. It was on this hole that Nick Faldo completed his supreme performance in the Johnnie Walker Asian Classic in 1993. Having watched Colin Montgomerie two putt from 20 feet, Faldo knew he had to hole from 12 feet to prevent a play-off. This was a day when Faldo had every confidence in his putter. He knew the ball was in the hole almost as soon as it left the putter head.

The New Zealander Simon Owen putts out on the final green during the 1990 qualifying rounds for the Alfred Dunhill Cup.

Rescued and revitalized after the war, during which it had been used for growing crops and as an army training school, Royal Selangor has become the regular venue of the Malaysian Open. Toughened and improved recently by the English architect Frank Pennink, it is now one of the best courses in Asia.

Grave Problems in a
Burial Ground

The Course Card

The Royal Selangor Golf Club, Kuala Lumpur Old course

Record: 64, T. Kono, Malaysian Open 1971

Hole	Yards	Par
1	428	4
2	405	4
3	512	5
4	164	3
5	346	4
6	463	4
7	187	3
8	388	4
9	493	5
10	467	4
11	422	4
12	391	4
13	488	5
14	207	3
15	579	5
16	351	4
17	147	3
18	435	4
Out	3,386	36
In	3,487	36
Total	**6,873**	**72**

The founding members of Malaysia's second oldest club, the Royal Selangor, must have been a singularly phlegmatic species of golfer. Sonorously, their early rules stated: "You cannot ground your club in addressing the ball, or move anything, however loose or dead it may be, when you find yourself in a grave."

For graves, on a course that included an old Chinese burial ground, were declared to be a hazard. No special mention was made of the long grass, despite the fact that to this day it is hung with bloodsucking leeches when the weather is humid. Unlike most Asian clubs of long standing, Selangor, which serves the Malaysian capital of Kuala Lumpur, has had only one change of address in its eighty years of existence. And this was not painful as the government, in acquiring the site of the first course after World War I, provided a more convenient and attractive alternative.

For four years during World War II the club served as the headquarters for the Japanese Army of Occupation. During that time the clubhouse suffered no real structural damage, but the two golf courses reverted back to jungle, except for patches of tapioca and a small airstrip. "The first impression on inspecting the property," reported a member in 1946, "was that golf would never again be played there."

He reckoned without the club's professional, Yorkshireman Tom Verity, and the members. After months of backbreaking work the main course was reopened for play by the end of the year. By mid-1947 a third nine was cleared and by March 1948 both full courses were in play. Verity, an outstanding character, was appointed professional in 1937 and he was to hold the post for twenty-seven years, leaving only to build new courses and to teach up-country. Some intangible quality departed from the club when he left.

The Royal Selangor Golf Club today is a hive of sporting activity. Besides its thirty-six holes, there are grass tennis courts, an Olympic-size swimming pool, a squash court, restaurant, and entertainment facilities for hundreds of people. It is something of a diplomatic listening post; the ambassadors of the U.S. and, most unexpectedly, the Soviet Union battle for the honors of lowest handicap, and two kings have graced the premises with regular attendance.

Thirty members founded the club at Petaling Hills, outside the city area, in 1893. No clubhouse was available for the first handicap competition, and notice was sent from a refreshment tent that "St. Andrews Rules, of course," would be used—a reminder that in 1893 golf had no set of standard rules. Leading clubs in Britain and elsewhere drew up their own until 1897, when it was agreed that those made by the Rules Committee of The Royal and Ancient Golf Club at St. Andrews would be applied universally.

In 1918 Selangor State took over Petaling Hills and paid for the construction of a new course and clubhouse. Few clubs have ever been blessed with such official help. Work began on the new site in 1920 and within a year nine holes of the main course were ready, together with the clubhouse. In the next year four grass and two hard tennis courts were laid down; the swimming pool did not appear until 1937.

The greens on both the Old and New courses were at first laid with an indigenous growth known derisively as "cow grass," a dwarf species that proved suitable for animals but which left much to be desired when used on greens.

Bermuda was used for the greens of the Old course for eleven years in the 1920s and 1930s, but the strain was never satisfactory and was replaced in 1935 by serangoon, successful in Singapore. A hybrid Bermuda strain, a world away from the original "cow grass," has now been put to use.

Maintenance difficulties are enormous in a country that, apart from its heat, has an annual rainfall of 160 inches. Green surfaces have the shape of upturned saucers—a characteristic of courses in the monsoon regions—to drain off the immense quantities of water that will flood a course in a matter of minutes.

Golf events in Malaysia are often held up or canceled because of rain, but one way to ensure protection is to hire a "Bumu," an expert in keeping rain away—sometimes apparently with good results. During the 1975 Malaysian Open Championship at Kuala Lumpur, heavy rain was forecast and arrived on schedule. The Asian hockey championships, held in a stadium less than a mile away, suffered badly and finished three weeks behind schedule. The golf championship had its Bumu. He came just after dawn on

For the Cautious Rather than the Bold

At 463 yards the 6th at Royal Selangor is really neither par four nor par five. Of course in championships this does not matter, since par has no meaning in a stroke-play scratch event except perhaps to rate the total score. The hole is barely reachable in two shots into a wind unless the fairway is dry and hard, which it seldom is. Downwind, of course, it is not the same problem. During the Malaysian Open, played each March, it is usually a drive and a 3- or 4-iron hole. But it is advisable to approach timidly: it is easy enough to get down in two from just short, but less likely from beyond.

The green is unusually narrow, being no more than 10 paces wide. This makes a tiny target, especially when fired at from 200 or more yards. It is guarded by a trap on either side, the right-hand one being a little shorter than the left. The green is elevated and of two levels, rising quite high at the back. It has gained something of a reputation because of the grain of its grass, which makes putting a tricky business. Knowledge of this makes the tee shot somehow more

difficult, since the player feels the need to gain as much length as possible in order to shorten the second shot. This has destroyed thousands of drives.

The tee shot is aimed at slightly higher ground, and there is one yawning trap on the left that is not particularly threatening unless the shot is hooked violently. On the right side is a line of thin trees, under which the broad-stemmed indigenous grass grows lush and thick. Running diagonally across the fairway about 30 yards from the green is the course's main storm drain, which catches plenty of over-ambitious second shots. Its stone and concrete lining can sometimes be spectacularly beneficial and many a second shot nose-diving to destruction has rammed the hard rock and rebounded high in the air to safety. However, for most it means a certain one-stroke penalty, which often leads to more as desperate recovery attempts overshoot the green in the effort to get too close. Sanely played, though, it is a hole of immense challenge and, once parred, great satisfaction.

each of the four mornings and set up his stand beneath a simple shelter behind the 17th tee. No one spoke to him, nor he to them. He burned a few sticks, chanting all the while in an undertone, except when he ate or took a short nap. No rain fell for four days, until the Malaysian Prime Minister presented the first prize to Australia's Graham Marsh. Then the heavens opened. In a matter of minutes the course and clubhouse precincts were awash. Had it fallen an hour earlier it would have been impossible to complete the event.

Royal Selangor is almost dead flat, which makes for easy walking, and the golf is pleasant when the sun is not high. But giant trees provide shade and the small stream that runs through the course adds its own freshness.

One gets the feeling that it is an easy course. This may be because each hole is a birdie proposition, or seems so. In the course of a championship the fortunes tend to fluctuate unpredictably and the explanation is often found in the grass on the fairways and greens.

Fairways are well-grassed and when freshly cut provide excellent lies. Greens require special preparation because of the rain, but at their best rival anything other than the softest bent grass. Despite the flatness of the fairways, the thick-bladed local grass gives a wide variation in lies. The way the ball sits very often determines its flight and destination, the influence of the grass overriding the skill and planning of the striker. For all that, championship golf at Selangor calls for special skills at the short end of the game, as a list of winners of the Malaysian Open shows.

Most holes dogleg around the massive trees. Numerous bunkers, strategically placed, provide the obstacles. In all, the Royal Selangor is a course in the highest category. In terms of architecture it is as the best-designed courses should be—all things to all golfers. It is a fearsome test from the back tees for the champions who come around frequently for the Malaysian Open, and at the same time real fun and pleasure for those with lesser gifts.

The 17th hole at Royal Selangor is a lovely par three over water.

The Course Card

Bali Handara
Country Club,
Bali

Hole	Yards	Par
1	500	5
2	180	3
3	450	4
4	180	3
5	400	4
6	410	4
7	400	4
8	411	4
9	527	5
10	412	4
11	180	3
12	410	4
13	410	4
14	180	3
15	540	5
16	432	4
17	442	4
18	560	5
Out	3,458	36
In	3,566	36
Total	**7,024**	**72**

Constructed almost entirely by hand labor under the supervision of the itinerant professional Guy Wolstenholme, Bali Handara is a fine reflection of, and response to, the golf boom in the Far East. The main problem in building a course on this beautiful island was the rainfall: up to an inch can fall every day during the two wet seasons.

The Golf Boom Reaches
An Idyllic Island

Even if it were possible to uphold the dubious claim that the Dutch invented golf, there is no evidence that they took it with them to the outposts of empire, as did the British. Rather, the game arrived in Indonesia—then under Dutch suzerainty—as an appendage to the tea and rubber plantations owned by British commercial interests.

Until after World War II there were fewer than a dozen courses throughout the 2,500-mile chain of islands that make up Indonesia—all but two belonged to the plantations. The Djakarta club, in the capital, was the most successful. Its eighteen holes were spread comfortably over 150 acres or more of park-like grounds not far from the city center.

After the war the club suffered a cruel blow. Half its property, nine holes beyond a road, was compulsorily acquired for a new university and the club is now confined to the 75 acres that originally contained only nine holes. Its holes are crowded in more ways than one and the total length of the course barely reaches 6,000 yards.

The election to president of General Suharto brought to power an enthusiastic golfer, and many of his ministers and senior army officers have dutifully followed his example. This growing interest in the game led, as it has done elsewhere in the world, to the need for a course of truly international quality and design. Djakarta Golf Club could never be that, because of its limited land space.

The choice for the site—and there could not have been a happier one—was Bali, at the eastern end of the Indonesian archipelago. Bali is an island of legendary beauty, little more than an hour's flying time from Djakarta, a volcanic structure sloping down through green forests and palm groves to the white sand of reef-protected beaches. It is the home of two and a half million Balinese.

General Ibnu Sutowo, the moving spirit behind the scheme, found his site high in the mountains where, at 4,000 feet, the weather is cool and the rainfall adequate for growing the best golf grass. The land included a dairy farm, on a gently sloping tract between two large and splendid lakes near the small town of Bedugal.

Thomson Wolveridge Fream and Storm were engaged as architects and Guy Wolstenholme, the expatriate English professional, took on the task of supervising the construction. He arrived in a downpour of rain in September 1973. The only

earth-moving machinery that Wolstenholme had at his disposal was an old-fashioned Russian steam-roller, converted into a bulldozer that crept along at less than walking pace. There was no other machinery available on the island, but there was something better—the wholehearted co-operation of the entire local population.

Altogether, 1,500 people, many of them women, worked on the course construction. The fairways were staked out, cleared up by the villagers, and finally hand-sown. Under Wolstenholme's careful supervision greens were built entirely with hand labor, frequently in heavy rain.

Bali has two wet seasons. During February—March and September—October rains fall almost every day, in the higher altitudes, arriving punctually at one o'clock in the afternoon and continuing until four, during which time an inch might fall. The natural patterns of water drainage on the site were carefully noted, and the course now has a drainage system second to none. It is possible to play less than half an hour after the afternoon rain has finished, or to get at least a few holes in before the sun disappears at six o'clock.

The course took its final shape in six months. Ron Fream of California selected the grasses, flown in from the United States, and an elaborate watering system arrived from Australia. The clubhouse is a beautiful building in the Indonesian style and all around it are small cottages in the same style to complete the setting. In every way the course fits in with its surrounding environment. From the clubhouse there is a view over the course and beyond it to the lake, its far side lost in the distance. Everything is a rich green except for the red tile roofs of the far village and the blue sky reflected in the lake.

From the course, the clubhouse is dwarfed by a forest-clad mountain, its heights wispy with cloud. Monkeys, deer, and pigs descend occasionally from the forest to cross the course, or to stop and feed before racing for cover at the approach of man.

The fairways, a superb blend of imported Kentucky

bluegrass and the local Bermuda strain, roll out like an expensive carpet at every hole. Bluegrass, as its name implies, has a gentle hue distinguishing it from other vegetation. When close clipped it is crisp and firm, ideal for iron play or long wood shots. In truth, fairways so perfect take something from the play. To handle the infinite variety of lies and stances on a seaside links, by contrast, is much more of a challenging task.

At Bali Handara the ball bounces and rolls truly, with a variation in proportion to the amount of rain that has fallen beforehand. The greens stand out as inspiring targets emphasized by the white sand of the bunkers, though these have not been overdone. Craters of sand would look extraordinarily inappropriate in a mountain setting; Bali Handara, like other courses in similar situations, is not a seaside links and should not be made to look like one. Golf is playable anywhere. It is one of an architect's jobs to arrange an arena for golfing in whatever natural circumstances there are and to get the best from them without destroying their character.

The trees, the flowers, the streams, and lakes at Bali Handara are unique to the course and are its real features, with the golf holes running over and between them. Bali Handara turned out even better than its designers' dreams.

Bali Handara is a wonderful subtropical course, making fine use of the wooded areas that line a number of holes.

Beauty Sweetens the Challenge

The 3rd hole at Bali Handara was the toughest to build, but in the end proved to be the most rewarding. It is a 450-yard par four, doglegging left, its fairway divided by a stream that rushes off the mountain behind. From a high teeing ground, the drive is over a garden of wild shrubs and flowers into a wide, safe field of fairway. The stream winds its way along the right of the 1st fairway, cutting it off from the shorter 2nd fairway, which is offset to the right. The second shot must then be hit across the water to the long green, which is well beyond. An imposing trap of white sand cuts in to the green on the right side. When the flag is set on this side its base is hidden by the sand because a gentle dividing ridge spurs out from the trap.

This is a hole of beauty and pleasure, presenting a basic challenge to players of all standards. To tempt the long hitter there is a short stretch of fairway, partially obscured by trees. This is the direct line to the green, but the penalties of failure are severe. There is the stream to consider and thick trees and undergrowth to trap the slice.

From the charming single-file track that leads to the tee, to the little wooden bridge across the stream and the walk away from the green through the trees, this hole epitomizes the magic and the fascination of Bali Handara.

Australasia

Sport is king in Australia, a land where top-class tennis players are taken for granted and an endless succession of pubescent Olympic hopefuls cleave the water like dolphins. In such a climate, golf—a game that can be played from youth to near-dotage—was bound to find enthusiastic support. The number of Australians who play golf ranges from 750,000 to twice that number, with the lower figure representing at least the solid nucleus of devotees. Either way, support for golf in Australia is every bit as great as in the United States and twice as great, *per capita*, as in Britain, which dispatched to the southern continent its first exemplars of golf during early Colonial days. There are now more than 1,600 courses in Australia, most of them concentrated in the populous southeast corner of the continent where the nation's first settlements were established. The antecedents of the earliest clubs are a little confused, for there were a number of false starts in Adelaide and Sydney. The Royal Melbourne, slipping through where others were stumbling, is the club with the longest unbroken existence, since 1891. The Royal Sydney and the Royal Adelaide soon followed, and by 1895 there were clubs in Perth and Tasmania. The best of Australia's courses are among the best in the world. There is a particular quality about those in the neighborhood of Melbourne, where the soil of the Sand Belt and the talents of architects like Alister Mackenzie and Dick Wilson have shaped testing golf in surroundings of great character. They have played their part in the breeding of great players who have made their mark around the world—Norman Von Nida, Peter Thomson (five-time winner of the British Open), Kel Nagle, Bruce Devlin, Bruce Crampton, Steve Elkington, Greg Norman, and others. In New Zealand, where the game got off to a start—albeit in a limited manner—about the same time as in Australia, golf has made great strides in recent years. With 500 courses it has more than Ireland, where the population is about the same.

1. Royal Melbourne 2. Royal Adelaide 3. Royal Sydney 4. Warakei 5. Paraparaumu

A Course to Humble Even the
Giants

The Course Card

Royal Melbourne
Golf Club,
Victoria
Championship
course

Record: 65, Sam Snead

Hole	Yards	Par
1	392	4
2	443	5
3	304	4
4	402	4
5	161	3
6	391	4
7	135	3
8	279	4
9	416	4
10	425	4
11	401	4
12	396	4
13	324	4
14	433	4
15	350	4
16	184	3
17	510	5
18	395	4
Out	2,923	35
In	3,418	36
Total	**6,341**	**71**

Something outstanding and exceptional was bound to emerge from the formation of the Royal Melbourne club. There was, to begin with, a dedication to the traditions of the game that stemmed through its earliest members and officers directly from St. Andrews. Later, after two changes of location to the site it now occupies, it was fashioned from a duneland setting akin to the old Scottish links. And finally the inspired architecture of its East and the West courses.

Championship events are now played over a composite eighteen holes, a beneficial expedient forced upon the organizers of the 1959 Canada Cup (now the World Cup) to avoid busy roads that cross both courses. It has been the venue for most of the prestigious Australian tournaments and several more besides, including three World Cups. When the Presidents Cup, the biennial encounter between the United States and the rest of the world, was looking for a venue for its first match outside the United States in December 1998, Royal Melbourne was the logical choice.

The necessary acreage of sandy dune left behind by a retreating sea, studded with native she-oaks and tea-trees, dwarf reed, heather, and bracken, was acquired by 1924, when it was decided to secure "the best expert advice." The choice of adviser was Dr. Alister Mackenzie, a celebrated Scottish golf architect. Mackenzie arrived in October 1926 and started work immediately with Alex Russell, Australian Open champion of 1924. Mackenzie was a designer of the highest skill, and the Royal Melbourne was in many ways his masterpiece. This is not to overlook Russell's contribution—evinced by the quality of the East course, which he designed and built after Mackenzie's departure.

As significant as the layout and overall design of the course is the scale and speed of its greens, the credit for which belongs to the former head greenskeeper Claude Crockford, who joined the staff in 1934. In many ways the course is as much his as it is Mackenzie's or Russell's.

Crockford himself undertook to rebuild the short, uphill 7th hole to the concept of the then best player of the

The best of Alex Russell and Alister Mackenzie, designers of the East and West courses respectively, are taken to produce the composite Melbourne championship course. A feature of both men's work is their skill in bunker placement and green contouring. The 3rd is Russell's creation—330 yards long, dipping into a hollow and up to a tiered green that falls to the left. In contrast, the 13th is Mackenzie's hole, a slightly longer par four that ends with the ball being played to a triangular green that falls away at the back.

Surrounded by sand, heather, and bracken, the sloping 5th provides a perfect example of a Royal Melbourne green. Renowned for the superb pace and texture of its greens, Australia's premier course ranks with any in the world and the variation in championship scores there (from Sam Snead's record 65 up to 105) is a good indication of the demands it makes even on the greatest of players. The course gained immensely in stature through the skills of its masterly head greenskeeper, Claude Crockford, who battled against flood and drought to maintain and even improve upon the designs of Alister Mackenzie and Alex Russell.

club, Ivo Whitton, after the original Mackenzie hole proved unsatisfactory. Crockford's 150-yard 7th is a rare gem of planning and construction. It was built on the sandy hill by horse and scoop like the rest of the course. It slopes in an intriguing line from back to front although there is adequate flat, or nearly flat, territory for the flagstick in one or two spots —a deception not always discovered until it is too late. It is surrounded by traps of good depth and formidable sides, with a foreground like a miniature natural park of small indigenous flora to add to its rugged appearance.

But Crockford's real memorials are the Melbourne greens; there are no truer or faster putting surfaces on earth. The greens are basically dry and firm and the grass sparse compared with the dense growth of most other courses. Every fifteen years or so, the turf is carefully cut into lengths of six feet by one foot across, lifted away to expose the root-mat and the lower six inches of soil, the home of most grass diseases. This is scraped away and replaced by sterile soil. Then the turf is relaid, keeping to the original contour.

To follow the Melbourne championship course is to experience a kaleidoscope of obstacles and emotions. The 1st is a 392-yard par four of huge width and openness. It is hardly possible to miss this fairway. The second shot— assuming one can reach the green—would be no harder if it weren't for the need to get somewhere near the flag to make the task of getting down in two a more reasonable proposition. As always at Melbourne, this is easier said than done.

The 2nd is an excellent par-five, especially when the wind is from the southwest. The tee shot must carry a formidable sand bunker on the short line and a player cannot hope to get home in two or near it unless he does. The second—if it reaches the green—runs past a crater of sand on the left and the green that looks so benign can be a holy terror when putting from a distance.

The 3rd hole is a Russell creation of 304 yards. Few holes of this length anywhere have its class. The tee shot aims out to a wide expanse except for a spread of sand on the right at the crown of the hill. Beyond, the fairway rushes down to a hollow before a two-tiered green that steps down from right to left, the third stage dropping into a final huge trap at its lowest and farthest left point. In addition the player is faced with a pitch over another deep monster on the right to get at the flag on the top right step—where it nearly always is on championship day.

There follows a dogleg par four, again by Russell, that climbs uphill to a green, two-tiered on the crown. The 5th is the first of the ingenious par threes that make this course so distinctive. It is a 170-yard shot across a small valley to a green that forms a step on the farther slope. Surrounding the green is a sea of sand, heather, and bracken and the slope before the green is so steep and "shaved" that a shot just feeble enough to land on the beveled front edge inevitably trickles back down to the foot of the slope. The green is deceptively fast and sloped from the back; holing out in two putts requires a keen eye and a steady hand.

The 6th hole is one of the world's best and a thrill to watch during a championship. It is a dogleg, starting from a high tee; the fairway turns at almost right angles around a wide area of perfectly natural ground scrub and sand, which can be crossed with sufficient power and direction.

The invitation is to bite off more than can be chewed. From the fairway there is a gentle slope up to a green set in a natural amphitheater that is guarded by a massive, deep trap on the left-hand side. The shot looks easy and receptive but there is a major problem of getting down in two from the back edge—which is usually the putt left when played into a stiff breeze and the second shot is a long iron. Putting across the green is no less examining, because the "line" is apt to turn almost the length of the putt. In the 1987 Australian Open this green became infamous as it provoked what may be the first "walk-out" ever staged by professional golfers. Sandy Lyle, that most genial of men, led the protest against a flag that had been placed on what he considered an impossible slope. He was supported by, among others, Greg Norman, who labeled it "completely unfair." The upshot was the final round was postponed until the following day when the pin was placed in a vaguely puttable position.

Following Crockford's new 7th, which offers no respite, is another jewel. The 8th is only 279 yards long but devilishly difficult. The green can be driven and often is, but in this lies the seeds of destruction. The fairway crosses a large valley and winds its way by circuitous route to the right until, having reached the hilltop, it turns back left to the small green surrounded by mild wilderness. Playing safe is no guarantee of four because even after a curtailed tee shot the pitch from below the hill is blind and therefore risky. It is a fine example of old-fashioned adventure.

The 9th hole is a man-sized par four that doglegs left to the horizon and a green of alarming undulation and fiendish speed. The 10th is one of the best holes on the course. It must have started its life as a par five because,

---

The Ultimate in Temptation

Above and below: The 8th hole at Royal Melbourne, above, is only 305 yards long —but woe betide any player who trifles with it.

It is a stiff test of a golf architect's skill to ask him to make something out of a hole of only 300 yards; few holes on earth of this length can be reckoned to be anything more than stop-gaps. The par-four 8th hole on the Royal Melbourne championship course is an exception. Granted the designers, Alister Mackenzie and Alex Russell, had a perfect piece of land to work with but the result nevertheless is quite unique. It makes the sternest demands on good and bad players alike, and no matter what the weather conditions scores here can vary from two to ten.

The 8th: 305 yards par 4

—— Bold line
----- Safe line

In golf course design two interesting themes run counter to each other. The one rather standard principle, that the farther one hits and the nearer one approaches the target the finer becomes the margin of error, is cleverly offset by the axiom that the more finely judged second shot gets progressively more difficult the farther one falls short of the green. Architects often attempt to incorporate these two themes into their design, but few succeed.

The sporting length of the 8th offers the ultimate in temptation—that of driving onto the green and perhaps holing the putt for an eagle. But the very real likelihood and the dire consequences of failure on a shot of that particular line and length are apt to inhibit the free swing and bring disaster. The hole crosses a pleasant valley from one crest to the next. Ordinarily, this would present no problems to the modern professional, except that on the direct line to the flag is a cavernous bunker. However, the designers have cleverly led the player toward the right where they offer a safe shot, provided it is not too long. Failure to reach the top of the crest leaves a shot to the flagstick which is mostly blind and, should the green be firm and fast, as it usually is, the pitch requires the utmost accuracy to hold the green. All around there is sand, except for a tiny apron in the form of a hollow, the excavation of which helped form the green.

The main feature of the hole is the enormous chasm of bunker which must be carried by the brave player who goes for the green. A man feels small indeed standing in there trying to get out.

instead of a straightforward fairway and green, the route winds away to the right and a higher level, drawing the play with it and so adding to the length and interest. The tee shot carries some large-scale Mackenzie traps and the second an expanse of Royal Melbourne native rough, thinned sufficiently for the ball not to be lost, but rugged enough to make escape an uncertain business.

Another beautiful par four is the 11th. The drive fires out on to a level area back-dropped by a forest of tea-trees, and there is no hint of what lies ahead until a hill is breasted at the 250-yard mark to reveal a spectacular target some 200 yards away across a shallow valley. The 12th (the 18th on the West course) leads back to the clubhouse. It is a par four of much merit, presenting a drive over a hill that is characterized by typical Mackenzie sand and a sharp dogleg turn to the right where the green is viewed, framed in several ominous white sandtraps.

The 324-yard 13th is a clever drive and a pitch made to a triangle green in which the apex points to the striker and the slope falls gently away to the back edge. The "falling away" technique was used again by Mackenzie at the 3rd at Augusta National. In the early days there was no doubt a choice of a high pitch or a run through a preceding small valley and steep bank close-shaved like the green. Nowadays, alas, everyone opts for the pitch. Perhaps the most powerful hole on the course, the 14th is 433 yards, and more a par five than a par four. The tee shot must carry over a hill with a savage seaside trap; the second shot, across a valley of sand and scrub, runs the gauntlet of steep-faced traps at the greenside. Again the fairway runs intriguingly to the left of the target and for once the green is comparatively flat. It was

here that Lee Trevino took a nine that cost him a win in the 1974 Chrysler Classic championship.

Lined along the right side with trees and the course boundary fence, the 15th is a dogleg sliding to the left with a green of fiendish undulations. It is, perhaps, the only place at which it is possible to go out-of-bounds; the 16th is a Russell par three of 184 yards up a gentle hill. The back of the green, to the left, is more like 200 yards distant, a factor to remember when selecting clubs. Australia's Bruce Crampton ran up a six here just when he and Bill Dunk looked to have the World Cup won in 1972.

At 510 yards the 17th is Melbourne's longest, but—incredibly—it was twice reached in two shots in 1958, first by Sam Snead, then by an Argentinian giant, Leopold Ruiz, with a drive and a 7-iron! There are cross-bunkers at the 400-yard mark and little else in the way of obstacles.

The last hole, 395 yards and invariably into wind, is one of the world's best finishing holes. With the green an island in a sea of sand it makes a formidable par four. It has characteristic undulation and ever-increasing speed when the chips are down. It makes the task of getting down in two little less than heroic and sometimes beyond one's capability, as the Scot Ronnie Shade found in the Eisenhower Trophy in 1968. From a yard or two short of the putting green and about 25 yards from the cup, his run-up swung away to the left and Britain lost the contest to the USA.

There are few, if any, courses in the world where the scores for a championship vary as much as they do at Melbourne. Sam Snead's 65 is the best—and 105 by Sam Surrudhin of Indonesia the worst. It is a course to humble the giants or confirm their greatness.

The 14th: 470 yards par 4

The 14th

Fairways that Wander to Deceive

The most difficult hole on the Royal Melbourne layout comes at a critical stage in the round—the 14th. It is a 433-yard par four that both twists and rolls spectacularly. It rises over a substantial hill before descending through a long, 200-yard valley and ending on about the same elevation at which it started. If one shoots straight for the green the hole also turns some 45 degrees after the tee shot; otherwise the approach must be planned to avoid the obstacles and then the line of attack can vary considerably.

But first there is one of those classic blind tee shots over a complex of Mackenzie, traps on the skyline. This must have been a fiendish hazard in the 1930s, when the balls flew shorter distances than they do now. Those who could not carry the bunkers must have been forced to go around them to the left, thus increasing the length of the hole to over 500 yards. Beyond the bunkers the fairway slopes downward, complicating the stance for the long

second, which is daunting enough, but the clear view from there of the various obstacles—and therefore possibilities—is frightening. There is rough to carry for the first part, and then the fairway twists and turns through three huge, deep bunkers that can bring disaster. Lee Trevino was caught in the heather overhanging the trap on the left side in the 1974 Chrysler Classic and ended up with a nine! Here again we see Mackenzie cleverly leading the golfer astray with a fairway that wanders away from the direct route, forcing him to play over the trouble.

The green is a subtle complex of gentle slopes that are almost invisible, but most often seen, alas, too late. For most golfers this hole is more of a par five than a four, and when the south wind blows strongly it becomes a par five for even the strongest. Before the tea-trees grew high along the way, the hole traversed a sea of natural white sand. It is a pity that was lost; however, the trees make the hole more attractive if no easier.

Royal Adelaide, vulnerable to winds, is a searching test combining the best of classic architecture with modern demands for length and accuracy. The nearest to a genuine links in Australia, its critical run home from the difficult 226-yard 12th is through narrow, thoughtfully bunkered fairways.

The Course Card

Royal Adelaide Golf Club, South Australia

Hole	Yards	Par
1	382	4
2	516	5
3	295	4
4	422	4
5	411	4
6	433	4
7	156	3
8	373	4
9	548	5
10	374	4
11	382	4
12	226	3
13	399	4
14	447	4
15	499	5
16	180	3
17	492	5
18	419	4
Out	3,536	37
In	3,418	36
Total	**6,954**	**73**

Taking on the Teetotalers—

and the Bishop

Golf came to Adelaide in 1869, among the steam-er trunks of South Australia's new governor, the Scotsman Sir James Fergusson. There were Scots enough already in residence (the administration of empire was a talent in which they were particularly distinguished) to help him establish the club with a small membership within a year of his arrival.

The early years were, at best, checkered. The golfing governor departed, having completed his term of office, and six years after it had been opened the first nine-hole course now lost beneath the Victoria Park racecourse was abandoned as unsuitable. The club remained in limbo for sixteen years. A new course was found, but it was an expedient, replaced in 1896 when the club merged with the palindromic Glenelg, in the southern suburbs of the city.

The new club was still called Adelaide but used the Glenelg course, nine holes were extended to eighteen with the advice of Scots golfer, Francis Maxwell, whose brother Robert won the British Amateur Championship in 1903.

In 1904, the club moved to its present site at Seaton, twenty-five minutes by train from the city center. The single-track railway line is still there but the station, beside which the clubhouse was built in the center of the 204-acre property, has been closed.

Soon after it acquired the Seaton course, Adelaide appointed its first professional—not surprisingly a Scotsman, Jack Scott, from Carnoustie. The appointment of a talented professional was critical to a young club, particularly one so far from Scotland, source and inspiration of all golfing mores. He made and repaired clubs, not the least of his functions in a climate that played havoc with woodwork; he taught, and in teaching laid the groundwork for the club's reputation; and he was the final arbiter on the game's rules and etiquette.

Scott remained at Adelaide for nearly twenty years and had the pleasure of seeing one of his protégés, Rufus Stewart, become the first South Australian to win the Australian Open in 1927.

An Echo of Scotland's Best

When the property at Seaton was chosen as the permanent site of the Adelaide Golf Club, much of it was white sand left stranded by the receding sea. After the fairways and greens had been made, little was left except an exciting-looking crater—the perfect natural feature around which to build a golf hole. Indeed, it became the 11th.

Modern requirements have stretched the hole to 382 yards. Although it is effectively shortened by the prevailing wind from the southwest, it requires a healthy hit from the tee to reach the crest of the hill from where the green can be viewed—set tidily and invitingly beyond the crater of wild sand that waits there so menacingly.

Two accurate long shots must be executed to find the target. Crafty players skirt the danger of the second by edging to the right. This might avoid the ultimate woe of a six or even a seven, but nobody can ever count on getting down in two from off the green and this route usually leads to a bogey five. But to pass this hole without taking on the carry is to miss what golf is all about, particularly at Royal Adelaide.

The 11th has wrecked countless hopes of a good card. Its features are so precious but, perhaps because it comes too early in the round, it has not received the recognition it deserves. It would have been ideal as a 17th hole, where its influence would have brought it fame.

The 11th hole at Royal Adelaide has wrecked countless hopes of a good card.

The hazards of golf are not always just those of the sandtrap and the water. The Adelaide club had to contend with the prim city fathers—led by a bishop—who deplored the club's use of youngsters as caddies on the Sabbath. The club thwarted an attempt by two of its members to stop the sale of alcohol at the club, and banished one of its member's free-range turkeys from the course.

To make worthwhile all their strenuous efforts to keep going, Alister Mackenzie arrived in 1926 to advise on modifications to the course. The work he carried out forms the basis of the present championship route, although in subsequent years the holes were constantly improved. Among Mackenzie's innovations was the removal of the need to play across the railway line, and the introduction of the sanddunes as features of the championship course.

Royal Adelaide (it acquired its Royal appendage in 1923) is perhaps the nearest course to a links that Australia has among its top championship venues. Its sand is in many places the natural hazard and rough. The 1st, 6th, 13th, 17th, and 18th holes were upgraded in the 1970s to give them more of the "seaside" character than they formerly had.

The whole layout has the flat appearance of a links, except for a rise in the center of the site where two tees, the 8th and 12th, are placed. Two huge craters of sand have been preserved to enhance the course's character.

Royal Adelaide has been host to the Australian Open plus a succession of other professional and amateur tournaments. It was also home to one of the most extraordinary incidents ever to take place on a golf course, concerning a shot played by Kevin Simmonds in a national amateur event. Simmonds hooked his drive at the second into the carriage of a passing train. Whereupon a passenger threw it back as the train approached the green, the ball finishing a yard or so from the hole. Sadly, we have to report that Simmonds missed what would have been golf's most astonishing albatross. Not a bad eagle three though.

Jim Ferrier, who attained world fame first as runner-up in the British Amateur in 1939 and the PGA Championship in 1947, won the double crown of Open and Amateur national titles at Royal Adelaide in 1938. Gary Player won the second of his seven Australian Open championships there in 1962 (an event in which Jack Nicklaus made his first appearance in Australia, finishing fifth). Player won with 278, five less than Ferrier's score twenty-four years earlier, but Ferrier was under

no pressure for he won by the enormous margin of 14 strokes from his contemporary, Norman Von Nida.

The final of the Australian Amateur in 1932 provided the most exciting contest in the championship's history. The defending champion, a seventeen-year-old left-handed prodigy, Harry Williams, was opposed by Dr. Reg Bettington, a triple Oxford Blue and captain of the New South Wales cricket team. Williams appeared to have his title safely in keeping when, two up, he hit his tee shot to six feet at the par-three 12th, the 30th hole of the contest. Bettington followed to 20 feet and courageously holed the putt before stepping back to watch Williams miss. Bettington took the lead by birding the next two holes. He stymied Williams on the 33rd green and birdied the 34th. A half in par-fives down the long 35th gave Bettington an incredible victory; Williams shot pars through the last seven holes, yet lost four of them.

Scoring of this kind was unknown in Australia in 1932. Both players were of the highest standard and Williams was recognized as the best player Australia had produced until then. He played little if any golf after 1939 and died suddenly at the age of forty-six. Bettington left Australia shortly afterward to settle in New Zealand and died in a car accident.

Although the match between Williams and Bettington was one of the most remarkable in the club's history, Royal Adelaide has seen much other quality golf and will continue to do so; in 1998 the Australian Open returns to the course for the eighth time.

Seaside Golf in a
City Saucer

The Course Card

Royal Sydney
Golf Club,
New South Wales

Hole	Yards	Par
1	277	4
2	549	5
3	182	3
4	427	4
5	435	4
6	154	3
7	563	5
8	302	4
9	359	4
10	419	4
11	438	4
12	384	4
13	514	5
14	194	3
15	443	4
16	563	5
17	210	3
18	402	4
Out	3,248	36
In	3,567	36
Total	**6,815**	**72**

A city whose premier golf course is little more than a ten-minute drive from its commercial and social heart is one where a dedicated golfer might be glad to live. The Royal Sydney is such a course, retaining the rugged look of a true links and surrounded by suburban houses.

In a land where sporting and athletic distinction is a matter of pride, the club is as much a feature of its city's life as the famous bridge and the billowing Opera House. Its membership roll reads like a who's who of New South Wales. Although formed as a men-only golf club in 1893, it is now a golf, tennis, and social club with 5,000 members and a waiting list of frustrating length.

The whole of the property is in the shape of a huge saucer. The center of the area is inclined to be wet and the course was laid out on the drier and sandier rim of the saucer, where good use was made of some useful undulations. The layout has peculiarities not found elsewhere. Many tees are sited against the club boundary on the higher grade with the fairways spread below and the greens in full view in the distance.

In its formative years the course was of nine holes and "rooms were taken at Mrs. Ebsworth's cottage for the use of members." In 1896 James Scott joined the club as its professional, his arrival coinciding with the extension of the course to eighteen holes, taking in some of the lower-lying area, and in 1897 the club received the title Royal. It went from strength to strength as the course improved in quality and it soon became host to the Australian Open,

previously held only at the Royal Melbourne Golf Club.

Royal Sydney is at its best on those clear, blue days that are characteristic of Sydney. Autumn and winter are particularly pleasant, when the course is at its greenest. In summer it browns somewhat, but a soft sea breeze ensures that outdoor activity is still enjoyable. Like most courses by the sea, there is rarely a day when the wind is absent. This is a precious commodity for golfers as it adds that extra dimension to the course, enhancing its adventure.

In October thunderstorms can wreck the golf. This almost happened in the 1969 Australian Open when Gary Player was struggling desperately to keep a narrow lead over Guy Wolstenholme. The skies to the south darkened in the late afternoon when Player was six slow holes from home. Lightning could be seen some miles away and amid the turbulence of the wind and the first shower Player and Bruce Devlin took shelter; they stayed there until ordered to resume. Wolstenholme played through it and lost by one stroke. Devlin and Lee Trevino finished close behind.

In 1988 Australia celebrated its bicentennial year and the Australian Open returned to Royal Sydney. The course was upgraded for the championship, the most significant change being the enlarging of several greens. This time an American prevailed, Mark Calcavecchia winning by six shots from his compatriot Mark McCumber. Calcavecchia called himself "lucky," but no one can enjoy so much fortune to win by such a margin without playing some superior golf as well.

The elegance of Royal Sydney 's layout diminishes the severity of its hazards in the eyes of less observant golfers. But its fairways are narrow, its rough fierce, and its bunkers numerous. The judging of distances too, can cause problems, and at holes such as the 13th, with its cross-bunkers some 280 yards from the tee, this can be crucial.

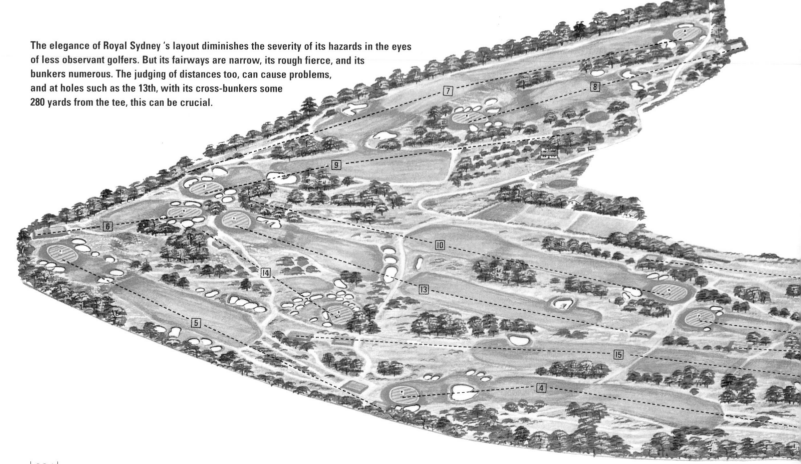

Perhaps he was lucky in that for once the wind did not blow and he was able to amass a staggering total of 19 under the card. Typically no one does well at Royal Sydney without a knowledge and command of the low, wind-escaping shot.

Except for five holes the course runs north and south, so that the shots called for have a repetition that can be destroying if the golfer is not particularly adept at playing into, or half across, a stout breeze. Most greens are surrounded by large bunkers designed by Alister Mackenzie and cut deep into the bare sand underneath. The ball will often plug into the soft white sand. The course begins with a drive-and-pitch hole. Originally it was almost drivable, but the task is harder now that the tee grounds have crept back uphill and there is a back tiger tee by the clubhouse door. Skirting the rim of the saucer, the course makes its way outward with three superb par fours and a par three from a high tee, until it turns around at the 6th, another par three from a high tee. The 7th is a stern par five and the 8th and 9th, two similar par fours, complete the half.

The best holes on the first nine are the 4th and 5th, both par fours. With the wind against they can be as much as a wooden club second shot for all but the mightiest hitters. The tees are higher than the fairways and the both greens demand a long shot gently uphill without being blind. These two holes are truly memorable. This first half is the shorter but by far the more interesting in the way of features. With a wind from the north it is very short, but never easy. There are many shots to the greens that have to carry all the way.

The second nine contains the longer 13th, 15th, and 16th that run more or less straight either north or south, so that no matter which way the wind blows one or two of them are into it and therefore out of range of two shots by anyone. From the 10th tee the course descends into the lower area and only rises again at the last green in the shadow of the clubhouse. These holes are plainer than the outward ones, but because most of them are straight they become a hard test of a golfer's technique. Stunted trees of indigenous variety separate these fairways and provide a savage penalty for waywardness.

The best holes inward are the long, par-five 13th, the 14th, and the final hole, which is aptly one of Australia's best. The 14th is a 194-yard par three. The green is surrounded by sand and, depending on ability, the aspect is either inspiring or wholly terrifying. A few years ago a tournament offered $100,000 to anyone who could make a hole in one but the professionals had a total of 440 shots without success. Then along came a club member, ID Magney, who swung mightily the very next day with a 4-wood and watched from the elevated tee as the ball hopped into the hole for an ace. Alas, the prize was now no longer available.

The final hole is a thrilling climax, a doglegging par four of 402 yards to a redan green, from which it is but a short step into the huge clubhouse and all it offers.

The 18th

No Place for the Nervous

The moment of truth in golf comes when a match is all square on the last tee. Every golfer is affected by the situation, the more so when he knows the 18th will test his stamina and nerve in the manner of Royal Sydney's closing hole. It is one of the best finishing holes in Australia. It is a par four of good length, doglegging to the left around a small copse of trees. The well-trapped green is set above the fairway on a kind of redan below the giant clubhouse. It slopes gently forward and, like the home hole on the Old Course at St. Andrews, has just enough subtlety to make putting a performance that is always worth watching.

The dogleg puts the slicer at a disadvantage since his shot curls away from the hole. However, the hooker can gain ground if he can hit the 235 yards to the corner. There is a temptation to bite off too much, which, in matches, can lead to over-caution if the second player to hit is intent on avoiding at all costs the mistake of his opponent. The approach presents an invitation to mis-hit in an instinctive effort to hit the shot high so that the green will receive it sympathetically. There is seldom the need. The green is large and usually soft enough to hold most shots.

The placing of the tee shot is critical at the 18th, where trees on both sides narrow the entrance to the green.

Golf Among
the Geysers

Whoever plays golf at Wairakei, above,
is conscious of a living earth.

Wairakei is among the more modern of New Zealand's major golf courses, implanted by the government's Tourist Hotel Corporation in the heart of lovely countryside, bubbling with geothermal activity, midway between Auckland and Wellington. It is not in fact a club at all, but a green fee facility open to all who spend their vacations in the neighborhood of the huge, trout-filled Lake Taupo and the hot thermal springs of Rotorua.

The popularity of the game in New Zealand was not reflected in the quality of courses available until Wairakei was built. In 1953 the NZGA met to approve courses for the New Zealand championships and only four were of international standards—Titirangi, Belmont, Paraparaumu, and Shirley. Architects were called in and courses were lengthened (there was nothing, until Wairakei, approaching 7,000 yards), bunkering was modernized and the game as a whole was tightened up. Finally, H. T. (Dooley) Coxhead, an accomplished golfer and a member of the Tourist Hotel Corporation, persuaded his colleagues that what their hotel at Wairakei needed was a championship golf course, after the manner of Gleneagles or White Sulphur Springs.

The man he found to do the job was Commander John Harris, a civil engineer and England's leading and most traveled golf course architect, whose father had constructed Moor Park, Wentworth, and Sunningdale in Britain. The possibilities of Wairakei must have appealed to him.

The course is set in gently rolling countryside with a few majestic spurs and a lattice of gullies and creeks.

Harris's layout made excellent use of the natural features and his sympathetic handling of the terrain made all but a little earth-moving unnecessary, apart from green-building and general fairway preparation. The construction was supervised by Michael Wolveridge, an Englishman whose keen appreciation of the subtleties of golf architecture had been enriched by a spell on the U.S. professional tour. When completed, Wairakei lacked only a fairway watering plan, a benefit excluded until later by the budget.

In its first year Wairakei came under heavy fire from the New Zealand Conference of Greenskeepers, who were "appalled" at the subsidence of the greens—which, like the rest of the course, were built on pumice, the "froth" of ancient volcanic lava. The subsidence was soon cured.

Wairakei makes few physical demands on the player. Walking is easy and mostly on the flat, with an occasional climb to the higher tees. The variety of holes, however, calls for a high degree of skill to match par—a skill beyond the reach of an average player. Many small creeks have to be cleared along the front nine and open-shouldered hitting is needed on the run in, making the course, from the championship tees at least, a handicap contest.

Whoever plays at Wairakei is conscious at all times of a living earth, for above the enclosing pine forests there rise the endless vapors of the Karapiti and Rogue bore holes. The Rogue is particularly awesome, its clouds of steam and spray rising to heights of 300 feet and more. It has given its name to Wairakei's most impressive hole, the 14th, 608 yards long from the back tee. The building of this hole exemplifies the importance of the construction supervisor's role in the creation of a golf course. Wolveridge improvised considerably as Wairakei was taking shape and for the end of the monster he dreamed up a banana-shaped green which is naturally set into a steep hill above the long, doglegged fairway. It poses permanently for brochure photographers.

The course as a whole can be played in three lengths—the Championship (6,977 yards), the Regular (5,960 yards), and the Hotel (5,193 yards). Par for the Championship and Regular routes is 72, and for the Hotel, 70.

The 14th

The Rogue with a Reputation

Flanked by soft hills and forestland, the long par-five 14th aims directly up a narrow valley toward a natural rogue borehole that belches forth clouds of sulphurous steam. Aptly named The Rogue, the hole has a reputation as the chief wrecker at Wairakei and it is an undoubted test of strength as well as skill. Its fairways wind past well-placed bunkers and beneath a tall pine tree toward an unusual green some 600 yards distant.

The main interest lies in the third shot to the green, which is large, elevated, and horseshoe-shaped; its left side is fraught with bunkers and hollows. The tougher pin spots are to the left and center and they demand a fairly lofted approach. This means, of course, that if a par five is to be attained in the usual manner, two mighty wood shots are needed before the final approach.

The Rogue is a special hole, vociferously attacked and defended with equal passion, but always memorable.

Wairakei, a splendidly natural course set amid a spectacular thermal region of the North Island, was built in response to the growing clamor of the early 1950s for a true championship course in New Zealand. It is long—but not too long— and imaginative in the siting and construction of its greens and traps.

	The Course Card		

Wairakei Hotel
International, North Island

Hole	Name	Yardage	Par
1	Wairakei	520	5
2	Pines	235	3
3	Karapiti	512	5
4	The Oak	872	4
5	High Pitch	179	3
6	Glen	488	4
7	Huka	869	4
8	Challenge	355	4
9	Hillside	455	4
10	Terrace	198	3
11	Ruapehu	358	4
12	Tongariro	298	4
13	The Plains	463	4
14	The Rogue	608	5
15	Flyover	205	3
16	Tauhara	411	4
17	Gap	434	4
18	Home	517	5
Out		3,485	36
In		3,492	36
Total		**6,977**	**72**

Man Conspires with Nature to Create
Adventure

The Course Card

Paraparaumu
Beach Golf Club,
Wellington

Record: 62, Bob
Charles Caltex 1968

Hole	Yards	Par
1	403	4
2	202	3
3	419	4
4	446	4
5	164	3
6	313	4
7	500	5
8	371	4
9	380	4
10	311	4
11	427	4
12	505	5
13	446	4
14	150	3
15	372	4
16	138	3
17	442	4
18	487	5
Out	3,198	35
In	3,278	36
Total	**6,476**	**71**

Paraparaumu Beach is an antipodean phenomenon—a real seaside links. Thirty-five miles north of Wellington in New Zealand's North Island, it is reached by a winding, circuitous route overlooking the Tasman Sea and the sentinel off-shore island of Kapiti.

The founder of the club, Stronach Patterson, and his colleague, D. O. Whyte, were attracted to Paraparaumu Beach and its linksland because in the 1920s no course of its kind existed in New Zealand or, for that matter, anywhere beyond the British Isles and the western fringes of mainland Europe. By 1930, Patterson, Whyte, and their colleagues had the support necessary to build their ideal links and Alex Russell, co-architect with Alister Mackenzie of Royal Melbourne, was chosen to design it.

Only a bare minimum of land could be afforded, but it was enough for Russell. Within its 130 acres he filled every square yard, either with natural, undulating fairways and carefully constructed tees and sandtraps, or with rough he left on the high dune tops. It says much for Russell's flair for architecture that the course bears no similarity at all to his work at Melbourne. The temptation was to duplicate the wide fairways and huge rolling greens that make Royal Melbourne such a distinctive course, but here they would have been out of place and Russell must have known it. Instead he drew upon his own experiences and observations in Britain, where he had traveled and played. The result must rank with Carnoustie or one of those happy courses along the Strathclyde coast, like Troon or Western Gailes. It is, nevertheless, different again from each of them—more a clever mixture of old and new, nature's sculpture and man's talent. Paraparaumu looks the way Troon would probably look if it had been built recently instead of eighty years ago.

To play the course in calm and sunny weather, or to battle gales from one quarter or another, is a satisfying and exciting adventure but it is best when the wind blows with moderate strength from the west. This is the prevailing wind, helping or hindering every stroke to some extent.

Bunkering is on a small scale—a sharp contrast to Russell's other courses, but here appropriate and sensible. There is a certain practicality in the creation of pot bunkers instead of the larger beach type. On some holes there are no artificial traps at all for the steep, close-cut slopes of the dunes serve as hazard enough.

The 1st hole, a 403-yard par four, heads off toward the mountains that form a distant backdrop. There is a 100-yard carry through a gap in the dunes leading to a large arena of fairway, with a gentle downslope giving a clear view of the green formed by low mounds and soft gathering undulations. The 1st green is typical of Paraparaumu: its small undulations, their crests only a yard or two apart, make putting a chancy business from a long way off. The small depressions tend to be lusher than the higher spots, creating variations in speed, and if a hole is cut on the crest of a bump, putting becomes an exceedingly difficult proposition.

The 2nd hole is difficult, a par three cleverly placed on the dune tops, the green having been made by ironing one into a suitable flatness. The target is not large, shyly hiding its shape behind a bump left judiciously on the apron: downwind from the back tee, the shot requires a 4- or 5-iron. Against the wind it can be a wood, and either way it is a par gratefully scored.

The 3rd fairway is reminiscent of the crumpled links of St. Andrews. The green is at eye-level with a sunken bunker hidden at the left front corner. Inevitably, it catches most pulled shots. The real hazard of the 3rd, though, is in over-hitting, because just beyond the center of the green is a steep, shaven slope that leads into a deep depression from which it takes luck to emerge without penalty.

The 4th is a 446-yard par four that runs along the foot of the highest ridge of the course. The 5th is a gem. Only 164 yards long, it rivals the famous Postage Stamp at Troon and Russell must have enjoyed creating it.

On the fairway of the 313-yard 6th, massive undulations can throw a straight drive off to the right or left, adding to the adventure of such a short shot. The 7th is a par five of quality requiring some stout hitting if the green is to be reached in two and the birdie thus gained. At the short 8th penalty, in the form of strong rough, awaits on either side of the plateau green. The second shot invites an inspired iron shot through a gap in the sandhills to a green nestling at the foot of the clubhouse hill; a large wild water channel runs alongside the left. Then follow three par fours and a par five reachable in two powerful shots.

At 446 yards the par-four 13th is one of the best holes in this part of the world. Nothing less than two perfect shots will get to the green. Of all holes the 13th, unique and thrilling, is the one that epitomizes Paraparaumu Beach. A golfer either loves or hates it; if he hates it he cannot like the links at all. Tantalizingly short, the 14th is a little drop shot par three made trickier by even a moderate wind. The 15th is a lovely par four, traversing between dunes up to a step like green that is difficult to hit from any line except the straight one.

The 16th is a gem of a three. It is cut into the side of a small hill with no bunker to guard it, but plenty of slope. The 17th, like the 13th, is enchanting. It has a split fairway on two levels offering a choice of routes. The lower, more direct route is easier for the first shot but fiendish for the second. The upper level is by far the best from which to approach, but it is necessarily more difficult to get there. From it, the passage is open to the green, still some 200 yards off and a daunting target. There is a steep and shaven slope off the left side, and the right is all traps and depressions; into a westerly wind it is often out of the reach of even the best players. But Gary Player played it in three into a gale in 1958, before he had become a world figure. He made another three, an eagle, at the final hole, too. The course record is 62, set long ago by Bob Charles. It has stood the test of time because it is a phenomenal score, on a course of real quality.

The 13th

Nature's Thrilling Invitation

As at many other holes at Paraparaumu, nature has played a great part in the creation of the 13th. Just like the very oldest courses on which the game of golf was born, it has many humps and hollows—some of them massive. It is most spectacular, for on a sunny day the view from the tee ground has few rivals in golf. The rough is splashed with the green and yellow of broom and the green can be seen against a backdrop of distant snow-capped mountains. The invitation is there to enjoy it and thrill to its stout golfing challenge.

The appeal of this hole can depend on a golfer's skills or, more pertinently perhaps, the distance he can strike the ball. It is 446 yards long and it takes a

massive drive from the back tee to reach the plateau halfway to the green. This is the ideal spot, offering a wonderful view of the slightly elevated green, about a 3-iron's carry across a huge hollow of fairway. Originally the green was a prepared saddle on the ridge without the back wall which members had demanded. Its addition has taken something away from the hole's uncompromising challenge but enough remains to make the 13th unique.

Paraparaumu's 13th hole is typical of the course. Its fairway undulates severely and it requires two precisely placed shots for a par.

The 13th hole at Paraparaumu offers an uncompromising challenge.

Since its completion in 1951 Paraparaumu has made a great contribution to New Zealand golf, hosting several national opens. It is a links course situated on a stretch of rolling dune land very much exposed to winds. Bob Charles, 1963 British Open champion, rates the 5th as "equal to any short hole in the world."

Africa

Most of Africa is a golfing void: the terrain alone sees to that. Beyond a sprinkling of courses in countries bordering the Mediterranean, such as Morocco (with its royal jewel at Rabat) and Tunisia, golf in Africa has thrived where the British influence was at one time strong — in Kenya, Rhodesia and, above all, in South Africa. The outstanding performances of South African golfers over the last fifty years bears witness enough to the quality of golf in their homeland and the attractive and testing courses on which they can hone their game. South Africa ranks about eighth in the world in the number of its golfers, but is among the van in their quality, with men like Bobby Locke, Gary Player and Ernie Els. Within the boundaries of the Republic there are courses of all types, ranging from true linksland challenges on the coastline of Natal to the many high veldt courses (there are at least eighty within a sixty-mile radius of Johannesburg) where, in the thin air, the ball flies like a space shot and every man is a superman when he drives from the tee. Golf traveled to Africa by troopship in the confused and unhappy decades before the Boer Wars. A six-hole course was laid out by a Scottish regiment near Cape Town in 1832 and the Cape Golf Club, the senior in South Africa, was born a few years later with a Scottish general as the midwife. Scotsmen, both professional and amateur, were in almost total charge of South African golf trophies for thirty years. Conditions in those early days were far removed from those of Scotland. Greens were more often than not compacted sand, and grass was a luxury only a few clubs could boast. Modern strains of grass and year-round automatic watering systems have long since overcome the drawbacks of an unreliable rainy season and, with courses of the caliber of Durban Country Club on the Indian Ocean coast and Royal Johannesburg, thousands of feet up in the Transvaal, South Africa can now lay claim to some of the most challenging layouts in the world.

1. Durban Country Club 2. Royal Johannesburg 3. Royal Rabat

The Thrill of
Anticipation and Uncertainty

Since the time it was first shaped from the bush and dunes of the Natal coast during the early years of the 1920s, the Durban Country Club course has achieved and maintained an excellence that keeps it at the forefront of South Africa's 250-odd courses.

The decision to build it grew largely from the misfortunes of the Royal Durban, South Africa's oldest club, which was host to the 1919 national championships: the course became so water-logged that the winner took 320 squelching strokes to finish. There was no guarantee that the low-lying course would not flood again and so Durban, one of the great cities of South Africa, was in danger of losing its place on the national tournament circuit.

There was already a need for a new course at Durban and pressure mounted after the 1919 debacle. A site was found and in 1920 the appropriately named George Waterman and Laurie Waters, four-time winner of the South African Open, began its design. The course was opened in 1922 and two years later Durban Country Club staged the first of its many South African Opens. Much of the history of the game in South Africa has been enacted there, and most of the great players have made their pilgrimage to it. Sid Brews, Bobby Locke, and Gary Player have had some of their greatest moments at the Country Club — and others they will want to forget. In 1998 Ernie Els won his third South African Open there, opening with a 64 that left him in a position of dominance he was not to relinquish.

The course saw Gary Player's first South African Open success in 1956, with 286. He returned in 1969 (having won the title another five times in the intervening thirteen years) to score 273, which included a then record round of 64 (the record now is 62, held by John Bland).

The Country Club is not long at 6,090 yards, and this was Arnold Palmer's only criticizm of it after his first experience there in 1963: "It would," he said, back in the days when the smaller, British ball was still legal, "be a much better course with the big ball." Palmer, with 71, lost his encounter to Player that time by a stroke, after Player had been out in 34 and Palmer had returned 34 for the second half.

To see the country club course at its best, it must be experienced in all its moods — especially in the wind, which blows often and puts a green out of reach of two shots when it could have been hit with a 7-iron only a matter of hours before. Suddenly all the bunkers then begin to make sense. The course has been updated on occasion — by Bob Grimsdell in 1959, and before him by the English architect, Colonel S. V. Hotchkin, the creator of Woodhall Spa, whose suggestions were adopted in 1928. Several tees have been resited and some holes have been renumbered, but basically the Durban Country Club has remained unchanged since 1922.

From the outset there was very little interference with the natural terrain but rather an accentuating of some of the site's original features. Grimsdell said: "The player is not shown everything at a glance, but is given the thrill of anticipation and uncertainty."

There are two distinct features — the holes on the dunes where either tee or green is elevated and surrounded by the natural bush, and those on the flatland, where trees still help shape the fairways but where the chances of a hanging lie are minimal — typically at the 5th, 6th, 7th, 10th, 11th, 14th, and 15th. They are no easier, but are not likely to cause so much apprehension.

The course's difficulties commence at the very first hole, where the golfer who flinches from the out-of-bounds on his right hand risks a hanging lie on the hump to his left. From it he can be out of sight of the green, set into a huge tree-covered dune. From the plateau green at the 1st there is a climb to the tee on the 2nd, where the shot is played from one ridge to another, over a deep, grassed hollow.

One of the largest memberships in the world enjoys the trials of the Durban Country Club course, automatic choice when the South African Open is held in Natal. At first sight it seems undemanding but many hazards are apparent only when the wind gusts off the ocean — across the sandhills that support the elevated tees and greens, and over the undulating fairways on the lowland part of the course.

The 18th at Durban Country Club, left, is driveable in favorable weather conditions.

The 3rd is everybody's favorite hole, played from an elevated tee at the highest point of the course into a valley. The ground rises again through a series of mounds, reaching like fingers on to the valley floor, to a green in the shadow of a tree-covered dune. Two shots are possible, but getting home with the second depends on the perfect placement of the first — and an ability to shut out the hazards lurking in the bush on both sides.

At the short 4th the golfer is coming off the dunes on to flatland, with the green, surrounded by slopes and mounds, looking deceptively small from the elevated tee. The 5th, 6th, and 7th take the corner on the flat, taxing neither the golfer's endurance nor his talents to any great extent, provided he is placing his shots well from the tee.

The 8th journeys back alongside the 3rd, playing in the opposite direction and with the high ground now causing more than a little concern: a 3-wood might not get the distance nor the height to hold the conical green, which is only partly visible. On the same level, the 9th tee looks down at a broad expanse of fairway — the green is somewhere to the right, out of sight. But for a time the pressure lifts.

The 10th and 11th are again on the flat, and length is the greatest prerequisite. There is a climb to the short 12th and the biggest concern again is to hold the green, as it is a long way back up the dune in the event of failure. Here Edward, Prince of Wales cut a ball down the bank and legend has it that he took 16 shots before he finally holed out.

Still on the parkland, the 13th tee is elevated — a pitch with the wedge for most players. A big second is required at the 14th and the 15th demands another short iron. None of the three is a really memorable hole. Now the player is back in the dunes, close to the sea. The 16th is a dogleg to the right where danger lurks on the right of the fairway along which runs a road bordered by dense bush. The 17th is a spectacular hole requiring a carefully placed drive to the rim of the valley on the right, for otherwise there is no sight of the green from the bottom of a deep basin in the fairway.

One can drive the 250-yard 18th in favorable weather. Whatever the conditions, the severe temptation to hit beyond one's capacity is always there and this makes it a fine finishing hole, demanding accuracy even from the faint-hearted. The way into the green is left, but a big pull finishes below the level of the fairway; a quick hook is dead in dense bush and a slice is invariably headed down a steep bank to the practice area below. Durban's 18th is among the shortest finishing holes anywhere in championship golf, but this in no way makes it easy to play.

"A little longer and the hole would be mediocre — just another drive and pitch," said Grimsdell. "But at this awkward and tempting distance it is just the finish needed for a course which rewards good golf but ruthlessly exposes all our weaknesses."

The Joy of Golf on
The High Veldt

The Course Card

Royal
Johannesburg
Golf Club,
Transvaal
East course

Hole	Yards	Par
1	473	5
2	228	3
3	418	4
4	444	4
5	145	3
6	530	5
7	384	4
8	489	5
9	366	4
10	469	4
11	467	4
12	186	3
13	359	4
14	398	4
15	199	3
16	448	4
17	354	4
18	468	5
Out	3,477	37
In	3,348	35
Total	**6,825**	**72**

To most golfers any mention of South Africa brings to mind Gary Player and Ernie Els, who have borne their country's standard in almost every land where the game is played. Since Player emerged as a player of outstanding skill in the late 1950s they have together preserved the name of South Africa as a nation capable of producing golfers of world class.

Compared with the United States, Britain, and Australia, the most powerful golfing nations, South Africa is small, but the fact that so many good players have emerged is a measure of their quality of the golf courses. In common with most countries the gospel of golf reached South Africa in the closing years of the last century, and as usual the missionaries were Scotsmen. The first appearance of the game, in an organized fashion, was on a six-hole course, laid out by the Royal Scots Regiment on rough and stony ground at Wynberg in 1882. Thereafter golf spread in fairly swift succession to the principal cities, but the South African Golf Union was not formed until 1910.

Johannesburg was only a mining camp when the first course was laid in 1890. It was rough and windswept, enthusiazm soon waned, and within the next few years the course was moved several times. This was not as great a problem as might be imagined; the ground was cleared for fairways, leaving all the natural hazards, of which rocks were a feature, and a tin was sunk wherever a hole was required; the sand greens followed later.

Meanwhile Johannesburg was expanding so swiftly that not until 1906 was the club able to find land free from the covetous reach of builders. Money was advanced by Sir George Farrar and Sir Abe Bailey for the purchase of a site, part of which is still in use. The construction of grass greens and tees, the first in Johannesburg, was a great step forward; a mule bus carried the members to and from the terminus of the trams into the city, and the

club settled to a generation of steady progress. As golf gained in popularity, and the membership increased, it was decided to have two courses, East and West. In 1933 more land was bought and construction began under the guidance of Bob Grimsdell, a golf architect of rare skill. There were many problems, not least ridding the ground of the coarse kikuyu grass that threatened the fairways and greens.

The East was recognized as the more difficult, but a gradual improvement in scoring, notably by Harold Henning in the Transvaal Open in 1955, prompted changes. These included the reshaping of fairways; the creation of new tees on many holes so that fairway bunkers would threaten the long driver; and new bunkers and hollows tightening some of the approaches. Now the course was a true championship test; Gary Player ranks it as one of the very best.

The course wanders quietly over wooded parkland. After the great sweep of the 1st, and a long short hole to a green plentifully trapped on the fade side, one is soon aware that this is a driver's course. The fairway bunkering at times is tight at around 250 yards, but one shrewdly placed bunker on the right side of the 3rd fairway is enough to make the golfer think on the tee. The 4th, the first of seven holes that curve to the right, and the 8th are outstanding driving holes, demanding length and exact placing for approaches to tightly guarded greens.

The short holes are of a high quality and vary in their demands; the 5th is a pitch that must carry to a slightly raised green embraced by bunkers, and so must the long iron to the 12th — beautifully set against a backdrop of willows — because the entrance to the green is angled to the line of flight. The 15th is possibly the most testing, for the plateau green makes the distance hard to judge.

Length is not the only criterion in the difficulty of a hole, and the 13th is a fine example. It swings to the left and a the tee. It can quicken fear in the mind of the golfer prone to hook because, as he stands on the 16th tee, he is aware that it follows the line of the hole too closely for comfort. Then at the last comes the challenging finish.

Needing big drives through a verdant valley, Royal Johannesburg's East course offers sheer golfing enjoyment tempered only by the abundant trees and strategic bunkers that narrow the fairways.

good drive means only a pitch home, though the entrance is narrow between bunkers; a thicket on the right threatens the approach from that side, and a mishit to the left may be caught by a pool that cuts into the line. Of the par fours only the 17th is shorter but the drive must carry a steep crest. Elsewhere the ground is gentle in its undulations, like the falling fairway of the splendid 11th hole. The drive must be placed as near as possible to a lone wattle tree, guarding the inside curve of the right-handed dogleg, for the most favorable position from which to carry a stream in front of the green. The stream that winds its way across the northern part of the course also comes into play at the 7th, where it slants across the fairway and must be carried from

The design of the holes is not necessarily the greatest problem. The greens demand careful reading because often the nap will more than counter the natural breaks of the ground. For a man to become a successful golfer in South Africa he must develop a firm putting stroke and a courageous attitude — and be a diligent observer of the greens.

Regardless of whether the visitor to Royal Johannesburg can manage this, he is sure to agree that the East course has few peers as a challenging and beautiful place to play golf.

The par-four 11th at Royal Johannesburg is the club's signature hole.

The 11th

Cole's Gamble Pays Off

The 11th, 511 yards long, is perhaps Royal Johannesburg's best hole. It is a gentle dogleg to the right, with a long carry from the tee but without fairway bunkers to inhibit the drive. At a strategic distance in front of the green a stream crosses the fairway diagonally. Closer to the green the fairway narrows considerably and toward the bank on the left side is a solitary bunker. The hole demands placement as opposed to the length so often required on many of the other holes. Yet, curiously, one of the best shots ever made there was also the longest — Bobby Cole's second from the rough in the second round of the 1974 South African Open, which Cole started in fourth place.

Played by a lesser player it would have been a desperation shot, a careless gamble in pursuit of a cause already lost. It was undeniably adventurous but it was the only shot with which Cole could be sure of a four after his drive had leaked left into the rough. His approach to the green was blocked by the stream and by some willows, some 220 yards distant. Cole knew that to reach the green from there his approach would have to be long and high enough to clear them.

Using wood, he hit the perfect shot to make his four. He was on his way to a 65 and a new record total of 272.

Bravura Golf —
Close to
the Casbah

The strong participating interest of King Hassan II and the need to attract tourists now means Morocco has over a dozen courses. By far the best is Royal Rabat, a long and demanding layout by Robert Trent Jones in a superb setting near the capital.

The Course Card

Royal Dar-es-
Salam,
Rabat
Red course

Record: 66, Howard
Clark, Moroccan
Open 1971

Hole	Yards	Par
1	409	4
2	233	3
3	454	4
4	424	4
5	569	5
6	443	4
7	430	4
8	574	5
9	199	3
10	483	5
11	464	4
12	567	5
13	389	4
14	210	3
15	396	4
16	430	4
17	225	3
18	563	5
Out	3,735	36
In	3,727	37
Total	**7,462**	**73**

As a broad generalization, golf course architec-ture falls into two schools, the "natural" and the "artificial". Like most labels, these words, with their emotive overtones, must be heavily qualified in each individual case. The designer whose instinctive approach is to leave the landscape looking as nearly undisturbed as possible must compromise when he works with terrain that is alien to the golfing ideal. Compromise is always at the designer's elbow raising insuperable objections: "The client insists … the budget does not permit … the land does not allow … "

Compromise is the last word to be applied to the work of Robert Trent Jones, the founder of the "artificial" school of architecture. Jones shapes his landscape and does not undertake a commission unless he is guaranteed the batteries of earth-moving machinery, the train-loads of topsoil, and the torrents of water needed to execute his bravura designs. His courses are stamped with a personality as distinctively as a signature. The vast tees, the sadistically molded greens, the extravagantly shaped bunkers and torture by water are the flourishes by which his name is inscribed.

The specification for Royal Rabat exactly matched his style. It was to be a course fit for a king — Hassan II of Morocco, the most enthusiastic golfer among contemporary royals. The championship layout, the Red course, was completed in 1971 and was the first of three courses at the club to come into play.

The drive to the clubhouse makes its way through the stands of cork oak from which Jones carved the course. The visitor's first feeling of anticipation is tinged by a more guarded feeling, almost of trepidation; he will come to an intimate familiarity with the cork oak, with its drab, olive-green leaves, gnarled branches and trunks that are stripped annually of their outer layer of bark, leaving them smooth, pink, and bare.

Between the trunks of these trees the visitor catches glimpses of brilliant green fairways and seemingly excessive blue expanses of water. The colors are exaggerated by the somber tints of the cork oak foliage and the twinge of fear that has attacked the visitor is soon confirmed by the view from the first, and subsequent, tees. Trent Jones clearly has a high regard for the cork oak, since he spared far too many of them in cutting out his avenues of fairways.

Every golfing instinct screams for an iron — or at most a 3-wood — off the tee, but the mathematical reality of the yardage demands that courage and driver be taken in both hands. What is more, the driving must be of high quality. The standard, unthinking boom straight down the middle may come to grief, for Jones slopes his fairways cunningly to deflect the ball toward his hungry bunkers. On nearly every hole the drive must be shaped, with draw or fade, if the ball is to finish in the prime position for an attack on the green.

Deception is the key to Jones's design and if he has failed to outwit the golfer with the demanding nature of the drive he has another trick in store for the approach. It looks fairly simple. His greens are invitingly large and will hold a well-struck shot. How can such targets be missed? To ask the question is to provide the answer, for any suspicion of complacency can send the ball away on a wayward course. But the cunning of the trick is that even if the ball finds the green it is by no means a formality to get down in two putts.

The two-putt zone on a Jones green is usually a small area and anything in the nature of an "outer" will need exceptional skill, or luck if the ball is to be caressed over those glassy undulations to within holing-out range.

And so it goes for eighteen tormenting holes. Some of them appear superficially to relax the challenge as the course moves into more open country, but it is an illusion. Artificial lakes are brought into play and, where they do not actually impinge on the target areas, their threatening proximity often induces the golfer to choose a "safe" line that turns out to be the road to some hazard from which his eye has been decoyed by the harmless water.

It is small wonder that the world's most skilled professionals have failed to completely master it. Although the Moroccan Open, a European Tour event, is frequently held there, no one has managed to better the 66 that Howard Clark shot in 1987. The par for the professionals is 72, and 73 for the amateurs, the one discrepancy being the 483-yard 10th that plays as a brute of a par four for the experts. As on all Trent Jones courses, it is the easiest thing in the world to drop a stroke at every hole without the suspicion of a mishit. Without showing some dazzle, the player will fail.

For lesser players, even off the extreme forward tees, Rabat provides a humbling if unforgettable experience.

The 9th

A Drug to
Make you Hook

Water is the most powerful hallucinatory drug known to golf. The sight of it anywhere near the target area causes an involuntary tightening of the grip, a slight acceleration of the normal speed of swing and, as often as not, a premature raising of the head in anxiety to see the ball pitch safely on dry land. Few holes in the world dispense this drug in such a powerful dosage as the 9th at Royal Rabat.

It is also one of the most picturesque holes to be found anywhere. The tee is set on the bank of a large lake with duck, geese, and flamingos in noisy regatta. Far across the lake — some 200 yards, but seemingly farther since water deceives the eye — the island green assumes minute proportions. It is connected to the mainland by

two hump-backed wooden bridges irresistibly reminiscent of a willow pattern plate. The golfer who is in serious action may be excused if he does not absorb the beauty of the scene.

The farthest tee demands a 3-iron at least and, if the wind is against, possibly even a driver. The urge to make certain of the carry often results in a forcing of the shot and consequently a hook. The ball may splash into the water left of the island or, more worryingly, pitch short on the upslope and roll back into the water. One contestant in the annual Moroccan Grand Prix, a professional with a notable tournament record, doggedly persevered with his idea of how the shot should be played and hit six balls into the lake before finally getting down in fourteen strokes.

Royal Rabat offers few more rewarding satisfactions then retracing one's footsteps across the wooden bridge with a three safely marked on the card — not that the golfer can afford to relax his concentration, for there are four more water holes still awaiting him and plenty of other problems besides.

The 9th hole may be Rabat's shortest but it is water all the way to an island green. Nothing but the most accurate iron will suffice.

There are, however, rewarding compensations for the eights and nines that blemish the scorecard, for this is golf at its most exotic. Where most clubs manage with a staff of a dozen, and often fewer, to maintain the course, here 500 men are kept busy grooming the fairways, raking the bunkers, and cosseting the greens. Their labors have produced a herbaceous wonderland of flowering shrubs as a foil to the cork oak and eucalyptus background. Walter Hagen's famous advice of "Never hurry, never worry, and always take time to smell the flowers" might have been coined for Rabat. Mimosa, bougainvillea, fuchsia, and

orange blossom provide splashes of color as dazzling as an impressionist's palette.

Geographically, the casbah seething with poverty and all manner of social deprivation is just down the road, but in every other sense it is a million miles away — another world, albeit still a Moroccan world. It would be a soulless golfer who could shrug off this juxtaposition with untroubled conscience, but in the narrow and unashamedly selfish context of golf, Royal Rabat represents an ideal that few inland courses can hope to achieve.

South America

South American golfers — players of the stature of Roberto de Vicenzo and Eduardo Romero — are better known to the world of golf than golf is in the continent where they learned their game. Of all the continents, South America has the slenderest golfing resources and most of them are concentrated in Argentina and Brazil. A scattering of courses have been built or are under construction in countries on the Caribbean shore like Venezuela, where Dick Wilson and Joe Lee laid out the taxing course at Lagunita Country Club as part of the sunlit circle of resort golf that now loops through the islands of the Spanish Main. But away from these areas, golf fades away almost to nothing. There is a handful of clubs in the Andean capital of Colombia (where the El Rincon course is a Trent Jones design), in Chile, Bolivia, and in Peru where, high in the thin air of the Andes, the visiting golfer from less dramatic altitudes is likely to exhaust himself merely teeing up. Golf arrived by railway in South America; to be exact, by railways in the making. The English and Scottish engineers who went to Argentina and Brazil to lay down the tracks at the turn of the century also laid down the first golf courses, in the neighborhood of Buenos Aires in Argentina and São Paulo in Brazil. Since that time the game has enjoyed steady rather than spectacular growth in popularity, although the facilities that there are — mostly for the better-off citizenry — possess outstanding qualities. The Jockey Club at Buenos Aires is a typical example. It has two courses dating from 1936, designed by the redoubtable Alister Mackenzie; the better known of the two, the Colorado (Red) course, was the venue for the World Cup in 1962 and 1970. It was fitting that, in the 1970 competition, the individual prize was won by Argentina's greatest golfing son, Roberto de Vicenzo, a man who had won his first Argentine Open in 1944 and gone on to add as much luster to the game as any of its finest champions.

1. The Jockey Club
2. Lagunita

A Superbly Groomed

Playground for the Rich

Although, as its name suggests, the Jockey Club's main interest is racing — the racetrack (and polo fields) adjoin the golf courses — it hosted the World Cup in 1970 when only nineteen players finished under the Red course's par of 292 for seventy-two holes.

The Course Card

Jockey Club, San Isidro Red course

Hole	Yards	Par
1	425	4
2	354	4
3	145	3
4	483	5
5	340	4
6	367	4
7	418	4
8	208	3
9	442	4
10	465	5
11	523	5
12	168	3
13	436	4
14	392	4
15	505	5
16	429	4
17	180	3
18	348	4
Out	3,182	35
In	3,446	37
Total	**6,628**	**72**

Golf is a sport for the well-to-do in Argentina and at the best known of its courses, the Jockey Club at Buenos Aires, it is merely an additional attraction to horse racing and polo. Its two courses at San Isidro are, however, none the worse for that; they were designed by Alister Mackenzie, whose imaginative flair has stamped the hallmark of greatness on golf courses worldwide.

The exclusive nature of golf in South America makes it hardly surprising that few golfers from the continent should have impressed themselves on the world stage, but one who certainly did was Roberto de Vicenzo.

Vicenzo is a folk hero among the golfers of Argentina and something of a demi-god at the Jockey Club. When he first went to America at the age of twenty-four, he could not speak a word of English. He did not have to; his driver spoke for him. His length astounded even Sam Snead and Ben Hogan, and he achieved it without even bothering to tee the ball up. He simply dropped the ball to the ground, pushed it

with the clubhead of his driver on to a tuft of turf, and then smashed the ball into the atmosphere with a hook that was under complete control.

Born of poor parents, Vicenzo learned the game at a golf course in Buenos Aires — not the Jockey Club — where he caddied with his four brothers (who all became professionals), and turned professional at the age of eighteen. By the time he retired at the age of fifty-two, he had won more than 140 tournaments, a record not even the evergreen Sam Snead has been able to approach. Among them have been more than twenty national championships won in fourteen different countries, an unapproachable record.

In 1970 World Cup was staged at the Jockey Club. (Among his many other records, Vicenzo has played in more of these matches than any other man.) Now he won the individual title for the second time, winning by a stroke over Australia's young David Graham, and Argentina finished second, 10 strokes behind Australia. It was a fitting climax to a career whose course was not yet run. In 1976, Vicenzo was invited to become an honorary member of the Royal and Ancient Golf Club of St. Andrews.

The Red course of the Jockey Club, which was used for the 1970 World Cup, is not really suited for a game of Vicenzo's immense strength. At 6,699 yards, it has not nearly the length with which he can ordinarily overpower his opponents. Yet it is in superb condition all year round, for Buenos Aires has no harsh winters or summers — sitting as it does about as far south of the equator as Atlanta is north of it and, being a port, it lies practically at sea level.

The 1st hole shoots directly away from the rear of the stately, U-shaped clubhouse and belies what is yet to come. At 425 yards it is long by the standards of any opening hole. Starting at about 150 yards from the tee and running nearly to the green on both sides of the fairway is what the members refer to as a pared de pinos, or a wall of pines. Approximately 260 yards from the tee, on the left — very strategically placed for professionals — is a large, banked bunker. This must be avoided at all costs, for it is nearly impossible to reach the green from out of it. Thus, it is wise to favor the right-hand side of the fairway off the tee. There is still another reason for doing so. All the trouble on the green lies on the left-hand side. First comes a cross-bunker lying slightly short of the green to the left, making any successful recovery from the fairway bunker all the more improbable. And running the length of the long green are two more thin bunkers, recovery from which is made more difficult by the undulating putting surface.

At 353 yards, the 2nd is more in keeping with the cunning of the course. A gigantic eucalyptus, not 100 yards to the right of the tee, makes the hole half-blind. A cross-bunker lies to the left at the landing area and another lies to the right just short of the green — which is small, as it should be, for the hole calls for nothing more than a three wood and a wedge. The 3rd, a 145-yard par three, is largely a matter of proper club selection. The green bends from right to left around a bunker. Another trap sits slightly short of the putting surface to the right, but this can easily be cleared. The one in the crook of the green must be avoided — and can be by using the proper club to carry the pin position.

At 483 yards, the 4th is short by the laws of any par-five, but the entire left side of the fairway is out of bounds. There are five bunkers on the hole, four of them scattered along the right-hand side of the fairway. The 5th protects the left side of the green. None of them presents a problem for three soft shots or two hard ones. This is the place for an early birdie. The 5th hole is one of those rare holes that only an architect of Mackenzie's imagination could pull off: a good, short par four. Only 340 yards long — a mere drive and a niblick or wedge — the hole must nevertheless be treated with respect. The entire left side is out of bounds and the tee shot

must carry a cross-bunker jutting into the fairway at the 220-yard mark. A sliced drive finds itself in another pared de pinos, ending with an ombú tree, a foliage typical of Argentina's pampas. The second shot, though short, must be precise, because the green is tightly guarded in front with three bunkers; the green is slickly undulated. The 6th, at 372 yards, lacks length and despite the small green is another promising birdie hole. The 7th is something else again, a full 418 yards and tightly bunkered off the tee. Two cross-bunkers intrude upon both sides of the fairway a good 230 yards off the tee and another lies to the right some 40 yards beyond them. The green is large and has a pot bunker that bites into its left side. To the right lies a mound covered with shrubs and trees that can leave an all but unplayable lie.

The par-three 8th is most notable for its beauty and its length — 208 yards. The green is very deep, widening considerably at the rear. As it widens, two bunkers lie to the left and right, along the slants it takes. There is no birdie here.

Next comes the swing – the crucial 9th and 10th holes that can make or break a round. The first is a very long par four, the second a short par five. After the 10th green the course makes an abrupt turn to the left. The 11th is another par five, but much more severe. For one thing, it is 50 yards longer than the 10th and, for another, it presents a much more severe dogleg, this time to the left. Bunkers to the right and left of the green are the main problems once the bend in the fairway has been cleared.

The 12th, at 168 yards, is a one-shotter to a very wide green full of curves, and any shot not reasonably close to the cup makes three-putting a distinct reality. At 436 yards, the 13th hole stands as the longest and probably the toughest par four on the course. The fairway is extremely narrow, as is the green. This, together with the fact that it is long and rises sharply to the rear, makes it difficult to hit and hold. Two bunkers to the left and another to the right mean that the second shot is not only long but must be accurate. The 14th is a straight forward par four just under 400 yards long. The 15th, a 505-yard par five, is much stiffer. Out-of-bounds lies along the entire left side of the hole and the right side is well bunkered. Three more traps flank the green. The 16th — par four, 429 yards — is an oddity in that it has only one bunker, lying right across the fairway, slightly beyond the 200-yard mark. The 17th presents a similar problem with its raised green and, although only 180 yards it is a tough a par three. The 18th is something of an anti-climax for people who are used to heroic finishing holes. It flies in a direct line toward the clubhouse and has not a single bunker on it. What is more, it is a mere 348 yards long; a 9-iron or a wedge will hit the green easily after an accurate drive. But weak as the last hole is, it cannot diminish the stature of the Jockey Club, which alone among South American courses conceived before World War II has any claims to greatness.

South America's
Busiest Course

The Course Card

Lagunita Country
Club, Caracas

Hole	Yards	Par
1	535	5
2	205	3
3	470	4
4	455	4
5	190	3
6	405	4
7	380	4
8	220	3
9	590	5
10	210	3
11	510	5
12	445	4
13	420	4
14	435	4
15	425	4
16	170	3
17	390	4
18	440	4
Out	3,450	35
In	3,445	35
Total	**6,895**	70

There are a number of outstanding country clubs in the vicinity of Caracas, a sprawling oil-rich city of more than two and a half million people. The Caracas Country Club is one, for the Venezuelan upper crust; another is Valle Arriba, with a membership of American businessmen and foreign diplomats; and a third is the Lagunita Country Club, in the suburb of El Hatillo, and its membership is a combination of the other two, mainly Spanish-speaking but with a high percentage of English-speakers, too.

The Lagunita golf club is part of a real estate development that includes expensive housing and covers more than one and a half square miles. It was bought by a group of local businessmen in 1956. The club now has 1,100 members, of which 700 are active golfers with handicaps — a high number by South American standards. Although the club is strictly private it is, nevertheless, the "buzziest" golf course on that continent, according to Freddy Alcántara, an authority throughout the Americas both as player and official.

"Lagunita is not a very long course by British or American standards," Alcántara reckoned. "It is only 6,895 yards at its extreme back tees. But, despite this, it is a tough course and it is beautifully designed. It is a true and fair test for championship players. For example, there is not a blind shot on the entire course, so you always know where you are going. Furthermore, the greens are very big, slick and fast-breaking. I would say the lack of length in its par fours is more than compensated by its par threes. They are long and very difficult and there are five of them. Hence the total par of only 70. They are the key holes on the course."

Lagunita was designed by Dick Wilson during the latter part of his career and was for the most part constructed under the supervision of Joe Lee, then Wilson's assistant. It was completed in 1962.

Lagunita has been host to the Venezuela National Amateur championship on a number of occasions and to the Simon Bolivar International Trophy, which was founded and organized by Alcántara. Its grandest day came in 1974 when it was chosen as the site for the twenty-second World Cup, and Sr. Alcántara's views of his home course turned out to be a bit conservative. Only three players in the entire field — Bobby Cole of South Africa, Hale Irwin of the United States, and Masashi "Jumbo" Ozaki of Japan — were able to break par over the 72-hole route; despite the fact that the official course record of 64 had been set by one of Lagunita's assistant professionals, Noel Machado (who also once unofficially shot the course in a startling 61).

The course at Lagunita is dominated by a large, modernistic clubhouse complete with ballroom and mandatory swimming pool. From its position on a hill, five holes can be seen, together with the practice range. The course fans out both to the left and to the right of the clubhouse, bending back on itself at the 2nd and 3rd and again at the 13th and 14th.

The 1st hole starts away from the left of the clubhouse and is a bit of an oddity in that it is a par five of 535 yards. Out-of-bounds lies along the left side — which is just as well, since the land has been turned into a quarry pit from which nobody could possibly play. The hole is a double dogleg with two cross-bunkers at the 220-yard mark, after which the fairway bends left for an easy second if the player chooses not to go for the green. Few players do, for the green is completely cut off in front and on both sides by bunkers. The quarry is avoided by laying up and playing into the green from the second dogleg. The 2nd is the first of those five treacherous par threes. It is 205 yards to the large, deep green, and that quarry still lies on the left. In a delightful understatement, the course notes describe the 2nd as "dangerous." The most difficult thing about the 3rd hole is its length: it is 470 yards, the maximum for a par four hole. Again, out-of-bounds lurks ominously on the left.

The 4th is one of the most interesting par fours on the course. It is 455 yards and demands a good drive to get past a dogleg that turns a complete ninety degrees and which cannot be cut because of three fairway bunkers and trees to the right. The green is shaped like a frying pan, with the handle protruding in front and guarded on either side by bunkers, with a flash trap to the rear. The 4th is not an easy par and no place to try to pick up a birdie.

The green of the 5th, a par three of 190 yards, is beautifully bunkered all around and to the left is another gravel pit. The 6th and 7th holes, both shortish comparatively uninteresting par fours, are followed by the longest par three on the course, the 220-yard 8th. It is the green that makes the hole, for it sharply inclines toward the approach and is well protected to the front and on both sides by bunkers. The prevailing wind at Lagunita blows across this hole from right to left. The 9th is a par five of 590 yards, the last third of which is uphill. There are no fairway bunkers and the hole needs none. The second shot must be played around a slight dogleg and requires something of a gargantuan effort to get anywhere near the green, which has two bunkers on either side. It is a truly fine par five.

The 10th tee, which sits just below the clubhouse, takes a long iron to carry 210 yards across a dip in the

Though Lagunita is not particularly long by modern championship standards, the club's confidence in its course was justified by the scores in the World Cup, held there in November 1974. Only three players among more than ninety broke the 72-hole par, all of them men in form: South African Open champion Bobby Cole, U.S. Open title holder Hale Irwin, and Japan's Masashi Ozaki, who led the world stroke averages that year.

Below right: The two courses at the Jockey Club were laid out by Alister Mackenzie. He structured the course with mounds and contouring combined with subtle bunkering.

ground to the green, which slopes severely toward the tee. The fairway of the 510-yard, par-five 11th is very wide, but out-of-bounds runs the entire length of the right side. The green is very narrow, long, and extremely fast. A cross-bunker sits just short of it for a lazy second shot and three more skirt the edges of the green. The 12th is one of the most treacherous holes on the course. A par four, 445 yards long, it is a sharp dogleg to the right with out of bounds all the way from tee to green. Three little bunkers and a copse at the angle of the dogleg make cutting it unfeasible. There are no bunkers around the huge green, but it is protected in front by a lake that runs clear to the putting surface. The second shot must carry the lake all the way.

The 13th and 14th, both medium-length par fours, are beautifully bunkered. At 435 yards, the 14th has plenty of length and no fewer than eight traps, three of them on the left side of the fairway in the landing area, where it bends slightly to the left. The ever-present out-of-bounds lies the complete length of the hole on the right. The elevated green is full of slopes and is practically encircled by five bunkers. The 15th — a favorite among the members — marches directly toward the clubhouse, as do the remaining holes. It is 425 yards, par four, and has three fairway bunkers to the left and close to the landing area. However, a gulley crosses the fairway and is played as a hazard. Out-of-bounds lies to the right of the fairway but can easily be avoided off the tee. A lateral water hazard, almost hidden, lies to the left of the green, which has but a single bunker directly in front of it. Also to the left of the green is another drainage ditch that is played as a hazard. All in all, it is a devious par four.

At only 170 yards, the 16th is the shortest hole on the course. However, the green is very large although fast and all but surrounded by bunkers. The 17th is short as par-fours go, only 390 yards, but it doglegs to the right with two fairway bunkers lying short of the bend.

Three more, front, right, and left, stand sentinel over every possible approach to the green. The 18th is a strong finishing hole, as it should be, 440 yards uphill to the clubhouse and against the prevailing wind. The fairway is wide, but bunkers lie on both sides of the landing area off the tee. The pear-shaped green is heavily bordered with rough and bunkers lie on both sides of its narrow entrance.

Lagunita, then, is a testing course and one that breeds a high degree of skill among those who play it regularly: the club are proud of the fact that over the years its membership has always included more than its fair share of scratch players.

Gazetteer

1 Nairn
2 Gullane
3 Gleneagles
4 Prestwick
5 Royal St. David's
6 Southport and Ainsdale
7 Little Aston
8 Formsby
9 Saunton
10 Burnham and Berrow
11 Royal Cinque Ports
12 Prince's
13 Berkshire
14 Hunstanton
15 Walton Heath
16 Wentworth
17 Royal Worlington and Newmarket
18 Royal West Norfolk
19 Woodhall Spa
20 Notts
21 Lahinch

22 Stavanger
23 Halmstad
24 Rungsted
25 Falkenstein
26 Frankfurter
27 Schloss Nippenburg
28 Haagsche
29 Royal Belgique
30 Royal Waterloo
31 Crans-sur-Sierre
32 Seefeld Wildmoos
33 Rome
34 Pevero
35 Glyfada
36 El Prat
37 La Manga
38 Estoril
39 Penina

40 Doral	65 The Honors
41 Jupiter Hills	66 Hazeltine
42 Ponte Vedra	67 Interlachen
43 Sea Island	68 Prairie Dunes
44 Palmetto Dunes	69 Oak Tree
45 Peachtree	70 Cherry Hills
46 Dunes	71 Colonial
47 Wild Dunes	72 Castle Pines
48 Country Club	73 Country Club
of North Carolina	74 Spyglass Hill
49 Cascades	75 Pasatiempo
50 Quaker Ridge	76 Riviera
51 Baltimore	77 Poppy Hills
52 Westchester	78 Edgewood
53 Concord	79 Mauna Kea
54 Oak Hill	80 Princeville
55 Canterbury	81 Hamilton
56 Scioto	82 St. George's
57 Inverness	83 Vancouver
58 NCR	84 Jasper
59 Muirfield Village	85 Vallescondido
60 Shoal Creek	86 Port Royal
61 Lakewood	
62 Chicago	
63 Butler National	
64 Sentry World	

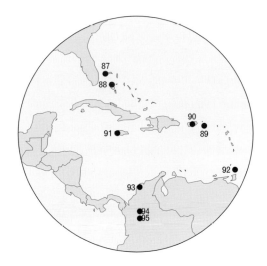

87 Lucayan
88 South Ocean
89 Fountain Valley
90 Cerromar
91 Tryall
92 Tobago
93 Club Lagos de Caujaral
94 El Rincon
95 Bogotá

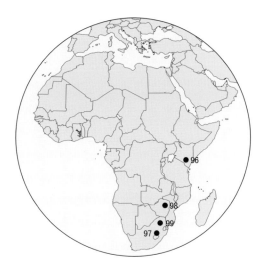

96 Karen
97 Houghton
98 Chapman
99 Gary Player

100 Kasugai
101 Nasu International
102 Yomiuri
103 Wack Wack
104 Navatanee
105 Delhi
106 New South Wales
107 Kingston Heath
108 Lake Karrinyup
109 Auckland
110 Christchurch

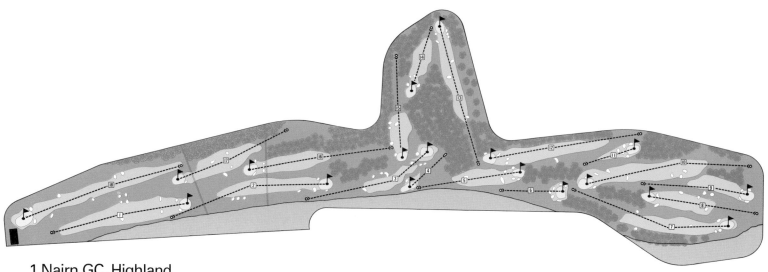

1 Nairn GC, Highland

The Nairn course was originally laid out on natural linksland by Archie Simpson in 1887 and modified two years later by Old Tom Morris and James Braid. It features large, undulating greens and deep bunkers, with panoramic views across the entrance of the Moray Firth to the mountains of Caithness. The sea plays its own part in the hazards at Nairn, and nowhere more than at the 5th — called Nets after the salmon nets on the shore. The tee shot over the beach needs judgment — and a long carry of 175 to 200 yards — to set up the best line for an exacting second shot to a semi-plateau green that is protected by bunkers to the front and side. The Scottish Professional Championship has been played here four times, with that famous pair John Panton and Eric Brown among its winners. In 1899 it became the first Scottish club to make an admission charge for a golf match. One hundred years later it will host the Walker Cup.

Record: 56, Ian Hutcheon, N. Scotland Amateur Stroke Play 1975

Nairn Card of the course

Hole	Yards	Par			
1	400	4	10	500	5
2	499	5	11	155	3
3	400	4	12	458	4
4	145	3	13	430	4
5	378	4	14	155	3
6	183	3	15	311	4
7	507	5	16	421	4
8	330	4	17	365	4
9	359	4	18	504	5
Out	**3,201**	**36**	**In**	**3,355**	**36**
			Total	**6,556**	**72**

2 Gullane GC, Lothian

Gullane No 1, the best of this small village's three fine courses, is often claimed to be the equal of nearby Muirfield. Certainly it has the same fine turf and true greens, plus the bonus of breathtaking views over the Firth of Forth to the hills of Fife. The 7th hole starts from the top of Gullane Hill, the course's highest point, and falls to the green 398 yards away. The back nine starts with a series of long, exacting holes. The 10th and 11th are both par fours of 466 and 471 yards — and they are followed by a very short par five of 480 yards set at cliff height, which is the lowest point on the course. Golf was played at Gullane from the start of the seventeenth century, and seven holes were laid down by 1844. Forty years later a full eighteen holes were in play, with two courses completed by 1900 and three by 1910.

Record: 64, J. B. Carr, Open Qualifying 1959

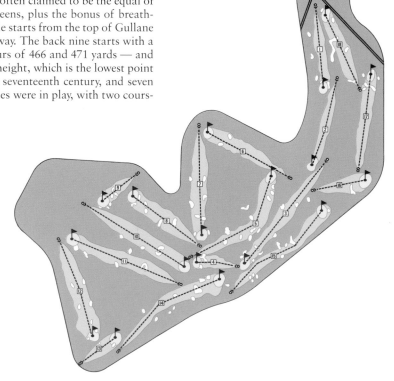

Gullane No1 Card of the course

Hole	Yards	Par			
1	302	4	10	466	4
2	379	4	11	471	4
3	496	5	12	480	5
4	144	3	13	170	3
5	450	4	14	435	4
6	324	4	15	537	5
7	398	4	16	186	3
8	332	4	17	390	4
9	151	3	18	355	4
Out	**2,976**	**35**	**In**	**3,490**	**36**
			Total	**6,466**	**71**

3 Gleneagles GC, Tayside

Designed by the legendary James Braid and Major C. K. Hutchinson, the King's course is one of four set on a sheltered moorland plateau. It is carved out of superb natural golfing country of rising hills splashed with purple heather and golden gorse, with sculptured bunkers that sparkle against tall stands of dark pine. The firm turf and immaculate greens combine to form a sequence of well-designed, memorable holes. The best is probably the 451-yard 13th, Braid's Brawest, where the fairway rolls narrowly away from the tee like an ocean swell between heather and bracken, demanding a long, straight drive to carry a ridge set with two deep bunkers. The approach to an elevated, well-trapped plateau green is deceptive, and par is an elusive reward.

Record: 62, Jose-Maria Olazabal, Bells Scottish Open

Gleneagles King's Course Card of the course

Hole	Yards	Par			
1	362	4	10	447	4
2	405	4	11	230	3
3	374	4	12	395	4
4	466	4	13	448	4
5	161	3	14	260	4
6	476	4	15	459	4
7	439	4	16	135	3
8	158	3	17	377	4
9	354	4	18	525	4
Out	**3,195**	**34**	**In**	**3,276**	**34**
			Total	**6,471**	**68**

4 Prestwick GC, Ayrshire

Prestwick Golf Club was host to the first Open championship in 1860 and twenty-four more thereafter, the last in 1924. There is a fascination in tackling these fabled holes, many of them little changed since those early days; the ghosts of Young Tom Morris, Braid, Taylor, and Vardon seem to stalk its narrow fairways still. The course lies on typical hard, humpy linksland, with deep bunkers, wild rough, a winding burn, and many blind shots over sandhills to the tiny greens. The most famous hole is probably the 500-yard, par-five 3rd, the Cardinal. Its main feature is a massive bunker set right on the dogleg, which has to be carried in the face of a solid revetment of uncompromising railroad ties.

Record: 67, Eric Brown, Dunlop Masters 1956

Prestwick Card of the course

Hole	Yards	Par			
1	346	4	10	453	4
2	168	3	11	194	3
3	500	5	12	515	5
4	382	4	13	461	4
5	206	3	14	363	4
6	400	4	15	348	4
7	431	4	16	296	4
8	431	4	17	391	4
9	458	4	18	288	4
Out	**3,342**	**35**	**In**	**3,309**	**36**
			Total	**6,651**	**71**

5 Royal St David's GC, Harlech, Gwynedd

Overlooked by the magnificent Harlech Castle, on reclaimed land of links-like character that is separated from the sea by sandhills, the Royal St. David's course is renowned for its beauty and its superb, large greens. The finishing stretch includes two of the finest holes, the 15th and 17th, both measuring 427 yards but requiring contrasting strategies. The 15th, with Mount Snowdon in the background, is bunkerless. The fairway is slightly doglegged right, winds between sandhills, and narrows toward a hollow just short of the green; it takes two good shots to get there against the prevailing wind. The 17th, usually downwind, needs extreme accuracy from the tee because of bunkers on the right of the narrow fairway and cross-bunkers that guard the green.

Record: 66, John Morgan, St David's Gold Cross 1951; T. J. Melia, J. L. Black

Royal St David's Card of the course

Hole	Yards	Par			
1	436	4	10	430	4
2	346	4	11	144	3
3	463	4	12	437	4
4	188	3	13	451	4
5	393	4	14	218	3
6	371	4	15	427	4
7	476	5	16	354	4
8	491	5	17	427	4
9	173	3	18	202	3
Out	**3,337**	**36**	**In**	**3,090**	**33**
			Total	**6,427**	**69**

6 Southport and Ainsdale GC, Merseyside

Embedded among the magnificent sandhills that reach down much of the South Lancashire coast are several courses of championship quality. The Southport and Ainsdale, or S & A links, is one of them. In 1906 there were nine rather undistinguished holes, but sixteen years later, with the help of James Braid, a tournament-class arena was built on a new site. Its challenging and demanding character is most apparent at the 16th, Gumbleys. This is a 510-yard par five, almost invariably played into the prevailing wind and requiring a tee shot between tight fairway bunkers to avoid the out-of-bounds railway area on the right. The second shot must clear the towering sandhills, or else an enormous, bunker covered with railroad ties. In 1933 Great Britain and Ireland won a rare Ryder Cup victory on this course and every time the Open is at Birkdale it is used as a qualifying course.

Record: 67, John Hammond Open Qualifying 1976, J. B. Dickinson, J. L. Plaxton, D. J. Russell, D. E. Vaughan

Southport and Ainsdale Card of the course

Hole	Yards	Par
1	200	3
2	520	5
3	418	4
4	316	4
5	477	4
6	386	4
7	480	5
8	157	3
9	482	5
Out	**3,406**	**37**
10	160	3
11	447	4
12	401	4
13	165	3
14	383	4
15	353	4
16	510	5
17	443	4
18	355	4
In	**3,197**	**35**
Total	**6,603**	**72**

7 Little Aston GC, Birmingham

As a true parkland course, set in splendid isolation within a few miles of the center of Birmingham, Little Aston offers more room for error from the tee than most courses of championship standard. This does not mean it presents a lesser test of golf, for the course demands accuracy of iron play to achieve anything like a good score. The holes were laid out in 1908 by Harry Vardon, who made full use of the excellent subsoil of sand and gravel. Three fine two-shotters, the 6th, 7th, and 8th, zigzag through the course, providing a challenging run to even the most accomplished of golfers. The 368-yard 7th is a classic short par four where both fairway traps and severe bunkering in front of the green must be avoided. The Dunlop Masters was held there five times, with such celebrated winners as Harry Weetman in 1953 and Bernard Hunt in 1963.

Little Aston Card of the course

Hole	Yards	Par	Hole	Yards	Par
1	390	4	10	438	4
2	437	4	11	398	4
3	505	5	12	491	5
4	316	4	13	164	3
5	160	3	14	313	4
6	426	4	15	566	5
7	374	4	16	402	4
8	394	4	17	364	4
9	197	3	18	389	4
Out	**3,199**	**35**	**In**	**3,525**	**37**
			Total	**6,724**	**72**

8 Formby GC, Merseyside

When golf started at Formby in 1884 the membership was limited to twenty-five, who paid one guinea a year for the privilege of playing nine completely natural holes. The site remains basically unchanged apart from the addition of nine more holes, a fine, sandy stretch between railway and sea and it was the sea that forced changes in 1978 to the 8th, 9th, and 10th holes. The first hole is typical of the course: the drive is menaced by an out-of-bounds railway on the right and the second shot requires extreme accuracy to find a flat, well-bunkered green. It was here that Sam Snead won his second World Senior title in 1965 by beating Charley Ward at the 37th hole. Formby has three times played host to the Amateur Championship, with Jack Reid and American Bob Dickson taking the honors in 1957 and 1967. In 1984 Jose-Maria Olazabal won a memorable final against Colin Montgomerie.

Record: 65, Neil Coles, Pro-Am 1974

Formby GC Card of the course

Hole	Yards	Par
1	415	4
2	381	4
3	518	5
4	312	4
5	162	3
6	402	4
7	377	4
8	493	5
9	450	4
Out	**3,510**	**37**
10	214	3
11	384	4
12	405	4
13	434	4
14	420	4
15	403	4
16	127	3
17	494	5
18	390	4
In	**3,271**	**35**
Total	**6,781**	**72**

9 Saunton GC, North Devon

As early as 1893 a nine-hole course existed in the fields of Braunton Burrows near Saunton, and in the 1920s it was developed into an eighteen-hole links by Herbert Fowler. Built among the sandhills, scrubland, and rushes, the course was closed in 1939; however, with the help of C. K. Cotton it was reopened in 1950 with new 1st, 17th, and 18th holes. The start is severe — there is only one par three in the first twelve holes — but the toughest hole at Saunton is the 16th. This 430-yard par four requires the drive to carry a high sandhill and draw to the left, following the dogleg. The long second is hit over a deep bunker into an elevated green wedged between sandhills, which disguise a subtle slope to the right.

Record: 69, Brian Huggett, J. Langmead

Saunton Card of the course

Hole	Yards	Par
1	470	4
2	476	5
8	402	4
4	444	4
5	112	3
6	370	4
7	428	4
8	380	4
9	382	4
Out	**3,464**	**36**
10	337	4
11	362	4
12	418	4
13	136	3
14	461	4
15	485	5
16	430	4
17	202	3
18	408	4
In	**3,239**	**35**
Total	**6,703**	**71**

10 Burnham and Berrow GC, Burnham-on-Sea

This is traditional links golf at its best — over and through the massive sandhills that skirt the north Somerset coast, with views of the Bristol Channel and the distant Glamorgan shore. Golf started here in 1891, and significant changes have been made over the intervening years to eliminate many of the blind shots that abounded at the turn of the century. Changes are still being made today. The finishing stretch of four holes is truly exacting with the 15th, a 479-yard par four, followed by a short par four, which demands a fine pitch shot when approaching the small raised green. The 201-yard 17th usually needs a wooden club and at the final hole trouble awaits the misplaced drive in the shape of sandy hills; an errant second shot usually finishes in a deep bunker.

Record: 66, Peter Baker, Tillman Trophy. 1986

Burnham and Berrow Card of the course

Hole	Yards	Par	Hole	Yards	Par
1	381	4	10	370	4
2	422	4	11	422	4
3	384	4	12	388	4
4	501	5	13	475	5
5	160	3	14	188	3
6	435	4	15	479	4
7	450	4	16	329	4
8	483	5	17	201	3
9	163	3	18	449	4
Out	**3,379**	**36**	**In**	**3,301**	**35**
			Total	**6,680**	**71**

11 Royal Cinque Ports GC, Deal

This superb natural links, one of the most challenging courses in Britain, opened in 1895. It has heavily bunkered fairways and well-protected greens. The only major alteration to the original layout occurred in 1938–39, when the direction of the 4th hole was reversed. Minor changes were also made to the 5th, 9th, and 14th holes. But the 16th, a 456-yard par four, is considered to be the best hole. The drive is uphill, requiring a carry of 150 yards to clear strategically placed fairway bunkers. An accurate approach shot must then be struck to pass through a channeled entrance on to the well-elevated green. The course was the setting for two early Open Championships; J.H. Taylor won his fourth Open victory there in 1909 and, in 1920, George Duncan carried off the title by two strokes.

Record: 65, Michael Bonallack, Brabazon Trophy 1964

Royal Cinque Ports Card of the course

Hole	Yards	Par	Hole	Yards	Par
1	325	4	10	362	4
2	364	4	11	382	4
3	453	4	12	418	4
4	153	3	13	400	4
5	494	5	14	215	3
6	304	4	15	420	4
7	358	4	16	456	4
8	164	3	17	360	4
9	383	4	18	396	4
Out	**2,998**	**35**	**In**	**3,409**	**35**
			Total	**6,407**	**70**

12 Prince's GC, Sandwich

Prince's, lying alongside Sandwich Bay, is a deceptive, stark links that is characterized by its flatness and the scarcity of sandtraps. Originally designed by Sir H. Mallaby-Deeley and P. M. Lucas, it was first played in 1907 when a large ridge of dunes — the Himalayas — dominated the course. World War II interrupted the golf and 1948 saw twenty-seven new championship holes, designed by J. S. F. Morrison and Sir Guy Campbell, come into play. The Blue is the championship course, no longer menaced by the dune ridge, but the wide, flat fairways make distance difficult to judge and the fast greens demand the greatest respect.

Record: 67, H. Weetman

Prince's Blue course Card of the course

Hole	Yards	Par	Hole	Yards	Par
1	502	5	10	574	5
2	567	5	11	197	3
3	186	3	12	466	4
4	451	4	13	438	4
5	388	4	14	479	5
6	411	4	15	528	5
7	188	3	16	179	3
8	356	4	17	416	4
9	397	4	18	407	4
Out	**3,446**	**36**	**In**	**3,684**	**37**
			Total	**7,130**	**73**

13 Berkshire GC, Ascot

In 1928 Herbert Fowler built thirty-six splendid holes for the Berkshire club, in the heart of rural England. The Red and Blue courses wind over rolling heathland and through quiet woods of pine, silver birch, and chestnut. The Red is unusual in that its eighteen holes comprise of six par fives, six par fours, and six par threes; of the short holes, the finest is the 221-yard 16th, where the outstanding plateau green can only be reached and held with a tightly controlled shot to its center. The 8th is the most difficult of the longer holes. The drive must be faced around the pines to leave the way clear for the second over a shallow valley on to the green. Holes from both courses are used to form the championship course.

Berkshire Red course Card of the course

Hole	Yards	Par	Hole	Yards	Par
1	518	5	10	187	3
2	146	3	11	338	4
3	481	5	12	328	4
4	394	4	13	484	5
5	182	3	14	436	4
6	353	4	15	477	5
7	201	3	16	221	3
8	427	4	17	529	5
9	477	5	18	177	3
Out	**3,179**	**36**	**In**	**3,177**	**36**
			Total	**6,356**	**72**

14 Hunstanton GC, Norfolk

This is an excellent example of open seaside golf, especially when played in the brisk winds common to this northern Norfolk coast. The course, laid out over gentle undulating linksland, was first played in 1892. Improvements over the next fifty years, mainly under the guidance of James Braid and James Sherlock, brought it up to championship standard. The front nine includes a fine short hole — the 7th — where the ball is driven from a raised tee, 162 yards over a deep hollow to a small, exposed plateau green guarded by an enormous forward bunker. On the back nine, sandhills cradle the fairways and punish any mishit stroke. The 13th, a 387-yard par four, is a testing hole where the dogleg to the left must be conquered by two long shots — the first from the tee and the second to carry some very rough country to an island target. The 16th needs a dropping shot over a large diagonal sandtrap invitingly positioned just short of the green. On May 31, 1974, and on the following two consecutive days, this hole was aced three times by a club member, R. J. Taylor.

Record: 65, Malcolm Gregson, Schweppes PGA championship 1967

Hunstanton Card of the course

Hole	Yards	Par		Yards	Par
1	343	4	10	372	4
2	532	5	11	439	4
3	443	4	12	356	4
4	165	3	13	387	4
5	424	4	14	216	3
6	332	4	15	476	5
7	162	3	16	188	3
8	483	5	17	446	4
9	508	5	18	398	4
Out	**3,392**	**37**	**In**	**3,278**	**35**
			Total	**6,670**	**72**

15 Walton Heath GC, Tadworth

The Old Course was designed by Herbert Fowler in 1904, and his additional nine holes were later extended to become the New course. Both resemble seaside courses in design and quality of turf, even though forty miles from the English Channel. The bunkers are large and deep, while the greens are big and consistent in pace in all weathers. The short and gentle first hole of the Old course belies the trials that follow, and the finish from the 14th is daunting. The 16th, a 499-yard par five, is critical, needing a long drive down a narrow heather-lined fairway and then a full-blooded shot to a green that is cut into a left-to-right slope, with a large bunker eating into the right-hand edge. Walton Heath was the venue of the 1981 Ryder Cup when arguably the strongest American side of all time — featuring Nicklaus, Miller, Trevino, Watson, Floyd, Irwin, Crenshaw, and Kite to name but eight — demolished the Europeans.

Record: 68, Ken Bousfield

Walton Heath Old course Card of the course

Hole	Yards	Par
1	310	4
2	447	4
3	285	4
4	453	4
5	395	4
6	400	4
7	176	3
8	485	5
9	395	4
Out	**3,346**	**36**
10	414	4
11	190	3
12	371	4
13	516	5
14	520	5
15	415	4
16	499	5
17	176	3
18	412	4
In	**3,513**	**37**
Total	**6,859**	**73**

16 Wentworth GC, Virginia Water

Rolling woodland and sandy subsoil create great golf courses and Wentworth, in Surrey's exclusive Virginia Water area, is an outstanding example. Designed by H. S. Colt, the East course, a delightful layout, opened in the early 1920s and was followed soon after by the West, the championship course. The Edinburgh opened in the 1990s but does not compare to the first two. Playing the West requires a combination of length and accurate placement of the tee. Twice a year it stages events on the European Tour: in the spring it is the Volvo PGA Championship; in the Fall it dons its colors of browns and golds to form a wonderful backdrop to the World Matchplay Championship.

Wentworth West course Card of the course

Hole	Yards	Par	Hole	Yards	Par
1	471	4	10	186	3
2	155	3	11	376	4
3	452	4	12	483	5
4	501	5	13	441	4
5	191	3	14	179	3
6	344	4	15	466	4
7	399	4	16	380	4
8	398	4	17	571	5
9	450	4	18	502	5
Out	**3,361**	**35**	**In**	**3,584**	**37**
			Total	**6,945**	**72**

17 Royal Worlington and Newmarket, Suffolk

Acclaimed as the best and most distinguished nine hole course in the country, this inland gem was constructed in 1890 under the guidance of Captain A. M. Ross, a local golfer, on a base of light sandy soil. This has enhanced the quality of the turf and led to true and unusually fast greens. The 5th is a stunning, bunkerless short hole that can be played with anything from a 5- to a 9-iron, and where the overlong shot is punished by the trees behind the green. The 7th is another fine par three, with a classic saucer green leaving only the top of the pin visible from the tee. In 1907 J. F. Ireland achieved the rare double of an ace at both the 5th and the 7th in the same round.

Record: 28, J. A. Floyd, 1949

Royal Worlington and Newmarket Card of the course

Hole	Yards	Par
1	476	5
2	224	3
3	361	4
4	495	5
5	157	3
6	458	4
7	165	3
8	460	4
9	299	4
Total	**3,074**	**35**

18 Royal West Norfolk GC, Brancaster

The vast bunkers covered with railroad ties, unyielding greens, and savage rough at this Brancaster course suggest all the elements of early links golf. A mixture of tidal marsh and undulating sand dunes threaten the often windswept fairways and form a formidable array of hazards for the erring shot. Horace Hutchinson and Holcombe Ingleby laid down the course in 1891, and despite alterations to their design by C.K. Hutchinson in 1928, its character remains little changed. The start is from an ancient rambling clubhouse out along the shoreline to its most easterly point, where the turn is taken. The 8th is on islands in the marsh; the harder and straighter the tee shot, the shorter and easier the second will be. At 478 yards, this par five needs heroism and strength. The 9th is a fine right-hand dogleg, a 404-yard par four, again played over the marsh, but this time with the added hazard of a creek short of the green. The back nine is some 310 yards shorter than the outward half, but is generally played into a strong wind, which compensates for the lack of length.

Royal West Norfolk Card of the course

Hole	Yards	Par	Hole	Yards	Par
1	410	4	10	151	3
2	449	4	11	478	5
3	407	4	12	386	4
4	128	3	13	317	3
5	421	4	14	432	4
6	186	3	15	188	3
7	486	5	16	346	4
8	478	5	17	377	4
9	404	4	18	384	4
Out	**3,369**	**36**	**In**	**3,059**	**34**
			Total	**6,428**	**70**

19 Woodhall Spa GC, Lincolnshire

Woodhall Spa is built on sandy soil and abounds in heather, silver birch, and pine trees. It features some of the most formidable bunkers in the country, particularly those that guard the three short holes, the 5th, 8th, and 12th. Against the wind, the 560-yard 9th is doubly severe, for the fairway is completely cut by a line of bunkers set 340 yards from the tee. Failure to clear this hazard, or playing short and safe, means that it is nearly impossible to reach the closely guarded green in three. Many championships have been held here, including the Brabazon Trophy and the ladies' home internationals, played between the countries of Great Britain and Ireland. The original Harry Vardon layout of 1905 was altered by H. S. Colt in 1912, and completely redesigned in the late 1920s by the owner, Colonel S. V. Hotchkin. It is now the home of the English Golf Union and a second course has been constructed on adjoining land.

Record: 66, F. W. Wood Lincolnshire Amateur Championship 1973

22 Woodhall Spa Card of the course

Hole	Yards	Par	Hole	Yards	Par
1	363	4	10	333	4
2	408	4	11	442	4
3	417	4	12	152	3
4	415	4	13	437	4
5	155	3	14	489	5
6	506	5	15	325	4
7	435	4	16	398	4
8	193	3	17	322	4
9	560	5	18	516	5
Out	**3,452**	**36**	**In**	**3,414**	**37**
			Total	**6,866**	**73**

20 Notts GC, Hollinwell

The spacious and testing Notts course was designed by Willie Park Jr. with the bunkers added by J. H. Taylor. The typical heathland course, opened in 1900, winds among silver birch, oak, gorse, and heather. At the difficult 8th, a 410-yard par four, the drive is crucial, requiring a 200-yard carry across Hollinwell lake and through a funnel of trees. The 205 yard 13th is played from an elevated tee down into a valley to a heavily bunkered green. Notts has been host to many professional and amateur events over the years, including the John Player Classic in 1970, when the $40,000 offered as first prize was a world record.

Record: 67, I. T. Simpson, 1981, I. Mackenzie

Notts Card of the course

Hole	Yards	Par	Hole	Yards	Par
1	376	4	10	362	4
2	430	4	11	365	4
3	511	5	12	430	4
4	455	4	13	205	3
5	193	3	14	380	4
6	533	5	15	440	4
7	403	4	16	355	4
8	410	4	17	480	5
9	178	3	18	457	4
Out	**3,489**	**36**	**In**	**3,531**	**36**
			Total	**7,020**	**72**

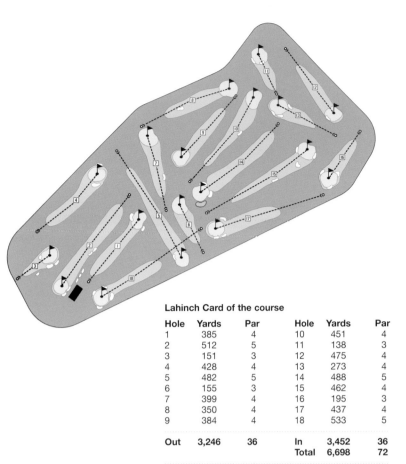

21 Lahinch GC, Country Clare

A barometer with hands hangs in the entrance to Lahinch Golf Club. Across its face is a message that reads "See goats" — for if they are in the shelter of the clubhouse foul weather is on the way and barometric pressures are neither here nor there. Laid out in 1893 by Old Tom Morris and remodeled thirty-three years later by Alister Mackenzie, it is characterized by massive sandhills, views of the ocean, and the dramatic Cliffs of Moher. Oddly, the most celebrated hole, the 155-yard 6th, The Dell, is probably the worst of a course that is stern yet essentially fair. From the tee the green is totally hidden and a mid-iron shot must be played over a hill. Judge the distance correctly and the ball is on the green in the hollow beyond; short or long and the next shot is from a precipitous bank. Club member John Burke was eight-time Irish Amateur champion, an Irish international from 1930 to 1949 and a member of the Walker Cup side in 1932.

Record: 67, Christy O'Connor, Irish Professional Championship 1961

Lahinch Card of the course

Hole	Yards	Par	Hole	Yards	Par
1	385	4	10	451	4
2	512	5	11	138	3
3	151	3	12	475	4
4	428	4	13	273	4
5	482	5	14	488	5
6	155	3	15	462	4
7	399	4	16	195	3
8	350	4	17	437	4
9	384	4	18	533	5
Out	**3,246**	**36**	**In**	**3,452**	**36**
			Total	**6,698**	**72**

22 Stavanger Golfklubb

Stavanger Golf Club was opened in 1956 and became an eighteen-hole course in 1963. A favorite among the more experienced Norwegian golfers, Stavanger is also the favorite course of King Olaf, and it is not hard to understand why. The towering conifers provide both an awesome backdrop and a testing trap to nearly every hole. At only 5,751 yards and with no par five beyond 500 yards, Stavanger is not the most demanding of courses, but the nonchalent should beware, Stavanger has enough to spoil the best of rounds.

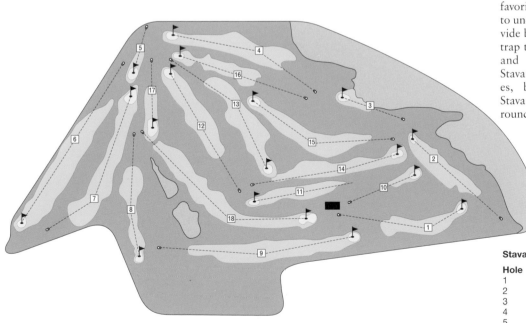

Stavanger Card of the course

Hole	Yards	Par	Hole	Yards	Par
1	290	4	10	168	3
2	280	4	11	312	4
3	160	3	12	332	4
4	415	4	13	362	4
5	116	3	14	364	4
6	452	5	15	355	4
7	408	4	16	312	4
8	326	4	17	184	3
9	453	5	18	462	5
Out	**2,900**	**36**	**In**	**2,851**	**35**
			Total	**6,698**	**71**

23 Halmstad GC, Tylösand

Halmstad Golf Club, in the picturesque West Coast town of Tylösand, midway between Malmo and Gothenberg, is a fine inland course not unlike Wentworth in Britain. The challenging eighteen-hole course, designed by Rafael Sandblom of Stockholm in 1938, and the less demanding nine-hole layout, are cut through predominantly pine forest on relatively flat, quick-drying sandy soil. Well-designed dogleg holes, such as the 6th, 8th, 9th, and 10th, four exceptional par fours, perceptive bunkering, and the ever-present trees combine to present a fine test of golf. An extremely comfortable and well-equipped clubhouse commands a central position and floodlit night putting competitions are a feature of the club's friendly, relaxed atmosphere. In 1958 it hosted the Scandinavian Amateur and Ladies' championships and there are frequent competitions to which visitors are encouraged, particularly during "Tylösand Week" in August, when the welcome is even warmer than usual.

Halmstad Card of the course

Hole	Yards	Par	Hole	Yards	Par
1	432	4	10	388	4
2	537	5	11	519	5
3	377	4	12	427	4
4	175	3	13	175	3
5	601	5	14	574	5
6	361	4	15	339	4
7	230	3	16	186	3
8	416	4	17	344	4
9	459	4	18	394	4
Out	3,588	36	In	3,346	36
			Total	6,934	72

24 Rungsted GC, Rungsted Kyst

The scene of many Scandinavian championships, Rungsted is distinguished by the problems of hilly terrain with deep ravines and encroaching beech woods. Its greatest weakness is the imbalance caused by the easiest holes, the 12th to the 15th, occurring together. At this point the play is building to a tough climax and these four cause a break in concentration before the final challenge, of which the centerpiece is the 17th. The drive here is threatened by out-of-bounds on the left and, as the ball loses height, it clears a belt of sheltering trees and may be caught by the prevailing westerly wind and carried into deep rough or the woods that lie on the right of the narrow fairway. Pinpoint accuracy from the tee is essential for any chance to attack the target with the second shot, which must negotiate trees short of the raised green. Ravines on either side await any ball that is slightly off the target, which is pear-shaped with possibilities for very difficult pin placings. Rungsted was designed by C. K. Mackenzie and opened in 1937. O. Bojensen made slight alterations to the course in 1969.

Record: 69, Olle Dahlgren, Johnnie Walker Cup 1973

Rungsted Card of the course

Hole	Yards	Par	Hole	Yards	Par
1	437	4	10	405	4
2	389	4	11	419	4
3	161	3	12	323	4
4	476	5	13	339	4
5	399	4	14	361	4
6	161	3	15	119	3
7	389	4	16	526	5
8	385	4	17	359	4
9	375	4	18	488	5
Out	3,172	35	In	3,339	37
			Total	6,511	72

25 Falkenstein GC, Hamburg

A fine natural course showing obvious signs of the game's Scottish origins, Falkenstein was laid out in 1930, by architects Alison and Morrison, on gently undulating ground with quick draining sandy subsoil that encourages the growth of heather, pines, and silver birch. Alterations were made later by Dr. Bernard von Limburger. The course features many well contrived dogleg holes, with the sparing but intelligent use of sandtraps. The massive 2nd, more than 550 yards, swings to the left past a giant bunker and presents the handicap golfer with a difficult third shot to a green that is guarded by sand on both sides. The 17th, another par five, is 80 yards shorter yet has vast areas of heather in front of the tee and crossing the fairway short of the green. In the German National Amateur of 1973, Rainer Falge scored an eagle three, only to lose the hole and the match to a spectacular holed second shot by Jens Harder, the eventual runner-up.

Record: 63, Sam Torrance, 1981

Falkenstein Card of the course

Hole	Yards	Par
1	329	4
2	558	5
3	241	3
4	477	5
5	406	4
6	419	4
7	358	4
8	182	3
9	424	4
Out	**3,394**	**36**
10	186	3
11	441	4
12	411	4
13	368	4
14	352	4
15	162	3
16	344	4
17	480	5
18	387	4
In	**3,131**	**35**
Total	**6,525**	**71**

26 Frankfurter GC, Frankfurt

With a total length of just under 6,800 yards, the Frankfurter Golf Club is decidedly short by modern championship standards. The difficulty here is in overcoming the very large greens, which demand second shot accuracy to get near the pin. The course is essentially flat, but the fairways are carved through forest and the problems set by the trees add to the scoring difficulties. The best hole is probably the 7th, a 220-yard par three that is flanked on the lip of the green by left and right bunkers; it requires a full-blooded tee shot into the heart of the target. Little has been done to the original H. S. Colt and John Morrison layout of 1928, and the course attracts a great international following because it is within easy reach of the city. The German Open has been held here on a number of occasions, including 1938, when Henry Cotton won the second of his trio of victories.

Record: 63, Dale Hayes, German Open 1969

Frankfurter Card of the course

Hole	Yards	Par	Hole	Yards	Par
1	415	4	10	360	4
2	425	4	11	175	3
3	465	4	12	400	4
4	170	3	13	435	4
5	555	5	14	375	4
6	335	4	15	490	5
7	220	3	16	175	3
8	410	4	17	505	5
9	425	4	18	435	4
Out	**3,420**	**35**	**In**	**3,350**	**36**
			Total	**6,770**	**71**

27 Schloss Nippenburg ETC

Schloss Nippenburg is Germany's first stadium golf course and has rightly won the title of PGA European Tour Course. Designed by Bernhard Langer, it was built upon derelict farmland and opened in June 1994. However it is not without its critics. After an amazing day of under-par scores at the 1996 Volvo German Open in which Paul Broadhurst hit a 62, Seve Ballesteros commented: "... it was no challenge."

Record: 62, Paul Broadhurst, German Open 1996

Schloss Nippenburg Card of the course

Hole	Yards	Par	Hole	Yards	Par
1	495	5	10	154	3
2	355	4	11	370	4
3	344	4	12	155	3
4	512	5	13	482	5
5	171	3	14	424	4
6	406	4	15	315	4
7	306	4	16	429	4
8	177	3	17	160	3
9	362	4	18	477	5
Out	**3128**	**36**	**In**	**2,966**	**35**
			Total	**6,094**	**71**

28 Haagsche GC, Wassenaar

The Dutch coastline is similar in many places to the best links country of the British Isles, and the Haagsche course is ideally sited for capitalizing on the best features of seaside golf. Designed in 1939 by British architects Colt, Alison, and Morrison, it has needed very little change. The 424-yard, par-five 6th is the best example of the course's exacting qualities. However, it was here, during the 1972 Dutch Open, that Jack Newton hit a spectacular shot. His massive second rolled across the green and into the cup for a double-eagle.

Record: 64, Peter Oosterhuis, Netherlands Open 1972

Haagsche Card of the course

Hole	Yards	Par	Hole	Yards	Par
1	493	5	10	476	5
2	371	4	11	392	4
3	347	4	12	163	3
4	181	3	13	369	4
5	478	5	14	344	4
6	424	4	15	368	4
7	323	4	16	286	4
8	201	3	17	146	3
9	350	4	18	493	5
Out	**3,168**	**36**	**In**	**3,349**	**36**
			Total	**6,517**	**72**

29 Royal Belgique GC, Tervuren

With a clubhouse that is a national monument and a course that was built by royal command, the Royal Golf Club de Belgique does justice to its auspicious origins. Tom Simpson laid out the eighteen holes on a clay subsoil in an area of parkland in 1904. He constructed nine short par fours, making club selection for the second shot a critical decision. Of the long par fours, the 17th is the most difficult. Doglegged right, and with the entrance to the fairway flanked by two large sandtraps, it demands a drive that must be as long as possible to line up the second with a clear shot. The spacious, stepped green is menaced by two bunkers guarding the front; three putts are certainly not uncommon here for the average golfer.

Record: 65, Flory van Donck, Belgian Open 1935

Royal Belgique Card of the course

Hole	Yards	Par	Hole	Yards	Par
1	491	5	10	349	4
2	420	4	11	417	4
3	156	3	12	194	3
4	415	4	13	523	5
5	511	5	14	325	4
6	204	3	15	514	5
7	373	4	16	336	4
8	361	4	17	419	4
9	336	4	18	305	4
Out	**3,272**	**36**	**In**	**3,382**	**37**
			Total	**6,654**	**73**

30 Royal Waterloo GC, Ohain

The first of Henry Cotton's three Open Championship victories, in 1934, came when he was the professional at the original Royal Waterloo Golf Club, whose course had been laid out eleven years earlier. In 1960 a new eighteen holes were designed by Fred Hawtree on a site at Ohain near Brussels. The greens are consistently slow, and the course is split into two distinct playing sections: the first ten holes and the finishing pair run over a wide, undulating plain with a scattering of small trees, but the 11th to the 16th climb and drop through a high beech wood. The dramatic contrast is best seen at the 13th, a 408-yard, par-four dogleg running through a wooded valley — a claustrophobic hole after the open plains. The course record was 67, set by Donald Swaelens, for many years the club's professional until his untimely death while still in his thirties.

Record: 65, Nick Faldo

Royal Waterloo Card of the course

Hole	Yards	Par
1	405	4
2	361	4
3	535	5
4	189	3
5	514	5
6	417	4
7	161	3
8	359	4
9	433	4
Out	**3,374**	**36**
10	403	4
11	424	4
12	193	3
13	408	4
14	392	4
15	161	3
16	480	5
17	527	5
18	486	5
In	**3,474**	**37**
Total	**6,848**	**73**

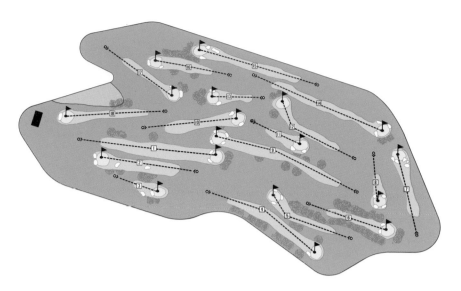

31 Crans-sur-Sierre GC, Valais

Few major championship courses are better known for their surroundings than their quality, but Crans-sur-Sierre, set on a high green mountain plateau 5,000 feet up in the Berner Alps, offers one of the most spectacular settings for golf anywhere. Completely encircled by high, snow-capped peaks, the course has been the venue for the Swiss Open and its successor, the European Masters, since 1939. Although unplayable for half the year, in summer it offers ideal conditions, its fairly level greens standing out against the tall stands of pines. The holes undulate gently and are reasonably wide open with minimal rough and a few strategically placed evergreens.

Record: 60, B. Dassu, Swiss Open 1971

Crans-sur-Sierre Card of the course

Hole	Yards	Par	Hole	Yards	Par
1	519	6	10	396	4
2	432	4	11	213	3
3	185	3	12	386	4
4	499	4	13	208	3
5	355	4	14	574	5
6	328	4	15	514	5
7	317	4	16	328	4
8	186	3	17	355	4
9	634	5	18	383	4
Out	3,455	36	In	3,356	36
			Total	6,811	72

32 Seefeld Wildmoos GC, Tirol

A major ski resort needs steep mountain slopes at high altitude, often densely wooded, with the longest possible snow season. Seefeld not only meets these criteria but also boasts a spectacular golf course. Designed by British architect Donald Harradine and located at 4,300 feet, it is carved out of some of the most fiendish golfing country imaginable. After the early holes over relatively level ground, the course climbs and plunges through forests of pine and birch, presenting some extraordinarily tight holes. Most memorable are the 9th, only 186 yards but a good 200 feet straight down the mountainside; and the 14th, a 656-yard par five running sharply downhill through the woods and reachable with two accurate long shots. Although under several feet of snow for almost half the year, the playing conditions in summer are excellent, the result of Herculean efforts by the club. Their endeavors have preserved a tight course where the emphasis is on percentage golf, particularly when approaching the elevated greens.

Record: 68 Gerhard König, Seefeld Pro-Am 1975

Seefeld Wildmoos Card of the course

Hole	Yards	Par	Hole	Yards	Par
1	519	5	10	405	4
2	437	4	11	317	4
3	328	4	12	520	5
4	388	4	13	180	3
5	252	3	14	656	5
6	388	4	15	416	4
7	574	5	16	335	4
8	284	4	17	191	3
9	186	3	18	372	4
Out	3,356	36	In	3,396	36
			Total	6,752	72

33 Rome GC, Aquasanta

Golf has been played at Aquasanta, with its reputedly medicinal waters, for more than seventy years. Here the Rome Golf Club, set in low hills and crossed by meandering streams, offers luxuriant golf in historic surroundings, with views of old aqueducts and the legendary Appian Way. The course is short by championship standards but tight enough to be testing. Strategically placed pines and other trees guard the fairways, and the network of streams form a hazard at several holes. The condition of this well-watered course is always superb, as might be expected of such an exclusive club. It is fairly level to play, with particularly featureless and deceptive greens.

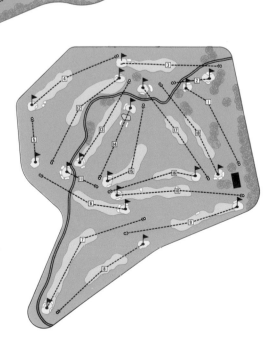

Rome Card of the course

Hole	Yards	Par	Hole	Yards	Par
1	334	4	10	470	4
2	137	3	11	129	3
3	350	4	12	439	4
4	387	4	13	379	4
5	211	3	14	359	4
6	378	4	15	365	4
7	544	5	16	350	4
8	394	4	17	417	4
9	427	4	18	400	4
Out	3,162	35	In	3,308	35
			Total	6,470	70

34 Pevero GC, Sardinia

The terrain at Pevero is so imposing and unyielding that it forced the architect, Robert Trent Jones, to follow its contours, developing nature's own golf holes rather than reshaping and building them with machines. The 4th, at 384 yards, starts an exhilarating sequence, plunging into a valley with distant views of Corsica to a green set along one slope. It is followed by a downhill par three with an enormous rock outcrop guarding the right and a lake to the left. The 6th is a par four, along, and across a lake, and it is succeeded by a 182-yard short hole back across the lake to a shallow green bunkered front and rear.

Record: 63, H. Jackson, Spanish Open, 1971

Pevero Card of the course

Hole	Yards	Par	Hole	Yards	Par
1	411	4	10	185	3
2	383	4	11	531	5
3	519	5	12	384	4
4	384	4	13	387	4
5	191	3	14	186	3
6	335	4	15	477	5
7	182	3	16	287	4
8	317	4	17	144	3
9	497	5	18	535	5
Out	**3,219**	**36**	**In**	**2,986**	**36**
			Total	**6,205**	**72**

35 Glyfada GC, Athens

Set between gently rolling mountain slopes and the sparkling Saronic Gulf, Glyfada is Greece's premier course. The eighteen holes, constructed in 1967, were designed by Donald Harradine, who cleverly lined each hole with umbrella pines to create the chief hazards. Athens airport, a mere 500 yards from the practice tee, is a source of constant noise and can become an almost intolerable distraction. Nevertheless, the course's narrow doglegs, fast greens, and pine-dominated rough provide excellent surroundings for Mediterranean-type golf. From the back tees there is enough length to test the best, making the course very tight and favoring players with powerful drives. The toughest hole is the 9th, a 397-yard par four, gently bending to the left with a deep hollow, often filled with water for tournament play, before the green.

Record: 67, Tony Lema

Glyfada Golf Club, Athens Card of the course

Hole	Yards	Par	Hole	Yards	Par
1	370	4	10	472	5
2	330	4	11	355	4
3	469	6	12	203	3
4	358	4	13	364	4
5	163	3	14	425	4
6	398	4	15	481	5
7	523	6	16	142	3
8	175	3	17	335	4
9	397	4	18	369	4
Out	**3,187**	**36**	**In**	**3,149**	**36**
			Total	**6,336**	**72**

36 Prat de Llobregat RGC, Barcelona

A flat, sandy coastal stretch south of Barcelona has given rise to the most untypical of all Spanish courses at El Prat — and without doubt one of the finest. Created by the late Javier Arana in 1954, it is a masterpiece of understatement, making excellent but far from penal use of the abundant umbrella pines; the emphasis is on strategic positioning from the tee, with subtle molding around the greens and minimal but significant bunkering. The course starts among pines close to the sea, but they are well spaced and the rough beneath is sparse. Then the holes move to more open country inland before turning along the shore to the clubhouse for the back nine. The second nine are slightly sterner, with the 14th epitomizing the whole course — it is a par four needing a long-iron second to a beautifully shaped green.

Record: 63, H. Jackson, Spanish Open, 1971

El Prat Card of the course

Hole	Yards	Par	Hole	Yards	Par
1	503	5	10	403	4
2	153	3	11	490	5
3	498	5	12	381	4
4	356	4	13	191	3
5	394	4	14	434	4
6	520	5	15	547	5
7	376	4	16	416	4
8	208	3	17	175	3
9	383	4	18	383	4
Out	**3,391**	**37**	**In**	**3,420**	**36**
			Total	**6,811**	**73**

37 La Manga GC, Murcia

In the mild climate of the Costa Blanca, south of Alicante, the fifty-four holes that form the North, South, and Princesa courses gaze out over the bay of Mar Menor. Set among more than 3,000 date palms, the courses are backed by a range of low, undulating mountains and distinguished by large bunkers, lakes, and "barancas," deep ravines that swallow any mishit ball. The tees and fairways are of the highest quality, with plenty of room to maneuver, and the greens are spacious. The South course is the championship layout and here the short 3rd creates some interesting problems. At 140 yards, with a lake lying prominently to the right, it would normally present little difficulty. Because it was so easy, Gary Player suggested that a shallow bunker be placed in the middle of the green. This effectively reduces its size by half and forces the golfer to go for whichever side the flag is located.

Record: 65, John O'Leary, Spanish Open 1975

La Manga South course Card of the course

Hole	Yards	Par	Hole	Yards	Par
1	375	4	10	390	4
2	390	4	11	380	4
3	140	3	12	520	5
4	545	5	13	430	4
5	360	4	14	230	3
6	435	4	15	395	4
7	340	4	16	405	4
8	205	3	17	210	3
9	510	5	18	595	5
Out	**3,300**	**36**	**In**	**3,555**	**36**
			Total	**6,855**	**72**

38 Estoril GC, Lisbon

Set on high ground behind the Lisbon resort of Estoril, with excellent views out to sea, this short but highly challenging course has been a regular venue for the Portuguese Open and Amateur Championships. Mackenzie Ross, who designed it in 1945, has made clever use of the pine and eucalyptus trees which, with the steeply sloping land, means that accuracy is more important than length. Placement off the tee, bold, well-struck approach shots and the regular quest of birdie-putts mark a round of golf here. At the 9th, with its 150 foot elevated tee, a deceptive mid-iron shot must be played on to the contoured green 171 yards away. Not only must the stroke be to the heart of the severely bunkered green but it also has to contend with a fluky wind that blows from left to right and threatens to carry the ball into the flanking trees.

Record: 62, Dale Hayes, Portuguese Open 1974

Estoril Card of the course

Hole	Yards	Par	Hole	Yards	Par
1	385	4	10	386	4
2	156	3	11	507	5
3	315	4	12	420	4
4	171	3	13	274	4
5	517	5	14	356	4
6	266	4	15	326	4
7	419	4	16	216	3
8	216	3	17	282	4
9	171	3	18	274	4
Out	**2,620**	**33**	**In**	**3,081**	**36**
			Total	**5,701**	**69**

39 Penina GC, Algarve

The brainchild of Henry Cotton, who was for many years its overlord, Penina has surmounted its major disadvantage of being absolutely flat. During its construction on an old rice field in 1964, 360,000 trees and shrubs were planted to separate the holes and provide visual relief as well as playing interest. The holes are imaginatively protected by a series of strategically sited drainage canals, lakes, and massive sandtraps. This calls for precise, nominated shots, and rewards the thoughtful approach rather than the heroic. The well-watered, elevated greens, which Doug Sanders rated the best he had ever putted on, are a major feature of this layout designed as part of a resort complex in the south of Portugal near Portimao. Since Cotton's day it has been completely upgraded and refurbished. A number of championships have been played there, including the 1976 World Amateur Team Championship. With tees up to 100 yards long, the Penina course can be extended to prodigious lengths for tournament play.

Penina Card of the course

Hole	Yards	Par
1	449	4
2	439	4
3	329	4
4	410	4
5	506	5
6	203	3
7	327	4
8	197	3
9	443	4
Out	**3,303**	**35**
10	547	5
11	537	5
12	434	4
13	227	3
14	431	4
15	348	4
16	230	3
17	492	5
18	492	5
In	**3,738**	**38**
Total	**7,041**	**73**

Doral Blue course Card of the course

Hole	Yards	Par
1	533	5
2	266	4
3	402	4
4	225	3
5	374	4
6	437	4
7	427	4
8	528	5
9	189	3
Out	**3,381**	**36**
10	543	5
11	351	4
12	608	5
13	246	3
14	415	4
15	183	3
16	379	4
17	426	4
18	437	4
In	**3,592**	**36**
Total	**6,973**	**72**

40 Doral CC, Miami, Fla.

Doral is the epitome of Florida resort golf. Ninety percent of the golfers who play there are winter vacationers, yet none of its six courses is in any way easy, the Blue undeniably being of championship caliber. Nicknamed the "Blue Monster" by professionals, largely because of the remarkable final hole, this Dick Wilson inspired layout also has a stunning 9th. The 437-yard, par-four 18th is an absolute dream of design, where water, on the left, has to be carried twice on the run into a green half encircled by the same lake. In all, Wilson built eight lakes during construction and the holes, interspersed by a few palm trees, were tailored around them. A redesign of several holes in 1996 has ensured the course remains a monster so far as competitors are concerned at the Doral Open, an important stop on the United States tournament circuit.

Jupiter Hills Card of the course

Hole	Yards	Par
1	512	5
2	439	4
3	176	3
4	573	5
5	421	4
6	379	4
7	411	4
8	384	4
9	192	3
Out	**3,487**	**36**
10	389	4
11	198	3
12	415	4
13	536	5
14	225	3
15	359	4
16	336	4
17	508	5
18	429	4
In	**3,428**	**36**
Total	**6,915**	**72**

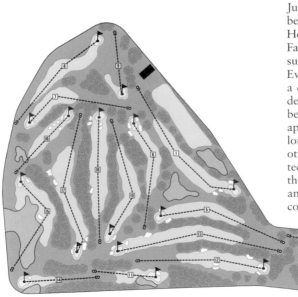

41 Jupiter Hills Club, Tequesta, Fla.

Jupiter Hills is an ultra-exclusive club, a joint financial venture between architect George Fazio and two old friends, comedian Bob Hope and auto industrialist William Ford. It has turned out to be Fazio's favorite course and one to which he is constantly making subtle improvements. It is nearly impossible to pick the best hole. Even Fazio cannot make up his mind, but sometimes cites the 11th, a delightful par three with a positively Machiavellian twist to its design. It has six tees and can be played at virtually any length between 198 yards and 120 yards, but it is the different angles of approach that the two tees offer that make the hole. The green is long and narrow and on one line straight away from the tees: on the other it is slightly angled and therefore easier to hit, though protected by water. But the outstanding characteristic of the course is that it is hilly — a full sixty feet from its lowest to its highest point, an unheard of amount of "drop" in the flatness of Florida's "golf coast" stretching from the Palm Beaches to Miami.

42 Ponte Vedra Inn & Club (Ocean Course), Ponte Vedra Beach, Fla.

Ponte Vedra Inn & Club is on Florida's Atlantic coast between Jacksonville and St. Augustine. Its Ocean Course was designed by British architect Herbert Bartram Strong, opened in 1933, and modified by Robert Trent Jones in the late 1940s. Jones made further changes in 1961 and added nine more holes, which in 1977 were joined to nine new holes designed by Joe Lee to create the Lagoon Course. The Ocean Course is a 6,484-yard test of skill featuring large mounds as back-drops for the fresh water lagoons that wind through the course. Water is only the most obvious hazard: fifteen- to twenty-foot-high mounds break up the otherwise flat Florida landscape and frequently obscure the greens. Ocean breezes can be brisk. The 4th hole, at 427 yards, is a difficult par four with water on either side of the fairway and in front of the green. The 11th, which tees off over water, is no easier, but perhaps the best known is the infamous "Island Ninth." A deceptively short par three at 140 yards, it features a green surrounded, except for a narrow walkway, by golf ball (and possibly alligator!) infested water. A short approach area offers a safe landing to those who underclub.

Ponte Vedra Ocean Course Card of the course

Hole	Yards	Par	Hole	Yards	Par
1	397	4	10	355	4
2	363	4	11	400	4
3	516	5	12	174	3
4	427	4	13	529	5
5	216	3	14	466	5
6	475	5	15	387	4
7	383	4	16	128	3
8	401	4	17	382	4
9	140	3	18	345	4
Out	**3,318**	**36**	**In**	**3,166**	**36**
			Total	**6,484**	**72**

43 Sea Island GC, Sea Is, Ga.

Sea Island's oceanside golf course was laid out in 1927 and 1929 on the Retreat Plantation — an early nineteenth century cotton farm — by the English architects H. S. Colt and Charles Alison. They designed two nine-holers which now form eighteen of the club's thirty-six holes. The Seaside is the front nine and rolls over the broad undulating fairways set among the dunes, edged by the ocean and surrounded by waterways and marshland. The Plantation course, which makes up the back nine, scythes through great forests of oak and pine, occasionally touching the marsh and often crossing or playing alongside the lagoons. The greens are well elevated and trapped on all sides. The 7th hole, White Heron, is a real equalizer, as the drive has to carry a broad marsh inlet where a stiff breeze can nudge the ball into the inlet. The alternative is to play to a thin peninsula of fairway, which leaves the second shot blind over two large bunkers with the brackish marsh threatening on the left. Bobby Jones first focused national attention on the club and his record of 67 stood for many years.

Record: 63, Sam Snead, 1958

Sea Island Card of the course

Hole	Yards	Par	Hole	Yards	Par
1	398	4	10	370	4
2	428	4	11	350	4
3	222	3	12	216	3
4	377	4	13	534	5
5	346	4	14	395	4
6	472	5	15	366	4
7	424	4	16	155	3
8	194	3	17	415	4
9	472	5	18	471	5
Out	**3,333**	**36**	**In**	**3,272**	**36**
			Total	**6,605**	**72**

Palmetto Dunes Card of the course

Hole	Yards	Par	Hole	Yards	Par
1	432	4	10	513	5
2	562	5	11	354	4
3	412	4	12	387	4
4	205	3	13	386	4
5	389	4	14	185	3
6	180	3	15	445	4
7	414	4	16	425	4
8	431	4	17	230	3
9	421	4	18	462	4
Out	**3,446**	**35**	**In**	**3,427**	**35**
			Total	**6,873**	**70**

44 Palmetto Dunes Resort, Hilton Head, S.C.

At the George Fazio course at Palmetto Dunes, in the South Carolina golfing Mecca of Hilton Head Island, each fairway runs parallel to another on its right and, with the exception of the 3rd and 16th, there is out-of-bounds on the left of every hole. A mark of Fazio's work is his extravagant shaping of teeing areas. Not for him the square-cut tees so common in golf. At Palmetto they sweep in elegant curves around lakes, while others are circular and laid one after another like giant stepping stones. At the par-three 17th the terraced tees advance down a slope to the lagoon, leaving the rolling green 230 yards away and protected by a large sandtrap. At the 421-yard par-four 9th a massive oak tree blocks any approach to the green from the right side of the fairway, and the short 4th green is split into three distinct levels. Oak, magnolia and palmetto trees, together with the ever-present threat of water, add to the danger and beauty of this most unusual course.

Record : 66 Buddy Alexander, 1975

49 Peachtree Card of the course

Hole	Yards	Par	Hole	Yards	Par
1	391	4	10	516	5
2	527	5	11	224	3
3	409	4	12	440	4
4	166	3	13	421	4
5	529	5	14	180	3
6	216	3	15	452	4
7	434	4	16	532	5
8	369	4	17	446	4
9	392	4	18	401	4
Out	**3,433**	**36**	**In**	**3,612**	**36**
			Total	**7,045**	**72**

45 Peachtree GC, Atlanta, Ga.

To speak of Peachtree in Atlanta is to speak of Bobby Jones, for it was he who was the inspiration behind it. His ideas were followed by architect Robert Trent Jones, and Peachtree has ever since been one of the premier golf clubs of Atlanta and the place that Bobby Jones considered his golfing home in his later years. The course was built during the late 1940s among azaleas and dogwood in the typically hilly countryside around Atlanta. Marching up and down these hills in the hot summer months can make it purgatory to play, but the anguish is more than compensated for during the other seasons — particularly the spring. The start is awesome, with an initial 391-yard par four, with two bunkers set in the dogleg which force the drive out to the right of the fairway. The 2nd is simple but superb. A 527-yard par five, it is bunkerless but has a green protected in front by a lake and stream. In 1989 Peachtree played host to an historic Walker Cup — the first victory on American soil by a side representing Great Britain and Ireland.

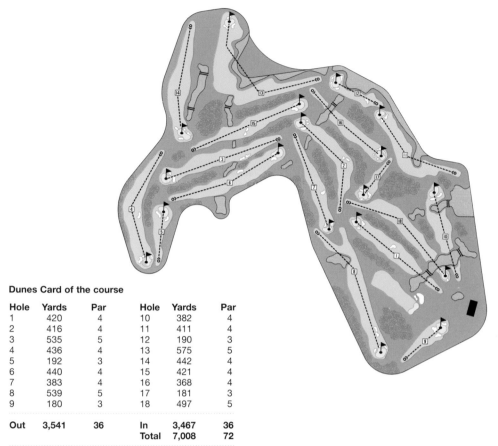

46 Dunes G & BC, Myrtle Beach, S.C

Dunes is the hub of a resort complex on the northeastern shores of South Carolina that today contains more than seventy golf courses. Dunes was designed by Robert Trent Jones back in 1947, and is easily one of his best. He built the course on land with a colorful history; it was a deer and turkey hunting ground before becoming an Air Force target range during World War II — somewhat hazardous territory to plough up into a golf course. Jones incorporated in the layout his favorite design features: long tees, well-defined fairway traps to give the player a target off the tee, and huge, elevated, sometimes tiered greens. The 13th, a 575-yard par five, is the most outstanding hole on the course. It doglegs so severely around Singleton Lake that the golfer feels he is going back on his tracks. The hole bends a full 110 degrees through the line of play, and to add to the difficulty the approach to the green is between two flanking green sidetraps supported by a single bunker on the far side. To make the green in two is a rare feat.

Dunes Card of the course

Hole	Yards	Par	Hole	Yards	Par
1	420	4	10	382	4
2	416	4	11	411	4
3	535	5	12	190	3
4	436	4	13	575	5
5	192	3	14	442	4
6	440	4	15	421	4
7	383	4	16	368	4
8	539	5	17	181	3
9	180	3	18	497	5
Out	3,541	36	In	3,467	36
			Total	7,008	72

47 Wild Dunes Beach and Racquet Club (Links Course), S.C

Both the Links and Harbor Courses at Wild Dunes are impressive achievements from designer Tom Fazio on land he described as an "architect's dream." The Links Course, opened in 1980, winds through marsh and sand for most of its 6,715 yards. Most of the elements of the course come into play on the par-three, 165-yard 4th hole: marshland at the edge of the tee and along the right side of the fairway; magnolia, oak, palm, and cedar trees in abundance; and a combination grass and sand bunker front and right of the green. The 10th hole begins a series of complete dune holes, which required no major earthwork to create. The 11th, 12th, and 13th also come with ocean views from the tees. The 15th brings back the marshland, which also borders the par-three, 175-yard 16th, where the championship tee is placed on a small peninsula in the salt-water lake. From there it's all carry over water and marshland to the green. The 17th and 18th are true links holes, with wild rolling dunes swept by strong ocean winds.

Wild Dunes Links Course Card of the course

Hole	Yards	Par	Hole	Yards	Par
1	501	5	10	331	4
2	370	4	11	376	4
3	400	4	12	192	3
4	165	3	13	427	4
5	505	5	14	489	5
6	421	4	15	426	4
7	359	4	16	175	3
8	203	3	17	379	4
9	451	4	18	540	5
Out	3,380	36	In	3,335	36
			Total	6,715	72

48 CC of North Carolina, Pinehurst, N.C.

Standing apart and aloof on the Sandhills of Pinehurst, the exclusive private Country Club of North Carolina has two eighteen-hole courses set amid an expanse of trees and water. The championship course is known as Dogwood, while the Cardinal course, designed in part by Robert Trent Jones, was extended to eighteen holes in 1981. The back nine of the championship layout is strengthened by the abundant water hazards, which affect all but the 10th and 12th. At the 206-yard 16th, the carry is all water to a green guarded to the front and back by enormous sandtraps. For the timid, a piece of fairway on the right offers refuge from the endless water, but taking the safe route may mean dropping a shot. The lake runs alongside the two home holes from the 17th tee and encroaches onto the final fairway before drifting away to leave an unhindered approach to the last green.

CC of North Carolina Card of the course

Hole	Yards	Par
1	425	4
2	421	4
3	160	3
4	382	4
5	513	5
6	441	4
7	450	4
8	221	3
9	578	5
Out	**3,591**	**36**
10	386	4
11	417	4
12	548	5
13	190	3
14	445	4
15	441	4
16	206	3
17	420	4
18	510	5
In	**3,563**	**36**
Total	**7,154**	**72**

49 Cascades GC, Hot Springs

One of the world's most elegant and successful golf swings — that of Sam Snead — was created on this demanding course at The Homestead, Virginia. Built in 1923 by William Flynn, it is rated by Snead as the best training course for budding professionals because it demands every shot in the book from an infinite variety of hilly lies. The first nine holes are extremely tight through dense woodland, but then the course opens out with more emphasis on length from the tee. The 449-yard 4th is typical of the opening holes, needing a firm drive to the left, with the approach being played from a difficult sidehill lie. It was here that Snead began his professional career in 1934 and where, in 1967, French girl Catherine Lacoste became the first non-American, the first amateur, and the youngest winner of the U.S. Women's Open.

Cascades Card of the course

Hole	Yards	Par		Hole	Yards	Par
1	394	4		10	375	4
2	412	4		11	191	3
3	283	4		12	476	5
4	198	3		13	438	4
5	576	5		14	408	4
6	369	4		15	222	3
7	425	4		16	525	5
8	141	3		17	491	5
9	450	4		18	192	3
Out	**3,248**	**35**		**In**	**3,318**	**36**
				Total	**6,566**	**71**

50 Quaker Ridge GC, Scarsdale, N.Y.

Designed by A.W. Tillinghast in 1916, this exacting course in rolling, heavily wooded country a short distance from New York is relatively unknown compared with its illustrious neighbor, Winged Foot. Typical of the examination set at Quaker Ridge is the ninety-degree dogleg 7th, which needs a precise drive to the right side of the fairway to give a sight of the green more than 200 yards away uphill. The second shot must carry a brook and two fairway bunkers to a green with sand on three sides. The shorter, par-four 11th is distinguished by a stream that crosses in front of the tee, threatens the left side of the fairway, and snakes back around the right side of the green. For good measure trees overhang the left side of the putting surface. Quaker Ridge has shunned the limelight of the big tournament circuit, but did play host to the Walker Cup in 1997. It resulted in an overwelming victory for the United States over a Great Britain and Ireland side that never came to terms with the slick, subtly contoured greens.

Quaker Ridge Card of the course

Hole	Yards	Par		Hole	Yards	Par
1	527	5		10	201	3
2	425	4		11	387	4
3	424	4		12	422	4
4	408	4		13	234	3
5	169	3		14	525	5
6	446	4		15	394	4
7	431	4		16	427	4
8	359	4		17	362	4
9	164	3		18	440	4
Out	**3,353**	**35**		**In**	**3,392**	**35**
				Total	**6,745**	**70**

51 Baltimore CC, Baltimore, Md.

Five Farms, which was once just the suburban course of the Baltimore Country Club, is now the hub of the club. It sits amid the rolling hills of Maryland's "huntcountry," where horses have always been the major sport but from which golf is fast taking over. Designed by the late, great genius of architecture, A.W. Tillinghast, the course is not overly bunkered and neither is it tremendously long. But those hills present numerous sidehill lies after mis-hit drives and the greens can get fearsomely slick, although remaining awesomely true. Baltimore has hosted a number of major events, including the exciting 1965 Walker Cup in which Britain and Ireland tied the U.S. team, so breaking a string of losses dating back to1938. In 1988 the Women's Open was held there, and was won by the Swede Liselotte Neumann.

Baltimore
Card of the course

Hole	Yards	Par
1	424	4
2	433	4
3	387	4
4	163	3
5	425	4
6	575	5
7	349	4
8	355	4
9	193	3
Out	**3,304**	**35**
10	378	4
11	424	4
12	388	4
13	158	3
14	500	5
15	425	4
16	422	4
17	175	3
18	385	4
In	**3,355**	**35**
Total	**6,659**	**70**

52 Westchester CC, N.Y.

Westchester County, a snug New York suburb within easy reach of the bustle of Manhattan, has more than its share of excellent golf courses and in particular Westchester Country Club, together with its near neighbors Quaker Ridge and Winged Foot, comprise a formidable trinity. The venue each year for the Buick Classic on the USPGA tour, the Westchester course is not long at a shade under 6,800 yards. But tight fairways and subtly contoured greens are married together to form a classic layout, one that eminently appeals to the game's shotmakers: Vijay Singh and Ernie Els have each won there twice in recent times.

Course record: 62, Peter Jacobsen, 1982

Westchester, CC
Card of the course

Hole	Yards	Par
1	190	3
2	384	4
3	408	4
4	419	4
5	565	5
6	133	3
7	326	4
8	464	4
9	505	5
Out	**3,394**	**36**
10	314	4
11	442	4
12	473	4
13	379	4
14	154	3
15	462	4
16	204	3
17	374	4
18	526	5
In	**3,328**	**35**
Total	**6,722**	**71**

53 Concord GC, Kiamesha Lake, N.Y.

The Concord Hotel and its two eighteen-hole courses are set in the woods of the Catskill Mountains about a two hour drive north of New York City. Before 1963 the resort had an eighteen-hole layout, the International, and a small nine-holer, the Challenger. To these the Texan architect Joe Finger added the Monster. This course is incredibly long, measuring, from the back tee, a standard 7,205 yards — which can be stretched to 7,672 yards in exceptional circumstances. Finger wanted the longer distance to be played only when there was a strong following wind, blowing off the mountains. The course borders on Kiamesha Lake and fine, though not extravagant, use of the water has been made on eight of the holes. The greens are grand, sprawling areas and the bunkering is subtle, in the true Finger style. At the 586-yard, par-five 4th, a lateral water hazard runs for 220 yards down the left-hand side, gradually encroaching on to the fairway and making the 4th a hole that even the elite find hard to master.

Concord Card of the course

Hole	Yards	Par	Hole	Yards	Par
1	530	5	10	417	4
2	443	4	11	172	3
3	415	4	12	531	5
4	586	5	13	412	4
5	211	3	14	154	3
6	382	4	15	447	4
7	224	3	16	556	5
8	443	4	17	399	4
9	432	4	18	451	4
Out	**3,666**	**36**	**In**	**3,539**	**36**
			Total	**7,205**	**72**

54 Oak Hill CC, Rochester, N.Y.

Before the 1956 U.S. Open at Oak Hill, Ben Hogan said that the East course was not tough enough to stage this premier event. After losing the championship to Cary Middlecoff by one shot, Hogan revised his opinion and nominated the 1st as the toughest opening hole he had ever faced. The first fairway appears generously wide, but accuracy from the tee is essential to afford any success with a second shot to a small green guarded by trees, expertly positioned bunkers, and a creek. This sets the tone for the entire course. During the second Open at Oak Hill in 1968, Lee Trevino served notice on the world that he was a force to be reckoned with when he won at Oak Hill with an Open-tying 275, four strokes better than defending champion Jack Nicklaus. In 1980, it was Jack's turn when he won the PGA with a magnificent 274. In 1995 the Ryder Cup at Oak Hill resulted in victory for Europe by the narrowest of margins. Everyone paid tribute to the challenge and the beauty of this course, which stands as a testimony to the skill of architect Donald Ross.

Oak Hill East Course Card of the course

Hole	Yards	Par	Hole	Yards	Par
1	447	4	10	432	4
2	410	4	11	195	3
3	206	3	12	374	4
4	570	5	13	596	5
5	419	4	14	325	4
6	175	3	15	178	3
7	432	4	16	440	4
8	430	4	17	458	4
9	425	4	18	452	4
Out	**3,514**	**35**	**In**	**3,450**	**35**
			Total	**6,964**	**70**

55 Canterbury GC, Cleveland, Ohio

Only ten miles from Cleveland, the Canterbury course was designed by New Yorker Herbert Strong in 1922 and modified a few years later by the club's professional, Jack Way. It is not excessively long, but the problems caused by the fourteen doglegs and the wind that blows off Lake Erie produce a course that favors the long hitter. From the 10th, a 605-yard monster, the run-in is very tough and has sealed the fate of many a player. When played into the wind the short, 232-yard 17th can require a wood to reach the raised double-tiered green, flanked by bunkers and guarded by out-of-bounds on the right. Then comes Canterbury's last and most difficult hole, its fairway uphill for 433 yards and lined with trees, with out-of-bounds to the right and a viciously trapped green. It is often said that if par is held on these three holes then victory is almost assured. The course has seen two U.S. Opens, in 1940 and 1946, and the 1973 PGA.

Canterbury Card of the course

Hole	Yards	Par
1	430	4
2	372	4
3	180	3
4	439	4
5	405	4
6	500	5
7	201	3
8	410	4
9	535	5
Out	**3,472**	**36**
10	360	4
11	165	3
12	372	4
13	490	5
14	385	4
15	358	4
16	605	5
17	232	3
18	438	4
In	**3,405**	**36**
Total	**6,877**	**72**

56 Scioto CC, Columbus, Ohio

Scioto is the course where Jack Nicklaus developed from a pudgy junior to a world beater. Designed by Donald Ross in 1912, it carries all the hallmarks of his best works — greens nestling into the terrain, gentle slopes on the approaches, full use of the ground's natural contours, and plenty of subtle problems that demand thought rather than power. The 438-yard 2nd is one of the great Ross holes. A stream crosses in front of the tee and runs up the left side of the fairway, which is bordered by trees and out-of-bounds on the right. Bunkers protect the tee shot landing area and the sloping green is guarded at the front. All four par-three holes on this magnificent course offer a stiff challenge. Toughest of all is the 238-yard 14th, a deceptive hole with a long carry over a rolling fairway. Scioto staged the 1926 U.S. Open (won by Bobby Jones), the Ryder Cup matches of 1931, and both the American PGA and Amateur Championships.

Scioto Card of the course

Hole	Yards	Par
1	410	4
2	438	4
3	377	4
4	194	3
5	438	4
6	527	5
7	372	4
8	505	5
9	162	3
Out	**3,423**	**36**
10	424	4
11	365	4
12	545	5
13	435	4
14	238	3
15	408	4
16	425	4
17	209	3
18	445	4
In	**3,494**	**35**
Total	**6,917**	**71**

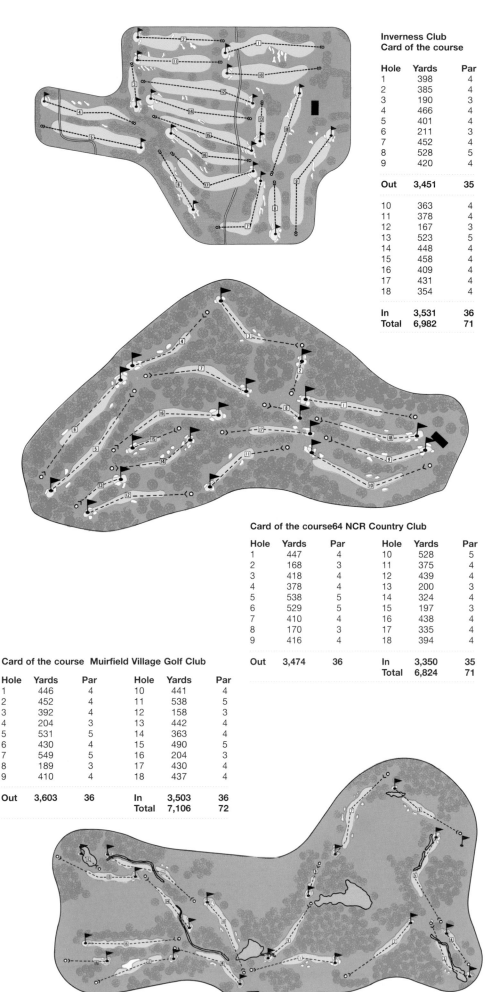

57 Inverness Club, Toledo, Ohio

The four U.S. Open Championships played at Inverness have all produced great drama — particularly in 1920 when big-hitting Ted Ray took the 275-yard shortcut over the trees at the dogleg 7th to score birdies in each round on his way to victory. The addition of twenty yards and the subsequent growth of the trees do not encourage today's professionals to attempt this shot. The original 1903 nine-hole course had another nine added by Donald Ross in 1919. The entire course has been remodelled several times since then. At the 401-yard, par-four 5th, for example, the correct approach is from the right side of the fairway, but this needs a long carry over a creek. Aiming left off the tee leaves a tricky long-iron second to a sloping bunker-less green. The 1993 PGA Championship at Inverness resulted in a win after a play-off for Paul Azinger. The vanquished was Greg Norman and it completed for the unfortunate Australian a Grand Slam of major championship play-off losses.

Inverness Club
Card of the course

Hole	Yards	Par
1	398	4
2	385	4
3	190	3
4	466	4
5	401	4
6	211	3
7	452	4
8	528	5
9	420	4
Out	3,451	35
10	363	4
11	378	4
12	167	3
13	523	5
14	448	4
15	458	4
16	409	4
17	431	4
18	354	4
In	3,531	36
Total	6,982	71

58 NCR CC, Kettering, Ohio

The NCR Country Club's South Course was one of two courses originally built in 1954 for the employees of the NCR Corporation. This 6,824-yard course, designed by Dick Wilson, has frequently been called a "thinking-man's course" because the premium here is on accuracy. The course winds through heavily wooded areas and rolling terrain and has no water hazards — a lack more than compensated for by the trees, traps, doglegs, and rough. The scenic 10th, a 528-yard par five, is a dogleg to a gorgeous green set in the face of a hill, surrounded by six traps. The toughest par three, the 228-yard 15th hole, calls for a demanding tee shot uphill to another heavily trapped green. Gary Player has suggested that golf architects today "could learn a lesson from this course," and Jack Nicklaus, admiring the sloping green of the 13th hole, said "What a job that architect Dick Wilson did!" NCR hosted the 1969 PGA Championship, won by Raymond Floyd, and the 1986 Women's Open, won by Jane Geddes.
Record: 66, Mike Podolski

Card of the course 64 NCR Country Club

Hole	Yards	Par	Hole	Yards	Par
1	447	4	10	528	5
2	168	3	11	375	4
3	418	4	12	439	4
4	378	4	13	200	3
5	538	5	14	324	4
6	529	5	15	197	3
7	410	4	16	438	4
8	170	3	17	335	4
9	416	4	18	394	4
Out	3,474	36	In	3,350	35
			Total	6,824	71

59 Muirfield Village GC, Ohio

Jack Nicklaus, who grew up in nearby Columbus, Ohio, selected the land for Muirfield Village and designed each hole with loving care. The course features downhills off elevated tees, heavy woods, tricky crosswinds in cold weather, and lakes and creeks that bring water into play on eleven holes. The dogleg 3rd hole, a par four at 392 yards, demands a precise drive: too long a shot finds bunkers to the right; too short and the shot to the green (over a lake) will be blocked by the trees or creek to the left. The 12th hole, the most picturesque, is a 158-yard par three set in an amphitheater valley. From the hill where the player tees off to the green cut into a hillside and trapped front and rear, there is water. Nicklaus says of his course: "Certainly, it's a tough, tough golf course. But it's a fair test . . . Golf to me is a game of precision more than power, and I think the course reflects that."

Card of the course Muirfield Village Golf Club

Hole	Yards	Par	Hole	Yards	Par
1	446	4	10	441	4
2	452	4	11	538	5
3	392	4	12	158	3
4	204	3	13	442	4
5	531	5	14	363	4
6	430	4	15	490	5
7	549	5	16	204	3
8	189	3	17	430	4
9	410	4	18	437	4
Out	3,603	36	In	3,503	36
			Total	7,106	72

Shoal Creek Card of the course

Hole	Yards	Par	Hole	Yards	Par
1	409	4	10	415	4
2	424	4	11	517	5
3	530	5	12	452	4
4	458	4	13	177	3
5	189	3	14	383	4
6	554	5	15	407	4
7	443	4	16	197	3
8	177	3	17	539	5
9	428	4	18	446	4
Out	3,612	36	In	3,533	36
			Total	7,145	72

60 Shoal Creek, Shoal Creek, Ala.

Opened in 1977, Shoal Creek soon hosted two prestigious events: the 1984 PGA Championship and the 1986 U.S. Amateur. Cradled in the lap of Oak and Double Oak Mountains, this sparkling Jack Nicklaus-designed course plays at 7,145 yards without a weak hole. Nicklaus describes the 555-yard 6th as the best par five he has created. The serpentine Shoal Creek meanders through the fairway and must be negotiated twice before reaching a slender, undulating green. The 428-yard, par-four 9th is a slight dogleg left, bunkered right at the turn, with water to the right of the fairway and on three sides of the green. The 10th and 11th holes both feature multitiered greens and the further windings of Shoal Creek. The 539-yard, par-five 17th is called the "Waterfall Hole," for the pond and waterfall that guard the front of the shallow green. To reach it in two requires shots both long and accurate to avoid the large bunker and woodlands on the right of the fairway and a large dogwood tree in the left center. The green, apparently flat has several subtle breaks in the center.

61 Lakewood GC, Point Clear, Ala.

Lakewood Golf Club is located on the eastern shore of Mobile Bay at the 140-year-old Grand Hotel, now owned by Marriott. Lakewood offers thirty-six holes of golf, the original eighteen holes designed by Perry Maxwell in 1946; nine holes added by Joe Lee in 1966; and nine more designed by Ron Garl in 1986. They are arranged in the Azalea and Dogwood courses, and the eighteen holes comprising the Dogwood course were the venue for the 1986 USGA Senior Women's Amateur Championship. A combination of the Maxwell and Lee designs, the Dogwood is 6,676 yards. It is characterized by pine trees and moss-draped oaks lining the fairways. The par fours and fives generally dogleg to some degree and lead through bayou-like vegetation that provides a natural habitat for beaver, duck, heron, and alligator.

Lakewood GC (Dogwood Course) Card of the course

Hole	Yards	Par
1	500	5
2	444	4
3	158	3
4	380	4
5	522	5
6	413	4
7	327	4
8	190	3
9	396	4
Out	3,330	36
10	388	4
11	430	4
12	530	5
13	236	3
14	438	4
15	406	4
16	436	4
17	145	3
18	337	4
In	3,346	35
Total	6,676	71

62 Chicago GC, Wheaton, Ill.

Chicago was one of the five clubs that formed the U.S. Golf Association in 1894 — the same year that the club moved to its present site at Wheaton from Belmont, where it had been inaugurated two years earlier. The guiding light in those times was the famed Charles Blair Macdonald, who constructed the first course before it was completely redesigned and rebuilt during 1921 with the assistance of Seth Raynor. At 413 yards, the 8th is slightly double doglegged and scarred by eight sandtraps, of which three abut a green that has a gently rolling surface and is set obliquely to the fairway. The club staged many early championships, including the U.S. Open three times and the U.S. Amateur on four occasions.

Record: 66, Bobby Jones, Walker Cup, 1928

Chicago GC Card of the course

Hole	Yards	Par	Hole	Yards	Par
1	450	4	10	139	3
2	440	4	11	410	4
3	219	3	12	414	4
4	536	5	13	149	3
5	320	4	14	351	4
6	395	4	15	393	4
7	207	3	16	525	5
8	413	4	17	382	4
9	406	4	18	425	4
Out	3,386	35	In	3,188	35
			Total	6,574	70

63 Butler National GC, Chicago, Ill.

Located in the Oak Brook suburb of Chicago, Butler National, designed by George Fazio, is a new course that demands patience and precision from the tee. The greens have become renowned for their mysterious undulations, so tricky that they defeat even those most familiar with them. Water has been used imaginatively, coming into play at eleven holes. It creates a potent problem from the back tee at the par-three 5th, where a 240-yard carry is needed to hit a peninsula green which is also backed on the right side by water. At the 435-yard, par-four 14th the same body of water has to be crossed twice en route to the green, making it the most challenging hole on the course.

64 Sentry World GC, Stevens Point, Wis.

Designed by Robert Trent Jones, Jr., Sentry World opened in late summer of 1982. It is a public course owned by Wisconsin's Sentry Insurance. Jones has described the 6,851-yard course as "very possibly my Mona Lisa," and it is easy to see why when surveying the spring-fed lakes and Sentry World's special characteristic, the five acres of flower beds. There are many tests for a golfer's game, with sinister bogs, sand traps (83 in all, including one that measures a full half-acre), hungry lakes and multitiered greens. The par-five, 513-yard 5th hole is exciting, as it hooks around an island in one of the lakes to a peninsular green that can be reached by two daring long shots. Another kind of hazard is provided by the gorgeous par-three 16th, the "Flower Hole": 90,000 multicoloured blooms hem both fairway and green. The flower beds are like water hazards, in that balls that stray into the marigolds and petunias cannot be retrieved.

65 The Honors Course, Chattanooga, Tenn.

Architect Pete Dye was given more than 200 acres of East Tennessee countryside to create The Honors Course, allowing him to design a course that reflects his belief that the architect must mold his idea to conform to the land. But Dye is not too much of a purist — the Honors called for the creation of two lakes, one larger than 20 acres in size. At 7,024 yards, the layout offers plenty of privacy among its widely spaced fairways. Players need to be free of distractions when facing the tricky, par-three 16th, with trees and a deep but subtle grass bunker to the left and one of the lakes to the right. Dye expects "many safe and somewhat timid" shots to find the bunker, facing "an interesting pitch back to the small green, since the lake still stands on the other side, ready for any missed shot." The 18th, a long, 451-yard par four, is crossed by two ravines en route to the large, severely contoured green surrounded by bunkers. The Honors Course tests every club in the bag and every shot in the repertoire of the seasoned golfer.

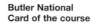

Butler National
Card of the course

Hole	Yards	Par
1	392	4
2	552	5
3	433	4
4	400	4
5	240	3
6	442	4
7	603	5
8	195	3
9	427	4
Out	**3,684**	**36**
10	433	4
11	190	3
12	469	4
13	193	3
14	435	4
15	578	5
16	385	4
17	454	4
18	470	4
In	**3,607**	**35**
Total	**7,291**	**71**

Sentry World Golf Course Card of the course

Hole	Yards	Par	Hole	Yards	Par
1	417	4	10	391	4
2	409	4	11	533	5
3	399	4	12	216	3
4	177	3	13	389	4
5	513	5	14	509	5
6	407	4	15	448	4
7	196	3	16	166	3
8	357	4	17	406	4
9	501	5	18	417	4
Out	**3,376**	**36**	**In**	**3,475**	**36**
			Total	**6,851**	**72**

The Honors Course Card of the course

Hole	Yards	Par	Hole	Yards	Par
1	401	4	10	435	4
2	520	5	11	562	5
3	195	3	12	355	4
4	433	4	13	394	4
5	459	4	14	156	3
6	546	5	15	443	4
7	437	4	16	168y	3
8	206	3	17	494	5
9	369	4	18	451	4
Out	**3,566**	**36**	**In**	**3,358**	**36**
			Total	**7,024**	**72**

66 Hazeltine National GC, Chaska, Minn.

Hazeltine, founded in the early 1960s by former USGA president Totten Heffelfinger, was designed by Robert Trent Jones. Heffelfinger specified a course capable of hosting a national championship, which Hazeltine did with the 1970 U.S. Open. Englishman Tony Jacklin triumphed then, but since that time Hazeltine has undergone many renovations in its quest for a finely balanced course. The keynote hole, and one of Jones' favorites, is the 16th, a 396-yard par-four that offers a severe examination of a player's skill and nerve. The fairway is guarded by Lake Hazeltine to the left and a small but menacing creek to the right, and the green beckons on a jutting peninsula surrounded by water — a challenging target even for the world's best shotmakers. In 1991 the U.S. Open returned to Hazeltine and this time it was won by Payne Stewart.

67 Interlachen CC, Edina, Minn.

Interlachen Country Club lies just west of the city of Minneapolis, Minnesota, in the suburb of Edina, and is blessed with an abundance and wide variety of trees. This is hallowed ground, the course having been designed by the legendary Donald Ross (1920) and having served as the site of the 1930 U.S. Open, won by Bobby Jones as the third leg of his "Grand Slam" that year. In 1930, Interlachen's 17th hole was the longest par three (262 yards) in Open history. The best Jones could do in four rounds was a bogey four (in the entire Open, the 17th gave up but two birdies). During the mid-1980s, Interlachen was restored by Geoffrey Cornish, holding to Ross' original concepts. It is customary to use the words "rolling fairways" to describe almost any golf course, but in the case of Interlachen, they may be taken literally, and no fewer than ten holes have elevated greens. Both factors proved too much for Great Britain and Ireland's Walker Cup team in 1993 — they were demolished 1995 by the USA.

68 Prairie Dunes GC, Hutchinson, Kan.

Prairie Dunes could hardly be farther from the sea, yet the superb course is played across rolling sandhills characteristic of a true Scottish links — an impression heightened by the severe rough, so unusual on American golf courses. Originally a nine-hole course, designed in 1937 by Perry Maxwell, it was extended to 6,339 yards over a period of twenty years by his son, J. Press Maxwell. The 420-yard, doglegged 8th is a classic. Thick rough prevents any thought of a short cut and a long iron second is necessary to reach a well-trapped, two-tier plateau green. The 169-yard 10th — played downwind, with a scrub-covered dune on the left, a cavernous bunker in front, a steep drop to deep rough on the right, and more bushes beyond — is a hole Scotland would be proud to own. Perhaps it was because Prairie Dunes reminded them of home that Great Britain and Ireland's Curtis Cup team achieved an historic first victory on American soil by the astonishingly comfortable margin of 13–5 in 1986.

Hazeltine National GC Card of the course

Hole	Yards	Par	Hole	Yards	Par
1	440	4	10	410	4
2	435	4	11	556	5
3	580	5	12	432	4
4	194	3	13	204	3
5	412	4	14	357	4
6	405	4	15	590	5
7	518	5	16	384	4
8	166	3	17	182	3
9	432	4	18	452	4
Out	**3,582**	**36**	**In**	**3,567**	**36**
			Total	**7,149**	**72**

Interlachen Country Club Card of the course

Hole	Yards	Par	Hole	Yards	Par
1	531	5	10	341	4
2	351	4	11	476	5
3	195	3	12	541	5
4	509	5	13	195	3
5	171	3	14	440	4
6	350	4	15	414	4
7	346	4	16	318	4
8	412	4	17	226	3
9	520	5	18	397	4
Out	**3,385**	**37**	**In**	**3,348**	**36**
			Total	**6,733**	**73**

74 Prairie Dunes Card of the course

Hole	Yards	Par	Hole	Yards	Par
1	424	4	10	169	3
2	150	3	11	450	4
3	325	4	12	327	4
4	160	3	13	357	4
5	439	4	14	337	4
6	382	4	15	197	3
7	507	5	16	420	4
8	420	4	17	497	5
9	399	4	18	379	4
Out	**3,206**	**35**	**In**	**3,133**	**35**
			Total	**6,339**	**70**

Hole	Yards	Par	Hole	Yards	Par
1	441	4	10	379	4
2	392	4	11	466	4
3	584	5	12	445	4
4	200	3	13	149	3
5	590	5	14	453	4
6	377	4	15	434	4
7	440	4	16	499	5
8	171	3	17	200	3
9	429	4	18	406	4
Out	3,624	36	In	3,391	35
			Total	7,015	71

69 Oak Tree GC, Edmond, Okla.

Architect Pete Dye calls his course at Oak Tree "the finest inland golf course I have ever built." Consistently acclaimed as one of America's best and host of the 1988 PGA Championship (won by Jeff Sluman), the Oak Tree course features not only the massive old oaks that give it its name, but also railroad ties, rock walls, and bridges that provide a variety of hazards. Large sand traps, strategically placed, guard greens that tend to slope right to left. On the par-four, 441-yard 1st, it's important to keep your drive to the right side of the fairway, away from the trees, for a clear shot over the lake to the green. The par-three 4th features the lake again, as well as the sloping right-to-left green. The back nine has its fair share of bunkers and traps. The finishing hole, a par four, 406-yard effort, tees off over water but the second shot should be played to the center of the green, avoiding a pot bunker to the right.

70 Cherry Hills CC, Denver, Colo.

Denver is the "mile-high" city and in its rarefied atmosphere the 6,955 yards of the Cherry Hills course play shorter than they read on the card. Designed by William Flynn in 1922 it was here, thirty-eight years later, that Arnold Palmer won his only U.S. Open. Ben Hogan named the 470-yard 14th one of the most difficult par fours in America. Its fairway rises from the tee with trees and out of bounds on the right; on the left, thick rough falls away to a creek. The hole then swings sharply to the left, offering a narrow opening to the green set between a deep bunker on the right and the ever-threatening creek that curls a round and behind the left edge. The 14th starts a demanding finish that includes a 194-yard par three to a very small green encircled by sand and trees. Then comes a short par-four 16th that demands supreme accuracy; an exacting 529-yard par five to an island green; and finally the 489-yard 18th often described as one of golf's finest last holes.

Record: 65, Arnold Palmer, US Open 1960

Cherry Hills Card of the course

Hole	Yards	Par	Hole	Yards	Par
1	355	4	10	434	4
2	415	4	11	556	5
3	325	4	12	203	3
4	433	4	13	384	4
5	541	5	14	470	4
6	170	3	15	194	3
7	394	4	16	400	4
8	230	3	17	529	5
9	433	4	18	489	5
Out	3,296	35	In	3,659	37
			Total	6,955	72

71 Colonial CC, Fort Worth, Texas

It is often said that Ben Hogan's success was partly due to the fact that, having played his early golf at Colonial, every other course in the world was easy in comparison. Designed in 1935 by John Bredemus and embellished by Perry Maxwell for the 1941 U.S. Open, it is 7,096 yards with a par of 70. Its trees, bunkers and river do not allow an all-out attack from the tee — placement rather than pure length being the key to success at every hole. This puts a premium on long, accurate second shots as at the 5th, a 466-yard, par-four dogleg to the right. A power fade from the tee may find the Trinity River under the trees, a long straight tee shot could overrun the fairway's bend into thick trees on the left. Yet anything less than a drive to the center of the fairway leaves an enormous shot to a green.

Record: 62, Joey Sindelar, 1985

Colonial Card of the course

Hole	Yards	Par	Hole	Yards	Par
1	572	5	10	416	4
2	401	4	11	609	5
3	470	4	12	435	4
4	226	3	13	172	3
5	466	4	14	431	4
6	415	4	15	436	4
7	453	4	16	176	3
8	192	3	17	387	4
9	405	4	18	434	4
Out	3,600	35	In	3,496	35
			Total	7,096	70

72 Castle Pines GC, Castle Rock, Colo.

Carved by Jack Nicklaus out of a scrub oak and pine forest north of Castle Rock, Colorado (near Denver), Castle Pines' 7,503-yard layout does not seem so long in the thin air of 6,600 feet above sea level. Here the ball carries about 10 percent farther than normal. Nicklaus disturbed very little of the terrain to create this course, in which fourteen holes are generally wooded, and the remaining four are open links with a Scottish flavor. On twelve of the eighteen holes, no other is visible. The most difficult hole is the 5th, a 477-yard par four that climbs to an elevated green guarded by mounds, five traps, and a collection bunker waiting in the front center of the green to punish any less than perfect approaches. Castle Pines is the home each year to one of the more unusual tournaments on the PGA Tour — the International — with its modified stableford format. Its roll call of winners includes Greg Norman, Davis Love, Jose-Maria Olazabal, and Phil Mickelson.

Castle Pines GC Card of the course

Hole	Yards	Par	Hole	Yards	Par
1	644	5	10	485	4
2	408	4	11	197	3
3	452	4	12	422	4
4	205	3	13	439	4
5	477	4	14	595	5
6	417	4	15	403	4
7	185	3	16	209	3
8	535	5	17	492	5
9	458	4	18	480	4
Out	**3,781**	**36**	**In**	**3,722**	**36**
			Total	**7,503**	**72**

73 Country Club of the Rockies, Edwards, Colo.

Situated high in the Rocky Mountains west of Vail, Colorado, the course at the Country Club of the Rockies, designed by Jack Nicklaus, has been acclaimed since its opening in 1985. The 7,000-foot elevation means both that the ball carries farther than normal in the thin mountain air and that the course is playable during the months of April through October only. The rest of the year, herds of deer and elk graze over the site, as they have for centuries. During the warm seasons, the 7,317-yard course boasts a Scottish links style layout with the mounds, characteristic of Nicklaus designs, that define fairways and protect greens. The par-four, 477-yard 12th hole plays downhill off the tee with mounds on either side. The second shot must cross the Eagle River, which comes into play and must be crossed on the 13th, 14th, and 15th holes as well.

Record: 67, Craig Stadler, Jerry Ford Invitational, 1986

Country Club of the Rockies Card of the course

Hole	Yards	Par	Hole	Yards	Par
1	453	4	10	446	4
2	389	4	11	180	3
3	566	5	12	477	4
4	209	3	13	573	5
5	429	4	14	156	3
6	427	4	15	415	4
7	571	5	16	463	4
8	162	3	17	586	5
9	400	4	18	415	4
Out	**3,606**	**36**	**In**	**3,711**	**36**
			Total	**7,317**	**72**

Spyglass Hill Card of the course

Hole	Yards	Par	Hole	Yards	Par
1	600	5	10	400	4
2	350	4	11	520	5
3	150	3	12	180	3
4	365	4	13	440	4
5	180	3	14	555	5
6	415	4	15	130	3
7	515	5	16	465	4
8	395	4	17	320	4
9	425	4	18	405	4
Out	**3,395**	**36**	**In**	**3,415**	**36**
			Total	**6,810**	**72**

74 Spyglass Hill GC, Pebble Beach, Calif.

Spyglass Hill is possibly the hardest of the courses on the Monterey Peninsula. The hilly land tumbles down toward the sea, leaving fairways lined with windswept cypress trees and Californian pines liberally laced with areas of brilliant white sand. The course, designed by Robert Trent Jones and opened in 1966, makes heavy demands on both the mental and physical resources of those who play. On a windy day it can become almost impossible and in fact is rarely played at its full championship length of 6,810 yards. The opening holes are a fearsome introduction to the course's difficulties. The 1st is an enormous 600 yards that needs thunderous stroke play even to approach a par. The course returns inland at the 6th, but trees now compound the problems set by the wind. The short 12th is played across a pond to a small, undulating green wedged between the water and a steep, bunkered rise. Over-clubbing can plug the ball in a trap or bounce it off the slope to roll back across the green and into the water.

75 Pasatiempo GC, Santa Cruz, Calif.

Pasatiempo, the brainchild of champion horsewoman and lady golfer Marion Hollins, was designed by Alister MacKenzie and completed in 1929. It is a 6,528-yard course that sprawls over the Santa Cruz hills. The front nine, deceptively simple holes that offer straight fairways flanked by trees and bunkers, don't prepare the golfer for the arroyos and dry stream of the back nine. Barrancas (Spanish for ravines) dot the fairways and guard the greens. A par-five, 445-yard, doglegged 10th hole sets the tone for the incoming nine. After a drive that must carry some 170–180 yards over a barranca, the player must use another wood for a downhill shot to a sloping fairway. A huge eucalyptus tree guards the green to the right and many a shot falls onto a bare lie among tree roots, caught by the extending branches. The 17th may offer some respite before the par-three, 187-yard closing hole, with towering trees on the right and a deep barranca on the way to a very tricky green.

76 Riviera CC, Pacific Palisades, Calif.

The golfing domain of show-business stars since its opening in 1926, this great Californian course, designed by George Thomas, plays host almost every year to the Los Angeles Open. It was here that Ben Hogan set his U.S. Open record of 276, which stood for nineteen years, and, in 1950, made his historic comeback to golf after a near-fatal car crash. Massive reconstruction work was undertaken in 1974 to restore the small meandering stream that had become, over fifty years, a 40 foot deep ravine; seventeen acres of land were reclaimed and the course was returned to its original glory. The spongy quality of the turf does not allow the ball to roll far and this makes the par fives extremely difficult, particularly the massive, 583-yard 17th. Yet power is not the only requirement, for there are subtle problems set by the winding barranca and the arrangement of bunkers. At the 167-yard 6th, sandtraps proliferate. The first bunker lies in the dead center of the fairway just short of the target; on the green itself there is a small shallow trap, and at the back a hillside bunker to swallow the over-clubbed stroke.

Riviera Card of the course

Hole	Yards	Par	Hole	Yards	Par
1	508	5	10	356	4
2	526	5	11	557	5
3	439	4	12	457	4
4	234	3	13	424	4
5	422	4	14	169	3
6	167	3	15	442	4
7	411	4	16	168	3
8	360	4	17	583	5
9	418	4	18	443	4
Out	**3,485**	**36**	**In**	**3,599**	**36**
			Total	**7,084**	**72**

Pasatiempo Golf Club Card of the course

Hole	Yards	Par	Hole	Yards	Par
1	497	5	10	445	4
2	438	4	11	406	4
3	218	3	12	386	4
4	394	4	13	490	5
5	197	3	14	422	4
6	518	5	15	145	3
7	345	4	16	408	4
8	178	3	17	363	4
9	491	5	18	187	3
Out	**3,276**	**36**	**In**	**3,252**	**35**
			Total	**6,528**	**71**

77 Poppy Hills GC, Pebble Beach, Calif.

Located on California's Monterey Peninsula, an area with an abundance of great golf courses, including the famed Spyglass Hill only a mile away, Poppy Hills Golf Course is in the Del Monte Forest. A public course designed by Robert Trent Jones, Jr., Poppy Hills opened in 1986. The course is close to the sea but incorporates water hazards with spare efficiency: the long (426-yard) par-four 5th offers a difficult second shot to the irregularly shaped green guarded by a pond on the right and bunkers to the left. The par-five 10th hole, at 510 yards, challenges the best golfer's approach shot as the green is nestled behind water. The back nine has its share of doglegs, including the 90 degree left dogleg on the 14th hole and a sharp right dogleg on the 439-yard, par-four 16th. Greens are typical of Robert Trent Jones, Jr., designs — large and rolling.

Poppy Hills
Card of the course

Hole	Yards	Par
1	413	4
2	162	3
3	406	4
4	560	5
5	426	4
6	181	3
7	388	4
8	380	4
9	557	5
Out	**3,473**	**36**
10	510	5
11	214	3
12	531	5
13	393	4
14	417	4
15	210	3
16	439	4
17	163	3
18	500	5
In	**3,377**	**36**
Total	**6,850**	**72**

78 Edgewood Tahoe, Stateline, Nev.

This public course, designed by George Fazio, opened for play in 1968. Adjacent to Lake Tahoe and at a breath-shortening elevation of 6,200 feet, the 7,725-yard course is as challenging as it is visually appealing. The 438-yard par four starting hole offers a wide landing area and a large green, but the second, a 493-yard, par-four, leads to a more severe two-tiered putting green. The toughest hole on the front nine, the 471-yard 9th, requires a long to mid-iron second shot after the dogleg right to make the par-four. The 11th and 12th holes, par four and three respectively, offer fair chances for birdies, but swirling winds make the 14th a challenge, and the winds combine with trees and water for the spectacular final three holes. Edgewood Tahoe hosted the 1985 U.S. Senior Open, won by Miller Barber.

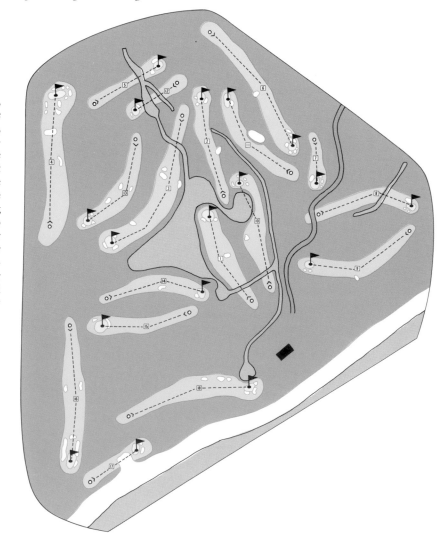

Edgewood Tahoe Card of the course

Hole	Yards	Par	Hole	Yards	Par
1	438	4	10	447	4
2	493	4	11	427	4
3	608	5	12	214	3
4	638	5	13	442	4
5	240	3	14	441	4
6	463	4	15	375	4
7	179	3	16	575	5
8	463	4	17	220	3
9	471	4	18	591	5
Out	**3,993**	**36**	**In**	**3,732**	**36**
			Total	**7,725**	**72**

79 Mauna Kea GC, Hawaii

Robert Trent Jones's incredibly tough masterpiece at Mauna Kea on the Big Island of Hawaii has been refined by his son Robert from a course that only the elite among playing professionals could hope to master. The younger Jones adapted the layout so that it became acceptable for the average player — though even without some of its original savagery it still presents a number of formidable challenges. Carved out of desolate volcanic lava beds beside the ocean and over the foothills of vast mountains, it has developed the lush beauty to be expected on these scenic islands. The 3rd, with its view over the pounding Pacific to a green perched above volcanic rock 210 yards away, is not solved in one shot. The green carries the Trent Jones characteristic of sharp borrows and lightning speed, which rewards only the lightest of touches. But not every hole is as severe.

Record: 64, Terry Dill, 1969

Mauna Kea
Card of the course

Hole	Yards	Par
1	383	4
2	394	4
3	210	3
4	413	4
5	593	5
6	344	4
7	204	3
8	530	5
9	427	4
Out	**3,498**	**36**
10	554	5
11	247	3
12	387	4
13	409	4
14	413	4
15	201	3
16	422	4
17	555	5
18	428	4
In	**3,616**	**36**
Total	**7,114**	**72**

Princeville Ocean
Card of the course

Hole	Yards	Par
1	415	4
2	610	5
3	180	3
4	360	4
5	520	5
6	435	4
7	200	3
8	350	4
9	390	4
Ocean	**3,460**	**36**

80 Princeville Makai GC, Hawaii

The championship course at Princeville on a beautiful tract of land on Kauai, the most westerly of the large Hawaiian islands, is undoubtedly one of the most outstanding examples of the courses designed by Robert Trent Jones Jr. Vast tees and large greens allow many combinations, lengths, and degrees of difficulty over a layout that features rolling fairways, strategic bunkers and generous use of lakes. The second hole is a fierce par five, where the second shot has to carry 100 yards of trouble. The winds play a big part at Princeville, the effect of which can be judged by the professionals' choice of clubs at the 180-yard, par-three 3rd. Played downwind it requires no more than a 9-iron, or even a wedge. The 60 foot elevated tee looks over the lake down on to the wide but shallow target, which is flanked at the back by two strategically placed bunkers.

Hamilton
Card of the course

Hole	Yards	Par
1	425	4
2	457	4
3	401	4
4	543	5
5	321	4
6	216	3
7	394	4
8	195	3
9	423	4
Out	**3,375**	**35**
10	343	4
11	451	4
12	385	4
13	220	3
14	424	4
15	381	4
16	181	3
17	550	5
18	440	4
In	**3,375**	**35**
Total	**6,750**	**70**

81 Hamilton G & CC, Ancaster, Ont.

Ancaster, as Hamilton is commonly known, epitomizes the country club ambience. The turf is lush and springy, while the heavily wooded surroundings give the property an elegant seclusion. The championship layout takes its front nine from the West course and the remainder from the South. Both were designed as nine-hole courses by H. S. Colt in 1914, and in 1974 an extra nine-holer, the East, was added by Robbie Robinson. From a promontory, the opulent clubhouse overlooks the strong finishing hole, a 440-yard par four where the fairway winds around an S-shaped stream to a saucer-like green. Because of the water, the tee shot is normally played as a lay-up and the approach to the large green calls for a wood or a low iron for even the longest hitter. The Canadian Open has been played at Ancaster twice, in 1930 and 1948. In the first, Tommy Armour shot a six-under-par 64 to set a course record that still stands today.

Record: 64, Tommy Armour, Canadian Open 1930; Jim Nelford, Canadian Am. Ch. 1977

St George's Card of the course

Hole	Yards	Par	Hole	Yards	Par
1	378	4	10	377	4
2	420	4	11	517	5
3	201	3	12	383	4
4	480	5	13	214	3
5	403	4	14	446	4
6	146	3	15	580	5
7	442	4	16	203	3
8	217	3	17	447	4
9	543	5	18	400	4
Out	**3,230**	**35**	**In**	**3,567**	**36**
			Total	**6,797**	**71**

82 St. George's GC, Islington, Ont.

St. George's is distinguished by its tight fairways and rolling terrain. Situated in downtown Toronto, the course was designed by Stanley Thompson and opened for play in 1928. It was known as the Royal York and associated with the Canadian Pacific Railway until the company relinquished its interest after World War II. Not only the fairways twist and roll — even a putt over a flat surface is a rare treat on the well-trapped greens. At the 14th, a 446-yard par-four, the drive must avoid out-of-bounds on the left and carry a knoll, leaving a mid-iron second shot down the hill to a green that is banked on the right and trapped on the left. The problems are intensified by a river that runs down the right side of the fairway and crosses just in front of the green. In the 1933 Canadian Open Joe Kirkwood, the eventual winner, was stymied behind a large oak at the 5th. He hit the ball out of the right and produced a total roundhouse hook to land the ball eight feet from the pin, and holed out for a birdie. **Record: 64, George Knudson, Canadian Open 1968**

83 Vancouver GC, Coquitlam, BC

Inspired by emigrant Scots, the Vancouver course was laid out in 1910 on a stretch of densely wooded, rolling coastal land. Giant pines and cedars line the narrow fairways, increasing the difficulty of the course and offering compensation for its lack of length. The front nine is considered the easier although the 6th is more than 600 yards and needs a subtle approach shot to an irregularly shaped green, protected by a small pond that lies in front and just off to the left. On the back nine, the 16th — aptly called Graves — is a deceptive par four of 371 yards. The hole doglegs sharply left, leaving the green unsighted from the championship tee. The drive must reach the crook of the fairway, where the second shot needs a firm blast with a mid-iron to make the small green, which sulks behind a single bunker and is encircled by trees. Before the urbanization of Vancouver, it took quite a trek through the British Columbian wilds to reach the club, which explains the old segregated dormitory accommodation in the original clubhouse.

Vancouver Card of the course

Hole	Yards	Par	Hole	Yards	Par
1	395	4	10	460	4
2	378	4	11	373	4
3	134	3	12	190	3
4	357	4	13	520	5
5	343	4	14	381	4
6	616	5	15	372	4
7	192	3	16	371	4
8	383	4	17	396	4
9	354	4	18	446	4
Out	**3,152**	**35**	**In**	**3,509**	**36**
			Total	**6,661**	**71**

84 Jasper Park GC, Alberta

Set in the rugged mountains of Alberta overlooking Lake Beauvert, Jasper Park has fairways that are invariably aligned with mountain peaks and roll through thick, rich woodland with breathtaking views over the valley, lake and river below. Originally designed in 1925 by Stanley Thompson, the course was rebuilt twenty years later and now follows an almost circular path, with the 9th at the farthest point in the traditional manner. Two par threes, the 12th (Tête Jaune) and 15th (The Bad Baby), are scintillating short holes to well-elevated greens. The 12th is played across two forward bunkers and against a backdrop of trees; to the right of the triangular green is a large waste of sand. The 15th is no better — the green is set in splendid isolation, and presents itself as a true target where only a direct hit by a well-weighted short-iron will bring results. The club has its own annual competition, suitably named the Totem Pole.

Jasper Park Card of the course

Hole	Yards	Par	Hole	Yards	Par
1	391	4	10	483	5
2	488	5	11	390	4
3	454	4	12	181	3
4	240	3	13	603	5
5	458	5	14	361	4
6	393	4	15	138	3
7	178	3	16	369	4
8	417	4	17	360	4
9	231	3	18	463	4
Out	**3,250**	**35**	**In**	**3,348**	**36**
			Total	**6,598**	**71**

85 Vallescondido GC, Mexico City

Vallescondido is a superior private course designed by Percy Clifford, with a membership that is restricted to 750 members. Situated just outside Mexico City, it sprawls over a beautiful valley; oak trees closely line the fairways and a meandering stream affects play on eight of the holes. The gently undulating ground means that sidehill lies often result from less than accurately positioned shots. This rolling nature of the layout means that good club selection can lead to the gaining of important yardage. On the front nine a small pond comes into play at the 165 yard, par-three 8th, while on the back nine a solitary lake affects the 10th, a 496-yard, par-five, and another small pond enters into the strategy of the short 15th. The 408-yard 4th ends with the green ninety degrees away from the initial line of play; the right of the fairway is flanked by sand and the green is effectively protected in front by a vast sandtrap.

Record: 68, Roberto de Vicenzo, 1975

Vallescondido Card of the course

Hole	Yards	Par	Hole	Yards	Par
1	408	4	10	496	5
2	323	4	11	359	4
3	668	5	12	218	3
4	408	4	13	468	4
5	219	3	14	574	5
6	400	4	15	255	3
7	530	5	16	420	4
8	165	3	17	443	4
9	434	4	18	405	4
Out	**3,455**	**36**	**In**	**3,638**	**36**
			Total	**7,093**	**72**

Port Royal Card of the course

Hole	Yards	Par
1	417	4
2	528	5
3	128	3
4	378	4
5	337	4
6	321	4
7	467	5
8	145	3
9	336	4
Out	**3,057**	**36**
10	302	4
11	427	4
12	157	3
13	348	4
14	331	4
15	340	4
16	125	3
17	475	5
18	377	4
In	**2,887**	**35**
Total	**5,944**	**71**

86 Port Royal GC, Southampton

Bermuda has so much golf to offer within its twenty-one square miles of land that it has been described as virtually one big golf club. Built in 1970, Port Royal was designed by Robert Trent Jones on high ground sweeping down to cliff edges overlooking the Atlantic, presenting a challenge considerably less lethal than many of his other designs. The greens are vast but gently contoured, and the surrounding bunkers do offer some leeway. From a tee on the cliff edge the spectacular short, 125-yard 16th is played across a yawning gap to a promontory that holds nothing more than the green, edged on three sides by sand. The course is over pleasantly undulating land where 200,000 new trees have been planted to blend in with the massive originals that survived the constructions. Three small lakes play their part — before the green at the 1st, on the left of the short 3rd, and left again of the driving area at the sweeping dogleg 17th.

Lucayan Card of the course

Hole	Yards	Par
1	373	4
2	170	3
3	540	5
4	431	4
5	383	4
6	389	4
7	210	3
8	489	5
9	429	4
Out	**3,414**	**36**
10	419	4
11	199	3
12	469	5
13	169	3
14	405	4
15	427	4
16	560	5
17	374	4
18	388	4
In	**3,410**	**36**
Total	**6,824**	**72**

87 Lucayan CC, Freepost

The towns of Lucayan and Freeport are the centers of the gambling enterprises that lure so many people to the Bahamas. However, the Lucayan Country Club is far from being a gambler's paradise: it is a conservative club with a membership largely composed of American and Canadian businessmen. The course, designed by Dick Wilson and opened in 1964, sits on a natural hilly area overlooking the Bell Channel. One of its most interesting features is the extraordinary natural hazard of white coral rock that lies off the fairway beyond the normal rough. If the ball lands here, finding it is a minor problem compared to the difficulties of playing out. There is only one lake on the course and this runs the final 200 yards down the left-hand side of the 17th to haunt any hook-prone right-hander. Lucayan was the last golf club which the late, vastly admired American professional Craig Wood represented. It was here that he shot a 66 a matter of days before his sixty-sixth birthday.

88 South Ocean GC, Nassau, New Providence

Designed by Joe Lee and completed in 1971, South Ocean is one of the best of the Bahamian courses. Situated on New Providence Island near Nassau, the capital, it has eighteen holes of completely separate and identifiable character, cut through dense tropical jungle. Water comes into play at seven holes and the vast greens are matched by enormous areas of sand, some with trees in the middle, a trademark of Lee's work. He has also resisted the modern temptation to make every par three a test of power rather than accuracy, and the 104-yard 11th — to an elongated green whose entrance is flanked by bunkers — is a welcome change, if no less demanding. Of the par fives, the 509-yard 16th is virtually a double dogleg, first round a lake on the right, then skirting a second stretch of water on the left before pitching to a green that is protected by four bunkers.

Record: 68, Lee Elder, Pro-Am 1973

South Ocean Card of the course

Hole	Yards	Par
1	487	5
2	375	4
3	359	4
4	150	3
5	367	4
6	492	5
7	333	4
8	193	3
9	397	4
Out	**3,153**	**36**
10	510	5
11	104	3
12	387	4
13	385	4
14	360	4
15	155	3
16	509	5
17	331	4
18	398	4
In	**3,139**	**36**
Total	**6,292**	**72**

89 Fountain Valley GC, St. Croix

At St. Croix on the Virgin Islands, an American protectorate, Robert Trent Jones has built a course of outstanding beauty and charm. Fountain Valley is on the floor of a valley that is filled with trees, water, and ravines, offering an awe-inspiring collection of views. Subtle teeing grounds are the key feature of the design, especially on the four short holes, three of which must be carried from the back tees, although alternative tees reduce the problem for the less accomplished. The first short hole is the 175-yard 5th, where the tees jut farther and farther out into the lake. From the championship teeing ground the shot requires a clear carry over the water, whereas from the ladies' tee the lake runs adjacent to the fairway, threatening any shot that is slightly hooked. The large green is trapped to the rear, penalizing those who over-club to ensure clearing the lake. Trade winds in the horseshoe-shaped valley both cool the course and add to its problems.

Fountain Valley Card of the course

Hole	Yards	Par	Hole	Yards	Par
1	510	5	10	395	4
2	400	4	11	487	5
3	407	4	12	310	4
4	467	4	13	470	5
5	175	3	14	190	3
6	595	5	15	400	4
7	419	4	16	389	4
8	180	3	17	235	3
9	470	4	18	410	4
Out	**3,623**	**36**	**In**	**3,286**	**36**
			Total	**6,909**	**72**

90 Cerromar Beach Hotel GC, Dorado

When Robert Trent Jones was invited to design a North and South course at Cerromar, just a short walk from his famous thirty-six-hole complex at Dorado Beach, the challenge to produce equally good-looking golf of a totally different style was irresistible. He achieved this by the more discreet use of the abundant water, particularly on the par-three and par-five holes, and by varying the greens from the large, contoured, sparsely bunkered type to the smaller, flatter, sand-surrounded designs. Although the combination of trees and water makes skillful shot-making essential on many holes, these hazards are pulled back from the line of play at others to offer scenically exciting and less demanding golf. The North course is used for championship play and its outstanding par threes call for the best stroke-making. At the 187-yard 4th the green is particularly narrow, well protected by inviting bunkers and flanked by water on the right. The 11th is played from a raised tee 193 yards away and into the prevailing wind, with a lateral water hazard threatening on the left of the green and a large bunker protecting the right side.

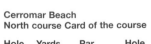

Cerromar Beach North course Card of the course

Hole	Yards	Par	Hole	Yards	Par
1	507	5	10	378	4
2	406	4	11	193	3
3	393	4	12	548	5
4	187	3	13	428	4
5	397	4	14	408	4
6	373	4	15	394	4
7	175	3	16	445	4
8	519	5	17	185	3
9	400	4	18	505	5
Out	**3,357**	**36**	**In**	**3,484**	**36**
			Total	**6,841**	**72**

91 Tryall G & BC, Hanover, Jamaica

Sandy Bay lies on the western tip of Jamaica on near-mountainous land that has superb views over the ocean. Here, in the breach of the trade winds, is the Tryall course, a fine layout that was conceived by Ralph Plummer. The ground was so hilly that it seemed unlikely that anybody could build a course of such outstanding merit, but somehow Plummer managed to do so. It seems that the drive is always either straight up a steep hill or disappearing down one, but in this lies the secret of success on this switchback course. If the ball is kept in the sort of play that Plummer envisaged then there are surprisingly few sidehill lies and — once the apparently inherent difficulty is seen to have evaporated — the golf becomes straightforward and steady. With the course's height there is generally a refreshing breeze blowing into the kitchen-hot valleys. Then, too, it is always pleasant to play through the palms and other tropical foliage. Tryall came to public prominence when it hosted the Johnnie Walker World Championship for five successive years from 1991. Fourteen new tees were built for the event, 400 yards added to the course's length, and the route was dramatically altered from that which normally greets members.

Tryall
Card of the course

Hole	Yards	Par
1	380	4
2	165	3
3	545	5
4	340	4
5	512	5
6	398	4
7	138	3
8	395	4
9	436	4
Out	**3,309**	**36**
10	137	3
11	491	5
12	178	3
13	375	4
14	434	4
15	372	4
16	362	4
17	402	4
18	338	4
In	**3,089**	**35**
Total	**6,398**	**71**

92 Tobago GC, Tobago

Commander John D. Harris has a string of designs in more than thirty countries to his credit, and the Tobago course at Mount Irvine Bay is one of his classics. Set in gently rising country along the coast, there are sea views from every hole, fine water features and an abundance of massive palm trees. The sharply doglegged 472-yard 9th is played from an elevated tee so that those who attempt the shortcut can clearly see the lake, trees, and sand that stand in their way. This is a feature of Harris's designs — he believes that every hazard should be visible, acting as lighthouse to guide the player along the correct path. The five par-three holes are particularly challenging; only two are less than 200 yards. The 215-yard 7th is considered the best. The shot is to a long, narrow green with sand on the right and a drop to a lake on the left. The lush tees, fairways and greens, all grassed in tifton, are amply watered by the course's subterranean irrigation network.

Tobago
Card of the course

Hole	Yards	Par
1	464	4
2	540	5
3	170	3
4	360	4
5	405	4
6	535	5
7	215	3
8	335	4
9	472	4
Out	**3,496**	**36**
10	485	5
11	445	4
12	215	3
13	510	5
14	225	3
15	445	4
16	445	5
17	195	3
18	395	4
In	**3,360**	**36**
Total	**6,856**	**72**

Lagos de Caujaral Card of the course

Hole	Yards	Par	Hole	Yards	Par
1	490	5	10	430	4
2	410	4	11	210	3
3	375	4	12	520	5
4	370	4	13	360	4
5	140	3	14	155	3
6	555	5	15	360	4
7	370	4	16	335	4
8	175	3	17	430	4
9	395	4	18	505	5
Out	**3,280**	**36**	**In**	**3,305**	**36**
			Total	**6,585**	**72**

93 Lagos de Caujaral GC, Barranquilla

Designer Joe Lee built many problems into this beautiful course; nine holes feature water — several of them threatened on both sides — while three par-fives have double doglegs, and three other holes have a seventy-five-foot drop from tee to fairway. Mercifully, at 6,585 yards, the length is not too demanding. Yet the strong trade winds can make even the most modest par four a drive and long-iron for the majority of golfers. The view from the elevated 1st tee is of a narrow fairway between dense trees to a well-trapped green — and this is the widest fairway on the course. The double water hazard is first featured at the 370-yard 4th, where the tee shot must carry 200 yards to an island fairway and counteract the prevailing wind pushing the ball toward the water on the right. It is then necessary to cross the water again to reach a green that is also virtually surrounded by two lakes, with bunkers to the left rear and right front.

94 El Rincon GC, Bogotá

"El Maestro" is the phrase that comes to the lips of El Rincon members when they express their feelings for the American architect Robert Trent Jones and the course he built for them. He finished his project on the outskirts of Bogota in 1953 and since then the only major change has been the redirecting of the two nines; the opening half was originally the back nine and vice versa. He planted numerous trees on the flat plain and sank a number of ponds that now come into play on eleven of the holes as subdued and controlled hazards. The fairways were planted with kikuyo grass and are lined by very strong rough, while the greens are swift, with a preponderance of typical Trent Jones breaks. All the qualities of the course are found in the 594-yard, par-five 15th. A pronounced dogleg to the left means that a carry of at least 250 yards is needed to ensure a good line for the second. The green is tucked behind a large water hazard and bunkered in front.

Record: 67, Dennis Watson, 1975

95 CC of Bogotá, Bogotá

The Country Club of Bogotá has two fine courses set against the splendid backdrop of the Andes. The championship layout, Los Fundadores, was designed in 1950 by Dr. Van Kleek, but eleven years later Robert Janis elongated the teeing grounds, reshaped the greens and added several new bunkers. The generally humid climate leaves the course moist for most of the year and keeps the fairways and greens in superb condition. The course offers a formidable challenge, its tight fairways hemmed in by two large lakes and an abundance of trees. The lush greens are well watered and true. Good driving is the key to success on this course. The uphill 18th is a daunting problem, 552 yards long and doglegging left around well-sited bunkers. The second, bedevilled by more fairway traps, is usually laid up short of water that cuts off the green.

96 Karen CC, Nairobi

Karen Country Club is situated on 216 acres of undulating woodland twelve miles west of Nairobi. The course was laid out in 1931 on farm land formerly owned by Baroness Karen von Blixen, after whom the district takes its name and where she wrote her classic novel *Out of Africa*. Red murrum claysoil renders the course hard underfoot during the long drought, but for most of the year the well-irrigated fairways are cool, green ribbons of turf winding through avenues of eucalyptus, acacias, and thorn bushes. The greens are mostly an experimental blend of native Bermuda with some South African bent, giving a surface that putts fairly. The 2nd, a 551-yard par five, demands both strength and skill. A dogleg of almost ninety degrees appears at the length of an excellent drive, and the second shot has to avoid a sandtrap in the middle of the fairway about sixty yards short of the green.

El Rincon Card of the course

Hole	Yards	Par
1	415	4
2	216	3
3	423	4
4	434	4
5	626	5
6	207	3
7	553	5
8	454	4
9	464	4
Out	3,792	36
10	430	4
11	438	4
12	555	5
13	390	4
14	202	3
15	594	5
16	179	3
17	465	4
18	471	4
In	3,724	36
Total	7,516	72

Bogotá Card of the course

Hole	Yards	Par
1	428	4
2	520	5
3	352	4
4	365	4
5	218	3
6	400	4
7	157	3
8	547	5
9	447	4
Out	3,444	36
10	225	3
11	444	4
12	453	4
13	552	5
14	380	4
15	206	3
16	408	4
17	447	4
18	552	5
In	3,667	36
Total	7,111	72

Karen Card of the course

Hole	Yards	Par	Hole	Yards	Par
1	350	4	10	362	4
2	562	5	11	404	4
3	538	5	12	308	4
4	387	4	13	457	4
5	205	3	14	142	3
6	475	4	15	528	5
7	166	3	16	190	3
8	369	4	17	467	4
9	443	4	18	540	5
Out	3,495	36	In	3,398	36
			Total	6,893	72

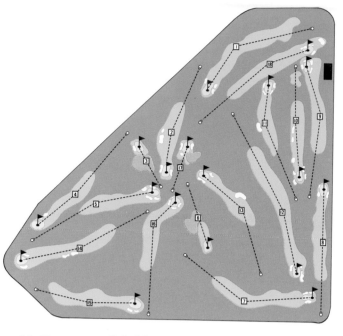

Houghton Card of the course		
Hole	Yards	Par
1	428	4
2	417	4
3	156	3
4	457	4
5	431	4
6	231	3
7	534	5
8	411	4
9	437	4
Out	3,502	35
10	372	4
11	420	4
12	586	5
13	453	4
14	523	5
15	443	4
16	392	4
17	156	3
18	474	4
In	3,819	37
Total	7,321	72

97 Houghton GC, Johannesburg

As with so many of the early South African courses, Houghton — first played in 1926 — was designed by the club professional, A.M. Copland. It was built on 155 acres of prime residential land that is now only three miles from Johannesburg City Hall. There are only three par-threes, and in the rarefied atmosphere of the Transvaal highveld (almost 6,000 feet above sea level) even the mediocre golfer finds himself suddenly two clubs longer; many of the par fours require a drive and a wedge or an 8-iron. The entire strategy of the course lies in the tight bunkering of the greens. The traps are cut into the putting surface and so positioned as to make accurate placement of the tee shot essential if there is to be any easy way to the pin. Particularly outstanding holes are the 4th, 5th, and 18th, all par-fours that reward only the finest shot-makers. The course has changed since the Dunlop Masters in the early 1960s — it is now played in a different direction, with several new tees and traps.

98 Chapman GC, Harare

In 1928 Salisbury Rayton Athletic Club laid out a nine-hole course with sand greens over a very rough patch of African bush country, and two years later a second nine was playable. After World War II substantial improvements were made with the financial help of Sir Henry Chapman, and the club was renamed in his honor. Many hardwood cedars and conifers were planted to line the fairways, and the greens were properly grassed; in 1961 the association with Rayton was severed, twenty-eight new bunkers were positioned and the Nyamaranga River was deepened and dammed to create yet more hazards. The river widens to a lake at the 6th, a long par four, and the average golfer may find that playing a safe lay-up second is more rewarding than going for the green with a long iron or a fairway wood. The 451-yard 11th has a hideous approach to the green; the second shot is a mid-iron and the target lies on the other side of a fairway divided by a stretch of water, surrounded by a cluster of bunkers and interspersed with a few trees and shrubs.

Record: 65 Simon Hobday, Zimbabwe Open, 1979

Chapman Card of the course		
Hole	Yards	Par
1	388	4
2	569	5
3	178	3
4	417	4
5	392	4
6	459	4
7	230	3
8	424	4
9	528	5
Out	3,585	36
10	368	4
11	451	4
12	400	4
13	152	3
14	547	5
15	458	4
16	431	4
17	191	3
18	547	5
In	3,545	36
Total	7,130	72

Gary Player Card of the course					
Hole	Yards	Par	Hole	Yards	Par
1	403	4	10	518	5
2	503	5	11	419	4
3	395	4	12	207	3
4	195	3	13	395	4
5	400	4	14	550	5
6	363	4	15	417	4
7	206	3	16	195	3
8	431	4	17	374	4
9	545	5	18	422	4
Out	3,441	36	In	3,497	36
			Total	6,938	72

99 Gary Player CC, South Africa

From the pyramid hotel that dominates the skyline to the lush, opulent greens it is plain to see that this course is not just soaked in sun, but it is also drenched in money. The course is famous for the Nedbank Million Dollar Golf Challenge that invites just twelve professionals to what many believe to be an exhibition of mere money-grabbing. Gary Player's course does, however, house some impressive holes. The par-five, 545-yard 9th is one of them. The drive must be straight to avoid trees on the left and a bunker on the right. The professional big-hitter could hit the green in two, however, staying on it is a different matter. The hole is a raised island and lies on the upper level of a split-level lake. The lay-up is advisable.

100 Kasugai CC, Nagoya

Kasugai's East and West courses were designed by Japan's leading architect Seichi Inoue in the hills to the west of Nagoya. Giant earth-moving machines were used in cutting off the tops of hills and filling the valleys to make the fairways — a common method of construction in Japan. What is left is still undulating and decidedly steep in places, which is much to the Japanese liking. The clubhouse, perched on the highest point, overlooks both layouts, which are well defined by many young conifers and small decorative ponds. These obstacles also serve to provide some challenge. For the 1975 Japan Open, played on the East course, additional fairway sandtraps and temporary trees were arranged to provide extra difficulty. Korai grass is used for the putting surfaces, giving the greens much variation in both texture and color from season to season. The East course is 6,856 yards of rambling holes over many hills, some of which are quite steep by world championship standards. This provides a problem of distance — an advantage to the long hitters but frustrating for those who have less power.

101 Nasu International CC, Tochigi

Situated on Japan's northernmost island, Nasu International Country Club is distinguished by its year-round, one-green putting system, which is contrary to the usual Japanese practice of providing winter and summer greens. The course has been carved through steep, hilly wood land that eventually makes the 6,825 yards play longer than the card reads, an effect exaggerated by the almost constant cross-winds and numerous sidehill lies. On the 6th and 7th, both par fours, the drive is blind, the fairways rising to a crest before dipping to well-trapped greens. The long, uphill 13th doglegs to the right around a bunker strategically placed to catch the sliced or the over-ambitious drive. The lay-up second then has to contend with the severe gusting winds to leave an untroubled short-iron to the target.

Kasugai East Card of the course

Hole	Yards	Par
1	415	4
2	395	4
3	498	5
4	199	3
5	416	4
6	460	4
7	182	3
8	511	5
9	407	4
Out	3,463	36
10	362	4
11	368	4
12	174	3
13	503	5
14	435	4
15	189	3
16	429	4
17	529	5
18	410	4
In	3,393	36
Total	6,856	72

Nasu Card of the course

Hole	Yards	Par
1	505	5
2	175	3
3	400	4
4	525	5
5	423	4
6	430	4
7	385	4
8	200	3
9	380	4
Out	3,423	36
10	490	5
11	360	4
12	200	3
13	500	5
14	412	4
15	460	4
16	410	4
17	150	3
18	420	4
In	3,402	36
Total	6,825	72

Yomiuri Card of the course

Hole	Yards	Par	Hole	Yards	Par
1	396	4	10	425	4
2	180	3	11	507	5
3	403	4	12	432	4
4	508	5	13	450	4
5	384	4	14	364	4
6	541	5	15	194	3
7	389	4	16	410	4
8	197	3	17	510	5
9	448	4	18	224	3
Out	3,446	36	In	3,516	36
			Total	6,962	72

102 Yomiuri CC, Tokyo

The Yomiuri Country Club, to the west of Tokyo, is part of a huge sporting complex built by the Yomiuri Newspaper Group. The course, which is of the highest class, was designed in 1964 by Seichi Inoue. He used his considerable experience to create holes that are adventurous without being unreasonable, avoiding a drawback that mars many courses in this mountainous country. At 6,962 yards it is well set for distance, particularly in the lushness that follows the mid-year wet season. It has a two-green system, which slightly interferes with the greenside trapping, but generally sand areas are punishing and fearsome. There are a number of blind shots from the teeing areas and many shots have to carry deep valleys, which are grassed as rough and where the wind can play strange tricks with the ball. Yomiuri has a high reputation amongst the professionals and top-class amateurs — a sentiment reflected by the decision of the Japan Golf Association to stage the World Cup there in 1966.

Wack Wack East Course
Card of the course

Hole	Yards	Par
1	421	4
2	431	4
3	357	4
4	352	4
5	576	5
6	431	4
7	344	4
8	156	3
9	429	4
Out	**3,497**	**36**
10	381	4
11	377	4
12	451	4
13	519	5
14	431	4
15	383	4
16	207	3
17	409	4
18	435	4
In	**3,593**	**36**
Total	**7,090**	**72**

103 Wack Wack G & CC, Manila

In 1933 a group of expatriate American businessmen in Manila bought a track of land at Mandaloyong and developed it into the Wack Wack course. Its name was inspired by the noise made by the innumerable flights of crows that were a pest to the players in the early days. The beautiful lake was created by damming a creek and has become an interesting hazard on several holes. During the 1960s the primitive table-top greens of the original construction were rebuilt along modern lines and several of the holes extended to bring the course up to 7,000 yards. The layout now leads the player over the gently undulating terrain, occasionally across streams and into the extremely well-trapped greens. At the end of the 1930s Wack Wack staged the first international Asian event, the Philippine Open. After World War II the club had a new lease on life and resumed the championship on a large scale, attracting players like Mangrum, Oliver, Burke, Harrison, and Furgol from the USA together with a large contingent of Australian and Taiwanese players.

Navatanee Card of the course

Hole	Yards	Par	Hole	Yards	Par
1	424	4	10	428	4
2	380	4	11	230	3
3	555	5	12	379	4
4	133	3	13	578	5
5	347	4	14	357	4
6	457	4	15	412	4
7	218	3	16	381	4
8	370	4	17	159	3
9	554	5	18	539	5
Out	**3,463**	**36**	**In**	**3,443**	**36**
			Total	**6,906**	**72**

104 Navatanee CC, Bangkok

Navatanee Golf Club possesses by far the best course in Thailand. Designed by Robert Trent Jones for its owner, Sukhum Navapan, this 6,906-yard, par-72 layout entertained the 1975 World Cup, from which all players departed with high praise for its championship qualities. The course construction converted a large swamp of rice paddies and wasteland into a vista of green fairways, white sand-traps and plenty of water, the familiar Trent Jones trademark. It is grassed in tifton from tee to cup, providing a lush carpet of superb lies for fairway play and — for such a hot climate — smooth putting surfaces. Jones has placed a variety of teeing grounds for most holes, so adapting the layout to suit every golfer's needs. The last four holes represent a thrilling finish for a round, with disaster lying in wait for any false step — even at the final hole, a torrid par five of 539 yards where a double water carry is particularly fearsome in any kind of wind.

Delhi GC
Card of the course

Hole	Yards	Par	Hole	Yards	Par
1	530	5	10	416	4
2	420	4	11	455	4
3	390	4	12	160	3
4	450	4	13	375	4
5	413	4	14	512	5
6	188	3	15	373	4
7	540	5	16	393	4
8	412	4	17	153	3
9	175	3	18	530	5
Out	**3,518**	**36**	**In**	**3,367**	**36**
			Total	**6,885**	**72**

105 Delhi GC, New Delhi

Built on the rubble of the old Mogul metropolis, the Delhi course, set amid the grandeur of such ancient architectural monuments, has a fascination and beauty all of its own. The fairways of pure couch grass — and the natural jungle rough have a verdant greenness after the monsoon rains that suggests coolness in an otherwise torrid climate. The layout has undergone several changes. At one time it ranged over wider territory, but the club now confines twenty-seven holes within a tight boundary, the main eighteen forming a championship course of high merit. It combines a need for length with a demand for extreme directness. Drives that curl into the wild bush rough are invariably unplayable, so necessitating the almost mandatory employment of an "agi-wallah," who performs the function of a fore-caddie while understudying the more responsible job of caddie. The club is a delightful meeting place for many of Delhi's sporting citizens and diplomats. Every two years it hosts the annual Indian Open championship, which is a part of the Asian tournament circuit.

New South Wales Card of the course

Hole	Yards	Par	Hole	Yards	Par
1	327	4	10	379	4
2	198	3	11	165	3
3	418	4	12	504	5
4	438	4	13	417	4
5	494	5	14	352	4
6	198	3	15	412	4
7	405	4	16	451	4
8	563	5	17	168	3
9	366	4	18	555	5
Out	**3,407**	**36**	**In**	**3,403**	**36**
			Total	**6,810**	**72**

106 New South Wales GC, Matraville

Laid out by Alister Mackenzie in 1928, the New South Wales course at Sydney offers magnificent, panoramic views over the Pacific Ocean to the east and Botany Bay to the south; the spot where Captain Cook landed in 1770 is less than a par four from the clubhouse. The land presents an unrivaled site for a course and the wind, ever-changing in both direction and strength, produces a stern challenge to golfers of all categories. The punishing undulations, bunkering, and rough combine with the wind to make the chance of a low score for the average handicap player a question of fine control over shots that must always travel in shallow trajectories. The l90-yard, par-three 6th, down among the rocks on the tip of the headland, is played over the water in the now immortal style of the 16th at Cypress Point. It is, perhaps, an early indicator of the influence Mackenzie was to have on golf course design.

Kingston Heath Card of the course

Hole	Yards	Par	Hole	Yards	Par
1	458	4	10	143	3
2	365	4	11	403	4
3	296	4	12	484	5
4	389	4	13	354	4
5	189	3	14	549	5
6	434	4	15	155	3
7	502	5	16	422	4
8	431	4	17	457	4
9	354	4	18	428	4
Out	**3,418**	**36**	**In**	**3,395**	**36**
			Total	**6,813**	**72**

107 Kingston Heath GC, Melbourne

Like many old clubs, Kingston Heath was born of necessity: an established club was forced off its course on municipal land near Melbourne city edge and so, faced with extinction, its members sought land farther out where the price was right and soil conducive. They chose a site for Kingston Heath on the same sandy tract of land as Royal Melbourne, and the eventual result looks like its half-brother. The design in 1925, was by Sydney professional Dan Souter, but three years later Alister Mackenzie undertook the bunkering. It is now a delightful mixture of flat and rising land, making easy walking and interesting golf. The holes vary in theme and, played for the first time, may even surprise. The fairways, lined by eucalyptus and tea-trees, are almost pure couch grass and lead on to greens that have fine surfaces of seaside bent, browntop and fescue mixed. The three par threes are classic in conception and offer a fine challenge for perceptive strokemaking. The course is on the regular championship roster and has accommodated the Open three times.

108 Lake Karrinyup GC, Western Australia

As its name suggests, Lake Karrinyup is constructed around a lake set in a natural basin surrounded by sandhills. The lake is the home of many forms of wildlife and from any angle mirrors the beauty of the course. Created by Alex Russell in 1927, it bears a marked similarity to his home course of Royal Melbourne in the arrangement of the generously wide, couch grass fairways, the grand sandtraps and the large, flowing greens. Eucalyptus and many species of native wild flowers flourish in the sandy soil, forming an indigenous and attractive setting for each hole. A wind from the Indian Ocean can affect the scores by adding to the problems already set by the water and the bush. The 8th, a 208-yard par-three, is the only hole that is played directly over the lake and a strong low-iron tee shot is often required when playing into the wind. The course is a popular venue for the Australian Open and amateur championships, with such winners such as Norman Von Nida in 1952 and Bruce Devlin in 1960.

**Lake Karrinyup
Card of the course**

Hole	Yards	Par
1	241	4
2	470	4
3	498	5
4	427	4
5	164	3
6	427	4
7	547	5
8	208	3
9	361	4
Out	**3,343**	**36**
10	372	4
11	492	5
12	164	3
13	421	4
14	284	4
15	531	5
16	438	4
17	197	3
18	405	4
In	**3,304**	**36**
Total	**6,647**	**72**

109 Auckland GC, Middlemore

Middlemore, as the Auckland Golf Club is known, after the district in which it thrives, has an atmosphere that is both special and unique, even for New Zealand. Its homely wooden clubhouse looks out on a parkland setting of exemplary tidiness and passivity. Tall rows of fifty-year-old pines divide some fairways, while others are open to the sky. Built on clay soil, it has periods of discomfort when it is either wet and sticky or bone dry. But these periods are fleeting, and between-times Middlemore is a soft and gently undulating, interesting course of championship dimensions containing a wide variety of obstacles and challenges. The club was opened in 1910 and within two years a full eighteen holes, designed by the professional F. G. Hood, were ready for play. It has hosted the New Zealand Open five times and the Amateur seven times. The members tend to be elderly, and they prefer the course cleanly cut with little rough. But it is easily and quickly converted into quite a daunting monster.

**Auckland
Card of the course**

Hole	Yards	Par
1	346	4
2	364	4
3	393	4
4	502	5
5	391	4
6	393	4
7	139	3
8	366	4
9	548	5
Out	**3,442**	**37**
10	110	3
11	272	4
12	347	4
13	205	3
14	327	4
15	379	4
16	366	4
17	451	5
18	335	4
In	**2,792**	**35**
Total	**6,234**	**72**

110 Christchurch GC, Shirley

Christchurch Golf Club has a golfing tradition stretching back to 1873 when, like many a similar club in distant British colonies, it began on another site sparked by the enthusiasm of a handful of Scots. Popularly known as Shirley, after the garden suburb in which it dwells, the course follows a route that takes it away to the 9th in the old Scottish tradition. The holes tumble over small bumps and hollows, follow boundary fences — much to the frustration of right-handed slicers — and leap, toward the end, over a tiny burn. Pines, broom, and gorse lend color and age to the backdrop. The best and most daunting hole is the 4th, a 484-yard par five that runs along the boundary fence, describing a gentle curve to the right. The green is made on the final step and is surrounded on three sides by the most punishing of indignities in golf, out-of-bounds. Here, the score for the unwitting, who opt to hit the green in two, often enters double figures. This feat needs either superb technique or an iron nerve. Playing short with an iron and pitching dead is best.

Christchurch Card of the course

Hole	Yards	Par	Hole	Yards	Par
1	351	4	10	400	4
2	329	4	11	142	3
3	146	3	12	454	5
4	484	5	13	368	4
5	542	5	14	348	4
6	400	4	15	426	4
7	185	3	16	521	5
8	399	4	17	373	4
9	420	4	18	314	4
Out	**3,256**	**36**	**In**	**3,346**	**37**
			Total	**6,602**	**73**

Index

World Atlas of Golf

The publishers would like to thank the following organizations & individuals for their kind permission to reproduce the photographs in this book:

Allsport/Simon Bruty 103/David Cannon 24, 67, 73, 79, 100–101, 133, 205/David Cannon 8–9, 12–13 /Vandystadt/Christian Petit 95/Andrew Redington 210–211, 214
St Andrews Links Trust/Masakuni Akiyama 27, 29, 30–31
Banff Springs Back Endpaper, 3–4, 166
Bridgeman Art Library/National Gallery, London 85
Corbis UK Ltd/Arthur Jones 47
Corbis-Bettmann 225/UPI 161 left
Peter Dazeley 38 Bottom, 39, 50, 53, 217

Golf Monthly/Press Association 58, 59/D.C. Thomson & Co. Ltd. 37
Hailey Sports Photographic 38 Top, 113, 114 Top, 114 Bottom, 224
Reed Consumer Books Ltd.
The Matthew Harris Golf Picture Library Front Endpaper, 2–3, 6–7, 10–11, 19, 20–21, 23, 34, 48, 75, 77, 107, 135, 181, 185
Hulton Getty Picture Collection 26
Killarney Golf & Fishing Club/Michael Diggin 81
L. C. Lambrecht 132
Brian Morgan Golf Photography 14–15 Bottom, 41, 118–119, 146, 149, 156, 158, 186, 193, 195, 206, 218–219
Olgiata Golf Club 93
Pinehurst County Club/Henedry 136

Tony Roberts Photography 200, 203, 209
Sea Pines Company, Inc. 128/David S. Soliday 14–15 Top
Phil Sheldon title, 10 left, 13, 18–19, 33, 35, 44–45, 46, 51, 57, 65/70 Top, 70–71, 106, 108, 109, 111, 115, 117, 122, 125, 127, 137 left, 143, 147, 151, 153, 156–157, 162–163, 163, 165, 189, 191, 198–199, 212–213, /Larry Petrillo 140–141, 175, 222–223/Jan Traylen 28, 61
U.S.G.A. ƒ, 123, 137 Right, 139, 140, 154, 155, 161 Right
Club Zur Vahr 90
Vilamoura 99
Visions in Golf/Mark Newcombe 170, 172–173, 178, 183